BARRON'S
STUDENTS' #1 CHOICE

PASS KEY

TO THE

TOEFL

TEST OF ENGLISH AS A FOREIGN LANGUAGE

*

Third Edition

Pamela J. Sharpe, Ph.D.
The Ohio State University

BARRON'S EDUCATIONAL SERIES, INC.

To my former students
at home and abroad

All inquiries should be addressed to:
Barron's Educational Series, Inc.
250 Wireless Boulevard
Hauppauge, New York 11788
http://www.barronseduc.com

Library of Congress Catalog Card No. 99-19549
International Standard Book No. 0-7641-7145-3 (book with compact disc)
International Standard Book No. 0-7641-0469-1 (book only)

Library of Congress Cataloging-in-Publication Data

Sharpe, Pamela J.
    Pass key to the TOEFL / Pamela J. Sharpe. — 3rd ed.
      p.   cm.
    "Material in this book was adapted from Barron's how to prepare for
the TOEFL, 9th ed., by Pamela J. Sharpe"—T.p. verso.
    ISBN 0-7641-7145-3
    1. Test of English as a Foreign Language Study guides. 2. English
language Textbooks for foreign speakers. 3. English language—
Examinations Study guides. I. Sharpe, Pamela J. Barron's how to
prepare for the TOEFL. II. Title.
PE1128.S523   1999
428'.0076—dc21   99-19549
                                              CIP

PRINTED IN THE UNITED STATES OF AMERICA
987654321

CONTENTS

INTRODUCTION

QUESTIONS AND ANSWERS CONCERNING THE TOEFL

REVIEW OF SECTION 1: LISTENING

REVIEW OF SECTION 2: STRUCTURE

REVIEW OF SECTION 3: READING

REVIEW OF WRITING ESSAYS

TOEFL MODEL TESTS

ANSWER KEYS FOR THE TOEFL REVIEW EXERCISES AND MODEL TESTS

EXPLANATORY ANSWERS FOR THE TOEFL MODEL TESTS

TRANSCRIPT FOR THE LISTENING SECTIONS OF THE TOEFL MODEL TESTS   433

To the Student

Barron's Pass Key to the TOEFL is the concise version of the classic *Barron's How to Prepare for the TOEFL*. Small enough to put in your purse, backpack, or book bag, this convenient book can always be in the right place when you have a few minutes to study—on the bus, while you wait for an appointment, or on break at work or school.

This concise version, *Pass Key to the TOEFL*, can be used to prepare for both the Paper and Pencil TOEFL and for the Computer-Based TOEFL. To make this book smaller, less expensive, and more convenient to carry with you, we have included four Model Tests in the book and the audio for two Model Tests on the compact disc. The larger version of this book, *Barron's How to Prepare for the TOEFL*, includes eight Model Tests in the book. The CD-ROM that supplements the book includes the audio for all eight Model Tests and the computer screens for four Computer-Assisted Model Tests as well as a Computer-Adaptive Model Test.

Ideally, you would use these two books for two different purposes. You would use this book, *Pass Key to the TOEFL*, to take the best advantage of your time while you are away from your computer or when you don't want to carry heavy materials. You would use the larger version of this book, *Barron's How to Prepare for the TOEFL*, and the CD-ROM that supplements it, when you have access to your computer.

Study thoughtfully, and take the TOEFL with confidence. It may well be the most important examination of your academic career. And this book can be an essential pass key to your success.

To the Teacher

Rationale for a TOEFL Preparation Course

Although *Barron's Pass Key to the TOEFL* may be perceived as a self-study guide for students who were preparing to take the TOEFL, in the years since its first publication, I have received letters from ESL teachers around the world who are using the book successfully for classroom study. In fact, in recent years, many special courses have been developed within the existing ESL curriculum to accommodate TOEFL preparation.

I believe that these TOEFL preparation courses respond to three trends within the profession. First, there appears to be a greater recognition on the part of many ESL teachers that student goals must be acknowledged and addressed. For the engineer, the businessperson, the doctor, or the preuniversity student, a satisfactory score on the TOEFL is one of the most immediate goals; for many, without the required score, they cannot continue their professional studies or obtain certification to practice their professions. They may have other language goals as well, such as learning to communicate more effectively or improving their writing, but these goals do not usually exert the same kinds of pressure that the required TOEFL score does.

Second, teachers have recognized and recorded the damaging results of test anxiety. We have all observed students who were so frightened of failure that they have performed on the TOEFL at a level far below that which their performance in class would have indicated. The standardized score just didn't correspond with the score in the gradebook. In addition, teachers have become aware that for some students, the TOEFL represents their first experience in taking a standardized test with a test book and a separate answer sheet or a computer-assisted test. The concepts of working within time limits, marking an answer grid or screen, and guessing to improve a score are often new and confusing to students, and they forfeit valuable points because they must concentrate on unfamiliar procedures instead of on language questions.

Third, teachers have observed the corresponding changes in student proficiency that have accompanied the evolutionary changes in ESL syllabus design. Since this book was first written, we have moved away from a grammatical syllabus to a notional functional syllabus, and at this writing, there seems to be growing interest in a content-based syllabus. Viewed in terms of what has actually happened in classrooms, most of us have emphasized the teaching of functions and meaning and de-emphasized the teaching of forms. As we did so, we noticed with pride the improvement in student fluency and with dismay the corresponding loss of accuracy. Some of our best, most fluent students received disappointing scores on the test that was so important to them.

Through these observations and experiences, teachers have concluded that (1) students need to work toward their own goals, (2) students need some time to focus on accuracy as well as on fluency, and (3) students need an opportunity to practice taking a standardized test in order to alleviate anxiety and develop test strategies. With the introduction of the Computer-Based TOEFL, the opportunity to gain experience taking a computer-assisted model test has also become important to student confidence and success. In short, more and more teachers have begun to support the inclusion of a TOEFL preparation course in the ESL curriculum.

Organization of a TOEFL Preparation Course

Organizing a TOEFL preparation course requires that teachers make decisions about the way that the course should be structured and the kinds of supplementary materials and activities that should be used.

Structuring

Some teachers have suggested that each review section in this book be used for a separate class; they are team teaching a TOEFL course. Other teachers direct their students to the language laboratory for independent study in listening comprehension three times a week, checking on progress throughout the term; assign reading and vocabulary study for homework; and spend class time on structure and writing. Still other teachers develop individual study plans for each student based on previous TOEFL part scores. Students with high listening and low reading scores concentrate their efforts in reading labs, while students with low listening and high reading scores spend time in listening labs.

Materials and Activities

Listening. Studies in distributive practice have convinced teachers of listening comprehension that a little practice every day for a few months is more valuable than a lot of practice concentrated in a shorter time. In addition, many teachers like to use two kinds of listening practice—intensive and extensive. Intensive practice consists of listening to problems like those in the "Review of Listening" in this book.

By so doing, the student progresses from short conversations through longer conversations to mini-talks, gaining experience in listening to simulations of the TOEFL examination. Extensive practice consists of watching a daytime drama on television, listening to a local radio program, or auditing a class. Creative teachers everywhere have developed strategies for checking student progress such as requiring a summary of the plot or a prediction of what will happen the following day on the drama; a one-sentence explanation of the radio program, as well as the name of the speaker, sponsor of the program, and two details; a copy of student notes from the audited class.

Structure. Of course, the focus in a review of structure for the TOEFL will be on form. It is form that is tested on the TOEFL. It is assumed that students have studied grammar prior to reviewing for the TOEFL, and that they are relatively fluent. The purpose of a TOEFL review then is to improve accuracy. Because accuracy is directly related to TOEFL scores and because the scores are tied to student goals, this type of review motivates students to pay attention to detail that would not usually be of much interest to them.

Among ESL teachers, the debate rages on about whether students should ever see errors in grammar. But many teachers have recognized the fact that students *do* see errors all the time, not only in the distractors that are used on standardized tests like the TOEFL and teacher-made tests like the multiple choice midterms in their grammar classes, but also in their own writing. They argue that students must be able to recognize errors, learn to read for them, and correct them.

The student preparing for the TOEFL will be required not only to recognize correct answers but also to eliminate incorrect answers, or distractors, as possibilities. The review of structure in this book supports recognition by alerting students to avoid certain common distractors. Many excellent teachers take this one step further by using student compositions to create personal TOEFL tests. By underlining four words or phrases in selected sentences, one phrase of which contains an incorrect structure, teachers encourage students to reread their writing. It has proven to be a helpful transitional technique for students who need to learn how to edit their own compositions.

Reading. One of the problems in a TOEFL preparation course is that of directing vocabulary study. Generally, teachers feel that encouraging students to collect words and develop their own word lists is the best solution to the problem of helping students who will be faced with the dilemma of responding to words from a possible vocabulary pool of thousands of words that may appear in context in the reading section. In this way, they will increase their vocabularies in an ordered and productive way, thereby benefiting even if none of their new words appears on the test that they take. Activities that support learning vocabulary in context are also helpful.

In order to improve reading, students need extensive practice in reading a variety of material, including newspapers and magazines as well as short excerpts from textbooks. In addition, students need to check their comprehension and time themselves carefully. Many teachers are using preparation books for the General Education Degree (GED) in special reading labs for students preparing for the TOEFL. Books such as *Barron's How to Prepare for the GED* contain passages at about the same level as those on the TOEFL and include comprehension questions after each passage. Teachers report that passages on natural science, social science, and general interest only should be assigned because literature passages often require that the student read and interpret poetry and plays, and these literary readings do not appear on the TOEFL. Again, it is well to advise students of the advantages of distributed practice. They should be made aware that it is better to read two passages every day for five days than to read ten passages in one lab period.

It is also necessary for students who are preparing for the Computer-Based TOEFL to practice reading from a computer screen. The skill of scrolling through text is different from the skill of reading a page in a book. To succeed on the TOEFL and after the TOEFL, students must develop new reading strategies for texts on screens.

Writing. There are many excellent ESL textbooks to help students improve their writing. Because the TOEFL limits the topics to opinion, persuasion, and argument, some teachers tend to emphasize these types of topics in composition classes.

The extensive list of writing topics published in the *Information Bulletin* for the Computer-Based TOEFL offers teachers an opportunity to use actual TOEFL topics in class. In order to help students organize their thoughts, the topics can be used as conversation starters for class discussion. In this way, students will have thought about the topics and will have formed an opinion before they are presented with the writing task on the TOEFL.

It is also a good idea to time some of the essays that students write in class so that they can become accustomed to completing their work within thirty minutes.

Although teachers need to develop grading systems that make sense for their teaching situations, the scoring guide that is used for the essay on the TOEFL is general enough to be adapted for at least some of the assignments in an ESL composition class. By using the guide, teachers can inform students of their progress as it relates to the scores that they can expect to receive on the essay they will write for the TOEFL.

Networking with ESL Teachers

One of the many rewards of writing is the opportunity that it creates to exchange ideas with so many talented colleagues. At conferences, I have met ESL teachers who use or have used one of the previous editions of this book; through my publisher, I have received letters from students and teachers from fifty-two nations. This preface and many of the revisions in this new edition were included because of comments and suggestions from those conversations and letters.

Thank you for your ideas. I hope that by sharing we can help each other and thereby help our students more. Please continue corresponding by mail or by e-mail.

Pamela Sharpe
1406 Camino Real
Yuma, Arizona 85364
Sharpe@toeflcenter.com

Acknowledgments

It is with affection and appreciation that I acknowledge my indebtedness to the late Dr. Jayne C. Harder, Director of the English Language Institute of the University of Florida, who initiated me into the science of linguistics and the art of teaching English as a foreign language.

I am also very grateful to my parents, Robert and Lilly Sharpe, for their enthusiastic encouragement during the preparation of the manuscript and for their assistance in typing and proofreading this and each of the previous editions; to the late Tom Clapp, for the maturity and confidence that I gained from our marriage; to Carole Berglie of Barron's Educational Series, Inc., for her insights and guidance in seeing the first edition of the manuscript through to publication; and to all of the editors at Barron's for their contributions to later editions, especially Marcy Rosenbaum and Debby Becak whose creativity contributed to making this the best edition yet.

With the permission of Mr. Frank Berlin, Sexton Educational Programs, New York, explanations for the listening comprehension problems have been adapted from previous work by the author.

With the permission of Educational Testing Service, the test instructions contained in this publication for the various sections of TOEFL have been reprinted from the *Information Bulletin* for the Paper and Pencil TOEFL and the Computer-Based TOEFL. The granting of this permission does not imply endorsement by ETS or the TOEFL program of the contents of this publication as a whole or of the practice questions that it contains. Since the types of questions in TOEFL and the instructions pertaining to them are subject to change, candidates who register to take TOEFL should read carefully the edition of the *Information Bulletin* that will be sent to them free of charge with their registration material.

With the assistance of Judy Peterson and the cooperation of Roxanne Nuhaily at the English Language Program, University of California, San Diego, the items for the Computer-Adaptive Model Test on the CD-ROM that supplements the larger version of this book were field tested; with the collaboration of Dr. Sherri McCarthy-Tucker, the items were analyzed and calibrated.

Finally, I would like to say a special thank you to my husband, John T. Osterman, for the unconditional love, the daily interest in and support for my writing career, and the best chapter in my life story.

Timetable for the TOEFL

TIMETABLE FOR THE PAPER AND PENCIL TOEFL
Total Time: 3 hours

Section 1 (40 Minutes)	Listening Comprehension	50 Questions
Section 2 (25 Minutes)	Structure and Written Expression	40 Questions
Section 3 (55 Minutes)	Reading Comprehension	50 Questions
TWE (30 Minutes)	Essay	1 Question

TIMETABLE FOR THE COMPUTER-BASED TOEFL
Total Time: 4.5 hours

Tutorial	Computer Skills	Variable
Section 1 (40–60 Minutes)	Listening	50 Questions
Section 2: Part One (15–20 Minutes)	Structure	20 Questions
Section 3 (70–90 Minutes)	Reading	45 Questions
Section 2: Part Two (30 Minutes)	Essay	1 Question

Note: Actual times will vary in accordance with the time the supervisor completes the preliminary work and begins the actual test. The time for the tutorial will vary from one person to another. Format and numbers of questions will also vary from one test to another. This timetable is a good estimate.

INTRODUCTION

Study Plan for the TOEFL

Many students do not prepare for the TOEFL. They do not even read the *Information Bulletin* that they receive from Educational Testing Service along with their registration forms. You have an advantage. Using this book, you have a study plan.

Barron's TOEFL Series

There are three books in the Barron's TOEFL series to help you prepare for the Test of English as a Foreign Language. Each book has a different purpose.

Barron's Practice Exercises for the TOEFL. A book for learners at an intermediate level who need preview and practice for the TOEFL. It includes a general preview of the TOEFL examination, a review of the most frequently tested problems, and more than a thousand exercises. Two separate cassette tapes accompany the book to give you practice in listening comprehension. You may have used *Barron's Practice Exercises for the TOEFL* before using this book.

Barron's How to Prepare for the TOEFL. A book for learners at high intermediate and advanced levels who need review and practice for the TOEFL. It includes questions and answers about the TOEFL examination, a detailed review for each section of the examination, practice exercises, and eight model tests similar to the actual TOEFL examination. Several sets of additional materials are available to supplement this book, including a separate package of cassette tapes, a separate package of audio compact discs, or the book may be accompanied by compact discs or a CD-ROM. A computer-adaptive test like that of the Computer-Based TOEFL is found on the CD-ROM.

Barron's Pass Key to the TOEFL. A pocket-sized edition of *Barron's How to Prepare for the TOEFL.* It is for high intermediate and advanced learners who need review and practice for the TOEFL and want to be able to carry a smaller book with them. It includes questions and answers about the TOEFL examination, basic tips on how to prepare for the TOEFL, and four model tests from *Barron's How to Prepare for the TOEFL.* One audio compact disc accompanies the book to give you practice in listening comprehension.

More About This Book

In preparing to take the TOEFL or any other language examination, it is very important to review the language skills for each section of the examination and to have an opportunity to take model tests that are similar to the actual examination.

Reviewing will help you recall some of the language skills you have studied in previous classes and other books. Taking model tests will give you the experience of taking a TOEFL before you take the actual examination.

Remember, the purpose of the book is to provide you with a concise review of the language skills for each section of the TOEFL examination and to provide you with opportunities to take model tests similar to the actual TOEFL examination.

By studying this book, you should renew and sharpen your skills, increase your speed, and improve your score.

Planning to Take the TOEFL

Study Plan I—For Intermediate Level Learners

- First, use *Barron's Practice Exercises for the TOEFL.*
- Then use this book, *Barron's Pass Key to the TOEFL.*

Study Plan II—For High Intermediate Level or Advanced Learners

- Use *Barron's How to Prepare for the TOEFL* with the CD-ROM for practice on computer-assisted tests.
- Use *Barron's Pass Key to the TOEFL* for preparation at times when you do not have a computer available.

Study Plan III—For Advanced Learners

- Use this book, *Barron's Pass Key to the TOEFL.*

A Ten-Week Calendar

Week One

- Read Chapter 2, "Questions and Answers Concerning the TOEFL."

- Write TOEFL Services for a copy of the *Information Bulletin.*
- Register for your test date.

Week Two

- Study Chapter 3, "Review of Section 1: Listening."
- Take the Listening Section of Model Test 1: Paper and Pencil TOEFL.
- Refer to the Answer Key in Chapter 8 and the Explanatory Answers in Chapter 9.
- Refer to the Chapter 10 "Transcript for the Listening Sections of the TOEFL Model Tests."

Week Three

- Begin Chapter 4, "Review of Section 2: Structure," the Patterns.
- Complete the Practice Exercises, and refer to the Answer Key in Chapter 8.
- Mark the Problems that you need to review again.

Week Four

- Continue Chapter 4, "Review of Section 2: Structure," the Style Problems.
- Complete the Practice Exercises, and refer to the Answer Key in Chapter 8.
- Mark the Problems that you need to review again.

Week Five

- Study Chapter 5, "Review of Section 3: Reading."
- Complete the Practice Exercises and refer to the Answer Key in Chapter 8.

Week Six

- Take all three sections of Model Test 1: Paper and Pencil TOEFL.
- Refer to the Answer Key in Chapter 8 and the Explanatory Answers in Chapter 9.

Week Seven

- Take all three sections of Model Test 2: Paper and Pencil TOEFL.

- Refer to the Answer Key in Chapter 8 and the Explanatory Answers in Chapter 9.

Week Eight
- Take all three sections of Model Test 3: Computer-Assisted TOEFL, and follow directions for marking in the book.
- Refer to the Answer Key in Chapter 8 and the Explanatory Answers in Chapter 9.

Week Nine
- Take all three sections of Model Test 4: Computer-Assisted TOEFL.
- Refer to the Answer Key in Chapter 8 and the Explanatory Answers in Chapter 9.

Week Ten
- Study all the Problems that you have marked in the Review Chapters.
- Review all the errors that you have made on the Model Tests.

Adjusting the Calendar

Ideally, you will have ten weeks to prepare for the TOEFL. But, if you have a shorter time to prepare, follow the plan in the same order, adjusting the time to meet your needs.

If you have taken the TOEFL before, you already know which section or sections are difficult for you. Look at the part scores on your score report. If your lowest score is on Section 1, Listening, then you should spend more time reviewing Section 1. If your lowest score is on Section 2 or Section 3, then you should spend more time reviewing them.

If you are participating in a TOEFL administration that includes an essay, you should plan time early in your study calendar to read Chapter 6, "Review of Writing Essays." Then, test yourself by taking one of the Model Test essays included in Chapter 7 every week.

For additional Model Tests and for practice marking your answers on a computer, use the larger version of this book, *Barron's How to Prepare for the TOEFL* and the CD-ROM that supplements it.

Plan for Preparation

To improve your scores most, follow this plan:

- *First,* concentrate on listening, structure, writing, and reading, instead of on vocabulary. Your score will improve, because when you are engaged in listening and reading, you are practicing skills that you can apply during the examination regardless of the content of the material. When you are reviewing structure, you are studying a system that is smaller than that of vocabulary, and, like the skills of listening and reading, has the potential for application on the TOEFL that you take. Many of the structures that you study will probably appear on the examination. But when you review lists of vocabulary, even very good lists, you may study hundreds of words and not find any of them on the examination. This is so because the system is very large. There are thousands of possible words that may be tested.

- *Second,* spend time preparing every day for at least an hour instead of sitting down to review once a week for seven hours. Even though you are studying for the same amount of time, research shows that daily shorter sessions produce better results on the test.

- *Finally,* do not try to memorize questions from this or any other book. The questions on the test that you take will be very similar to the questions in this book, but they will not be exactly the same.

What you should try to do as you use this and your other books is learn how to apply your knowledge. Do not hurry through the practice exercises. While you are checking your answers to the model tests, *think* about the correct answer. Why is it correct? Can you explain the answer to yourself before you check the explanatory answer? Is the question similar to others that you have seen before?

Plan for Additional Preparation

Although this book should provide you with enough review material, some of you will want to do more in order to prepare for the TOEFL. Suggestions for each section follow.

- *To prepare for Section 1,* Listening, listen to radio and television newscasts and weather reports, television documentaries, lectures on educational television stations, and free lectures sponsored by clubs and universities. Attend movies in English. Try to make friends with speakers of American English and participate in conversations.

- *To prepare for Section 2,* Structure, use an advanced grammar review book. If you are attending an English course, do not stop attending.

- *To prepare for Section 3,* Reading, read articles in English newspapers and magazines, college catalogs and admissions materials, travel brochures, and entries that interest you from American and English encyclopedias. Try to read a variety of topics—American history, culture, social science, and natural science.

- *To prepare for the essay,* Writing, refer to the TOEFL *Information Bulletin* for the Computer-Based TOEFL or visit the TOEFL web site at www.toefl.org. Actual essay topics for the TOEFL are listed in the TOEFL *Bulletin* and on the web site.

A Good Start

Learn to relax. If you start to panic in the examination room, close your eyes and say "no" in your mind. Tell yourself, "I will not panic. I am prepared." Then take several slow, deep breaths, letting your shoulders drop in a relaxed manner as you exhale.

Concentrate on the questions. Do not talk. Concentrate your attention. Do not look at anything in the test room except the answers that correspond to the question you are working on.

Do not think about your situation, the test in general, your score, or your future. If you do, force yourself to return to the question.

If you do not understand a problem and you do not have a good answer, do your best. Then stop thinking about it. Be ready for the next problem.

Do not cheat. In spite of opportunity, knowledge that others are doing it, desire to help a friend, or fear that you will not make a good score, *do not cheat.*

On the TOEFL, cheating is a very serious matter. If you are discovered, your test will not be scored. Legal action may be taken by Educational Testing Service (ETS).

Suggestions for Success

Your attitude will influence your success on the TOEFL examination. You must develop patterns of positive thinking. To help in developing a positive attitude, memorize the following sentences and bring them to mind after each study session. Bring them to mind when you begin to have negative thoughts.

I know more today than I did yesterday.
I am preparing.
I will succeed.

Remember, some tension is normal and good. Accept it. Use it constructively. It will motivate you to study. But don't panic or worry. Panic will cause loss of concentration and poor performance. Avoid people who panic and worry. Don't listen to them. They will encourage negative thoughts.

You know more today than you did yesterday.
You are preparing.
You will succeed.

QUESTIONS AND ANSWERS CONCERNING THE TOEFL

The TOEFL is the Test of English as a Foreign Language.

Almost one million students from 180 countries register to take the TOEFL every year at 1,275 test centers in the United States and in their home countries. Some of them do not pass the TOEFL because they do not understand enough English. Others do not pass it because they do not understand the examination.

The following questions are commonly asked by students as they prepare for the TOEFL. To help you, they have been answered here.

TOEFL Programs

What is the purpose of the TOEFL?

Since 1963 the TOEFL has been used by scholarship selection committees of governments, universities, and agencies such as Fulbright, the Agency for International Development, AMIDEAST, Latin American Scholarship Program, and others as a standard measure of the English proficiency of their candidates. Now some professional licensing and certification agencies also use TOEFL scores to evaluate English proficiency.

The majority of admissions committees of colleges and universities in the United States require foreign applicants to submit TOEFL scores along with transcripts and recommendations in order to be considered for admission. Some colleges and universities in Canada and other English-speaking countries also require the TOEFL for admissions purposes.

Many universities use TOEFL scores to fulfill the foreign language requirement for doctoral candidates whose first language is not English.

Which TOEFL testing programs are available now?

Three TOEFL testing programs are available—the Paper and Pencil TOEFL, the Computer-Based TOEFL, and the Institutional TOEFL. The Paper and Pencil TOEFL and the Computer-Based TOEFL programs are the official administrations. The Institutional TOEFL is not an official administration.

What is the Paper and Pencil TOEFL program?

The Paper and Pencil TOEFL continues to be offered once a month on regularly scheduled Fridays and Saturdays at designated test centers in fourteen countries throughout the world, including Bangladesh, Bhutan, Cambodia, Hong Kong, India, Japan, Korea, Laos, Macau, Pakistan, the People's Republic of China, Thailand, Taiwan, and Vietnam. In these countries, the Paper and Pencil TOEFL is the official administration.

Refer to the TOEFL *Information Bulletin* for specific dates. Be sure that you order the TOEFL *Bulletin* for the Paper and Pencil TOEFL.

What is the Computer-Based TOEFL program?

The Computer-Based TOEFL was introduced July, 1998, in the United States, Canada, Latin America, Europe, Australia, Africa, the Middle East, and a limited number of Asian nations. The Computer-Based TOEFL will be phased in, replacing the Paper and Pencil TOEFL worldwide by 2001. A list of test centers established for the purpose of administering the Computer-Based TOEFL program appears in the free TOEFL *Information Bulletin* available from TOEFL Services. Be sure that you order the TOEFL *Information Bulletin* for the Computer-Based TOEFL program.

What is the Institutional TOEFL program?

More than 1,200 schools, colleges, universities, and private agencies administer the Institutional TOEFL. The Institutional TOEFL is the same length, format, and difficulty as the official Paper and Pencil TOEFL, but the dates and the purposes of the Institutional TOEFL are different from those of the official TOEFL.

The dates for the Institutional TOEFL usually correspond to the beginning of an academic session on a college or university calendar.

The Institutional TOEFL is used for admission, placement, eligibility, or employment only at the school or agency that offers the test.

If you plan to use your scores for a different college, university, or agency, you should take one of the official TOEFL tests, either the Paper and Pencil TOEFL or the Computer-Based TOEFL.

How can I order an *Information Bulletin?*

There are three ways to order a TOEFL *Information Bulletin.*

e-mail	toefl@ets.org
download	www.ets.org
FAX	1-609-771-7500
mail	TOEFL Services
	P.O. Box 6151
	Princeton, NJ 08541-6151
	U.S.A.

Be sure that you request the correct TOEFL *Information Bulletin* for your test. Ask for either the Paper and Pencil *Information Bulletin* or the Computer-Based *Information Bulletin.*

It is correct to limit your correspondence by FAX or mail to two sentences. For example:

REQUEST FOR THE TOEFL *INFORMATION BULLETIN*

(write your address here)
(write the date here)

TOEFL Services
P.O. 6151
Princeton, NJ 08541-6151
U.S.A.

Dear TOEFL Representative:

Please send me a copy of the TOEFL *Information Bulletin* for the (write Paper and Pencil or Computer-Based TOEFL here).

Thank you for your earliest attention.

Sincerely yours,

(write your name here)

The TOEFL *Bulletin* is also available overseas in U.S. embassies and advising offices of the United States Information Service (USIS), binational centers, IIE and AMIDEAST Counseling

Centers, Fulbright offices, and ETS Regional Registration Centers, as well as in Sylvan Technology Centers.

May I choose the Paper and Pencil TOEFL or the Computer-Based TOEFL?

When the Computer-Based TOEFL is phased in for the country where you will take your TOEFL, you must take the Computer-Based TOEFL. All Paper and Pencil TOEFL tests will be replaced.

Which language skills are tested on the TOEFL?

In general, the same four language skills are tested in all TOEFL programs. Listening, structure, writing, and reading are tested in three separate sections:

Section 1   Listening
Section 2   Structure
Section 3   Reading

There are some differences in the types of questions used to test the language skills, however. Charts that outline the differences between the Paper and Pencil TOEFL and the Computer-Based TOEFL are printed at the beginning of each Review Chapter in this book.

Does the TOEFL have a composition section?

Paper and Pencil TOEFL

The Paper and Pencil TOEFL does not have a composition section, but if you take the TOEFL in August, October, December, February, or May, you will also take the TWE (Test of Written English).

Computer-Based TOEFL

The Computer-Based TOEFL has a Writing Section. On the TWE and on the Writing Section, you must write a short essay on an assigned topic.

The essay should be about 300 words long. The topic is typical of academic writing requirements at colleges and universities in North America. You have 30 minutes to finish writing. Both the Test of Written English and the Writing Section are described in greater detail in Chapter 6 of this book.

Are all the TOEFL tests the same length?

Paper and Pencil TOEFL

All of the forms of the Paper and Pencil TOEFL are the same length.

Computer-Based TOEFL

The forms for the Computer-Based TOEFL vary in length. Items are selected by the computer based on the level of difficulty and the number of correct responses from previous items. Difficult items are worth more points than average or easy items.

Is the Computer-Based TOEFL fair?

The Computer-Based TOEFL is fair because the computer is constantly adjusting the selection of items based on your responses. It allows you to achieve that maximum number of points that you are capable of based on your English language proficiency. In addition, everyone receives the same test content and the same proportion of question types—multiple choice and computer-assisted.

What if I have little experience with computers?

There is a Tutorial at the beginning of the Computer-Based TOEFL to help you become familiar with the computer before you begin your test. In the Tutorial, you will review how to use a mouse, how to scroll, and how to answer all the question types on the test.

If you would like to work through the Tutorial before the day of your Computer-Based TOEFL, you can request a free CD-ROM Sampler from ETS. In the United States and Canada, call 1-800-446-3319. From other countries, call 1-619-771-7243. Or, if you have access to the web, you can use the Sampler by visiting the TOEFL web site at http://www.toefl.org. There are also a few samples of the Tutorial in the TOEFL *Information Bulletin*.

Registration

How do I register for the TOEFL?

Paper and Pencil TOEFL

The TOEFL *Information Bulletin* has a registration form in it. Using the directions in the TOEFL *Bulletin*, fill out the form and mail it to your local representative. Be sure to sign the form and include your registration fee. The address for your local representative is included in the TOEFL *Bulletin*.

Computer-Based TOEFL

There are three ways to register for the Computer-Based TOEFL. If you plan to pay by credit card—VISA, MasterCard, or American Express—you may register by phone. Call Sylvan Candidate Services at 1-800-468-6335, or phone your Regional Registration Center. The phone numbers for the regional centers are listed in the TOEFL *Bulletin*. If you plan to pay by check, money order, or credit card, you may register by mail. To arrange a test in the United States, Canada, Puerto Rico, or a U.S. territory, return the Voucher Request Form in your *Bulletin*, along with your registration fee to TOEFL Services in Princeton, New Jersey. There is a mailing label provided in the *Bulletin*. To arrange a test in all other locations where the Computer-Based TOEFL is offered, return the International Test Scheduling Form to your Regional Registration Center. There are mailing labels provided in the TOEFL *Bulletin*. Be sure to sign the form and include your registration fee.

You will be asked to choose two days of the week and two months of the year as well as two test centers. If there are no appointments available on the dates you have requested, you will be assigned a date close to the request you have made.

Institutional TOEFL

The school, college, university, or agency that administers the Institutional TOEFL should have registration forms available. Fees vary.

The school, college, university, or agency will return your registration form and the registration fee to TOEFL Services along with the forms and fees of all of the other applicants for the Institutional Testing.

When should I register for the TOEFL?

If you are taking the TOEFL as part of the application process for college or university admission, plan to take the test early enough for your score to be received by the admission office in time to be considered with your application. Usually, a test date at least two months before the admission application deadline allows adequate time for your scores to be considered with your admission application.

Test centers often receive more requests than they can accommodate on certain dates. Try to schedule your appointment by phone or mail at least a month before the date you prefer to take the TOEFL.

What are the fees for the TOEFL?

Paper and Pencil TOEFL

In most countries, the registration fee is $80 U.S., but the cost may vary slightly from one country to another. For exact fees in local currency, refer to the TOEFL *Information Bulletin*.

Computer-Based TOEFL

In the United States, Canada, Puerto Rico, and U.S. territories, the registration fee is $100 U.S. The fee may be paid by check, credit card, money order, bank draft, or U.S. postal money order.

In other countries, the registration fee was originally advertised as $125 U.S., but TOEFL Services is now offering the Computer-Based TOEFL worldwide at $100 U.S. Because of rates of exchange, the actual cost may vary from one country to another. For exact fees in local currency, and options for payment, refer to the TOEFL *Information Bulletin*.

Which credit cards will be accepted?

Only MasterCard, VISA, and American Express may be used to pay for TOEFL registration fees and services.

What can I do if I have currency exchange restrictions?

TOEFL Services can issue a Fee Certificate to a friend or family member living in a country where U.S. dollars are available. The friend or family member can send the certificate to you, and you can use it to pay your TOEFL registration fee. The certificate costs $140 U.S., and is valid for one year.

Will Educational Testing Service (ETS) confirm my registration?

Paper and Pencil TOEFL

If you register for the Paper and Pencil TOEFL, you will receive an Admission Ticket.

You must complete the ticket and take it with you to the test center on the day of the test. You will also receive a Photo File Record to which you must attach a passport-sized photograph. Your photograph will be made available to the institutions that receive your scores.

If you have not received the Admission Ticket two weeks before the date of your TOEFL test, call TOEFL Services in Princeton, New Jersey at 1-609-771-7100 or call your local representative. The phone numbers for local representatives are listed in the TOEFL *Information Bulletin.*

Computer-Based TOEFL

If you register for the Computer-Based TOEFL, you will receive an Appointment Confirmation Number. If you do not receive an Appointment Confirmation Number, or if you lose your Appointment Confirmation Number, call TOEFL Services at 1-609-771-7100 in the United States or call your Regional Registration Center outside the United States. The phone numbers for Regional Registration Centers are listed in the TOEFL *Information Bulletin.*

May I change the date or cancel my registration?

Paper and Pencil TOEFL

Test date changes and cancellations are not permitted for the Paper and Pencil TOEFL; however, you may receive absentee credit. If you do not take the Paper and Pencil TOEFL, write "absentee credit" across your Admission Ticket and send it to TOEFL Services. It must arrive within sixty days of your test date for you to receive $10 cash or $10 credit toward registration for a different date.

Computer-Based TOEFL

In the United States, Canada, Puerto Rico, and U.S. territories, call Sylvan Candidate Services at 1-800-468-6335. Be sure to call by noon two business days before the date of your appointment, or you will not receive a partial reimbursement of your registration fee. If you want to choose a different date, you may be asked to pay a rescheduling fee of $20.

In all other locations, call your Regional Registration Center by noon five business days before the date of your appointment, or you will not receive a partial reimbursement of your registration fee. If you want to choose a different date, you may be asked to pay a rescheduling fee of $20.

You must provide your Appointment Confirmation Number when you call. You will be given a Cancellation Number.

How should I prepare the night before the TOEFL?

Don't go to a party the night before you take your TOEFL examination. But don't try to review everything that you have studied in this book either. By going to a party, you will lose the opportunity to review a few problems that may add valuable points to your TOEFL score. But by trying to review everything, you will probably get confused, and you may even panic.

Select a limited amount of material to review the night before you take the TOEFL.

And remember, you are not trying to score 100 percent on the TOEFL examination. No one knows everything. If you answer 75 percent of the questions correctly, you will receive an excellent score.

May I register on the day of the TOEFL?

Registration of candidates on the day of the TOEFL is not permitted under any circumstances at test centers in the United States or abroad.

Test Administration

Where are the test centers?

Paper and Pencil TOEFL

Test centers are listed in the TOEFL *Information Bulletin*. Be sure to check the chart to make sure that the center you wish to use will be offering the Paper and Pencil TOEFL on the date you have chosen.

Computer-Based TOEFL

Sylvan Technology Centers will be administering the Computer-Based TOEFL at two different types of test centers throughout the world. Permanent centers will be open all year. Mobile centers will be open on certain specified dates. Be sure to check the TOEFL *Information Bulletin* to make sure that the center will be offering the Computer-Based TOEFL on the date you have chosen.

After you have taken the Computer-Based TOEFL, it may not be possible for you to contact administrators at your test center if it is a mobile center. In that case, you can call TOEFL Services or the Regional Registration Center where you arranged for your test. Telephone numbers are listed in the TOEFL *Information Bulletin*.

What kind of room will be used for the TOEFL?

Paper and Pencil TOEFL

The rooms vary greatly from one test site to another. Rooms used for the Paper and Pencil TOEFL tend to be large. The seats are usually school desks. It is a good idea to wear clothing that allows you to adjust to warm or cold room temperatures.

Computer-Based TOEFL

Rooms used for the Computer-Based TOEFL are much smaller. There are only six to fifteen students at individual computer stations. Each student has a headset. It is a good idea to wear clothing that allows you to adjust to warm or cold room temperatures.

What should I take with me to the examination room?

Paper and Pencil TOEFL

Take three sharpened number two pencils with erasers on them, your Admission Ticket, and Photo Identification Form. In addition to your photo identification, you must have official identification with you.

It would be helpful to take a watch, although most examination rooms will have clocks. Books, dictionaries, tape recorders, cellular phones, pagers, highlighters, pens, and notes are not permitted in the examination room.

Computer-Based TOEFL

Take your Appointment Confirmation Number; your Computer-Based TOEFL Voucher, if you registered by mail or FAX; and your official identification.

You will not need a watch because the computer screen has a clock face on it. Books, dictionaries, tape recorders, cellular phones, pagers, highlighters, pens, and notes are not permitted in the examination room. Some centers will have lockers for you to store your possessions, but it is really better not to take with you anything that you cannot take into the examination room.

What kind of identification is required?

Paper and Pencil TOEFL

The test center supervisor will not admit you if you do not have official identification. In the United States, only your valid passport will be accepted. The supervisor will not allow you to enter with an expired passport or a photocopy of your passport. In other countries, your valid passport is still the best identification, but if you do not have a passport, you may refer to the TOEFL *Bulletin* for special directions.

Be sure that your photo identification and your passport picture look like you do on the day of the examination. If not, you may not be admitted to the examination room.

Be sure to use the same spelling and order of your name on your registration materials, Admission Ticket, Answer Sheet, and any correspondence that you may have with either TOEFL Services or your Regional Registration Center.

Computer-Based TOEFL

In the United States, only your valid passport will be accepted. In other countries, your valid passport is still the best identification, but if you do not have a passport, you may refer to the TOEFL *Bulletin* for special directions.

Your photograph will be taken at the test center and reproduced on all official score reports sent to institutions. Your identification will be checked against the new photograph. In addition, all Computer-Based TOEFL sessions will be videotaped.

Be sure to use the same spelling and order of your name on your registration materials or phone registration, the Test Center Log that you will sign when you enter the test area, the forms on the computer screens, and any correspondence that you may have with TOEFL Services, Sylvan Technology Centers, or other local representatives.

Will I sign a Confidentiality Statement?

Paper and Pencil TOEFL

There is no Confidentiality Statement required for the Paper and Pencil TOEFL.

Computer-Based TOEFL

Before you begin the Computer-Based TOEFL, you will be asked to sign a Confidentiality Statement. You will agree to keep confidential the content of all test questions. The purpose of this procedure is to protect the security of the test.

Where should I sit?

You will be assigned a seat. You may not select your own seat.

It is usually better not to sit with friends anyway. You may find yourself looking at friends instead of concentrating on your test materials. You may even be accused of cheating if it appears that you are communicating in some way.

What if I am late?

Paper and Pencil TOEFL

Report to the test center no later than the time on your Admission Ticket. No one will be admitted after the test materials have been distributed.

Computer-Based TOEFL

Report to the test center thirty minutes before the appointment time for your TOEFL. You will need a half hour to check in. If you arrive late, you may not be admitted, and your fee will not be refunded.

How long is the testing session of the TOEFL?

Paper and Pencil TOEFL

The total time for the testing session of the Paper and Pencil TOEFL is two hours. Since the instructions are not included as part of the timed sections, the actual time that you will spend in the examination room will be about three hours. When the TWE is given with the TOEFL, the total time will be about three and one half hours. When you finish, you must sit quietly until the supervisor dismisses the group.

Computer-Based TOEFL

The time for the Computer-Based TOEFL will vary, depending on your familiarity with computers. There is a computer Tutorial at the beginning of the session for those who need some practice using the computer before taking the Computer-Based TOEFL. In general, the Computer-Based TOEFL takes four to four and a half hours, including the Tutorial. When you finish, you may leave the room quietly.

How much time do I have to complete each of the sections?

It is wise to work as rapidly as possible without compromising accuracy. Check the Timetable for the TOEFL on page xiii.

Are breaks scheduled during the TOEFL?

Paper and Pencil TOEFL

There are no breaks scheduled during the Paper and Pencil TOEFL.

Computer-Based TOEFL

There is a ten-minute break scheduled during the Computer-Based TOEFL. It usually occurs between the Structure and the Reading Sections.

Is there a place to eat lunch at the test centers?

Some of the testing centers are conveniently located near restaurants, but many, especially the mobile centers, are not. You may want to take a snack with you to eat before or after your test.

How can I complain about a test administration?

If you feel that the test situation was not fair, you have a right to register a complaint. Within three days of the date of the test, write a letter to Test Administration Services. The FAX number is 1-609-520-1092. Include the date of your test, the city, and the country. Explain why you feel that the test was not fair.

Examination

What kinds of questions are found on the TOEFL?

Paper and Pencil TOEFL

All the questions on the Paper and Pencil TOEFL are multiple choice.

Computer-Based TOEFL

The majority of the questions on the Computer-Based TOEFL are multiple choice. There are also some other types of questions on the Computer-Based TOEFL. These questions will have special directions on the screen. You will have many examples of them in the Model Tests in this book.

How do I answer the test questions?

Paper and Pencil TOEFL

Read the four possible answers in your test book, and mark the corresponding space on the answer sheet, which will be provided for you at the test center.

There are two versions of the Answer Sheet—a horizontal and a vertical version. We have included both versions of answer sheets with the Model Tests included in this book. Because it takes a little longer to finish an examination when you mark the answers on a separate sheet, always use the answer sheets when you take the Paper and Pencil Model Tests in this book.

Computer-Based TOEFL

When you are presented with a multiple choice question, read the four possible answers on the screen, point the arrow and click beside the answer that you choose. The oval will change from white to black. When you are presented with other types of questions, follow the directions on the screen.

How do I mark the answers?

Paper and Pencil TOEFL

Before the examination begins, the supervisor will explain how to mark the answer sheet. Be sure to fill in the space completely.

MARKING THE ANSWER SHEET: PAPER AND PENCIL TOEFL

One question is shown in the test book. One answer is marked on the Answer Sheet.

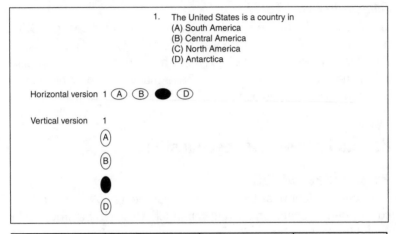

Computer-Based TOEFL

Before the examination begins, you will have an opportunity to practice marking the answers to questions on the computer screen. The Tutorial will include all the different types of questions on the Computer-Based TOEFL.

MARKING THE ANSWER SCREEN: COMPUTER-BASED TOEFL

One question is shown on the computer screen. One answer is marked on the screen. The screen is printed on the following page.

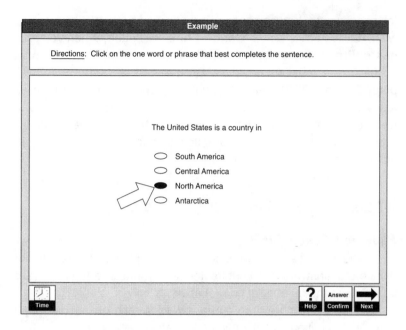

May I make marks in the test book?

Paper and Pencil TOEFL

You are not allowed to make marks in your test book for the Paper and Pencil TOEFL. You may not underline words or write notes in the margins of the test book. It is considered cheating.

Computer-Based TOEFL

There is no test book for the Computer-Based TOEFL. All of the questions and the answer options are presented on the computer screen.

May I change an answer?

Paper and Pencil TOEFL

You may erase an answer on the Answer Sheet if you do so carefully and completely. Stray pencil marks may cause inaccurate scoring by the test-scoring machine.

Computer-Based TOEFL

On the first two sections of the Computer-Based TOEFL, Listening and Structure, you can change your answer by clicking on the new answer. You can change your answer as many times as you wish, until you click on the **Confirm Answer** button. When you click on **Confirm Answer**, you move to the next question, and you cannot go back to a previous question. On the third section of the Computer-Based TOEFL, Reading, you can change your answer as many times as you wish. You may go on to the next question and back to the previous questions. The CD-ROM that supplements this book will provide you with practice in choosing and changing answers on the computer screen.

If I am not sure of an answer, should I guess?

Paper and Pencil TOEFL

If you are not sure of an answer, you should guess. The number of incorrect answers is not subtracted from your score. Your score is based upon the number of correct answers only.

Do not mark more than one answer for each question. Do not leave any questions blank on your Answer Sheet.

Computer-Based TOEFL

Answer every question. Your score will be based not only on the difficulty of the questions but also on the number of questions answered.

How should I guess?

Paper and Pencil TOEFL

First, eliminate all of the possibilities which you know are NOT correct. Then, if you are almost sure of an answer, guess that one.

If you have no idea of the correct answer for a question, choose one letter and use it for your "guess" answer throughout the entire examination.

By using the same letter each time that you guess, you will probably answer correctly 25 percent of the time.

The "guess" answer is especially useful for finishing a section quickly. If the supervisor tells you to stop working on a section before you have finished it, answer all of the remaining questions with the "guess" answer.

Computer-Based TOEFL

In the first two sections, Listening and Structure, eliminate the incorrect answers, then guess, but do not use a "guess answer" to finish these sections quickly. You will receive a lower score for random guessing.

On the third section, Reading, try to manage your time so that you can finish all of the questions, but if you have only a minute or two left, try to answer all of the remaining questions. Use a "guess answer." Even random guessing will increase your score on the Reading Section.

What should I do if I discover that I have marked my answers incorrectly?

Paper and Pencil TOEFL

Do not panic. Notify the supervisor immediately.

If you have marked one answer in the wrong space on the Answer Sheet, the rest of the answers will be out of sequence. Ask for time at the end of the examination to correct the sequence. The TOEFL test supervisor may or may not allow you to do this.

If you have marked the answers in the test book instead of on the Answer Sheet, ask for your test book to be attached to your Answer Sheet and included in the supervisor's "Irregularities Report."

To save time finding the number on the Answer Sheet that corresponds to the problem you are reading, to avoid mismarking, and to save space on your desk, use your test book as a marker on your Answer Sheet. As you advance, slide the book down underneath the number of the question that you are marking on the Answer Sheet.

Computer-Based TOEFL

It is not possible to mark your screen incorrectly because the computer program will present only one question on each screen. If you change your mind after you have confirmed a response on the Listening or Structure Sections, the computer will not allow you to return to a previous question on these two sections, and you will not be able to change the answer that you have confirmed.

As you see, it is very important to be sure of the answer before you click on **Confirm Answer**.

May I choose the order of the sections on my TOEFL?

You may not choose the order. Listening, Structure, and Reading are tested in that order. The essay is written last. When you have finished with a section, you may not work on any other section of the test.

What if I cannot hear the tape for the Listening Section?

Paper and Pencil TOEFL

It is the responsibility of the supervisor for the Paper and Pencil TOEFL to make sure that everyone is able to hear the tape. If you cannot hear it well, raise your hand and ask the supervisor to adjust the volume.

Computer-Based TOEFL

You will have your own headset for the Computer-Based TOEFL. Before the Listening Section begins, you will have an opportunity to adjust the volume yourself.

May I keep my test?

Paper and Pencil TOEFL

TOEFL Services makes copies of test books available for Paper and Pencil TOEFLs taken on specific dates listed in the TOEFL *Information Bulletin.* They are called "disclosed" tests. If you take the TOEFL on one of the specified dates, you must bring a 15.3 cm x 22.8 cm self-addressed envelope with enough stamps attached to mail 43 grams. Your test book will then be mailed to you by the test supervisor the week after the test. This service is free. If you do not have a self-addressed stamped envelope, you may not request your test later.

TOEFL Services will also mail you a copy of your Answer Sheet, a list of the correct answers, and a cassette tape recording of the Listening Comprehension Section. To receive these materials, complete the order form on the inside cover of your test book and mail it along with the fee printed on the form to TOEFL Services.

If you try to take your test book without the permission of your test supervisor, your test will not be scored. In addition, TOEFL Services may take legal action against you.

Computer-Based TOEFL

The Computer-Based TOEFL does not offer any "disclosed" tests at this time.

What can I do if I do not appear to take the test?

Paper and Pencil TOEFL

If you do not appear to take the test, you have a right to request a partial refund. If you enter the examination room, you cannot request a partial refund. You must make your request within sixty days of the date of the TOEFL test. Ask for "absentee credit" when you write to the TOEFL Office. The refund is $10.

Computer-Based TOEFL

There is a $60 refund, if you cancel your test five business days before the date of your appointment, or if you decide not to use your Computer-Based Test Voucher.

Score Reports

How is my TOEFL scored?

Paper and Pencil TOEFL

Total Paper and Pencil TOEFL scores range from 310 to 677.

First, each of the three sections of the TOEFL is graded on a scale from 31 to 68. Then the scores from the three sections are added together. Finally, the sum is multiplied by 10 and divided by 3.

For example, the following scores were received on the three sections.

Listening Comprehension	52
Structure and Written Expression	48
Vocabulary and Reading Comprehension	50
	150

150 x 10 = 1500 ÷ 3 = 500 Total TOEFL Score

Computer-Based TOEFL

Total Computer-Based TOEFL scores range from 0 to 300.

First, each of the three sections of the TOEFL is graded on a scale from 0 to 30. Then the scores from the three sections are added together. Finally, the sum is multiplied by 10 and divided by 3.

For example, the following scores were received on the three sections.

Listening	23
Structure and Writing	25
Reading	<u>27</u>
	75

75 x 10 = 750 ÷ 3 = 250 Total TOEFL Score

How do I interpret my score?

There are no passing or failing scores on the TOEFL. Each agency or university will evaluate the scores according to its own requirements. Even at the same university, the requirements may vary for different programs of study, levels of study (graduate or undergraduate), and degrees of responsibility (student or teaching assistant).

The admissions policies summarized on the next page are typical of U.S. universities, assuming, of course, that the applicant's documents other than English proficiency are acceptable.

TYPICAL ADMISSIONS POLICIES OF AMERICAN UNIVERSITIES

Paper and Pencil TOEFL Score	Policy	Computer-Based TOEFL Score
650 or more	admission assured for graduate students	280 or more
600–649	admission assured for undergraduate students	250–279
550–599	admission probable for graduate students	213–249
500–549	admission probable for undergraduate students	173–212
450–499	individual cases reviewed	133–172
449 or less	referral to English language program probable	132 or less

Refer to the TOEFL *Information Bulletin* for a detailed chart of percentile ranks for total TOEFL scores. This will help you interpret your score relative to the scores of others taking the examination.

How do the scores on the Paper and Pencil TOEFL compare with those on the Computer-Based TOEFL?

A concordance table is a table that shows comparisons. A concordance table for the Paper and Pencil TOEFL and the Computer-Based TOEFL has been mailed to all institutions that use TOEFL scores for admissions decisions. A copy of the concordance table is available now on the ETS web site and will be printed in future editions of the TOEFL *Information Bulletin*.

A shorter version of the table is printed below:

Paper-Based TOEFL	Computer-Based TOEFL
677	300
650	280
600	250
550	213
500	173
450	133
400	97

If I score very poorly on one part of the TOEFL, is it still possible to receive a good total score?

If you feel that you have done very poorly on one part of a section, do not despair. You may receive a low score on one part of a section and still score well on the total examination if your scores on the other parts of that section and the other sections are good.

When can I see my scores?

Paper and Pencil TOEFL

You are entitled to four copies of your test results, including one personal copy for yourself and three Official Score Reports.

You will receive your copy about five weeks after you take the test.

TOEFL Services also offers score reporting by phone. To use this service, you must have your Admission Ticket, a credit card, and a touch-tone phone. Call 1-609-771-7267 from six in the morning to ten at night, New York time. The fee for this service is a $10 charge to your credit card plus a charge to your telephone bill for the long distance call.

Scores are available by phone approximately one month after the date of your test. For exact dates, refer to the TOEFL *Bulletin*.

Computer-Based TOEFL

After you complete your Computer-Based TOEFL, you can view your estimated score on the screen. You will be able to see section scores for both Listening and Reading, as well as the multiple choice part of the Structure Section, but the essay, which is included as half of the Structure score, will not have been graded. The estimated score that you will see shows a total score range based on a very poorly written essay or on a very well written essay.

You are entitled to five copies of your test results, including one personal copy for yourself and four Official Score Reports.

Your official scores for all sections will be mailed to you about two weeks after you take your Computer-Based TOEFL, but you will have a very good idea how you performed on the test after you see the estimate. No score reporting by phone is currently available for the Computer-Based TOEFL.

What can I do if I question my score report?

Paper and Pencil TOEFL

Occasionally, the computer will score an Answer Sheet incorrectly because of the way you have marked it. If you feel your score is much, much lower than you expected, you have a right to request that your Answer Sheet be hand scored.

Two people will score your Answer Sheet independently. If their results are different from that of the computer, your score will be changed. The cost of this service is $20 for the TOEFL and $45 for the TWE. You must make your request within six months of the date of the test.

To make a request, write a letter to TOEFL Services.

Computer-Based TOEFL

The TOEFL *Bulletin* for the Computer-Based TOEFL includes a request form to arrange for your essay to be rescored by two graders who have not seen it previously. The fee for this service is $45.

May I cancel my scores?

Paper and Pencil TOEFL

If you do not want your Paper and Pencil TOEFL scores to be reported, you have a right to cancel them. To cancel your test scores, you must complete the score cancellation section of your TOEFL Answer Sheet, and you must write, call, or FAX TOEFL Services. If your request is received at TOEFL Services within seven days of the date of the test, your scores will not be reported.

Computer-Based TOEFL

Before you view your scores, you may cancel them. If you do, they will not be sent to any institutions or to you. You will not know how you performed. If you view your scores, you may not cancel them. You will then choose four institutions to receive your score report. All of this is arranged by responding to questions on the computer screen.

How will the agencies or universities of my choice be informed of my score?

Paper and Pencil TOEFL

Five weeks after the testing, your Official Score Reports will be forwarded directly to the agencies and/or universities that you designated on an information section at the top of the TOEFL Answer Sheet on the day of the examination.

You may send your personal copy to an institution or agency, but the score will probably have to be confirmed by an official at TOEFL Services before you can be admitted. Scores more than two years old cannot be reported or verified.

Computer-Based TOEFL

Two weeks after the testing, your Official Score Reports will be forwarded directly to the agencies and/or universities that you designated on the information section on the computer screen on the day of the examination.

Personal copies of score reports are not accepted by institutions without confirmation by TOEFL Services. Scores more than two years old are not considered valid.

How can I send additional reports?

Paper and Pencil TOEFL

There is a form in the TOEFL *Bulletin* that you can use to have Official Score Reports sent to institutions that were not listed on your Answer Sheet.

You may also request Official Score Reports by phone. To use this service, you must have your Admission Ticket, a credit card, and a touch-tone phone. Call 1-609-771-7267 from six in the morning to ten at night, New York time. The fee for this service is a $12 charge to your credit card per call, an $11 charge per score report, plus a charge to your telephone bill for the long distance call. Official Score Reports will be mailed three days after your telephone request.

Computer-Based TOEFL

There is a form in the TOEFL *Bulletin* that you can use to have Official Score Reports sent to institutions that were not listed on your computer screen. No score reporting by phone is currently available for the Computer-Based TOEFL.

May I take the TOEFL more than one time?

Paper and Pencil TOEFL

You may take the Paper and Pencil TOEFL as many times as you wish in order to score to your satisfaction.

Computer-Based TOEFL

You may not take the Computer-Based TOEFL more than once a month. For example, if you take the Computer-Based TOEFL in July, you must wait until August to take it again.

If I have already taken the TOEFL, how will the first score or scores affect my new score?

TOEFL scores are considered to be valid for two years. If you have taken the TOEFL more than once, but your first score report is dated more than two years ago, TOEFL Services will not report your score.

If you have taken the TOEFL more than once in the past two years, TOEFL Services will report the score for the test date you request on your Score Request Form.

How difficult is the TOEFL?

The level of difficulty of the TOEFL is directly related to the average level of proficiency in English of the candidates who take the examination.

This means that each question will probably be answered correctly by 50 percent of the candidates.

Is there a direct correspondence between proficiency in English and a good score on the TOEFL?

There is not always a direct correspondence between proficiency in English and a good score on the TOEFL. Many students who are proficient in English are not proficient in how to approach the examination. That is why it is important to prepare by using this book.

What is the relationship between my score on the Model Tests in this book and my score on the TOEFL?

It is not possible to calculate a TOEFL score from a score that you might receive on a Model Test in this book. This is so because the actual TOEFL examination has a wider variety of problems.

The Model Tests in this book have been especially designed to help you improve your total TOEFL score by improving your knowledge of the types of problems that most often appear on the TOEFL. These problem types are repeated throughout the four Model Tests so that you will have practice in recognizing and answering them.

By improving your ability to recognize and correctly answer those types of problems that most often appear on the TOEFL, you will improve your total TOEFL score.

Thousands of other students have succeeded by using this book. You can be successful, too.

Updates

Visit my web site at **www.toeflcenter.com**
for the latest information about the TOEFL.

This web site helps students and professionals prepare
for the Test of English as a Foreign Language (TOEFL). You are
invited to write to <u>Dr. Pamela Sharpe,</u> learn from <u>friends</u> around the
world who have recently taken the test, <u>practice</u> with the type of
examples that appear on the TOEFL, and visit The TOEFL Center
<u>Bookstore.</u> The TOEFL Center web site also has information about
<u>scholarships</u> and <u>news</u> about the TOEFL.

| *Dear*
Dr. Sharpe | *The Practice*
Page | *The TOEFL Center*
Bookstore | *TOEFL News* | *Scholarship*
Opportunities |

*TOEFL is a registered trademark of Educational Testing Service. The TOEFL Center bears
sole responsibility for this web site's content and is not connected with the Educational
Testing Service.*

REVIEW OF SECTION 1: LISTENING

Overview of the Listening Section

QUICK COMPARISON
PAPER AND PENCIL TOEFL AND COMPUTER-BASED TOEFL
SECTION 1

Paper and Pencil TOEFL Listening Comprehension	Computer-Based TOEFL Listening
There are fifty questions—thirty on Part A; twenty on Parts B and C.	There are fewer questions.
There are three types of questions—short conversations; longer conversations and class discussions; mini-talks and lectures.	There are three types of questions—short conversations; longer conversations and class discussions; mini-talks and lectures.
The three types of questions are presented in three separate parts. Part A has short conversations; Part B has long conversations and class discussions; Part C has mini-talks and lectures.	The three types of questions are presented in three sets. The first set has short conversations; the second set has longer conversations and class discussions; the third set has lectures.
Everyone taking the TOEFL answers the same questions.	The computer selects questions based on your level of language proficiency.
There are no pictures or visual cues.	Each short conversation begins with a picture to provide orientation. There are several pictures and visual cues with each longer conversation and lecture.

You hear the questions, but they are not written out for you to read.

The questions are written out on the computer screen for you to read while you hear them.

Everyone taking the TOEFL proceeds at the same pace. You cannot pause the tape.

You may control the pace by choosing when to begin the next conversation or lecture.

The section is timed. At the end of the tape, you must have completed the section.

The section is timed. A clock on the screen shows the time remaining for you to complete the section.

You may not replay any of the conversations or lectures.

You may not replay any of the conversations or lectures.

All of the questions are multiple choice.

Most of the questions are multiple choice, but some of the questions have special directions.

Every question has only one answer.

Some of the questions have two answers.

You answer on a paper Answer Sheet, filling in ovals marked (A), (B), (C), and (D).

You click on the screen in the oval that corresponds to the answer you have chosen, or you follow the directions on the screen.

You can return to previous questions, erase, and change answers on your Answer Sheet.

You cannot return to previous questions. You can change your answer before you click on **Confirm Answer**. After you click on **Confirm Answer**, you will see a screen that notifies you to get ready to listen to the next conversation or lecture. You cannot go back.

You may not take notes.

You may not take notes.

Review of Problems and Questions for the Listening Section

This Review can be used to prepare for both the Paper and Pencil TOEFL and the Computer-Based TOEFL. For the most part, the same types of problems are tested on both the Paper and Pencil TOEFL and the Computer-Based TOEFL; however, the Informal Conversations in Problem 9 and the Tours in Problem 13 are found only on the Paper and Pencil TOEFL.

Most of the questions on both the Paper and Pencil TOEFL and the Computer-Based TOEFL are multiple choice. Some of the questions on the Computer-Based TOEFL are computer-assisted. The computer-assisted questions have special directions on the screen.

Although the computer-assisted questions in this book are numbered, and the answer choices are lettered A, B, C, D, the same questions on the CD-ROM that accompanies the larger version of this book, *Barron's How to Prepare for the TOEFL,* are not numbered and lettered. You need the numbers and letters in the book to refer to the Answer Key, the Explanatory Answers, and the Transcript for the Listening Section. On the CD-ROM, you can refer to other chapters by clicking on the screen. The questions on the CD-ROM that is available to supplement the larger version are like those on the Computer-Based TOEFL.

Types of Problems in Short Conversations

 Details

Details are specific facts stated in a conversation.

In some short conversations, you will hear all of the information that you need to answer the problem correctly. You will NOT need to draw conclusions.

When you hear a conversation between two speakers, you must remember the details that were stated.

EXAMPLE

| Man: | Front desk. How may I help you? |
| Woman: | I'd like to arrange a wake-up call for tomorrow morning at seven o'clock, please. |

| Narrator: | When does the woman want to get up tomorrow? |
| Answer: | Seven o'clock in the morning. |

2   Idiomatic expressions

Idiomatic expressions are words and phrases that are character-istic of a particular language with meanings that are usually different from the meanings of each of the words used alone.

In some short conversations, you will hear idiomatic expres-sions, such as "to kill time," which means to wait.

When you hear a conversation between two speakers, you must listen for the idiomatic expressions. You will be expected to recog-nize them and restate the idiom or identify the feelings or attitudes of the speaker.

It will help you if you study a list of common idioms as part of your TOEFL preparation.

EXAMPLE

| Man: | I'm single. In fact, I've never been married. |
| Woman: | No kidding! |

| Narrator: | What does the woman mean? |
| Answer: | She is surprised by the man's statement. |

3   Suggestions

A *suggestion* is a recommendation.

In some short conversations, you will hear words and phrases that make a suggestion, such as "you should," "why don't you," or "why not."

When you hear the words and phrases that introduce a suggestion, you must be able to recognize and remember what the speaker suggested, and who made the suggestion.

EXAMPLE

Woman:	Do you know if there is a Lost and Found on campus? I left my book bag in this room earlier, and it's gone.
Man:	Too bad. Look, why don't you check with your teacher first? Maybe someone in your class turned it in.
Narrator:	What does the man suggest that the woman do?
Answer:	Ask her teacher about the book bag.

4   Assumptions

An *assumption* is a statement accepted as true without proof or demonstration.

In some short conversations, an assumption is proven false, and the speaker or speakers who had made the assumption express surprise.

When you hear a conversation between two speakers, you must be able to recognize remarks that register surprise, and draw conclusions about the assumptions that the speaker may have made.

EXAMPLE

Woman:	Let's just e-mail our response to Larry instead of calling.
Man:	*Larry* has an e-mail address?
Narrator:	What had the man assumed about Larry?
Answer:	He would not have an e-mail address.

5   Predictions

A *prediction* is a guess about the future based on evidence from the present.

In some short conversations, you will be asked to make predictions about the future activities of the speakers involved.

When you hear a conversation between two speakers, you must listen for evidence from which you may draw a logical conclusion about their future activities.

EXAMPLE

Man:	Could you please book me on the next flight out to Los Angeles?
Woman:	I'm sorry, sir. Continental doesn't fly into Los Angeles. Why don't you try Northern or Worldwide?
Narrator:	What will the man probably do?
Answer:	He will probably get a ticket for a flight on Northern or Worldwide Airlines.

6   Implications

Implied means suggested, but not stated. In many ways, implied conversations are like prediction conversations.

In some short conversations, you will hear words and phrases or intonations that will suggest how the speakers felt, what kind of work or activity they were involved in, or where the conversation may have taken place.

When you hear a conversation between two speakers, you must listen for information that will help you draw a conclusion about the situation.

EXAMPLE

Woman:	Where's Anita? We were supposed to go to the library to study.
Man:	Well, here is her coat, and her books are over there on the chair.
Narrator:	What does the woman imply about Anita?
Answer:	Anita has not left for the library yet.

7   Problems

A *problem* is a situation that requires discussion or solution.

In some short conversations, you will hear the speakers discuss a problem.

When you hear a discussion between two speakers, you must be able to identify what the problem is. This may be more difficult because different aspects of the problem will also be included in the conversation.

EXAMPLE

Woman:	It only takes two hours to get to New York, but you'll have a six-hour layover between flights.
Man:	Maybe you could try routing me through Philadelphia or Boston instead.
Narrator:	What is the man's problem?
Answer:	His flight connections are not very convenient.

8   Topics

A *topic* is a main theme in a conversation or in a piece of writing.

In some short conversations, the speakers will discuss a particular topic.

When you hear a conversation, you must be able to identify the main topic from among several secondary themes that support the topic.

EXAMPLE

Man:	Tell me about your trip to New York.
Woman:	It was great! We saw the Statue of Liberty and the Empire State Building and all of the tourist attractions the first day, then we saw the museums the second day and spent the rest of the time shopping and seeing shows.
Narrator:	What are the man and woman talking about?
Answer:	The woman's trip.

Types of Problems in Longer Conversations

9 Informal Conversations

Informal conversations are conversations between friends or with service personnel in stores or restaurants.

In some longer conversations, you will hear an informal exchange between two speakers.

When you hear a conversation, you must be able to summarize the important ideas. You will usually NOT be required to remember small details.

It will help you to review the short conversations in this chapter.

EXAMPLE

Ted Parker:	Are you Mrs. Williams?
Mrs. Williams:	Why, yes!
Ted Parker:	I'm Ted Parker. I talked with you on the telephone earlier today.
Mrs. Williams:	Oh, good.
Ted Parker:	Let me show you what we have in a new Oldsmobile Cutlass.
Mrs. Williams:	I want to look at last year's model, too, if you have any.
Ted Parker:	I have one. A red Delta 88, with 2,000 miles on it. It was a demonstrator.
Mrs. Williams:	A demonstrator?
Ted Parker:	That means that only the sales staff have driven it.
Mrs. Williams:	Oh, well, let's just look at the new ones then.
Ted Parker:	Okay. Everything on this side of the lot is the Cutlass model. You said on the phone that you are looking for automatic. Did you have any idea of other options that you'd like to have on the car?

	Air conditioning, power windows, maybe cruise control?
Mrs. Williams:	Just air conditioning…and an FM radio.
Ted Parker:	Then I suggest that you just spend some time looking at the cars in the last row there. Those six. They have the options and the prices on the sticker on the window, and if you have any questions, I'll be glad to help you.
Mrs. Williams:	Thank you.
Ted Parker:	Let me just say that the best way to know whether you want a car is to drive it. So, when you find something you think you may be interested in, we can take it out for a test drive and let you get the feel of it.
Mrs. Williams:	Okay. That sounds like a good idea.

Question:	Who is the man?
Answer:	A car salesman.
Question:	What is the woman looking for?
Answer:	A new Oldsmobile.
Question:	Besides automatic shift, what options does the woman want?
Answer:	Only air conditioning and a radio.
Question:	What will the woman probably do?
Answer:	Take the car for a test drive.

10 Academic Conversations

Academic conversations are conversations between students and professors or other academic personnel on a college or university campus.

In some longer conversations, you will hear an academic conversation between two speakers.

When you hear a conversation, you must be able to summarize the main ideas. You may also be asked to recall important details.

EXAMPLE

Marcy:	Do you have a minute, Dr. Peterson?
Dr. Peterson:	Sure. Come on in, Marcy. What's the problem?
Marcy:	Well, I'm not sure. I got this letter, and I don't understand it very well.
Dr. Peterson:	Let's see it.
Marcy:	It's from the Financial Aid Office. Are they going to cancel my student aid?
Dr. Peterson:	I would hope not. Hmmmn. Oh, I see. Here's what happened. You are only registered for three hours next semester.
Marcy:	That's true, but I plan to register for another class during open registration. I heard about a new environmental science course, and I'm waiting for it to be assigned a sequence number.
Dr. Peterson:	Well, then, you don't have a problem. You see, the terms of your grant require that you take at least six hours per semester.
Marcy:	I know, but I've never gotten a letter before.
Dr. Peterson:	I think it's a new procedure. Don't worry about it. Just be sure to sign up for at least three more hours before the beginning of the semester.
Marcy:	Thanks, Dr. Peterson. I'm really glad you were in your office today.
Question:	What is Marcy's problem?
Answer:	She has received a letter from the Financial Aid Office.
Question:	Why did Marcy receive a letter?
Answer:	She did not register for six hours this semester.

Question: What had Marcy planned to do?
Answer: Register for three more hours during open registration.

Question: How does Marcy feel when she leaves Dr. Peterson's office?
Answer: Relieved.

Types of Problems in Talks and Lectures

 11 Class Discussions

Class discussions are conversations that occur in classrooms.

In some talks, you will hear a class discussion between two, three, or more speakers.

When you hear a discussion, you must be able to summarize the important ideas. You will usually NOT be required to remember small details.

It will help you to audit some college classes.

EXAMPLE

Miss Richards: Good morning. My name is Miss Richards, and I'll be your instructor for Career Education 100. Before we get started, I'd appreciate it if you would introduce yourselves and tell us a little bit about why you decided to take this class. Let's start here....

Bill: I'm Bill Jensen, and I'm a sophomore this term, but I still haven't decided what to major in. I hope that this class will help me.

Miss Richards: Good, I hope so, too. Next.

Patty: I'm Patty Davis, and I'm majoring in foreign languages, but I'm not sure what kind of job I can get after I graduate.

| Miss Richards: | Are you a sophomore, too, Patty? |
| Patty: | No. I'm a senior. I wish I'd taken this class sooner, but I didn't know about it until this term. |

| Miss Richards: | Didn't your advisor tell you about it? |
| Patty: | No. A friend of mine took it last year, and it helped her a lot. |

| Miss Richards: | How did you find out about the course, Bill? |
| Bill: | The same way Patty did. A friend of mine told me about it. |

| Question: | In what class does this discussion take place? |
| Answer: | Career Education. |

| Question: | What are the two students talking about? |
| Answer: | They are introducing themselves. |

| Question: | Why is the woman taking the course? |
| Answer: | To help her find a job after graduation. |

| Question: | How did the students find out about the course? |
| Answer: | From friends who had taken it. |

12 Radio Programs

Radio programs are short talks that provide information about the news.

In some talks, you will hear information about the news.

When you hear a talk, you must be able to summarize the information. You will usually NOT be required to remember small details.

It will help you to listen to feature news programs on radio and television. Listen carefully. Ask yourself questions to test your ability to remember the information.

EXAMPLE

This is Morning News Magazine, and I'm Jack Stevens. I'll be your host while Mark Watkins is on assignment in the Middle East.

Today's story is about the flight from the cities. Everyone knows that it's happening, but only recently have we been able to determine where the people are going. To the suburbs? To the fringes of the city? Surprisingly not. In a marked reversal of U.S. migration patterns, nonmetropolitan areas have started growing faster than metropolitan areas. City dwellers are leaving to settle in small-town America.

Census figures confirm both the shrinkage of many urban areas and the revival of small towns, a trend that began to become apparent in the last two decades. For example, while the national population increased by 4.8 percent from 1970–1975, towns of 2,500 to 25,000 persons rose 7.5 percent, and the smallest towns with populations of less than 2,500 rose 8.7 percent, or nearly double the national rate.

Recent surveys consistently show that a majority of people, including four out of ten big-city dwellers, prefer life outside the urban environment. They associate small towns with a feeling of community and a sense of security.

Tomorrow's report will focus on crime control. Till then, this is Jack Stevens wishing you a good morning.

Question:	What is the topic of this talk?
Answer:	Migration out of the cities.
Question:	Where are many people moving?
Answer:	To small towns.
Question:	Which areas have experienced the most growth?
Answer:	The towns with a population of 2,500 or fewer people.
Question:	According to surveys, why are people moving?
Answer:	Because people feel secure in small towns.

13 Tours

Tours are short talks that provide factual information about a tourist attraction.

In some talks, you will hear a talk by a tour guide.

When you hear a talk, you must be able to summarize the important ideas. You must also be able to answer questions that begin with the following words: *who, what, when, where, why?*

It will help you to listen to travel programs on radio and television. Listen carefully. Ask yourself questions to test your ability to remember the information.

EXAMPLE

Welcome to the Lincoln Memorial, located, as you can see, on the west bank of the Potomac River, on the axis of the Capitol Building and the Washington Monument.

The structure itself was designed by Henry Bacon in 1912 and completed ten years later at a cost of 2.9 million dollars.

The outer walls of the memorial are white Colorado marble, 189 feet long and 118 feet 8 inches wide. The thirty-six outer columns are also of marble, representing the thirty-six states that were in the Union at the time of Lincoln's death. The name of each state is cut into stone above the column.

Inside the memorial, the walls are Indiana limestone and the floor is pink Tennessee marble. Three commemorative features include the huge seated statue of Lincoln and two inscribed stone tablets.

The marble statue occupies the place of honor, centrally located, as you will note, and facing the Washington Monument and the Capitol Building. The statue is 19 feet high and

19 feet wide, made of twenty-eight blocks of Georgia white marble. Because of the immense size, it took two men four years to complete the carving.

On the north wall, inscribed in stone, is Lincoln's Second Inaugural Address; on the south wall, similarly inscribed, is the Gettysburg Address.

There is a mural above each inscription, representing the two greatest accomplishments of Lincoln's presidency—the emancipation of the slaves and the unification of the North and South after the Civil War.

This memorial is open daily from eight o'clock in the morning to midnight. Stay as long as you like, and be sure to ask one of the park service employees if you have any questions.

Question:	What material was used in the construction of most of the Lincoln Memorial?
Answer:	Marble.
Question:	Why are there thirty-six columns?
Answer:	There is one for each state in the Union at the time of Lincoln's death.
Question:	What other buildings can be seen from the memorial?
Answer:	The Capitol Building and the Washington Monument.
Question:	When is the memorial open?
Answer:	Every day from 8 a.m. to midnight.

14   Academic Talks

Academic talks are short talks that provide orientation to academic courses and procedures.

In some talks, you will hear academic talks on a variety of college and university topics.

When you hear a talk, you must be able to summarize the main ideas. You must also be able to answer questions about important details. You will usually not be asked to remember minor details.

EXAMPLE

Since we'll be having our midterm exam next week, I thought I'd spend a few minutes talking with you about it. I realize that none of you has ever taken a class with me before, so you really don't know what to expect on one of my exams.

First, let me remind you that I have included a very short description of the midterm on the syllabus that you received at the beginning of the semester. So you should read that. I also recommend that you organize and review your notes from all of our class sessions. I'm not saying that the book is unimportant, but the notes should help you to identify those topics that we covered in greatest detail. Then, you can go back to your book and reread the sections that deal with those topics. I also suggest that you take another look at the articles on reserve in the library. They have information in them that is not in the book, and although we didn't talk much about them in class, I do feel that they are important, so you can expect to see a few questions from the articles on the exam. Oh, yes, I almost forgot. Besides the twenty-five objective questions, there will be five essay questions, and you must choose three.

EXAMPLE

Question: What does the speaker mainly discuss?
Answer: The midterm exam.

Question: When will the students take the exam?
Answer: Next week.

Question: According to the professor, what should the students do to prepare?
Answer: Study their notes, the articles on reserve, and appropriate sections of the book.

Question: What is the format of the exam?
Answer: Twenty-five objective questions and five essay questions.

15 Lectures

Lectures are short talks that provide information about academic subjects. They are like short lectures that might be heard in a college classroom.

In some talks, you will hear academic information in a short lecture.

When you hear a lecture, you must be able to summarize the important ideas. You must also be able to answer questions that begin with the following words: *who, what, when, where, why?*

It will help you to listen to documentary programs on radio and television. Programs on educational broadcasting networks are especially helpful. Listen carefully. Ask yourself questions to test your ability to remember the information.

EXAMPLE

Ernest Hemingway began his writing career as an ambitious young American newspaperman in Paris after the first

World War. His early books, including *The Sun Also Rises,* were published in Europe before they were released in the United States.

Hemingway always wrote from experience rather than from imagination. In *Farewell to Arms,* published in 1929, he recounted his adventures as an ambulance driver in Italy during the war. In *For Whom the Bell Tolls,* published in 1940, he retold his memories of the Spanish Civil War.

Perhaps more than any other twentieth-century American writer, he was responsible for creating a style of literature. The Hemingway style was hard, economical, and powerful. It lured the reader into using imagination in order to fill in the details.

In 1952, Hemingway published *The Old Man and the Sea,* a short, compelling tale of an old fisherman's struggle to haul in a giant marlin that he had caught in the Gulf of Mexico. Some critics interpreted it as the allegory of man's struggle against old age; others interpreted it as man against the forces of nature. This book was the climax of Hemingway's career. Two years later he was awarded the Nobel prize for literature.

Question:	What theme did Hemingway use for many of his books?
Answer:	War.
Question:	What was the Hemingway style?
Answer:	Short and powerful.
Question:	What prize did Hemingway win after he wrote *The Old Man and the Sea?*
Answer:	The Nobel prize for literature.
Question:	What advice would Hemingway probably give to other writers?
Answer:	Write from experience about things you have seen and people you have known.

TYPES OF QUESTIONS

Multiple Choice Questions

Paper and Pencil TOEFL

1. What theme did Hemingway use for many of his books?
    (A) War
    (B) Romance
    (C) Travel
    (D) Sports

2. What was the Hemingway style?
    (A) Long descriptions
    (B) Imaginative details
    (C) Short sentences
    (D) Difficult symbolism

3. What prize did Hemingway win after he wrote *The Old Man and the Sea?*
    (A) The Nobel prize for literature
    (B) The European prize for best book of 1952
    (C) The lifetime achievement award for literature
    (D) The American newspapers prize for young writers

4. What advice would Hemingway probably give to other writers?
    (A) Write for a newspaper before you begin writing novels
    (B) Create your own style of literature
    (C) Write from experience about things you have seen and people you have known
    (D) Travel in order to meet interesting people

Answer Sheet

1. ● Ⓑ Ⓒ Ⓓ
2. Ⓐ Ⓑ ● Ⓓ
3. ● Ⓑ Ⓒ Ⓓ
4. Ⓐ Ⓑ ● Ⓓ

Computer-Based TOEFL

What theme did Hemingway use for many of his books?
- ● War
- ○ Romance
- ○ Travel
- ○ Sports

What was the Hemingway style?
- ○ Long descriptions
- ○ Imaginative details
- ● Short sentences
- ○ Difficult symbolism

What prize did Hemingway win after he wrote *The Old Man and the Sea?*
- ● The Nobel prize for literature
- ○ The European prize for best book of 1952
- ○ The lifetime achievement award for literature
- ○ The American newspapers prize for young writers

What advice would Hemingway probably give to other writers?
- ○ Write for a newspaper before you begin writing novels
- ○ Create your own style of literature
- ● Write from experience about things you have seen and people you have known
- ○ Travel in order to meet interesting people

Computer-Assisted Questions

Two-Answer Questions. On some of the computer-assisted questions, you will be asked to select two answers. Both answers must be correct to receive credit for the question.

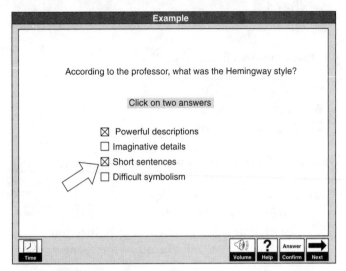

Visual Questions. On some of the computer-assisted questions, you will be asked to select a visual. The visual may be a picture, a drawing, or a diagram.

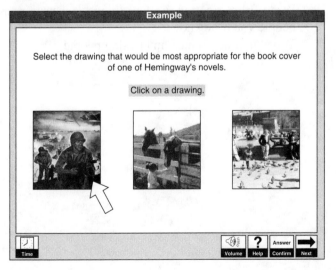

Sequencing Questions. On some of the computer-assisted questions, you will be asked to sequence events in order. The events could be historical events or the steps in a scientific process.

All answers must be sequenced correctly to receive credit for the question.

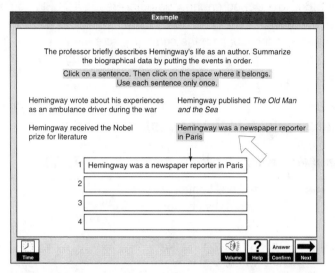

Classification Questions. On some of the computer-assisted questions, you will be asked to classify information by organizing it in categories.

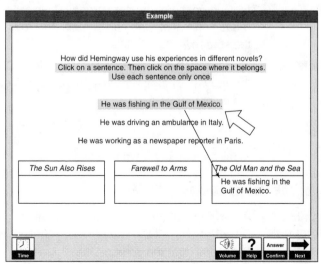

Computer Tutorial for the Listening Section

In order to succeed on the Computer-Based TOEFL, you must understand the computer vocabulary used for the test, and you must be familiar with the icons on the computer screens that you will see on the test. First, review the vocabulary. Then study the computer screens in this Tutorial.

Testing Tools: Vocabulary, Icons, and Keys

General Vocabulary for the Computer-Based TOEFL

Mouse	A small control with one or two buttons on it.
Mouse Pad	A rectangular pad where you move the *mouse*.
Arrow	A marker that shows you where you are moving on the computer screen. Move the *mouse* on the *mouse pad* to move the **Arrow** on the screen.
Click	To depress the button on the *mouse* is to **Click** the *mouse*. **Click** the *mouse* to make changes on the computer screen.
Icon	A small picture or a word or a phrase in a box. Move the *arrow* to the **Icon** and *click* on the **Icon** to tell the computer what to do.

Icons for the Computer-Based TOEFL

Dismiss Directions	An example of an *icon*. *Click* on **Dismiss Directions** to tell the computer to remove the directions from the screen.

Oval   The *icon* beside the answers for the multiple choice test questions. Move the *arrow* to the **Oval** and *Click* on one of the **Ovals** to choose an answer.

Next   An example of an *icon*. To see the next question on the screen, *click* on **Next** first and then *click* on **Confirm Answer**.

Confirm   An example of an *icon*. *Click* on **Confirm Answer** after you *click* on **Next** to see the next question on the screen. Remember, *click* on **Next**, **Confirm Answer** in that order.

Help   An example of an *icon*. *Click* on the question mark to see a list of the *icons* and directions for the section.

Time   An *icon* of a clock in the bottom left corner of the screen. *Click* on the clock face to hide or show the time you have left to finish the section of the test you are working on. Five minutes before the end of each section of the test, the clock will appear automatically. Remember, the time appears in numbers at the top of the screen, not on the clock face. You cannot use the clock during the recording.

Specific Vocabulary for Section 1

Volume   One additional *icon* at the bottom of the screen in the Listening Section. *Click* on **Volume** to go to a screen with an *up arrow* and a *down arrow*. *Click* on the *up arrow* to make the recording louder. *Click* on the *down arrow* to make the recording softer. Remember, you can change the volume while the speaker is giving directions, but not after the directions have concluded.

COMPUTER SCREENS FOR THE COMPUTER-BASED TOEFL

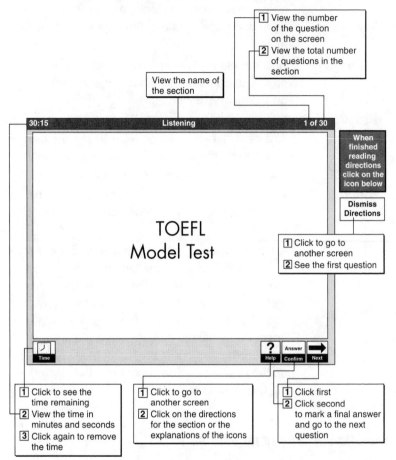

View the name of the section

1 View the number of the question on the screen
2 View the total number of questions in the section

30:15   Listening   1 of 30

When finished reading directions click on the icon below

Dismiss Directions

TOEFL Model Test

1 Click to go to another screen
2 See the first question

Time

? Help   Answer Confirm   Next

1 Click to see the time remaining
2 View the time in minutes and seconds
3 Click again to remove the time

1 Click to go to another screen
2 Click on the directions for the section or the explanations of the icons

1 Click first
2 Click second to mark a final answer and go to the next question

TIP: When the icons are black, you can click on them. When they are gray, they are not functioning. For example, **Answer Confirm** is gray until you click on **Next**. Then **Answer Confirm** is black. Remember the order to click on these two icons.

Computer Screens for Section 1

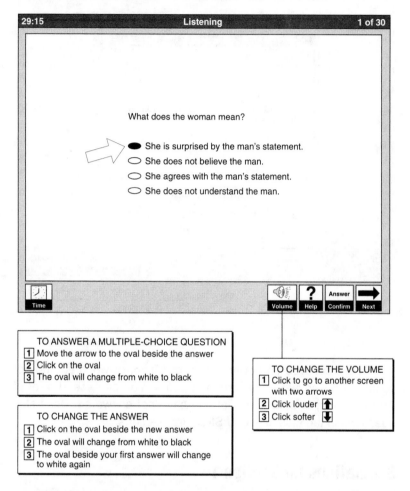

TO ANSWER A MULTIPLE-CHOICE QUESTION
1 Move the arrow to the oval beside the answer
2 Click on the oval
3 The oval will change from white to black

TO CHANGE THE ANSWER
1 Click on the oval beside the new answer
2 The oval will change from white to black
3 The oval beside your first answer will change
to white again

TO CHANGE THE VOLUME
1 Click to go to another screen
with two arrows
2 Click louder ⬆
3 Click softer ⬇

TIP: Most of the questions on the Computer-Based TOEFL are
multiple choice. When you learn to move the arrow to the oval and
click on the oval, you will be able to answer most of the questions.

TIP: When you do not answer a question, or when you do not confirm your answer, this screen appears. You can spend a lot of time returning to questions that you have not answered. Don't skip questions in the Listening and Structure Sections.

Simulations for Section 1

In order to prepare for the experience that you will have on the Computer-Based TOEFL, you can use the CD-ROM that supplements the larger version of this book, *Barron's How to Prepare for the TOEFL*. Locate the Listening Section on Model Tests 5–8. The computer will simulate the Listening Section on the Computer-Based TOEFL. These Model Tests are computer-assisted.

As part of your study plan, be sure to review all of the questions in all of the Model Tests. Use the Explanatory Answers on the CD-ROM or on pages 385–431. Finally, take the Cumulative Model Test on the CD-ROM. This test is computer-adaptive, which means that the computer will select questions for you at your level of language proficiency.

If you choose not to purchase the larger version of this book, or you do not have a computer, you can still simulate some of the features of the Computer-Based TOEFL. In Section 1 of Model Tests 3–4 in Chapter 7, the questions are written out for you to read while you listen to them. This is different from the Paper and Pencil TOEFL. Instead of the CD-ROM, you may be using either an audio compact disc or a cassette. Pause the tape or compact disc occasionally to give yourself more control of the time for each question. But be careful not to pause too often or you will not be able to complete all of the questions within the total time allowed for the section.

Advice for the Listening Section: Computer-Based TOEFL

Be sure to adjust the volume before you begin. Before you begin the Listening Section on the actual TOEFL examination, you will have an opportunity to adjust the volume on your headset. Be sure to do it before you dismiss the directions and begin the test. After the test has begun, you may not adjust the volume.

Do not let the visuals of people distract you from listening to the short conversations. We all respond in different ways to pictures. If you become too involved in looking at the pictures, you may pay less attention to the recording. For the most part, the pictures of people are for orientation to the short conversation. After you look briefly at the picture, give your full concentration to the conversation. If you take the Model Tests on the CD-ROM that supplements the larger version of this book, *Barron's How to Prepare for the TOEFL*, first practice by watching the screen during the short conversation and then by closing your eyes or looking away during the conversation. Find the best way for you to listen to this part of the test.

Focus on the visuals of objects, art, specimens, maps, charts, and drawings in the talks. In general, the pictures of people are for orientation to the talks, whereas the visuals of objects, art, specimens, maps, charts, and drawings support the meaning of the talks. Do not focus on the pictures of people. Do focus on the other visuals that appear during the talks. They could reappear in a question. When you take the Model Tests, practice selective attention. Disregard the pictures of the lecturer and the students, and be alert to the other visuals.

Be sure to read the question while you are hearing it. The questions will be shown on the screen while you are hearing them. If you find that it is to your advantage to close your eyes or look away during the short conversations, be sure to give your full attention to the screen again while the question is being asked. During the questions for longer conversations and talks, watch the screen carefully. By using the Model Tests, you will be able to develop a rhythm for interacting with the screen that is to your advantage.

REVIEW OF SECTION 2: STRUCTURE

Overview of the Structure Section

Paper and Pencil TOEFL *Structure and Written* *Expression*	*Computer-Based TOEFL* *Structure*
There are two types of questions—incomplete sentences and sentences with underlined words and phrases.	There are two types of questions—incomplete sentences and sentences with underlined words and phrases.
The two types of questions are presented in separate parts. Part A has incomplete sentences, and Part B has sentences with underlined words and phrases.	The two types of questions are presented at random in one continuous section. You may see two incomplete sentences, one sentence with underlined words and phrases, another incomplete sentence, and so forth.
There are forty questions— fifteen on Part A and twenty-five on Part B.	There are between twenty and thirty questions.
All of the questions are multiple choice.	All of the questions are multiple choice.
Everyone taking the TOEFL answers the same questions.	The computer will select questions based on your level of proficiency.
Every question has only one answer.	Every question has only one answer.

You have twenty-five minutes to complete the section.

You may control the pace by choosing when to begin the next question, but the section is timed. A clock on the screen shows the time remaining for you to complete the section.

You answer on a paper answer sheet, filling in ovals marked (A), (B), (C), and (D).

You click on the screen either in the oval or on the underlined word or phrase.

You can return to previous questions, erase, and change answers on your answer sheet.

You cannot return to previous questions. You can change your answer before you click on **Confirm Answer**. After you click on **Confirm Answer**, you will see the next question. You cannot go back.

The score on Section 2 is not combined with the score on the essay in the Test of Written English (TWE).

The score on Section 2 is combined with the score on the essay in the Writing Section.

Review of Problems and Questions for the Structure Section

This Review can be used to prepare for both the Paper and Pencil TOEFL and the Computer-Based TOEFL. For the most part, the same types of problems are tested on both the Paper and Pencil TOEFL and the Computer-Based TOEFL. All of the questions on both the Paper and Pencil TOEFL and the Computer-Based TOEFL are multiple choice. Computer-assisted questions do not have special directions.

Strategies and Symbols for Review

Strategies

How will this Review of Structure help you?

It won't teach you every rule of English grammar, but it will provide you with a review of the problems in structure and written expression that are most commonly tested on the TOEFL.

Use this review to study and to check your progress. Follow three easy steps for each problem.

1. *Review the generalization.* First, read the explanation and study the word order in the chart. Then, close your eyes, and try to see the chart in your mind.

2. *Study the examples.* Focus on the examples. First, read them silently, noting the difference between the correct and incorrect sentences. Then, read the underlined parts of the correct sentences aloud.

3. *Check your progress.* First, complete the exercise. Each exercise has two questions—one similar to Part A and the other similar to Part B on the Structure and Written Expression Section of the TOEFL. Then, check your answers, using the Answer Key in Chapter 8 of this book.

If you are studying in an English program, use this review with your grammar book. After your teacher presents a grammar rule in class, find it in this review. Refer to the generalization, study the examples, and check your progress by completing the exercise.

When you go to your next grammar class, you will be more prepared. When you go to your TOEFL examination, you will be more confident. With preparation, you can succeed in school and on the TOEFL.

Symbols

In order for you to use the patterns and rules of style in this review, you must understand five kinds of symbols.

Abbreviations. An abbreviation is a shortened form. In the patterns, five abbreviations, or shortened forms, are used: *S* is an abbreviation for *Subject,* *V* for *Verb,* *V Ph* for *Verb Phrase,* *C* for *Complement,* and *M* for *Modifier.*

Small Letters. Small letters are lowercase letters. In the patterns, a verb written in small (lowercase) letters may not change form. For example, the verb *have* may not change to *has* or *had* when it is written in small letters.

Capital Letters. Capital letters are uppercase letters. In the patterns, a verb written in capital (uppercase) letters may change form. For example, the verb *HAVE* may remain as *have,* or may change to *has* or *had,* depending upon agreement with the subject and choice of tense.

Parentheses. Parentheses are curved lines used as punctuation marks. The following punctuation marks are parentheses: (   ). In the patterns, the words in parentheses give specific information about the abbreviation or word which precedes them. For example, *V (present)* means that the verb in the pattern must be a present tense verb. *N (count)* means that the noun in the pattern must be a countable noun.

Alternatives. Alternatives are different ways to express the same idea. In the patterns, alternatives are written in a column. For example, in the following pattern, there are three alternatives:

had would have could have	participle

The alternatives are *had, would have,* and *could have.* Any one of the alternatives may be used with the participle. All three alternatives are correct.

PATTERNS

Patterns are the parts of a sentence. In some books, *patterns* are called *structures*. In *patterns,* the words have the same order most of the time.

Some of the most important patterns are summarized in this review section. Remember, the generalizations in the charts and explanations for each pattern refer to the structure in the examples. There may be similar structures for which these generalizations are not appropriate.

1 Missing Main Verb

Remember that every English sentence must have a subject and a main verb.

S	V	
The sound of the dryer	bothers	my concentration

Avoid using an *-ing* form, an infinitive, an auxiliary verb, or another part of speech instead of a main verb.

EXAMPLES

INCORRECT: The prettiest girl in our class with long brown hair and brown eyes.

CORRECT: The prettiest girl in our class <u>has</u> long brown hair and brown eyes.

INCORRECT: In my opinion, too soon to make a decision.

CORRECT: In my opinion, <u>it is</u> too soon to make a decision.

INCORRECT: Do you know whether the movie that starts at seven?

CORRECT: Do you know whether the movie that starts at seven <u>is</u> good?

or

Do you know whether the movie <u>starts</u> at seven?

INCORRECT: Sam almost always a lot of fun.
 CORRECT: Sam <u>is</u> almost always a lot of fun.

INCORRECT: The book that I lent you having a good bibliography.
 CORRECT: The book that I lent you <u>has</u> a good bibliography.

EXERCISES

Part A: Choose the correct answer.

Arizona _____ a very dry climate.
   (A) has
   (B) being
   (C) having
   (D) with

Part B: Choose the incorrect word or phrase and correct it.

Venomous snakes <u>with</u> modified teeth connected to
             (A)

<u>poison glands</u> <u>in which</u> the venom <u>is secreted</u> and stored.
   (B)   (C)   (D)

Verbs that Require an Infinitive in the Complement

Remember that the following verbs require an infinitive for a verb in the complement.

agree	claim	deserve	hesitate	manage
appear	consent	expect	hope	mean
arrange	decide	fail	intend	need
ask	demand	forget	learn	offer

| plan | pretend | refuse | tend | wait |
| prepare | promise | seem | threaten | want |

S	V	C (infinitive)	M
We	had planned	to leave	day before yesterday

Avoid using an *-ing* form after the verbs listed. Avoid using a verb word after *want*.

EXAMPLES

| INCORRECT: | He wanted speak with Mr. Brown. |
| CORRECT: | He <u>wanted</u> <u>to speak</u> with Mr. Brown. |

| INCORRECT: | We demand knowing our status. |
| CORRECT: | We <u>demand</u> <u>to know</u> our status. |

| INCORRECT: | I intend the inform you that we cannot approve your application. |
| CORRECT: | I <u>intend</u> <u>to inform</u> you that we cannot approve your application. |

| INCORRECT: | They didn't plan buying a car. |
| CORRECT: | They didn't <u>plan</u> <u>to buy</u> a car. |

| INCORRECT: | The weather tends improving in May. |
| CORRECT: | The weather <u>tends</u> <u>to improve</u> in May. |

EXERCISES

Part A: Choose the correct answer.

One of the least effective ways of storing information is learning _____ it.
  (A) how repeat
  (B) repeating
  (C) to repeat
  (D) repeat

Part B: Choose the incorrect word or phrase and correct it.

Representative democracy seemed <u>evolve</u> <u>simultaneously</u>
                                 (A)   (B)
<u>during</u> the eighteenth and nineteenth centuries in Britain,
  (C)
Europe, and <u>the United States.</u>
                    (D)

Verbs that Require an *-ing* Form in the Complement

Remember that the following verbs require an *-ing* form for a verb in the complement:

admit	*enjoy*	*recall*
appreciate	*finish*	*recommend*
avoid	*keep*	*regret*
complete	*mention*	*risk*
consider	*miss*	*stop*
delay	*postpone*	*suggest*
deny	*practice*	*tolerate*
discuss	*quit*	*understand*

S	V	C (-ing)	M
He	enjoys	traveling	by plane

Avoid using an infinitive after the verbs listed.

Forbid may be used with either an infinitive or an *-ing* complement, but *forbid from* is not idiomatic.

EXAMPLES

INCORRECT:	She is considering not to go.
CORRECT:	She is <u>considering</u> not <u>going</u>.
INCORRECT:	We enjoyed talk with your friend.
CORRECT:	We <u>enjoyed</u> <u>talking</u> with your friend.
INCORRECT:	Hank completed the writing his thesis this summer.
CORRECT:	Hank <u>completed</u> <u>writing</u> his thesis this summer.
INCORRECT:	I miss to watch the news when I am traveling.
CORRECT:	I <u>miss</u> <u>watching</u> the news when I am traveling.
INCORRECT:	She mentions stop at El Paso in her letter.
CORRECT:	She <u>mentions</u> <u>stopping</u> at El Paso in her letter.

EXERCISES

Part A: Choose the correct answer.

Strauss finished _____ two of his published compositions before his tenth birthday.
    (A) written
    (B) write
    (C) to write
    (D) writing

Part B: Choose the incorrect word or phrase and correct it.

<u>Many</u> people have stopped <u>to smoke</u> <u>because</u> they are afraid
  (A)   (B)   (C)
that it <u>may be</u> harmful to their health.
        (D)

Verb Phrases that Require an *-ing* Form in the Complement

Remember that the following verb phrases require an *-ing* form for a verb in the complement:

approve of	*do not mind*	*keep on*
be better off	*forget about*	*look forward to*
can't help	*get through*	*object to*
count on	*insist on*	*think about*
		think of

S	V Ph	C (-ing)	M
She	forgot about	canceling	her appointment

Avoid using an infinitive after the verb phrases listed. Avoid using a verb word after *look forward to* and *object to*.

Remember that the verb phrase *BE likely* does not require an *-ing* form but requires an infinitive in the complement.

EXAMPLES

INCORRECT: She is likely knowing.
CORRECT: She is likely to know.

INCORRECT: Let's go to the movie when you get through to study.
CORRECT: Let's go to the movie when you get through studying.

INCORRECT: We can't help to wonder why she left.
CORRECT: We can't help wondering why she left.

INCORRECT: I have been looking forward to meet you.
CORRECT: I have been looking forward to meeting you.

INCORRECT: We wouldn't mind to wait.
CORRECT: We wouldn't mind waiting.

EXERCISES

Part A: Choose the correct answer.

Many modern architects insist on _____ materials native to the region that will blend into the surrounding landscape.

    (A) use
    (B) to use
    (C) the use
    (D) using

Part B: Choose the incorrect word or phrase and correct it.

During Jackson's administration, those <u>who</u> did not approve of
                                                 (A)

<u>permit</u> common people in the White House <u>were shocked</u> by
  (B)   (C)

the president's insistence that they <u>be invited</u> into the mansion.
                                           (D)

5   Irregular Past Forms

Remember that past forms of the following irregular verbs are not the same as the participles:

Verb Word	Past Form	Participle
be	was/were	been
beat	beat	beaten
become	became	become
begin	began	begun
bite	bit	bitten
blow	blew	blown
break	broke	broken
choose	chose	chosen
come	came	come

Verb Word	*Past Form*	*Participle*
do	did	done
draw	drew	drawn
drink	drank	drunk
drive	drove	driven
eat	ate	eaten
fall	fell	fallen
fly	flew	flown
forget	forgot	forgotten
forgive	forgave	forgiven
freeze	froze	frozen
get	got	gotten or got
give	gave	given
go	went	gone
grow	grew	grown
hide	hid	hidden
know	knew	known
ride	rode	ridden
run	ran	run
see	saw	seen
shake	shook	shaken
show	showed	shown
shrink	shrank	shrunk
sing	sang	sung
speak	spoke	spoken
steal	stole	stolen
swear	swore	sworn
swim	swam	swum
take	took	taken
tear	tore	torn
throw	threw	thrown
wear	wore	worn
weave	wove	woven
withdraw	withdrew	withdrawn
write	wrote	written

S	V (past)	M
The concert	began	at eight o'clock

Avoid using a participle instead of a past for simple past statements.

EXAMPLES

INCORRECT: They done it very well after they had practiced.
CORRECT: They <u>did</u> it very well after they had practiced.

INCORRECT: Before she run the computer program, she had checked it out with her supervisor.
CORRECT: Before she <u>ran</u> the computer program, she had checked it out with her supervisor.

INCORRECT: We eat dinner in Albuquerque on our vacation last year.
CORRECT: We <u>ate</u> dinner in Albuquerque on our vacation last year.

INCORRECT: My nephew begun working for me about ten years ago.
CORRECT: My nephew <u>began</u> working for me about ten years ago.

INCORRECT: I know that you been forty on your last birthday.
CORRECT: I know that you <u>were</u> forty on your last birthday.

EXERCISES

Part A: Choose the correct answer.

Before the Angles and the Saxons _____ to England, the Iberians had lived there.
(A) coming
(B) come
(C) came
(D) did come

Part B: Choose the incorrect word or phrase and correct it.

When Columbus <u>seen</u> the New World, he <u>thought</u> that he
      (A)   (B)

<u>had reached</u> the East Indies <u>by way of</u> a Western route.
    (C)   (D)

6   Factual Conditionals—Absolute, Scientific Results

Remember that *absolute conditionals* express scientific facts. *Will* and a verb word expresses the opinion that the result is absolutely certain.

CONDITION			RESULT		
If	S	V (present) ,	S	V (present)	
If	a catalyst	is used ,	the reaction	occurs	more rapidly

or

CONDITION			RESULT		
If	S	V (present) ,	S	will	verb word	
If	a catalyst	is used ,	the reaction	will	occur	more rapidly

Avoid using *will* and a verb word instead of the present verb in the clause beginning with *if.* Avoid using the auxiliary verbs *have, has, do,* and *does* with main verbs in the clause of result.

EXAMPLES

INCORRECT: If water freezes, it has become a solid.
CORRECT: If <u>water</u> <u>freezes,</u> <u>it</u> <u>becomes</u> a solid.
                or
               If <u>water</u> <u>freezes,</u> <u>it</u> <u>will become</u> a solid.

INCORRECT: If children be healthy, they learn to walk at about eighteen months old.

CORRECT: If <u>children</u> <u>are</u> healthy, <u>they</u> <u>learn</u> to walk at about eighteen months old.

or

If <u>children</u> <u>are</u> healthy, <u>they</u> <u>will learn</u> to walk at about eighteen months old.

INCORRECT: If orange blossoms are exposed to very cold temperatures, they withered and died.

CORRECT: If <u>orange blossoms</u> <u>are exposed</u> to very cold temperatures, <u>they</u> <u>wither and die</u>.

or

If <u>orange blossoms</u> <u>are exposed</u> to very cold temperatures, <u>they</u> <u>will wither and die</u>.

INCORRECT: If the trajectory of a satellite will be slightly off at launch, it will get worse as the flight progresses.

CORRECT: If <u>the trajectory</u> of a satellite <u>is</u> slightly off at launch, <u>it</u> <u>gets</u> worse as the flight progresses.

or

If <u>the trajectory</u> of a satellite <u>is</u> slightly off at launch, <u>it</u> <u>will get</u> worse as the flight progresses.

INCORRECT: If light strikes a rough surface, it diffused.

CORRECT: If <u>light</u> <u>strikes</u> a rough surface, <u>it</u> <u>diffuses</u>.

or

If <u>light</u> <u>strikes</u> a rough surface, <u>it</u> <u>will diffuse</u>.

EXERCISES

Part A: Choose the correct answer.

If water is heated to 212 degrees F. _____ as steam.

    (A) it will boil and escape

    (B) it is boiling and escaping

    (C) it boil and escape

    (D) it would boil and escape

Part B: Choose the incorrect word or phrase and correct it.

If a live sponge is <u>broken</u> into pieces, each piece <u>would turn</u>
            (A)   (B)
into a new sponge <u>like</u> <u>the original one.</u>
                   (C)   (D)

7   Factual Conditionals—Probable Results for the Future

Remember that *will* and a verb word expresses the opinion that the results are absolutely certain. In order of more to less probable, use the following modals: *will, can, may.*

If	S	V (present)		,	S	will can may	verb word	
If	we	find	her address	,	we	will	write	her

S	will can may	verb word		if	S	V (present)	
We	will	write	her	if	we	find	her address

Avoid using the present tense verb instead of a modal and a verb word in the clause of result.

EXAMPLES

INCORRECT: If you put too much water in rice when you cook it, it got sticky.

CORRECT: If <u>you</u> <u>put</u> too much water in rice when you cook it, <u>it</u> <u>will get</u> sticky.

                            or

       <u>It</u> <u>will get</u> sticky, if <u>you</u> <u>put</u> too much water in rice when you cook it.

INCORRECT: If they have a good sale, I would have stopped by on my way home.

CORRECT: If <u>they</u> <u>have</u> a good sale, <u>I</u> <u>will stop</u> by on my way home.

         or

I <u>will stop</u> by on my way home, <u>if</u> <u>they</u> <u>have</u> a good sale.

INCORRECT: We will wait if you wanted to go.
CORRECT: <u>We</u> <u>will wait</u> <u>if</u> <u>you</u> <u>want</u> to go.

         or

<u>If</u> <u>you</u> <u>want</u> to go, <u>we</u> <u>will wait</u>.

INCORRECT: If you listen to the questions carefully, you answer them easily.

CORRECT: If <u>you</u> <u>listen</u> to the questions carefully, <u>you</u> <u>will</u> <u>answer</u> them easily.

         or

<u>You</u> <u>will answer</u> them easily <u>if</u> <u>you</u> <u>listen</u> to the questions carefully.

INCORRECT: If we finished our work a little early today, we'll attend the lecture at the art museum.

CORRECT: If <u>we</u> <u>finish</u> our work a little early today, <u>we'll attend</u> the lecture at the art museum.

         or

<u>We'll attend</u> the lecture at the art museum <u>if</u> <u>we</u> <u>finish</u> our work a little early today.

EXERCISES

Part A: Choose the correct answer.

If services are increased, taxes _____.

    (A) will probably go up

    (B) probably go up

    (C) probably up

    (D) going up probably

Part B: Choose the incorrect word or phrase and correct it.

If you don't <u>register</u> before <u>the last day</u> of regular registration,
           (A)   (B)

you <u>paying</u> <u>a late fee</u>.
   (C)   (D)

8   Contrary-to-Fact Conditionals—Change in Conditions *Unless*

Remember that there is a subject and verb that determines the change in conditions after the connector *unless*.

S	V	unless	S	V	
Luisa	won't return	unless	she	gets	a scholarship

Avoid deleting *unless* from the sentence; avoid deleting either the subject or the verb from the clause after *unless*.

EXAMPLES

INCORRECT: I can't go I don't get my work finished.
CORRECT: I can't go <u>unless</u> <u>I get</u> my work finished.

INCORRECT: They are going to get a divorce unless he stopping drugs.
CORRECT: They are going to get a divorce <u>unless</u> <u>he</u> <u>stops</u> taking drugs.

INCORRECT: You won't get well unless you are taking your medicine.
CORRECT: You won't get well <u>unless</u> <u>you</u> <u>take</u> your medicine.

INCORRECT: Dean never calls his father unless needs money.
CORRECT: Dean never calls his father <u>unless</u> <u>he</u> <u>needs</u> money.

INCORRECT: We can't pay the rent unless the scholarship check.
CORRECT: We can't pay the rent <u>unless</u> <u>the scholarship check</u> <u>comes</u>.

EXERCISES

Part A: Choose the correct answer.

Football teams don't play in the Super Bowl championship
_____ either the National or the American Conference.
   (A) unless they win
   (B) but they win
   (C) unless they will win
   (D) but to have won

Part B: Choose the incorrect word or phrase and correct it.

Usually <u>boys</u> cannot <u>become</u> Boy Scouts <u>unless completed</u>
    (A)   (B)   (C)
<u>the fifth grade</u>.
    (D)

9   Importance—Subjunctive Verbs

Remember that the following verbs are used before *that* and the verb word clause to express importance.

ask	propose
demand	recommend
desire	request
insist	require
prefer	suggest
	urge

S	V	that	S	verb word	
Mr. Johnson	prefers	that	she	speak	with him personally

Avoid using a present or past tense verb instead of a verb word. Avoid using a modal before the verb word.

Note: The verb *insist* may be used in non-subjunctive patterns in the past tense. For example: *He* insisted *that I* was *wrong*.

EXAMPLES

INCORRECT: The doctor suggested that she will not smoke.
CORRECT: The doctor <u>suggested</u> that she not <u>smoke.</u>

INCORRECT: I propose that the vote is secret ballot.
CORRECT: I <u>propose</u> that the vote <u>be</u> secret ballot.

INCORRECT: The foreign student advisor recommended that she studied more English before enrolling at the university.
CORRECT: The foreign student advisor <u>recommended</u> that she <u>study</u> more English before enrolling at the university.

INCORRECT: The law requires that everyone has his car checked at least once a year.
CORRECT: The law <u>requires</u> that everyone <u>have</u> his car checked at least once a year.

INCORRECT: She insisted that they would give her a receipt.
CORRECT: She <u>insisted</u> that they <u>give</u> her a receipt.

EXERCISES

Part A: Choose the correct answer.

Less moderate members of Congress are insisting that changes in the social security system _____ made.
    (A) will
    (B) are
    (C) being
    (D) be

Part B: Choose the incorrect word or phrase and correct it.

<u>Many</u> architects prefer that a dome <u>is used</u> to roof buildings that
  (A)   (B)

need <u>to conserve</u> <u>floor space.</u>
      (C)   (D)

10   Importance—Impersonal Expressions

Remember that the following adjectives are used in impersonal expressions.

essential
imperative
important
necessary

it is	adjective	infinitive	
It is	important	to verify	the data

or

it is	adjective	that	S	verb word	
It is	important	that	the data	be	verified

Avoid using a present tense verb instead of a verb word. Avoid using a modal before the verb word.

EXAMPLES

INCORRECT: It is not necessary that you must take an entrance examination to be admitted to an American university.

CORRECT: <u>It is not necessary</u> <u>to take</u> an entrance examination to be admitted to an American university.

or

It is not necessary that you take an entrance examination to be admitted to an American university.

INCORRECT: It is imperative that you are on time.
CORRECT: It is imperative to be on time.

or

It is imperative that you be on time.

INCORRECT: It is important that I will speak with Mr. Williams immediately.
CORRECT: It is important to speak with Mr. Williams immediately.

or

It is important that I speak with Mr. Williams immediately.

INCORRECT: It is imperative that your signature appears on your identification card.
CORRECT: It is imperative to sign your identification card.

or

It is imperative that your signature appear on your identification card.

INCORRECT: It is essential that all applications and transcripts are filed no later than July 1.
CORRECT: It is essential to file all applications and transcripts no later than July 1.

or

It is essential that all applications and transcripts be filed no later than July 1.

EXERCISES

Part A: Choose the correct answer.

It is necessary _____ the approaches to a bridge, the road design, and the alignment in such a way as to best accommodate the expected traffic flow over and under it.

    (A) plan
    (B) to plan
    (C) planning
    (D) the plan

Part B: Choose the incorrect word or phrase and correct it.

It is essential that vitamins <u>are</u> supplied either by foods <u>or</u>
                               (A)   (B)
<u>by supplementary tablets</u> for normal growth <u>to occur.</u>
            (C)   (D)

11   Purpose—Infinitives

Remember that an infinitive can express purpose. It is a short form of *in order to*.

S	V	C	infinitive (purpose)	
Laura	jogs		to stay	fit
She	takes	vitamins	to feel	better

Avoid expressing purpose without the word *to* in the infinitive. Avoid using *for* instead of *to*.

EXAMPLES

INCORRECT: Wear several layers of clothing for keep warm.
CORRECT: Wear several layers of clothing <u>to keep</u> warm.

INCORRECT:	David has studied hard the succeed.
CORRECT:	David has studied hard <u>to succeed</u>.

INCORRECT:	Don't move your feet when you swing for play golf well.
CORRECT:	Don't move your feet when you swing <u>to play</u> golf well.

INCORRECT:	Virginia always boils the water twice make tea.
CORRECT:	Virginia always boils the water twice <u>to make</u> tea.

INCORRECT:	Wait until June plant those bulbs.
CORRECT:	Wait until June <u>to plant</u> those bulbs.

EXERCISES

Part A: Choose the correct answer.

In the Morrill Act, Congress granted federal lands to the states
_____ agricultural and mechanical arts colleges.

 (A) for establish
 (B) to establish
 (C) establish
 (D) establishment

Part B: Choose the incorrect word or phrase and correct it.

Papyrus <u>was used</u> <u>for to make</u> not only paper <u>but also</u> sails,
     (A)   (B)   (C)

baskets, <u>and</u> clothing.
      (D)

12   Passives—Word Order

Remember that in a passive sentence the actor is unknown or not important. The subject is not the actor.

Passive sentences are also common in certain styles of scientific writing.

S	BE	participle	
State University	is	located	at the corner of College and Third

Avoid using a participle without a form of the verb BE.

EXAMPLES

INCORRECT: My wedding ring made of yellow and white gold.
CORRECT: My wedding ring is made of yellow and white gold.
(It is the *ring*, not the person who made the ring, that is important.)

INCORRECT: If your brother invited, he would come.
CORRECT: If your brother were invited, he would come.
(It is your *brother*, not the person who invited him, that is important.)

INCORRECT: Mr. Wilson known as Willie to his friends.
CORRECT: Mr. Wilson is known as Willie to his friends.
(It is *Mr. Wilson*, not his friends, that is important.)

INCORRECT: References not used in the examination room.
CORRECT: References are not used in the examination room.
(It is *references*, not the persons using them, that are important.)

INCORRECT: Laura born in Iowa.
CORRECT: Laura was born in Iowa.
(It is *Laura*, not her mother who bore her, that is important.)

EXERCISES

Part A: Choose the correct answer.

In the stringed instruments, the tones _____ by playing a bow across a set of strings that may be made of wire or gut.

(A) they produce
(B) producing
(C) are produced
(D) that are producing

Part B: Choose the incorrect word or phrase and correct it.

<u>Work</u> is often <u>measure</u> in units <u>called</u> foot pounds.
(A) (B)   (C)   (D)

13   Belief and Knowledge—Anticipatory *It*

Remember that an anticipatory *it* clause expresses belief or knowledge. Anticipatory means before. Some *it* clauses that go before main clauses are listed below:

It is believed
It is hypothesized
It is known
It is said
It is thought
It is true
It is written

Anticipatory *it*	that	S	V	
It is believed	that	all mammals	experience	dreams

Avoid using an *-ing* form, a noun, or an infinitive instead of a subject and verb after an anticipatory *it* clause.

EXAMPLES

INCORRECT: It is hypothesized that the subjects in the control
group not to score as well.

CORRECT: It is hypothesized that the subjects in the control
group will not score as well.

INCORRECT: It is generally known that she leaving at the end of
the year.

CORRECT: It is generally known that she is leaving at the end of
the year.

INCORRECT: It is said that a buried treasure near here.

CORRECT: It is said that a buried treasure was hidden near here.

INCORRECT: It is believed that a horseshoe bringing good luck.

CORRECT: It is believed that a horseshoe brings good luck.

INCORRECT: It is thought that our ancestors building this city.

CORRECT: It is thought that our ancestors built this city.

EXERCISES

Part A: Choose the correct answer.

_____ Giant Ape Man, our biggest and probably one of our
first human ancestors, was just about the size of a male gorilla.

(A) It is believed that
(B) That it is
(C) That is believed
(D) That believing

Part B: Choose the incorrect word or phrase and correct it.

That it is believed that most of the earthquakes in the world
            (A)   (B)

occur near the youngest mountain ranges—the Himalayas,
      (C)   (D)

the Andes, and the Sierra Nevadas.

14   Predictions—*Will Have* + Participle

Remember that *will have* followed by a participle and a future adverb expresses a prediction for a future activity or event.

adverb (future)	S	will	have	participle	
By the year 2010,	researchers	will	have	discovered	a cure for cancer

Avoid using *will* instead of *will have*.

EXAMPLES

INCORRECT: You will finished your homework by the time the movie starts.

CORRECT: You will have finished your homework by the time the movie starts.

INCORRECT: Jan will left by five o'clock.

CORRECT: Jan will have left by five o'clock.

INCORRECT: Before school is out, I have returned all of my library books.

CORRECT: Before school is out, I will have returned all of my library books.

INCORRECT: We have gotten an answer to our letter by the time we have to make a decision.

CORRECT: We will have gotten an answer to our letter by the time we have to make a decision.

INCORRECT: Before we can tell them about the discount, they will bought the tickets.

CORRECT: Before we can tell them about the discount, they will have bought the tickets.

EXERCISES

Part A: Choose the correct answer.

By the middle of the twenty-first century, the computer
_____ a necessity in every home.
(A) became
(B) becoming
(C) has become
(D) will have become

Part B: Choose the incorrect word or phrase and correct it.

<u>It is believed</u> that <u>by 2010</u> immunotherapy <u>have succeeded</u> in
    (A)   (B)   (C)
<u>curing</u> a number of serious illnesses.
  (D)

15 Missing Auxiliary Verb—Active

Remember that some main verbs require auxiliary verbs.

	BE	-ing	
Mom	is	watering	her plants

	HAVE	participle	
Mom	has	watered	her plants

	MODAL	verb word	
Mom	should	water	her plants

Avoid using *-ing* forms without BE, participles without HAVE, and verb words without modals when *-ing*, a participle, or a verb word function as a main verb.

EXAMPLES

INCORRECT: The party is a surprise, but all of her friends coming.
 CORRECT: The party is a surprise, but all of her friends
are coming.

INCORRECT: She read it to you later tonight.
 CORRECT: She will read it to you later tonight.

INCORRECT: The sun shining when we left this morning.
 CORRECT: The sun was shining when we left this morning.

INCORRECT: We gone there before.
 CORRECT: We have gone there before.

INCORRECT: I can't talk with you right now because the doorbell
ringing.
 CORRECT: I can't talk with you right now because the doorbell
is ringing.

EXERCISES

Part A: Choose the correct answer.

The giraffe survives in part because it _____ the vegetation
in the high branches of trees where other animals have not
grazed.
　　(A) to reach
　　(B) can reach
　　(C) reaching
　　(D) reach

Part B: Choose the incorrect word or phrase and correct it.

According to some scientists, the earth losing its outer
　　　(A)　　　　　　　　　　　　　　　　　(B) (C)
atmosphere because of pollutants.
　　　　　　　(D)

16   Missing Auxiliary Verb—Passive

Remember that the passive requires an auxiliary BE verb.

S		BE	participle
The plants		are	watered
The plants	have	been	watered
The plants	should	be	watered

Avoid using a passive without a form of BE.

EXAMPLES

INCORRECT: The phone answered automatically.
CORRECT: The phone is answered automatically.

INCORRECT: They have informed already.
CORRECT: They have been informed already.

INCORRECT: These books should returned today.
CORRECT: These books should be returned today.

INCORRECT: The plane delayed by bad weather.
CORRECT: The plane was delayed by bad weather.

INCORRECT: My paper has not typed.
CORRECT: My paper has not been typed.

EXERCISES

Part A: Choose the correct answer.

Hydrogen peroxide_____as a bleaching agent because it
effectively whitens a variety of fibers and surfaces.

(A) used
(B) is used
(C) is using
(D) that it uses

Part B: Choose the incorrect word or phrase and correct it.

If a rash <u>occurs</u> within twenty-four hours <u>after taking</u> a new
       (A)   (B)

<u>medication</u>, the treatment <u>should discontinued</u>.
   (C)   (D)

17   Object Pronouns after Prepositions

Remember that personal pronouns used as the object of a preposition should be object case pronouns.

	preposition	pronoun (object)
I would be glad to take a message	for	her

Remember that the following prepositions are commonly used with object pronouns:

among	of
between	to
for	with
from	

Avoid using a subject pronoun instead of an object pronoun after a proposition.

EXAMPLES

INCORRECT: The experiment proved to my lab partner and I that prejudices about the results of an investigation are often unfounded.

CORRECT: The experiment proved <u>to</u> my lab partner and <u>me</u> that prejudices about the results of an investigation are often unfounded.

INCORRECT:	Of those who graduated with Betty and he, Ellen is the only one who has found a good job.
CORRECT:	Of those who graduated <u>with</u> Betty and <u>him,</u> Ellen is the only one who has found a good job.
INCORRECT:	Among we men, it was he who always acted as the interpreter.
CORRECT:	Among <u>us</u> men, it was he who always acted as the interpreter.
INCORRECT:	The cake is from Jan and the flowers are from Larry and we.
CORRECT:	The cake is from Jan and the flowers are <u>from</u> Larry and <u>us.</u>
INCORRECT:	Just between you and I, this isn't a very good price.
CORRECT:	Just <u>between</u> you and <u>me,</u> this isn't a very good price.

EXERCISES

Part A: Choose the correct answer.

Since the earth's crust is much thicker under the continents, equipment would have to be capable of drilling through 100,000 feet of rock to investigate the mantle _____ .

(A) beneath them
(B) beneath their
(C) beneath its
(D) beneath they

Part B: Choose the incorrect word or phrase and correct it.

According to Amazon legends, men <u>were forced</u> to <u>do</u> all of the
                                      (A)   (B)

household tasks for the women warriors <u>who</u> governed and
                                                   (C)

protected the cities <u>for they.</u>
                           (D)

18   **Relative Pronouns that Refer to Persons and Things**

Remember that *who* is used to refer to persons, and *which* is used to refer to things.

	someone	who	
She is	the secretary	who	works in the international office

Avoid using *which* instead of *who* in reference to a person.

	something	which	
This is	the new typewriter	which	you ordered

Avoid using *who* instead of *which* in reference to a thing.

EXAMPLES

INCORRECT: The people which cheated on the examination had to leave the room.

CORRECT: The people who cheated on the examination had to leave the room.

INCORRECT: There is someone on line two which would like to speak with you.

CORRECT: There is someone on line two who would like to speak with you.

INCORRECT: Who is the man which asked the question?
CORRECT: Who is the man who asked the question?

INCORRECT: The person which was recommended for the position did not fulfill the minimum requirements.

CORRECT: The person who was recommended for the position did not fulfill the minimum requirements.

INCORRECT: The student which receives the highest score will be awarded a scholarship.

CORRECT: The student <u>who</u> receives the highest score will be awarded a scholarship.

EXERCISES

Part A: Choose the correct answer.

Charlie Chaplin was a comedian _____ was best known for his work in silent movies.

    (A) who
    (B) which
    (C) whose
    (D) what

Part B: Choose the incorrect word or phrase and correct it.

Absolute zero, the temperature at <u>whom</u> <u>all substances</u> have
                         (A)   (B)

zero thermal energy and thus, <u>the lowest</u> possible temperatures,
                                     (C)

<u>is</u> unattainable in practice.
(D)

19   Count Nouns

Remember that *count nouns* have both singular and plural forms. Plural numbers can precede *count nouns* but not *noncount* nouns.

There are several categories of *count nouns* that can help you organize your study. Some of them are listed here.

    1. Names of persons, their relationships, and their occupations:
        one boy   *two boys*
        one friend   *two friends*
        one student   *two students*

2. Names of animals, plants, insects:

one dog	*two dogs*
one flower	*two flowers*
one bee	*two bees*

3. Names of things with a definite, individual shape:

one car	*two cars*
one house	*two houses*
one room	*two rooms*

4. Units of measurement:

one inch	*two inches*
one pound	*two pounds*
one degree	*two degrees*

5. Units of classification in society:

one family	*two families*
one country	*two countries*
one language	*two languages*

6. Containers of noncount solids, liquids, pastes, and gases:

one bottle	*two bottles*
one jar	*two jars*
one tube	*two tubes*

7. A limited number of abstract concepts:

one idea	*two ideas*
one invention	*two inventions*
one plan	*two plans*

Number (plural)	Noun (count-plural)
sixty	years

Avoid using a singular *count noun* with a plural number.

EXAMPLES

INCORRECT: We have twenty dollar left.
CORRECT: We have twenty dollars left.

INCORRECT:	I hope that I can lose about five pound before summer.
CORRECT:	I hope that I can lose about <u>five</u> <u>pounds</u> before summer.
INCORRECT:	Several of the people in this class speak three or four language.
CORRECT:	Several of the people in this class speak <u>three or four</u> <u>languages</u>.
INCORRECT:	The temperature has risen ten degree in two hours.
CORRECT:	The temperature has risen <u>ten</u> <u>degrees</u> in two hours.
INCORRECT:	The teacher has ordered two book, but they aren't in at the bookstore.
CORRECT:	The teacher has ordered <u>two</u> <u>books</u>, but they aren't in at the bookstore.

EXERCISES

Part A: Choose the correct answer.

A desert receives less than twenty-five _____ of rainfall every year.

(A) centimeter
(B) a centimeter
(C) centimeters
(D) of centimeters

Part B: Choose the incorrect word or phrase and correct it.

<u>In 1950</u> it was <u>naively</u> predicted that <u>eight or ten computer</u>
  (A)   (B)   (C)
would be sufficient <u>to handle</u> all of the scientific and business
                        (D)
needs in the United States.

20   Noncount Nouns

Remember that *noncount* nouns have only one form. They are used in agreement with singular verbs. The word *the* does not precede them.

There are categories of *noncount* nouns that can help you organize your study. Some of them are listed here.

1. Food staples that can be purchased in various forms:
   bread
   meat
   butter

2. Construction materials that can change shape, depending on what is made:
   wood
   iron
   grass

3. Liquids that can change shape, depending on the shape of the container:
   oil
   tea
   milk

4. Natural substances that can change shape, depending on natural laws:
   steam, water, ice
   smoke, ashes
   oxygen

5. Substances with many small parts:
   rice
   sand
   sugar

6. Groups of things that have different sizes and shapes:

clothing	(a coat, a shirt, a sock)
furniture	(a table, a chair, a bed)
luggage	(a suitcase, a trunk, a box)

7. Languages:
   Arabic
   Japanese
   Spanish

8. Abstract concepts, often with endings -ness, -ance, -ence, -ity:
   beauty
   ignorance
   peace

9. Most -ing forms:
   learning
   shopping
   working

noun (noncount)	verb (singular)	
Friendship	is	important

Avoid using *the* before a *noncount* noun. Avoid using a plural verb with a noncount noun.

EXAMPLES

INCORRECT:	The happiness means different things to different people.
CORRECT:	<u>Happiness</u> means different things to different people.
INCORRECT:	Toshi speaks the Japanese at home.
CORRECT:	Toshi speaks <u>Japanese</u> at home.
INCORRECT:	Bread are expensive in the grocery store on the corner.
CORRECT:	<u>Bread is</u> expensive in the grocery store on the corner.

INCORRECT: I like my tea with the milk.
 CORRECT: I like my tea with <u>milk</u>.

INCORRECT: If you open the door, airs will circulate better.
 CORRECT: If you open the door, <u>air</u> will circulate better.

EXERCISES

Part A: Choose the correct answer.

_____ at 212 degrees F. and freezes at 32 degrees F.
(A) Waters boils
(B) The water boils
(C) Water boils
(D) Waters boil

Part B: Choose the incorrect word or phrase and correct it.

<u>The religion</u> attempts <u>to clarify</u> <u>mankind's</u> relationship with a
    (A)   (B)   (C)
<u>superhuman power</u>.
         (D)

21   Nouns with Count and Noncount Meanings

Remember that some nouns may be used as *count* or as *noncount* nouns depending on their meanings. Materials and abstract concepts are *noncount* nouns, but they may be used as *count* nouns to express specific meanings.

Count noun	Specific meaning	Noncount noun	General meaning
an agreement agreements	an occasion or a document	agreement	abstract concept all agreements
a bone bones	a part of a skeleton	bone	construction material

a business businesses	a company	business	abstract concept all business transactions
a cloth cloths	a piece of cloth	cloth	construction material
a decision decisions	an occasion	decision	abstract concept all decisions
an education educations	a specific person's	education	abstract concept all education
a fire fires	an event	fire	material
a glass glasses	a container	glass	construction material
a history histories	a historical account	history	abstract concept all history
an honor honors	an occasion or an award	honor	abstract concept all honor
a language languages	a specific variety	language	abstract concept all languages
a life lives	a specific person's	life	abstract concept all life
a light lights	a lamp	light	the absence of darkness
a noise noises	a specific sound	noise	abstract concept all sounds
a pain pains	a specific occasion	pain	abstract concept all pain
a paper papers	a document or sheet	paper	construction material
a pleasure pleasures	a specific occasion	pleasure	abstract concept all pleasure
a silence silences	a specific occasion	silence	abstract concept all silence
a space spaces	a blank	space	the universe
a stone stones	a small rock	stone	construction material
a success successes	an achievement	success	abstract concept all success
a thought thoughts	an idea	thought	abstract concept all thought

a time times	a historical period or moment	time	abstract concept all time
a war wars	a specific war	war	the general act of war all wars
a work works	an artistic creation	work	employment abstract concept all work

	a document	
I have	a paper	due Monday

	construction material	
Let's use	paper	to make the present

Avoid using *count* nouns with specific meanings to express the general meanings of *noncount* nouns.

EXAMPLES

INCORRECT: Dr. Bradley will receive special honor at the graduation.

CORRECT: Dr. Bradley will receive a special honor at the graduation.
(an award)

INCORRECT: She needs to find a work.

CORRECT: She needs to find work.
(employment)

INCORRECT: My neighbor dislikes a noise.

CORRECT: My neighbor dislikes noise.
(all sounds)

INCORRECT: We need glass for the juice.

CORRECT: We need a glass for the juice.
or
We need glasses for the juice.
(containers)

INCORRECT: A war is as old as mankind.
  CORRECT: <u>War</u> is as old as mankind.
            (the act of war)

EXERCISES

Part A: Choose the correct answer.

It is generally believed that an M.B.A. degree is good preparation for a career in _____ .

(A) a business
(B) business
(C) businesses
(D) one business

Part B: Choose the incorrect word or phrase and correct it.

<u>A space</u> is the last frontier for <u>man</u> to <u>conquer</u>.
  (A)   (B)   (C)   (D)

22 Noncount Nouns that Are Count Nouns in Other Languages

Remember that many nouns which are *count* nouns in other languages may be *noncount* nouns in English. Some of the most troublesome have been listed for you below.

advice	*homework*	*money*	*poetry*
anger	*ignorance*	*music*	*poverty*
courage	*information*	*news*	*progress*
damage	*knowledge*	*patience*	
equipment	*leisure*	*permission*	
fun	*luck*		

	Ø	Noun (noncount)
Did you do your		homework?

Avoid using *a* or *an* before *noncount* nouns.

EXAMPLES

INCORRECT: Do you have an information about it?

CORRECT: Do you have information about it?

INCORRECT: Counselors are available to give you an advice before you register for your classes.

CORRECT: Counselors are available to give you advice before you register for your classes.

INCORRECT: George had a good luck when he first came to State University.

CORRECT: George had good luck when he first came to State University.

INCORRECT: A news was released about the hostages.

CORRECT: News was released about the hostages.

INCORRECT: Did you get a permission to take the placement test?

CORRECT: Did you get permission to take the placement test?

EXERCISES

Part A: Choose the correct answer.

Fire-resistant materials are used to retard _____ of modern aircraft in case of accidents.

(A) a damage to the passenger cabin

(B) that damages to the passenger cabin

(C) damage to the passenger cabin

(D) passenger cabin's damages

Part B: Choose the incorrect word or phrase and correct it.

<u>A progress</u> <u>has been made</u> toward <u>finding</u> <u>a cure</u> for AIDS.
  (A)   (B)   (C)   (D)

23   Singular and Plural Expressions of Noncount Nouns

Remember that the following singular and plural expressions are idiomatic:

a piece of advice	*two pieces of advice*
a piece of bread	*two pieces of bread*
a piece of equipment	*two pieces of equipment*
a piece of furniture	*two pieces of furniture*
a piece of information	*two pieces of information*
a piece of jewelry	*two pieces of jewelry*
a piece of luggage	*two pieces of luggage*
a piece of mail	*two pieces of mail*
a piece of music	*two pieces of music*
a piece of news	*two pieces of news*
a piece of toast	*two pieces of toast*
a loaf of bread	*two loaves of bread*
a slice of bread	*two slices of bread*
an ear of corn	*two ears of corn*
a bar of soap	*two bars of soap*
a bolt of lightning	*two bolts of lightning*
a clap of thunder	*two claps of thunder*
a gust of wind	*two gusts of wind*

	a	singular	of	noun (noncount)
A folk song is	a	piece	of	popular music

	number	plural	of	noun (noncount)
I ordered	twelve	bars	of	soap

Avoid using the noncount noun without the singular or plural idiom to express a singular or plural.

EXAMPLES

INCORRECT: A mail travels faster when the zip code is indicated on the envelope.

CORRECT: A piece of mail travels faster when the zip code is indicated on the envelope.

INCORRECT: There is a limit of two carry-on luggages for each passenger.

CORRECT: There is a limit of two pieces of carry-on luggage for each passenger.

INCORRECT: Each furniture in this display is on sale for half price.

CORRECT: Each piece of furniture in this display is on sale for half price.

INCORRECT: I'd like a steak, a salad, and a corn's ear with butter.

CORRECT: I'd like a steak, a salad, and an ear of corn with butter.

INCORRECT: The Engineering Department purchased a new equipment to simulate conditions in outer space.

CORRECT: The Engineering Department purchased a new piece of equipment to simulate conditions in outer space.

EXERCISES

Part A: Choose the correct answer.

Hybrids have one more _____ per plant than the other varieties.

    (A) corns

    (B) ear of corn

    (C) corn ears

    (D) corn's ears

Part B: Choose the incorrect word or phrase and correct it.

A few tiles on Skylab were the only equipments that failed
 (A)   (B)   (C)
to perform well in outer space.
 (D)

24   Infinitive and *-ing* Subjects

Remember that either an infinitive or an *-ing* form may be used as the subject of a sentence or a clause.

S (infinitive)	V	
To read a foreign language	is	even more difficult

S (*-ing*)	V	
Reading quickly and well	requires	practice

Avoid using a verb word instead of an infinitive or an *-ing* form in the subject. Avoid using *to* with an *-ing* form.

EXAMPLES

INCORRECT: To working provides people with personal satisfaction as well as money.

CORRECT: To work provides people with personal satisfaction as well as money.

             or

Working provides people with personal satisfaction as well as money.

INCORRECT: The sneeze spreads germs.

CORRECT: To sneeze spreads germs.

             or

Sneezing spreads germs.

INCORRECT: Shoplift is considered a serious crime.
  CORRECT: To shoplift is considered a serious crime.
                        or
             Shoplifting is considered a serious crime.

INCORRECT: The rest in the afternoon is a custom in many countries.
  CORRECT: To rest in the afternoon is a custom in many countries.
                        or
             Resting in the afternoon is a custom in many countries.

INCORRECT: To exercising makes most people feel better.
  CORRECT: To exercise makes most people feel better.
                        or
             Exercising makes most people feel better.

EXERCISES

Part A: Choose the correct answer.

_____ trees is a custom that many people engage in to celebrate Arbor Day.
  (A) The plant
  (B) Plant
  (C) Planting
  (D) To planting

Part B: Choose the incorrect word or phrase and correct it.

Spell correctly is easy with the aid of a number of
 (A)   (B)
word processing programs for personal computers.
        (C)   (D)

25   Nominal *That* Clause

Remember that sometimes the subject of a verb is a single noun. Other times it is a long noun phrase or a long noun clause.

One example of a long noun clause is the *nominal that* clause. Like all clauses, the *nominal that* clause has a subject and verb. The *nominal that* clause functions as the main subject of the main verb which follows it.

Nominal *that* clause S	V	
That vitamin C prevents colds	is	well known

EXAMPLES

INCORRECT: That it is that she has known him for a long time influenced her decision.

CORRECT: That she has known him for a long time influenced her decision.

INCORRECT: It is that we need to move is sure.

CORRECT: That we need to move is sure.

INCORRECT: Is likely that the library is closed.

CORRECT: That the library is closed is likely.

INCORRECT: She will win is almost certain.

CORRECT: That she will win is almost certain.

INCORRECT: That is not fair seems obvious.

CORRECT: That it is not fair seems obvious.

EXERCISES

Part A: Choose the correct answer.

_____ migrate long distances is well documented.
   (A) That it is birds
   (B) That birds
   (C) Birds that
   (D) It is that birds

Part B: Choose the incorrect word or phrase and correct it.

That <u>it is</u> the moon influences only <u>one kind</u> of tide is not
    (A)   (B)

<u>generally</u> <u>known</u>.
  (C)   (D)

26   Noncount Nouns with Qualifying Phrases—*The*

Remember, *the* is used with count nouns. You have also learned that *the* can be used before an *-ing* noun that is followed by a qualifying phrase.

In addition, *the* can be used before a noncount noun with a qualifying phrase.

The	noncount noun	Qualifying Phrase	
The	art	of the Middle Ages	is on display

EXAMPLES

INCORRECT: Poetry of Carl Sandburg is being read at the student union on Friday.

CORRECT: <u>The</u> poetry <u>of Carl Sandburg</u> is being read at the student union on Friday.

INCORRECT:	Poverty of people in the rural areas is not as visible as that of people in the city.
CORRECT:	The poverty of people in the rural areas is not as visible as that of people in the city.

INCORRECT:	Science of genetic engineering is not very old.
CORRECT:	The science of genetic engineering is not very old.

INCORRECT:	History of this area is interesting.
CORRECT:	The history of this area is interesting.

INCORRECT:	Work of many people made the project a success.
CORRECT:	The work of many people made the project a success.

EXERCISES

Part A: Choose the correct answer.

_____ of Country-Western singers may be related to old English ballads.

    (A) The music
    (B) Music
    (C) Their music
    (D) Musics

Part B: Choose the incorrect word or phrase and correct it.

Philosophy of the ancient Greeks has been preserved in the
    (A)   (B)
scholarly writing of Western civilization.
    (C)   (D)

27   *No* Meaning *Not Any*

Remember that *no* means *not any*. It may be used with a singular or plural count noun or with a noncount noun.

no	noun (count singular) noun (count plural)	verb (singular) verb (plural)
No No	tree trees	grows above the tree line grow above the tree line

no	noun (noncount)	verb (singular)	
No	art	is	on display today

Avoid using the negatives *not* or *none* instead of *no*. Avoid using a singular verb with a plural count noun.

EXAMPLES

INCORRECT:	There is not reason to worry.
CORRECT:	There is <u>no reason</u> to worry.

INCORRECT:	None news is good news.
CORRECT:	<u>No news</u> is good news.

INCORRECT:	We have not a file under the name Wagner.
CORRECT:	We have <u>no file</u> under the name Wagner.

INCORRECT:	None of cheating will be tolerated.
CORRECT:	<u>No cheating</u> will be tolerated.

INCORRECT:	Bill told me that he has none friends.
CORRECT:	Bill told me that he has <u>no friends</u>.

EXERCISES

Part A: Choose the correct answer.

At Woolworth's first five-and-ten-cent store, _____ more than a dime.

    (A) neither items cost
    (B) items not cost
    (C) items none costing
    (D) no item cost

Part B: Choose the incorrect word or phrase and correct it.

Some religions <u>have</u> <u>none</u> deity but <u>are</u> philosophies that
        (A) (B)   (C)

function <u>instead of religions.</u>
          (D)

28   *Almost All of the* and *Most of the*

Remember that *almost all of the* and *most of the* mean all except a few, but *almost all of the* includes more.

almost all (of the) most (of the)	noun (count—plural)	verb (plural)	
Almost all (of the) Most (of the)	trees in our yard trees	are are	oaks oaks

almost all (of the) most (of the)	noun (noncount)	verb (singular)
Almost all (of the) Most (of the)	art by R. C. Gorman art by R. C. Gorman	is expensive is expensive

Avoid using *almost* without *all* or *all of the*. Avoid using *most of* without *the*.

EXAMPLES

INCORRECT: Almost the states have a sales tax.
CORRECT: Almost all of the <u>states</u> have a sales tax.
             or
      Almost all <u>states</u> have a sales tax.
             or
      Most of the <u>states</u> have a sales tax.
             or
      <u>Most</u> <u>states</u> have a sales tax.

INCORRECT:	Most of teachers at State University care about their students' progress.
CORRECT:	Almost all of the teachers at State University care about their students' progress.

or

Almost all teachers at State University care about their students' progress.

or

Most of the teachers at State University care about their students' progress.

or

Most teachers at State University care about their students' progress.

INCORRECT:	My cousin told me that most of people who won the lottery got only a few dollars, not the grand prize.
CORRECT:	My cousin told me that almost all of the people who won the lottery got only a few dollars, not the grand prize.

or

My cousin told me that almost all people who won the lottery got only a few dollars, not the grand prize.

or

My cousin told me that most of the people who won the lottery got only a few dollars, not the grand prize.

or

My cousin told me that most people who won the lottery got only a few dollars, not the grand prize.

INCORRECT:	Most the dictionaries have information about pronunciation.
CORRECT:	Almost all of the dictionaries have information about pronunciation.

or

Almost all dictionaries have information about pronunciation.

or

Most of the dictionaries have information about pronunciation.

or

Most dictionaries have information about pronunciation.

INCORRECT: Is it true that most Americans watches TV every night?

CORRECT: It is true that almost all of the Americans watch TV every night?

or

Is it true that almost all Americans watch TV every night?

or

Is it true that most of the Americans watch TV every night?

or

Is it true that most Americans watch TV every night?

EXERCISES

Part A: Choose the correct answer.

_____ fuel that is used today is a chemical form of solar energy.

(A) Most of
(B) The most
(C) Most
(D) Almost the

Part B: Choose the incorrect word or phrase and correct it.

Almost the plants known to us are made up of
  (A)   (B)
a great many cells, specialized to perform different tasks.
      (C)   (D)

29   **Nouns that Function as Adjectives**

Remember that when two nouns occur together, the first noun describes the second noun; that is, the first noun functions as an adjective. Adjectives do not change form, singular or plural.

	noun	noun
All of us are foreign	language	teachers

Avoid using a plural form for the first noun even when the second noun is plural. Avoid using a possessive form for the first noun.

EXAMPLES

INCORRECT: May I borrow some notebooks paper?
CORRECT: May I borrow some notebook paper?

INCORRECT: All business' students must take the Graduate Management Admission Test.
CORRECT: All business students must take the Graduate Management Admission Test.

INCORRECT: I forgot their telephone's number.
CORRECT: I forgot their telephone number.

INCORRECT: There is a sale at the shoes store.
CORRECT: There is a sale at the shoe store.

INCORRECT: Put the mail on the hall's table.
CORRECT: Put the mail on the hall table.

EXERCISES

Part A: Choose the correct answer.

_____ is cheaper for students who maintain a B average because they are a better risk than average or below-average students.

(A) Automobile's insurance
(B) Insurance of automobiles
(C) Automobile insurance
(D) Insurance automobile

Part B: Choose the incorrect word or phrase and correct it.

Sex's education is instituted to help the student understand the
    (A)   (B)

process of maturation, to eliminate anxieties related to
                            (C)   (D)

development, to learn values, and to prevent disease.

30   Hyphenated Adjectives

Remember that it is common for a number to appear as the first in a series of hyphenated adjectives. Each word in a hyphenated adjective is an adjective and does not change form, singular or plural.

	a	adjective	—	adjective	noun
Agriculture 420 is	a	five	—	hour	class

a	adjective	—	adjective	—	adjective	noun	
A	sixty	—	year	—	old	employee	may retire

Avoid using a plural form for any of the adjectives joined by hyphens even when the noun that follows is plural.

EXAMPLES

INCORRECT:	A three-minutes call anywhere in the United States costs less than a dollar when you dial it yourself.
CORRECT:	A three-minute call anywhere in the United States costs less than a dollar when you dial it yourself.

INCORRECT:	They have a four-months-old baby.
CORRECT:	They have a four-month-old baby.

INCORRECT:	Can you make change for a twenty-dollars bill?
CORRECT:	Can you make change for a twenty-dollar bill?

INCORRECT:	A two-doors car is cheaper than a four-doors model.
CORRECT:	A two-door car is cheaper than a four-door model.

INCORRECT:	I have to write a one-thousand-words paper this weekend.
CORRECT:	I have to write a one-thousand-word paper this week-end.

EXERCISES

Part A: Choose the correct answer.

The evolution of vertebrates suggests development from a very simple heart in fish to a _____ in man.

    (A) four-chamber heart
    (B) four-chambers heart
    (C) four-chamber hearts
    (D) four-chamber's heart

Part B: Choose the incorrect word or phrase and correct it.

The MX is a four-stages rocket with an 8,000-mile range,
       (A)   (B)   (C)
larger than that of the Minuteman.
    (D)

31   Cause-and-Result—*So*

Remember that *so* is used before an adjective or an adverb followed by *that*. The *so* clause expresses cause. The *that* clause expresses result.

CAUSE				RESULT			
S	V	so	adverb adjective	that	S	V	
She	got up	so	late	that	she	missed	her bus
The music	was	so	loud	that	we	couldn't talk	

Avoid using *as* or *too* instead of *so* in clauses of cause. Avoid using *as* instead of *that* in clauses of result.

EXAMPLES

INCORRECT: He is so slow as he never gets to class on time.
CORRECT: He is <u>so slow that</u> he never gets to class on time.

INCORRECT: This suitcase is as heavy that I can hardly carry it.
CORRECT: This suitcase is <u>so heavy that</u> I can hardly carry it.

INCORRECT: We arrived so late as Professor Baker had already called the roll.
CORRECT: We arrived <u>so late that</u> Professor Baker had already called the roll.

INCORRECT: He drives so fast as no one likes to ride with him.
CORRECT: He drives <u>so fast that</u> no one likes to ride with him.

INCORRECT: Preparing frozen foods is too easy that anyone can do it.
CORRECT: Preparing frozen foods is <u>so easy that</u> anyone can do it.

EXERCISES

Part A: Choose the correct answer.

Oil paints are _____ they have become the most popular painter's colors.
    (A) so versatile and durable that
    (B) so versatile and durable than
    (C) such versatile and durable as
    (D) such versatile and durable

Part B: Choose the incorrect word or phrase and correct it.

By the mid-nineteenth century, land was such expensive in large
                    (A)   (B)
cities that architects began to conserve space by designing
                                         (C)   (D)
skyscrapers.

32   Exact Similarity—*the Same as* and *the Same*

Remember that *the same as* and *the same* have the same meaning, but *the same as* is used between the two nouns compared, and *the same* is used after the two nouns or a plural noun.

noun		the same as	noun
This coat	is	the same as	that one

noun		noun		the same
This coat	and	that one	are	the same

noun (plural)		the same
These coats	are	the same

Avoid using *to* and *like* instead of *as*. Avoid using *the same* between the two nouns compared.

EXAMPLES

INCORRECT:	That car is almost the same like mine.
CORRECT:	That car is almost <u>the same as</u> <u>mine</u>.

or

That car and mine are almost <u>the same</u>.

INCORRECT:	My briefcase is exactly the same that yours.
CORRECT:	My briefcase is exactly <u>the same as</u> <u>yours</u>.

or

My briefcase and yours are exactly <u>the same</u>.

INCORRECT:	Is your book the same to mine?
CORRECT:	Is your book <u>the same as</u> <u>mine</u>?

or

Are your book and mine <u>the same</u>?

INCORRECT:	Are this picture and the one on your desk same?
CORRECT:	Are this picture and the one on your desk <u>the same</u>?

or

Is this picture <u>the same as</u> <u>the one</u> on your desk?

INCORRECT:	The teacher gave Martha a failing grade on her composition because it was the same a composition he had already read.
CORRECT:	The teacher gave Martha a failing grade on her com position because it was <u>the same as</u> <u>a composition</u> he had already read.

or

The teacher gave Martha a failing grade on her composition because it and a composition he had already read were <u>the same</u>.

EXERCISES

Part A: Choose the correct answer.

Although we often use "speed" and "velocity" interchangeably, in a technical sense, "speed" is not always _____ "velocity."
(A) alike
(B) the same as
(C) similar
(D) as

Part B: Choose the incorrect word or phrase and correct it.

When two products are <u>basically</u> <u>the same as</u>, <u>advertising</u> can
                (A)   (B)   (C)

<u>influence</u> the public's choice.
  (D)

33   General Similarity—*Like* and *Alike*

Remember that *like* and *alike* have the same meaning, but *like* is used between the two nouns compared, and *alike* is used after the two nouns or a plural noun.

noun		like	noun
This coat	is	like	that one

noun		noun		alike
This coat	and	that one	are	alike

noun (plural)		alike
These coats	are	alike

Avoid using *as* instead of *like*. Avoid using *like* after the two nouns compared.

EXAMPLES

INCORRECT: The weather feels as spring.
CORRECT: The weather feels <u>like</u> <u>spring</u>.

INCORRECT: These suits are like.
CORRECT: This suit is <u>like</u> <u>that suit</u>.
         or
These suits are <u>alike</u>.

INCORRECT: Your recipe for chicken is like to a recipe that my mother has.
CORRECT: Your recipe for chicken is <u>like</u> <u>a recipe</u> that my mother has.
         or
Your recipe for chicken and a recipe that my mother has are <u>alike</u>.

INCORRECT: I want to buy some shoes same like the ones I have on.
CORRECT: I want to buy some shoes <u>like</u> <u>the ones</u> I have on.
         or
The shoes I want to buy and the shoes I have on are <u>alike</u>.

INCORRECT: Anthony and his brother don't look like.
CORRECT: Anthony doesn't look <u>like</u> <u>his brother</u>.
         or
Anthony and his brother don't look <u>alike</u>.

EXERCISES

Part A: Choose the correct answer.

Although they are smaller, chipmunks are _____ most other ground squirrels.

(A) like to
(B) like as
(C) like
(D) alike

Part B: Choose the incorrect word or phrase and correct it.

The first living structures to appear on earth thousands of years
  (A)   (B)

ago were alike viruses.
(C)   (D)

34   General Difference—*to Differ from*

Remember that *differ* is a verb and must change forms to agree with the subject.

	DIFFER	from	
This one	differs	from	the rest

Avoid using BE with *differ*. Avoid using *than*, *of*, or *to* after *differ*.

EXAMPLES

INCORRECT: Sharon is different of other women I know.
CORRECT: Sharon is different from other women I know.
                    or
            Sharon differs from other women I know.

INCORRECT: Do you have anything a little different to these?
CORRECT: Do you have anything a little different from these?
                  or
            Do you have anything that differs a little from these?

INCORRECT: The campus at State University different from that of City College.
CORRECT: The campus at State University differs from that of City College.
                  or
            The campus at State University is different from that of City College.

INCORRECT: Jayne's apartment is very differs from Bill's even though they are in the same building.

CORRECT: Jayne's apartment <u>is</u> very <u>different from</u> Bill's even though they are in the same building.

or

Jayne's apartment <u>differs from</u> Bill's even though they are in the same building.

INCORRECT: Customs differ one region of the country to another.

CORRECT: Customs <u>differ from</u> one region of the country to another.

or

Customs <u>are</u> <u>different from</u> one region of the country to another.

EXERCISES

Part A: Choose the correct answer.

Modern blimps like the famous Goodyear blimps _____ the first ones in that they are filled with helium instead of hydrogen.

(A) differ from
(B) different from
(C) is different from
(D) different

Part B: Choose the incorrect word or phrase and correct it.

<u>Crocodiles</u> <u>different from</u> alligators in that they have
   (A)   (B)

<u>pointed snouts</u> and long lower teeth that stick out when their
     (C)

mouths <u>are closed</u>.
      (D)

35 Comparative Estimates—Multiple Numbers

Remember that the following are examples of multiple numbers:

half	four times
twice	five times
three times	ten times

	multiple	as	much many	as	
Fresh fruit costs	twice	as	much	as	canned fruit
We have	half	as	many	as	we need

Avoid using *so* instead of *as* after a multiple. Avoid using *more than* instead of *as much as* or *as many as*. Avoid using the multiple after *as much* and *as many*.

EXAMPLES

INCORRECT: This one is prettier, but it costs twice more than the other one.

CORRECT: This one is prettier, but it costs <u>twice as much as</u> the other one.

INCORRECT: The rent at College Apartments is only half so much as you pay here.

CORRECT: The rent at College Apartments is only <u>half as much as</u> you pay here.

INCORRECT: Bob found a job that paid as much twice as he made working at the library.

CORRECT: Bob found a job that paid <u>twice as much as</u> he made working at the library.

INCORRECT: The price was very reasonable; I would gladly have paid three times more than he asked.

CORRECT: The price was very reasonable; I would gladly have paid <u>three times as much as</u> he asked.

INCORRECT: We didn't buy the car because they wanted as much twice as it was worth.

CORRECT: We didn't buy the car because they wanted <u>twice as much as</u> it was worth.

EXERCISES

Part A: Choose the correct answer.

After the purchase of the Louisiana Territory, the United States had _____ it had previously owned.

(A) twice more land than

(B) two times more land than

(C) twice as much land as

(D) two times much land than

Part B: Choose the incorrect word or phrase and correct it.

With American prices for sugar at three times <u>as much</u> the world
                                                (A)

price, manufacturers <u>are</u> beginning <u>to use</u> fructose blended with
                      (B)   (C)

pure sugar, <u>or</u> sucrose.
            (D)

36 Comparative Estimates—*More Than* and *Less Than*

Remember that *more than* or *less than* is used before a specific number to express an estimate that may be a little more or a little less than the number.

	more than	number	
Steve has	more than	a thousand	coins in his collection

	less than	number	
Andy has	less than	a dozen	coins in his pocket

Avoid using *more* or *less* without *than* in estimates. Avoid using *as* instead of *than*.

EXAMPLES

INCORRECT: More one hundred people came to the meeting.
CORRECT: More than one hundred people came to the meeting.

INCORRECT: We have lived in the United States for as less than seven years.
CORRECT: We have lived in the United States for less than seven years.

INCORRECT: The main library has more as one million volumes.
CORRECT: The main library has more than one million volumes.

INCORRECT: A new shopping center on the north side will have five hundred shops more than.
CORRECT: A new shopping center on the north side will have more than five hundred shops.

INCORRECT: There are most than fifty students in the lab, but only two computers.
CORRECT: There are more than fifty students in the lab, but only two computers.

EXERCISES

Part A: Choose the correct answer.

In the Great Smoky Mountains, one can see _____ 150 different kinds of trees.
  (A) more than
  (B) as much as
  (C) up as
  (D) as many to

Part B: Choose the incorrect word or phrase and correct it.

Pelé scored <u>more as</u> 1,280 goals <u>during his career</u>, <u>gaining</u> a
            (A)   (B)   (C)
reputation as <u>the best</u> soccer player of all time.
              (D)

37 Comparative Estimates—*As Many As*

Remember that *as many as* is used before a specific number to express an estimate that does not exceed the number.

	as many as	number	
We should have	as many as	five hundred	applications

Avoid using *as many* instead of *as many as*. Avoid using *much* instead of *many* before a specific number.

Note: Comparative estimates with *as much as* are also used before a specific number that refers to weight, distance, or money. For example, *as much as* ten pounds, *as much as* two miles, or *as much as* twenty dollars.

EXAMPLES

INCORRECT: We expect as much as thirty people to come.
CORRECT: We expect <u>as many as</u> <u>thirty</u> people to come.

INCORRECT: There are as many fifteen thousand students attending summer school.
CORRECT: There are <u>as many as</u> <u>fifteen thousand</u> students attending summer school.

INCORRECT: The children can see as much as twenty-five baby animals in the nursery at the zoo.
CORRECT: The children can see <u>as many as</u> <u>twenty-five</u> baby animals in the nursery at the zoo.

INCORRECT: Many as ten planes have sat in line waiting to take off.
CORRECT: <u>As many as</u> <u>ten</u> planes have sat in line waiting to take off.

INCORRECT: State University offers as much as two hundred major fields of study.
CORRECT: State University offers <u>as many as</u> <u>two hundred</u> major fields of study.

EXERCISES

Part A: Choose the correct answer.

It has been estimated that _____ one hundred thousand men participated in the gold rush of 1898.

(A) approximate
(B) until
(C) as many as
(D) more

Part B: Choose the incorrect word or phrase and correct it.

It is generally accepted that the common cold <u>is caused</u> <u>by</u>
                                                    (A)   (B)

<u>as much as</u> forty strains of viruses <u>that</u> may be present in the
    (C)   (D)

air at all times.

38 Degrees of Comparison—Superlative Adjectives

Remember that superlatives are used to compare more than two.

	the	most (least) adjective (two + syllables) adjective -est (one syllable) adjective -est (two + syllables ending in -y)
An essay test is	the	most difficult
An essay test is	the	hardest
An essay test is	the	trickiest

Avoid using a comparative -er form when three or more are compared.

EXAMPLES

INCORRECT: She is more prettier than all of the girls in our class.
CORRECT: She is <u>the prettiest</u> of all of the girls in our class.

INCORRECT: New York is the larger of all American cities.
CORRECT: New York is <u>the largest</u> of all American cities.

INCORRECT: Of all of the candidates, Alex is probably the less qualified.
CORRECT: Of all of the candidates, Alex is probably <u>the least</u> qualified.

INCORRECT: Although there are a number of interesting findings, a
              most significant results are in the abstract.

CORRECT: Although there are a number of interesting findings,
              <u>the</u> <u>most</u> <u>significant</u> results are in the abstract.

INCORRECT: In my opinion, the more beautiful place in Oregon is
              Mount Hood.

CORRECT: In my opinion, <u>the</u> <u>most</u> <u>beautiful</u> place in Oregon is
              Mount Hood.

EXERCISES

Part A: Choose the correct answer.

The blue whale is _____ known animal, reaching a length
of more than one hundred feet.

    (A) the large
    (B) the larger
    (C) the largest
    (D) most largest

Part B: Choose the incorrect answer and correct it.

<u>The</u> <u>more</u> important theorem of all in plane geometry <u>is</u> <u>the</u>
(A) (B)   (C)(D)
Pythagorean Theorem.

39 Degrees of Comparison—Irregular Adjectives

Remember that some very common adjectives have irregular
forms. Some of them are listed for you on the next page.

Adjective	Comparative— to compare two	Superlative— to compare three or more
bad	*worse*	*the worst*
far	*farther*	*the farthest*
	further	*the furthest*
good	*better*	*the best*
little	*less*	*the least*
many	*more*	*the most*
much	*more*	*the most*

	irregular comparative	than	
This ice cream is	better	than	the other brands

	irregular superlative	
This ice cream is	the best	of all

Avoid using a regular form instead of an irregular form for these adjectives.

EXAMPLES

INCORRECT: The lab is more far from the bus stop than the library.

CORRECT: The lab is <u>farther from</u> the bus stop than the library.

or

The lab is <u>further from</u> the bus stop than the library.

INCORRECT: The badest accident in the history of the city occurred last night on the North Freeway.

CORRECT: The <u>worst</u> accident in the history of the city occurred last night on the North Freeway.

INCORRECT: These photographs are very good, but that one is the better of all.

CORRECT: These photographs are very good, but that one is <u>the best</u> of all.

INCORRECT: Please give me much sugar than you did last time.

CORRECT: Please give me <u>more</u> sugar than you did last time.

INCORRECT: This composition is more good than your last one.
CORRECT: This composition is <u>better</u> than your last one.

EXERCISES

Part A: Choose the correct answer.

_____ apples are grown in Washington State.
(A) Best
(B) The most good
(C) The best
(D) The better

Part B: Choose the incorrect word or phrase and correct it.

<u>Because</u> a felony is <u>more bad</u> than a misdemeanor, the
  (A)   (B)
punishment is <u>more severe</u>, and often includes a jail sentence
            (C)
<u>as well as</u> a fine.
  (D)

40   Double Comparatives

Remember that when two comparatives are used together, the first comparative expresses cause and the second comparative expresses result. A comparative is *more* or *less* with an adjective, or an adjective with *-er*.

CAUSE				RESULT			
The	comparative	S	V,	the	comparative	S	V
The	more	you	review,	the	easier	the patterns	will be

Avoid using *as* instead of *the*. Avoid using the **incorrect** form *lesser* Avoid omitting *the*. Avoid omitting *-er* from the adjective.

EXAMPLES

INCORRECT: The more you study during the semester, the lesser
you have to study the week before exams.

CORRECT: The more you study during the semester, the less you
have to study the week before exams.

INCORRECT: The faster we finish, the soon we can leave.

CORRECT: The faster we finish, the sooner we can leave.

INCORRECT: The less one earns, the lesser one must pay in income
taxes.

CORRECT: The less one earns, the less one must pay in income
taxes.

INCORRECT: The louder he shouted, less he convinced anyone.

CORRECT: The louder he shouted, the less he convinced anyone.

INCORRECT: The more you practice speaking, the well you will do
it.

CORRECT: The more you practice speaking, the better you will
do it.

EXERCISES

Part A: Choose the correct answer.

It is generally true that the lower the stock market falls,

_____ .

(A) higher the price of gold rises
(B) the price of gold rises high
(C) the higher the price of gold rises
(D) rises high the price of gold

Part B: Choose the incorrect word or phrase and correct it.

The higher the solar activity, the intense the auroras or polar
                                  (A)   (B)

light displays in the skies near the earth's geomagnetic poles.
                               (C)   (D)

41 Illogical Comparatives—General Similarity and Difference

Remember that comparisons must be made with logically comparable nouns. You can't compare *the climate* in the north with *the south.* You must compare *the climate* in the north with *the climate* in the south.

Remember that *that of* and *those of* are used instead of repeating a noun to express a logical comparative. An example with *different from* appears below.

noun (singular)		different	from	that	
Football in the U.S.	is	different	from	that	in other countries

noun (plural)		different	from	those	
The rules	are	different	from	those	of soccer

Avoid omitting *that* and *those.* Avoid using *than* instead of *from* with *different.*

EXAMPLES

INCORRECT: The food in my country is very different than that in the United States.

CORRECT: The food in my country is very <u>different from</u> <u>that</u> in the United States.

INCORRECT: The classes at my university are very different from State University.

CORRECT: The classes at my university are very <u>different from</u> <u>those</u> at State University.

INCORRECT:	The English that is spoken in Canada is similar to the United States.
CORRECT:	The English that is spoken in Canada is <u>similar to that</u> of the United States.

INCORRECT:	Drugstores here are not like at home.
CORRECT:	Drugstores here are not <u>like those</u> at home.

INCORRECT:	The time in New York City differs three hours from Los Angeles.
CORRECT:	The time in New York City <u>differs</u> three hours <u>from that</u> of Los Angeles.

EXERCISES

Part A: Choose the correct answer.

One's fingerprints are _____ .

   (A) different from those of any other person

   (B) different from any other person

   (C) different any other person

   (D) differs from another person

Part B: Choose the incorrect word or phrase and correct it.

Perhaps the colonists were <u>looking for</u> a climate <u>like England</u>,
                            (A)   (B)

when they decided <u>to settle</u> the North American continent
                       (C)

<u>instead of</u> the South American continent.
   (D)

42   Addition—*Besides*

Remember that *besides* means *in addition to. Beside* means *near.*

	noun adjective	
besides		
Besides	our dog,	we have two cats and a canary
Besides	white,	we stock green and blue

	beside	noun
We sat	beside	the teacher

Avoid using *beside* instead of *besides* to mean *in addition*.

EXAMPLES

INCORRECT:	Beside Marge, three couples are invited.
CORRECT:	<u>Besides</u> Marge, three couples are invited.

INCORRECT:	Beside Domino's, four other pizza places deliver.
CORRECT:	<u>Besides</u> Domino's, four other pizza places deliver.

INCORRECT:	To lead a well-balanced life, you need to have other interests beside studying.
CORRECT:	To lead a well balanced life, you need to have other interests <u>besides</u> studying.

INCORRECT:	Beside taxi service, there isn't any public transportation in town.
CORRECT:	<u>Besides</u> taxi service, there isn't any public transportation in town.

INCORRECT:	Janice has lots of friends beside her roommate.
CORRECT:	Janice has lots of friends <u>besides</u> her roommate.

EXERCISES

Part A: Choose the correct answer.

_____ a mayor, many city governments employ a city manager.

    (A) Beside

    (B) Besides

    (C) And

    (D) Also

Part B: Choose the incorrect word or phrase and correct it.

To receive a degree from an American university, one must take
    (A)

many courses beside those in one's major field.
           (B)   (C)   (D)

43   Cause—*Because of* and *Because*

Remember that *because of* is a prepositional phrase. It introduces a noun or a noun phrase. *Because* is a conjunction. It introduces a clause with a subject and a verb.

	because	S	V
They decided to stay at home	because	the weather	was bad
or			
	because of	noun	
They decided to stay at home		because of	the weather

Avoid using *because of* before a subject and verb. Avoid using *because* before a noun which is not followed by a verb.

EXAMPLES

INCORRECT: Classes will be canceled tomorrow because a national holiday.

CORRECT: Classes will be canceled tomorrow because it is a national holiday.

or

Classes will be canceled tomorrow because of a national holiday.

INCORRECT: She was absent because of her cold was worse.

CORRECT: She was absent because her cold was worse.

or

She was absent because of her cold.

INCORRECT: John's family is very happy because his being awarded a scholarship.

CORRECT: John's family is very happy because he has been awarded a scholarship.

or

John's family is very happy because of his being awarded a scholarship.

INCORRECT: She didn't buy it because of the price was too high.

CORRECT: She didn't buy it because the price was too high.

or

She didn't buy it because of the price.

INCORRECT: It was difficult to see the road clearly because the rain.

CORRECT: It was difficult to see the road clearly because it was raining.

or

It was difficult to see the road clearly because of the rain.

EXERCISES

Part A: Choose the correct answer.

_____ in the cultivation of a forest, trees need more careful planning than any other crop does.

(A) Because the time and area involved

(B) For the time and area involving

(C) Because of the time and area involved

(D) As a cause of the time and area involved

Part B: Choose the incorrect word or phrase and correct it.

Many roads and railroads were built in the 1880s because of the

                      (A)   (B)   (C)

industrial cities needed a network to link them with

                               (D)

sources of supply.

44 Correlative Conjunctions—Inclusives
not only . . . but also

Remember that *not only . . . but also* are correlative conjunctions. They are used together to include two parallel structures (two nouns, adjectives, verbs, adverbs).

	not only	parallel structure	but also	parallel structure
One should take	not only	cash	but also	traveler's checks
Checks are	not only	safer	but also	more convenient

Avoid using *only not* instead of *not only*. Avoid using *but* instead of *but also*.

Avoid using the incorrect pattern:

not only	parallel structure	but	parallel structure	also
not only	cash	but	traveler's checks	also
	safer	but	more convenient	also

EXAMPLES

INCORRECT: The program provides only not theoretical classes but also practical training.

CORRECT: The program provides <u>not only</u> theoretical classes <u>but also</u> practical training.

INCORRECT: The new models are not only less expensive but more efficient also.

CORRECT: The new models are <u>not only</u> less expensive <u>but also</u> more efficient.

INCORRECT: The objective is not to identify the problem but also to solve it.

CORRECT: The objective is <u>not only</u> <u>to identify</u> the problem <u>but also</u> <u>to solve</u> it.

INCORRECT: Not only her parents but her brothers and sisters also live in Wisconsin.

CORRECT: <u>Not only</u> <u>her parents</u> <u>but also</u> <u>her brothers and sisters</u> live in Wisconsin.

INCORRECT: To complete his physical education credits, John took not only swimming also golf.

CORRECT: To complete his physical education credits, John took <u>not only</u> <u>swimming</u> <u>but also</u> <u>golf</u>.

EXERCISES

Part A: Choose the correct answer.

Amniocentesis can be used not only to diagnose fetal disorders _____ the sex of the unborn child with 95 percent accuracy.

(A) but determining
(B) but also determining
(C) but to determine
(D) but also to determine

Part B: Choose the incorrect word or phrase and correct it.

The deadbolt is <u>the best</u> lock for entry doors <u>because</u> it is <u>not only</u>
        (A)   (B)   (C)
inexpensive but <u>installation is easy.</u>
                  (D)

PROBLEM 45   Future Result—*When*

Remember that *when* introduces a clause of condition for future result.

RESULT		CONDITION		
S	V (present) V (will + verb word)	when	S	V (present)
The temperature The temperature	drops will drop	when when	the sun the sun	sets sets

Avoid using *will* instead of a present verb after *when*.

EXAMPLES

INCORRECT: I will call you when I will return from my country.
   CORRECT: I will call you <u>when</u> <u>I</u> <u>return</u> from my country.

INCORRECT: Marilyn plans to work in her family's store when she will get her M.B.A.
   CORRECT: Marilyn plans to work in her family's store <u>when</u> <u>she</u> <u>gets</u> her M.B.A.

INCORRECT: He will probably buy some more computer software when he will get paid.
   CORRECT: He will probably buy some more computer software <u>when</u> <u>he</u> <u>gets</u> paid.

INCORRECT: She will feel a lot better when she will stop smoking.
   CORRECT: She will feel a lot better <u>when</u> <u>she</u> <u>stops</u> smoking.

INCORRECT: When Gary will go to State University, he will be a teaching assistant.
   CORRECT: <u>When</u> <u>Gary</u> <u>goes</u> to State University, he will be a teaching assistant.

EXERCISES

Part A: Choose the correct answer.

Bacterial spores germinate and sprout _____ favorable conditions of temperature and food supply.
   (A) when encountering of
   (B) when they encounter
   (C) when they will encounter
   (D) when the encounter of

Part B: Choose the incorrect word or phrase and correct it.

In <u>most states</u> insurance agents <u>must pass</u> an examination
     (A)   (B)

<u>to be licensed</u> when they <u>will complete</u> their training.
     (C)   (D)

46   Indirect Questions

Remember that question words can be used as conjunctions. Question words introduce a clause of indirect question.

Question words include the following:

who	*why*
what	*how*
what time	*how long*
when	*how many*
where	*how much*

S	V	question word	S	V
I	don't remember	what	her name	is

V	S		question word	S	V
Do	you	remember	what	her name	is?

Avoid using *do, does,* or *did* after the question word. Avoid using the verb before the subject after the question word.

EXAMPLES

INCORRECT: I didn't understood what did he say.
CORRECT: I didn't understand <u>what he said</u>.

INCORRECT: Do you know how much do they cost?
CORRECT: Do you know <u>how much they cost</u>?

INCORRECT: I wonder when is her birthday.
  CORRECT: I wonder <u>when</u> her birthday <u>is</u>.

INCORRECT: Could you please tell me where is the post office?
  CORRECT: Could you please tell me <u>where</u> the post office <u>is</u>?

INCORRECT: Can they tell you what time does the movie start?
  CORRECT: Can they tell you <u>what time</u> the movie <u>starts</u>?

EXERCISES

Part A: Choose the correct answer.

Recently, there have been several outbreaks of disease like legionnaire's syndrome, and doctors don't know

_____.

    (A) what is the cause
    (B) the cause is what
    (C) is what the cause
    (D) what the cause is

Part B: Choose the incorrect word or phrase and correct it.

In Ground Control Approach, <u>the air traffic controller</u> <u>informs</u>
                                           (A)   (B)
the pilot how far <u>is the plane</u> from <u>the touchdown point.</u>
                (C)   (D)

47   Negative Emphasis

Remember that negatives include phrases like *not one, not once, not until, never, never again, only rarely,* and *very seldom.* Negatives answer the question, *how often?* They are used at the beginning of a statement to express emphasis. Auxiliaries must agree with verbs and subjects.

negative	auxiliary	S	V	
Never	have	I	seen	so much snow

Avoid using a subject before the auxiliary in this pattern.

EXAMPLES

INCORRECT: Never again they will stay in that hotel.
CORRECT: Never again will they stay in that hotel.

INCORRECT: Only rarely an accident has occurred.
CORRECT: Only rarely has an accident occurred.

INCORRECT: Very seldom a movie can hold my attention like this one.
CORRECT: Very seldom can a movie hold my attention like this one.

INCORRECT: Not one paper she has finished on time.
CORRECT: Not one paper has she finished on time.

INCORRECT: Not once Steve and Jan have invited us to their house.
CORRECT: Not once have Steve and Jan invited us to their house.

EXERCISES

Part A: Choose the correct answer.

Not until the Triassic Period _____ .
    (A) the first primitive mammals did develop
    (B) did the first primitive mammals develop
    (C) did develop the first primitive mammals
    (D) the first primitive mammals develop

Part B: Chose the incorrect word or phrase and correct it.

Only rarely wins the same major league baseball team the World
(A)   (B)
Series two years in a row.
          (C)   (D)

48   Duration—*For* and *Since*

Remember that *for* is used before a quantity of time. *For* expresses duration. *For* answers the question, *how long?* *Since* is used before a specific time. *Since* expresses duration too, but *since* answers the question, *beginning when?*

Remember that a quantity of time may be several days—a month, two years, etc. A specific time may be Wednesday, July, 1960, etc. You will notice that the structure *HAVE* and a participle is often used with adverbs of duration.

S	HAVE	participle		for	quantity of time
She	has	been	in the U.S.	for	six months

S	HAVE	participle		since	specific time
She	has	been	in the U.S.	since	June

Avoid using *for* before specific times. Avoid using *before* after HAVE and a participle.

EXAMPLES

INCORRECT: Mary has been on a diet since three weeks.
 CORRECT: Mary has been on a diet for three weeks.

INCORRECT: She has been living here before April.
 CORRECT: She has been living here since April.

INCORRECT: We haven't seen him since almost a year.
  CORRECT: We haven't seen him <u>for</u> <u>almost a year</u>.

INCORRECT: We have known each other before 1974.
  CORRECT: We have known each other <u>since</u> <u>1974</u>.

INCORRECT: He has studied English since five years.
  CORRECT: He has studied English <u>for</u> <u>five years</u>.

EXERCISES

Part A: Choose the correct answer.

Penguins, the most highly specialized of all aquatic birds, may live _____ twenty years.

   (A) before
   (B) since
   (C) for
   (D) from

Part B: Choose the incorrect word or phrase and correct it.

Because national statistics on crime have only been kept

<u>for 1930</u>, it is not possible <u>to make</u> judgments about crime
  (A) (B)   (C)
<u>during the early years</u> of the nation.
       (D)

49   Generalization—*As a Whole* and *Wholly*

Remember that *as a whole* means generally. *Wholly* means completely. *As a whole* is often used at the beginning of a sentence or a clause. *Wholly* is often used after the auxiliary or main verb.

generally as a whole	S	V	
As a whole	the news	is	correct

S	V	completely wholly	
The news	is	wholly	correct

Avoid using *wholly* instead of *as a whole* at the beginning of a sentence or clause to mean generally. Avoid using *as whole* instead of *as a whole*.

EXAMPLES

INCORRECT: Wholly, we are in agreement.
  CORRECT: As a whole, we are in agreement.
          (generally)

INCORRECT: The house and all of its contents was as a whole con-
            sumed by the fire.
  CORRECT: The house and all of its contents was wholly con-
            sumed by the fire.
          (completely)

INCORRECT: The teams are not rated equally, but, wholly, they are
            evenly matched.
  CORRECT: The teams are not rated equally, but, as a whole, they
            are evenly matched.
          (generally)

INCORRECT: Wholly, Dan's operation proved to be successful.
  CORRECT: As a whole, Dan's operation proved to be successful.
          (generally)

INCORRECT: As whole, people try to be helpful to tourists.
  CORRECT: As a whole, people try to be helpful to tourists.
          (generally)

EXERCISES

Part A: Choose the correct answer.

_____ the Gulf Stream is warmer than the ocean water surrounding it.
   (A) Wholly
   (B) Whole
   (C) As a whole
   (D) A whole as

Part B: Choose the incorrect word or phrase and correct it.

Although <u>there are</u> exceptions, <u>as whole</u>, the male of the bird
       (A)   (B)

species is <u>more</u> <u>brilliantly</u> colored.
      (C)   (D)

50 Sentences and Clauses

Remember that a main clause, also called an independent clause, can function as a separate sentence. A subordinate clause, also called a dependent clause, must be attached to a main clause. A dependent clause is often marked with the clause marker *that*.

SENTENCE		
Main Clause (Sentence)	Clause Marker - - - - - - - - - - - Dependent Clause	
We were glad	that	the box came

Avoid using the clause marker with dependent clauses as sentences. Avoid using the clause marker *that* with a sentence that has no dependent clause following it.

EXAMPLES

INCORRECT:	Utensils and condiments that are found on the table by the door.
CORRECT:	<u>Utensils and condiments</u> <u>are found</u> on the table by the door.
INCORRECT:	During final exam week, that the library when opening all night.
CORRECT:	During final exam week, <u>the library</u> <u>is open</u> all night.
INCORRECT:	The weather that is very rainy this time of year.
CORRECT:	<u>The weather</u> <u>is</u> very rainy this time of year.
INCORRECT:	All of the dorms that are located on East Campus.
CORRECT:	All of the <u>dorms</u> <u>are located</u> on East Campus.
INCORRECT:	During our vacation, that we suspended the newspaper delivery.
CORRECT:	During our vacation, <u>we</u> <u>suspended</u> the newspaper delivery.

EXERCISES

Part A: Choose the correct answer.

Of all the cities in Texas,_____.

    (A) that San Antonio is probably the most picturesque
    (B) San Antonio is probably the most picturesque
    (C) probably San Antonio the most picturesque
    (D) the most picturesque probably that San Antonio

Part B: Choose the incorrect word or phrase and correct it.

<u>Thunder</u> <u>that</u> is audible from distances as far away <u>as</u> ten <u>miles</u>.
  (A)   (B)   (C)   (D)

STYLE

Style is a general term that includes elements larger than a single grammatical pattern or structure. In most grammar books, *style* means *sentence structure*—that is, how the parts of a sentence relate to each other.

Some of the most important elements of style are summarized in this review section.

Point of View—Verbs

In all patterns, maintain a point of view, either present or past.

Avoid changing from present to past tense, or from past to present tense in the same sentence.

EXAMPLES

INCORRECT: He was among the few who want to continue working on the project.

CORRECT: He is among the few who want to continue working on the project.

> *or*

He was among the few who wanted to continue working on the project.

INCORRECT: It is an accepted custom for a man to open the door when he accompanied a woman.

CORRECT: It is an accepted custom for a man to open the door when he accompanies a woman.

> *or*

It was an accepted custom for a man to open the door when he accompanied a woman.

INCORRECT: She closed the door and hurries away to class.

CORRECT: She closes the door and hurries away to class.

or

She <u>closed</u> the door and <u>hurried</u> away to class.

INCORRECT: We receive several applications a day and with them
             had been copies of transcripts and degrees.

CORRECT: We <u>receive</u> several applications a day and with them
             <u>are</u> copies of transcripts and degrees.

or

We <u>received</u> several applications a day and with them
<u>were</u> copies of transcripts and degrees.

INCORRECT: Mr. Davis tried to finish his research, but he found
             only part of the information that he needs.

CORRECT: Mr. Davis <u>tries</u> to finish his research, but he <u>finds</u>
             only part of the information that he <u>needs</u>.

or

Mr. Davis <u>tried</u> to finish his research, but he <u>found</u>
only part of the information that he <u>needed</u>.

EXERCISES

Part A: Choose the correct answer.

The first transistor was basically a small chip made of germani-
um onto one surface of which two pointed wire contacts
_____ side by side.

   (A) are made
   (B) made
   (C) were made
   (D) making

Part B: Choose the incorrect word or phrase and correct it.

<u>Because</u> early balloons were at the mercy of <u>shifting</u> winds, they
  (A)   (B)

<u>are</u> not considered a practical means of transportation
(C)

<u>until the 1850s.</u>
    (D)

Point of View—Verbs and Adverbs

In all patterns, avoid using past adverbs with verbs in the present tense.

EXAMPLES

INCORRECT: Between one thing and another, Charles does not finish typing his paper last night.

CORRECT: Between one thing and another, Charles <u>did</u> not finish typing his paper <u>last night</u>.

INCORRECT: In 1990, according to statistics from the Bureau of Census, the population of the United States is 250,000,000.

CORRECT: <u>In 1990</u>, according to statistics from the Bureau of Census, the population of the United States <u>was</u> 250,000,000.

INCORRECT: We do not receive mail yesterday because it was a holiday.

CORRECT: We <u>did</u> not receive mail <u>yesterday</u> because it <u>was</u> a holiday.

INCORRECT: Mary does not finish her homework in time to go with us to the football game yesterday afternoon.

CORRECT: Mary <u>did</u> not finish her homework in time to go with us to the football game <u>yesterday afternoon</u>.

INCORRECT: Although there are only two hundred foreign students studying at State University in 1990, there are more than five hundred now.

CORRECT: Although there <u>were</u> only two hundred foreign students studying at State University <u>in 1990</u>, there are more than five hundred now.

EXERCISES

Part A: Choose the correct answer.

Iron_____ for weapons and tools in the Bronze Age following the Stone Age.

    (A) is generally used
    (B) generally used
    (C) was generally used
    (D) used generally

Part B: Choose the incorrect word or phrase and correct it.

The Nineteenth Amendment to the Constitution gives women
             (A)   (B)

the right to vote in the elections of 1920.
      (C)   (D)

3   Agreement—Modified Subject and Verb

In all patterns, there must be agreement of subject and verb.

Avoid using a verb that agrees with the modifier of a subject instead of with the subject itself.

EXAMPLES

INCORRECT: His knowledge of languages and international relations aid him in his work.

   CORRECT: His knowledge of languages and international relations aids him in his work.

INCORRECT: The facilities at the new research library, including an excellent microfilm file, is a among the best in the country.

   CORRECT: The facilities at the new research library, including an excellent microfilm file, are among the best in the country.

INCORRECT: All trade between the two countries were suspended
pending negotiation of a new agreement.

CORRECT: All <u>trade</u> between the two countries <u>was</u> suspended
pending negotiation of a new agreement.

INCORRECT: The production of different kinds of artificial
materials are essential to the conservation of our
natural resources.

CORRECT: The <u>production</u> of different kinds of artificial
materials <u>is</u> essential to the conservation of our
natural resources.

INCORRECT: Since the shipment of supplies for our experiments
were delayed, we will have to reschedule our work.

CORRECT: Since the <u>shipment</u> of supplies for our experiments
<u>was</u> delayed, we will have to reschedule our work.

EXERCISES

Part A: Choose the correct answer.

Groups of tissues, each with its own function, _____ in
the human body.

    (A) it makes up the organs

    (B) make up the organs

    (C) they make up the organs

    (D) makes up the organs

Part B: Choose the incorrect word or phrase and correct it.

The Zoning Improvement Plan, <u>better known as</u> zip codes,
                                  (A)

<u>enable</u> postal clerks <u>to speed</u> the routing of <u>an</u> ever-increasing
  (B)   (C)   (D)

volume of mail.

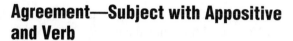

Agreement—Subject with Appositive and Verb

Remember that there must be agreement of subject and verb. An appositive is a word or phrase that follows a noun and defines it. An appositive usually has a comma before it and a comma after it.

In all patterns, avoid using a verb that agrees with words in the appositive after a subject instead of with the subject itself.

EXAMPLES

INCORRECT: The books, an English dictionary and a chemistry text, was on the shelf yesterday.

CORRECT: The books, an English dictionary and a chemistry text, were on the shelf yesterday.

INCORRECT: Three swimmers from our team, Paul, Ed, and Jim, is in competition for medals.

CORRECT: Three swimmers from our team, Paul, Ed, and Jim, are in competition for medals.

INCORRECT: Several pets, two dogs and a cat, needs to be taken care of while we are gone.

CORRECT: Several pets, two dogs and a cat, need to be taken care of while we are gone.

INCORRECT: State University, the largest of the state-supported schools, have more than 50,000 students on main campus.

CORRECT: State University, the largest of the state-supported schools, has more than 50,000 students on main campus.

INCORRECT: This recipe, an old family secret, are an especially important part of our holiday celebrations.

CORRECT: This recipe, an old family secret, is an especially important part of our holiday celebrations.

EXERCISES

Part A: Choose the correct answer.

Cupid, one of the ancient Roman gods, _____.
- (A) were a little winged child
- (B) representing as a little winged child
- (C) was represented as a little winged child
- (D) a little winged child

Part B: Choose the incorrect word or phrase and correct it.

Columbus, Ohio, the capital of the state, <u>are</u> not only <u>the largest</u>

(A)   (B)

city in Ohio <u>but also</u> a typical metropolitan area, often <u>used</u>

(C)   (D)

in market research.

5   Agreement—Verb-Subject Order

There and *here* introduce verb-subject order. The verb agrees with the subject following it.

there	V	S
There	are	the results of the election

here	V	S
Here	is	the result of the election

Avoid using a verb that does not agree with the subject.

EXAMPLES

INCORRECT: There was ten people in line already when we
            arrived.
CORRECT: There were ten people in line already when we
            arrived.

INCORRECT: There have been very little rain this summer.
CORRECT: There has been very little rain this summer.

INCORRECT: Here are their house.
CORRECT: Here is their house.

INCORRECT: There has been several objections to the new policy.
CORRECT: There have been several objections to the new policy.

INCORRECT: I think that there were a problem.
CORRECT: I think that there was a problem.

EXERCISES

Part A: Choose the correct answer.

In a suspension bridge_____ that carry one or more flexible
cables firmly attached at each end.
   (A) there is two towers on it
   (B) there are two towers
   (C) two towers there are
   (D) towers there are two

Part B: Choose the incorrect word or phrase and correct it.

There is about 600 schools in the United States that use the
    (A)   (B)   (C)
Montessori method to encourage individual initiative.
                    (D)

6   Agreement—Noun and Pronoun

In all patterns, there must be agreement of noun and pronoun.

Avoid using a pronoun that does not agree in number with the noun to which it refers.

EXAMPLES

INCORRECT:	If you want to leave a message for Mr. and Mrs. Carlson, I will be glad to take them.
CORRECT:	If you want to leave a message for Mr. and Mrs. Carlson, I will be glad to take it.
INCORRECT:	Al is interested in mathematics and their applications.
CORRECT:	Al is interested in mathematics and its applications.
INCORRECT:	It is easier to talk about a problem than to resolve them.
CORRECT:	It is easier to talk about a problem than to resolve it.
INCORRECT:	Although their visas will expire in June, they can have it extended for three months.
CORRECT:	Although their visas will expire in June, they can have them extended for three months.
INCORRECT:	In spite of its small size, these cameras take very good pictures.
CORRECT:	In spite of their small size, these cameras take very good pictures.

Exercises

Part A: Choose the correct answer.

A college bookstore that sells used textbooks stocks _____ along with the new ones on the shelf under the course title.
   (A) its
   (B) their
   (C) a
   (D) them

Part B: Choose the incorrect word or phrase and correct it.

Magnesium, <u>the lightest</u> of our structural metals, has an
                   (A)

important place <u>among</u> common engineering materials
                        (B)

<u>because of</u> <u>their</u> weight.
       (C)   (D)

Agreement—Subject and Possessive Pronouns

In all patterns, there must be agreement of subject pronoun and possessive pronouns that refer to the subject.

Subject Pronouns	Possessive Pronouns
I	*my*
you	*your*
he	*his*
she	*her*
it	*its*
we	*our*
you	*your*
they	*their*

Remember that *it* refers to a small baby. Avoid using *it's* instead of *its* as a possessive pronoun. *It's* means *it is*.

EXAMPLES

INCORRECT: Those of us who are over fifty years old should get their blood pressure checked regularly.

CORRECT: <u>Those of us</u> who are over fifty years old should get <u>our</u> blood pressure checked regularly.

INCORRECT: Our neighbors know that when they go on vacation, we will get its mail for them.

CORRECT: Our neighbors know that when <u>they</u> go on vacation, we will get <u>their</u> mail for them.

INCORRECT: A mother who works outside of the home has to prepare for emergencies when she cannot be there to take care of your sick child.

CORRECT: A mother who works outside of the home has to prepare for emergencies when <u>she</u> cannot be there to take care of <u>her</u> sick child.

INCORRECT: Wine tends to lose their flavor when it has not been properly sealed.

CORRECT: Wine tends to lose <u>its</u> flavor when <u>it</u> has not been properly sealed.

INCORRECT: Optional equipment on a car can add several hundred dollars to it's resale value when you trade it in.

CORRECT: Optional equipment on a car can add several hundred dollars to <u>its</u> resale value when you trade <u>it</u> in.

EXERCISES

Part A: Choose the correct answer.

The television programs we allow _____ to watch influence their learning.

    (A) a children
    (B) our children
    (C) our child
    (D) their childs

Part B: Choose the incorrect word or phrase and correct it.

Although maple trees are <u>among</u> the most colorful varieties
                        (A)

<u>in the fall</u>, they lose <u>its</u> leaves <u>sooner than</u> oak trees.
    (B)   (C)   (D)

Verbal Modifiers— *-ing* and *-ed* Forms

-ing forms and *-ed* forms may be used as verbals. Verbals function as modifiers.

An introductory verbal modifier with *-ing* or *-ed* should immediately precede the noun it modifies. Otherwise, the relationship between the noun and the modifier is unclear and the sentence is illogical.

Avoid using a noun immediately after an introductory verbal phrase which may not be logically modified by the phrase.

EXAMPLES

INCORRECT: After graduating from City College, Professor Baker's studies were continued at State University, where he received his Ph.D. in English.

CORRECT: <u>After graduating</u> from City College, <u>Professor Baker</u> continued his studies at State University, where he received his Ph.D. in English.

INCORRECT: Returning to her room, several pieces of jewelry were missing.

CORRECT: <u>Returning</u> to her room, <u>she</u> found that several pieces of jewelry were missing.

INCORRECT: Having been delayed by heavy traffic, it was not possible for her to arrive on time.

CORRECT: <u>Having been delayed</u> by heavy traffic, <u>she</u> arrived late.

INCORRECT: Accustomed to getting up early, the new schedule was not difficult for him to adjust to.

CORRECT: Accustomed to getting up early, he had no difficulty adjusting to the new schedule.

INCORRECT: After finishing his speech, the audience was invited to ask questions.

CORRECT: After finishing his speech, he invited the audience to ask questions.

EXERCISES

Part A: Choose the correct answer.

_____ air traffic controllers guide planes through conditions of near zero visibility.

  (A) They talk with pilots and watch their approach on radar,
  (B) Talking with pilots and watching their approach on radar,
  (C) Talk with pilots and watch their approach on radar,
  (D) When they talked with pilots and watched their approach on radar,

Part B: Choose the incorrect word or phrase and correct it.

Have designed his own plane, *The Spirit of St. Louis,* Lindbergh
   (A)

flew from Roosevelt Field in New York across the ocean to
   (B)   (C)

Le Bourget Field outside Paris.
            (D)

Verbal Modifiers—Infinitives of Purpose to Introduce Instructions

An infinitive that expresses purpose may be used as an introductory verbal modifier. Remember that a verb word follows the infinitive. The verb word expresses a manner to accomplish the purpose.

Avoid using a noun or *to* with an *-ing* form instead of the infinitive of purpose. Avoid using an *-ing* form or a passive construction after an introductory verbal modifier.

EXAMPLES

INCORRECT:	To protect yourself from dangerous exposure to the sun's rays, using a sun screen.
CORRECT:	To protect yourself from dangerous exposure to the sun's rays, use a sun screen.
INCORRECT:	Prepare for the TOEFL, study thirty minutes every day for several months.
CORRECT:	To prepare for the TOEFL, study thirty minutes every day for several months.
INCORRECT:	In order to take advantage of low air fares, to buy your tickets well in advance.
CORRECT:	In order to take advantage of low air fares, buy your tickets well in advance.
INCORRECT:	To taking action pictures, always use a high-speed film.
CORRECT:	To take action pictures, always use a high-speed film.
INCORRECT:	The send letters and packages from the United States overseas, use Global Mail or DHL Delivery.
CORRECT:	To send letters and packages from the United States overseas, use Global Mail or DHL Delivery.

EXERCISES

Part A: Choose the correct answer.

To relieve pressure in the skull,_____ into the blood.

    (A) you will inject a strong solution of pure glucose
    (B) to inject a strong solution of pure glucose
    (C) a strong solution of glucose will inject purely
    (D) inject a strong solution of pure glucose

Part B: Choose the incorrect word or phrase and correct it.

To estimate how much <u>it will cost</u> <u>to build</u> a home, <u>finding</u> the
                (A)   (B)   (C)

total square footage of the house and multiply <u>by cost</u> per
                                         (D)

square foot.

10   **Parallel Structure—In a Series**

In all patterns, ideas of equal importance should be expressed by the same grammatical structure.

Avoid expressing ideas in a series by different structures.

EXAMPLES

INCORRECT: Jane is young, enthusiastic, and she has talent.
  CORRECT: Jane is <u>young,</u> <u>enthusiastic,</u> and <u>talented.</u>

INCORRECT: We learned to read the passages carefully and under lining the main ideas.
  CORRECT: We learned <u>to read</u> the passages carefully and <u>to underline</u> the main ideas.

INCORRECT: The duties of the new secretary are to answer the tele phone, to type letters, and book keeping.
  CORRECT: The duties of the new secretary are <u>to answer</u> the tele phone, <u>to type</u> letters, and <u>to do</u> the bookkeeping.

INCORRECT: The patient's symptoms were fever, dizziness, and his head hurt.
  CORRECT: The patient's symptoms were <u>fever,</u> <u>dizziness,</u> and <u>headaches.</u>

INCORRECT: Professor Williams enjoys teaching and to write.
  CORRECT: Professor Williams enjoys <u>teaching</u> and <u>writing.</u>

EXERCISES

Part A: Choose the correct answer.

In a hot, sunny climate, man acclimatizes by eating less, drinking more liquids, wearing lighter clothing, and _____.
(A) skin changes that darken
(B) his skin may darken
(C) experiencing a darkening of the skin
(D) darkens his skin

Part B: Choose the incorrect word or phrase and correct it.

The aims of the European Economic Community <u>are to</u>
                                               (A)

eliminate tariffs between member countries; <u>developing</u> common
                                             (B)

policies for agriculture, labor, welfare, trade, and <u>transportation;</u>
                                                      (C)

and <u>to abolish</u> trusts and cartels.
    (D)

11 Parallel Structure—After Correlative Conjunctions

Remember that ideas of equal importance are introduced by correlative conjunctions:

both...and
not only...but also

Avoid expressing ideas after correlative conjunctions by different structures.

EXAMPLES

INCORRECT:	She is not only famous in the United States, but also abroad.
CORRECT:	She is famous not only in the United States, but also abroad.

INCORRECT:	The exam tested both listening and to read.
CORRECT:	The exam tested both listening and reading.

INCORRECT:	He is not only intelligent but also he is creative.
CORRECT:	He is not only intelligent but also creative.

INCORRECT:	Flying is not only faster but also it is safer than traveling by car.
CORRECT:	Flying is not only faster but also safer than traveling by car.

INCORRECT:	John registered for both Electrical Engineering 500 and to study Mathematics 390.
CORRECT:	John registered for both Electrical Engineering 500 and Mathematics 390.

EXERCISES

Part A: Choose the correct answer.

Both historically and _____, Ontario is the heartland of Canada.

(A) in its geography
(B) geographically
(C) also its geography
(D) geography

Part B: Choose the incorrect word or phrase and correct it.

The cacao bean was cultivated by the Aztecs not only to drink
          (A)   (B)

but also currency.
 (C)   (D)

12   Redundancy—Unnecessary Phrases

In all patterns, prefer simple, direct sentences to complicated, indirect sentences. Find the Subject-Verb-Complement-Modifier, and determine whether the other words are useful or unnecessary.

S	V	C	M
Lee	learned	English	quickly

Avoid using an adjective with such phrases as *in character* or *in nature.*

Avoid using the redundant pattern instead of an adverb such as *quickly.*

in a	adjective	manner
in a	quick	manner

EXAMPLES

INCORRECT:	The key officials who testified before the Senate committee responded in a manner that was evasive.
CORRECT:	The key officials who testified before the Senate committee responded evasively.
INCORRECT:	Mr. Davis knows a great deal in terms of the condition of the situation.
CORRECT:	Mr. Davis knows a great deal about the situation.
INCORRECT:	It was a problem which was very difficult in character and very delicate in nature.
CORRECT:	The problem was difficult and delicate.
INCORRECT:	The disease was very serious in the nature of it.
CORRECT:	The disease was very serious.

INCORRECT: Mary had always behaved in a responsible manner.
CORRECT: <u>Mary</u> <u>had always behaved</u> <u>responsibly</u>.

EXERCISES

Part A: Choose the correct answer.

Waitresses and waiters who serve _____ deserve at least a
20 percent tip.
    (A) in a courteous manner
    (B) courteously
    (C) with courtesy in their manner
    (D) courteous

Part B: Choose the incorrect word or phrase and correct it.

Hummingbirds move <u>their</u> wings so <u>rapid a way</u> that they appear
                              (A)   (B)
<u>to be hanging</u> <u>in the air</u>.
        (C)   (D)

PROBLEM 13

Redundancy—Repetition of Words with the Same Meaning

In all patterns, avoid using words with the same meaning consecutively in a sentence.

EXAMPLES

INCORRECT: The money that I have is sufficient enough for my
                    needs.
CORRECT: The money that I have is <u>sufficient</u> for my needs.

INCORRECT: Bill asked the speaker to repeat again because he had
                    not heard him the first time.
CORRECT: Bill asked the speaker <u>to repeat</u> because he had not
                    heard him the first time.

INCORRECT: The class advanced forward rapidly.
  CORRECT: The class <u>advanced</u> rapidly.

INCORRECT: She returned back to her hometown after she had
              finished her degree.
  CORRECT: She <u>returned</u> to her hometown after she had finished
              her degree.

INCORRECT: I am nearly almost finished with this chapter.
  CORRECT: I am <u>nearly</u> finished with this chapter.
                              or
              I am <u>almost</u> finished with this chapter.

EXERCISES

Part A: Choose the correct answer.

Famous for his _____ punctuation, typography, and language, Edward Estlin Cummings published his collected poems
in 1954.

   (A) new innovations for
   (B) innovations in
   (C) newly approached
   (D) innovations newly approached in

Part B: Choose the incorrect word or phrase and correct it.

The idea of a submarine is <u>an old ancient one,</u> dating from
                                       (A)
<u>as early as</u> <u>the fifteenth century</u> when Drebbel and Da Vinci
     (B)   (C)
<u>made</u> preliminary drawings.
  (D)

14   Redundancy—Repetition of Noun by Pronoun

In all patterns, avoid using a noun and the pronoun that refers to it consecutively in a sentence. Avoid using a pronoun after the noun it refers to, and *that*.

EXAMPLES

INCORRECT: My teacher he said to listen to the news on the radio in order to practice listening comprehension.

CORRECT: <u>My teacher</u> said to listen to the news on the radio in order to practice listening comprehension.

INCORRECT: Steve he plans to go into business with his father.

CORRECT: <u>Steve</u> plans to go into business with his father.

INCORRECT: My sister she found a store that imported food from our country.

CORRECT: <u>My sister</u> found a store that imported food from our country.

INCORRECT: Hospitalization that it covers room, meals, nursing, and additional hospital expenses such as lab tests, X-rays, and medicine.

CORRECT: <u>Hospitalization</u> covers room, meals, nursing, and additional hospital expenses such as lab tests, X-rays, and medicine.

INCORRECT: Anne she wants to visit Washington, D.C., before she goes home.

CORRECT: <u>Anne</u> wants to visit Washington, D.C., before she goes home.

EXERCISES

Part A: Choose the correct answer.

A perennial is_____ for more than two years, such as trees and shrubs.

   (A) any plant that it continues to grow
   (B) any plant it continuing to grow
   (C) any plant that continues to grow
   (D) any plant continuing growth

Part B: Choose the incorrect word or phrase and correct it.

Advertising it provides most of the income for magazines, news-
      (A)   (B)   (C)

papers, radio, and television in the United States today.
                           (D)

Transitive and Intransitive Verbs— *Raise* and *Rise*

PROBLEM 15

A transitive verb is a verb that takes a complement. An intransitive verb is a verb that does not take a complement.

The following pairs of verbs can be confusing. Remember that *raise* is a transitive verb; it takes a complement. *Rise* is an intransitive verb; it does not take a complement.

Transitive		
Verb word	*Past*	*Participle*
raise	raised	raised

Intransitive		
Verb word	*Past*	*Participle*
rise	rose	risen

Remember that *to raise* means to move to a higher place or to cause to rise. *To rise* means to go up or to increase.

Raise and rise are also used as nouns. A *raise* means an increase in salary. A *rise* means an increase in price, worth, quantity, or degree.

S	RAISE	C	M
Heavy rain	raises	the water level of the reservoir	every spring
Heavy rain	raised	the water level of the reservoir	last week

S	RISE	C	M
The water level	rises		when it rains every spring
The water level	rose		when it rained last week

EXAMPLES

INCORRECT: The cost of living has raised 3 percent in the past year.

CORRECT: The cost of living has risen 3 percent in the past year.

INCORRECT: The flag is risen at dawn by an honor guard.

CORRECT: The flag is raised at dawn by an honor guard.
(An honor guard raises the flag.)

INCORRECT: Kay needs to rise her grades if she wants to get into graduate school.

CORRECT: Kay needs to raise her grades if she wants to get into graduate school.

INCORRECT: The landlord has risen the rent.

CORRECT: The landlord has raised the rent.

INCORRECT: The smoke that is raising from that oil refinery is black.

CORRECT: The smoke that is rising from that oil refinery is black.

EXERCISES

Part A: Choose the correct answer.

The average elevation of the Himalayas is twenty thousand feet, and Mount Everest _____ to more than twenty-nine thousand feet at its apex.

    (A) raises
    (B) rises
    (C) roses
    (D) arises

Part B: Choose the incorrect word or phrase and correct it.

When the temperature is <u>risen</u> to <u>the burning point</u> without a
                     (A)   (B)

source of escape <u>for the heat</u>, spontaneous combustion <u>occurs.</u>
                (C)   (D)

PROBLEM 16   Transitive and Intransitive Verbs— *Lay* and *Lie*

Remember that *lay* is a transitive verb; it takes a complement. *Lie* is an intransitive verb; it does not take a complement.

Transitive		
Verb word	*Past*	*Participle*
lay	laid	laid

Intransitive		
Verb word	*Past*	*Participle*
lie	lay	lain

Remember that *to lay* means to put, to place or to cause to lie. *To lie* means to recline or to occupy a place.

The past form of the verb *to lie* is *lay.*

S	LAY	C	M
The postman	lays	the mail	on the table every day
The postman	laid	the mail	on the table yesterday

S	LIE	C	M
He	lies		on the sofa to rest every day after work
He	lay		on the sofa to rest yesterday after work

EXAMPLES

INCORRECT:	Her coat was laying on the chair.
CORRECT:	Her coat was lying on the chair.
INCORRECT:	I have lain your notebook on the table by the door so that you won't forget it.
CORRECT:	I have laid your notebook on the table by the door so that you won't forget it.
INCORRECT:	Key West lays off the coast of Florida.
CORRECT:	Key West lies off the coast of Florida.
INCORRECT:	Why don't you lay down for awhile?
CORRECT:	Why don't you lie down for awhile?
INCORRECT:	Linda always forgets where she lies her glasses.
CORRECT:	Linda always forgets where she lays her glasses.

EXERCISES

Part A: Choose the correct answer.

The geographic position of North America, _____
in the early days of the European settlement.

  (A) laying between the Atlantic and the Pacific Oceans, isolating it

  (B) isolating it as it laid between the Atlantic and the Pacific Oceans

  (C) lying between the Atlantic and the Pacific Oceans, isolated it

  (D) isolating it between the Atlantic and the Pacific Oceans as it was layed

Part B: Choose the incorrect word or phrase and correct it.

Melanin, a pigment that <u>lays</u> under the skin, <u>is</u> responsible for
               (A)   (B)

skin color, including the variations that <u>occur</u> <u>among</u> different
                                    (C)   (D)

races.

Transitive and Intransitive Verbs—
Set and *Sit*

Remember that *set* is a transitive verb; it takes a complement.
Sit is an intransitive verb; it does not take a complement.

Transitive		
Verb word	*Past*	*Participle*
set	set	set

Intransitive		
Verb word	*Past*	*Participle*
sit	sat	sat

Remember that *to set* means to put, to place, or to cause to sit.
To sit means to occupy a place on a chair or a flat surface.

S	SET	C	M
The students	set	the lab equipment	on the table every class
The students	set	the lab equipment	on the table last class period

S	SIT	C	M
The equipment	sits		on the table every class
The equipment	sat		on the table last class period

EXAMPLES

INCORRECT: Please sit the telephone on the table by the bed.
CORRECT: Please <u>set</u> <u>the telephone</u> on the table by the bed.

INCORRECT: Won't you set down?
CORRECT: Won't <u>you</u> <u>sit</u> down?

INCORRECT: Their house sets on a hill overlooking a lake.
CORRECT: Their <u>house</u> <u>sits</u> on a hill overlooking a lake.

INCORRECT: Let's sit your suitcases out of the way.
CORRECT: Let's <u>set</u> <u>your suitcases</u> out of the way.

INCORRECT: Terry has set there waiting for us for almost an hour.
CORRECT: <u>Terry</u> <u>has sat</u> there waiting for us for almost an hour.

EXERCISES

Part A: Choose the correct answer.

When Jacqueline Kennedy was first lady, she collected many beautiful antiques and _____ them among the original pieces in the White House.

    (A) sat
    (B) set
    (C) sit
    (D) sits

Part B: Choose the incorrect word or phrase and correct it.

Hyde Park, the family estate <u>of Franklin D. Roosevelt</u>, <u>sets</u> on
                                    (A)   (B)

top of a bluff <u>overlooking</u> <u>the Hudson River.</u>
               (C)   (D)

Similar Verbs—*Make* and *Do*

Verb word	Past	Participle
do	did	done

Verb word	Past	Participle
make	made	made

Remember that *to do* and *to make* have similar meanings, but *do* is often used before complements that describe work and chores. *To make* is often used before complements that are derived from verbs.

DO an assignment	MAKE an agreement	(to agree)
the dishes	an announcement	(to announce)
a favor	an attempt	(to attempt)
homework	a decision	(to decide)
the laundry	a discovery	(to discover)
a paper	an offer	(to offer)
research	a profit	(to profit)
work	a promise	(to promise)

S	DO	C	M
We	do	our homework	before class every day
We	did	our homework	before class yesterday

S	MAKE	C	M
We	make	an agreement	with each other every semester
We	made	an agreement	with each other last semester

EXAMPLES

INCORRECT: I really don't mind making the homework for this class.

CORRECT: I really don't mind doing the homework for this class.

INCORRECT: Did you do a mistake?

CORRECT: Did you make a mistake?

INCORRECT: Please make me a favor.

CORRECT: Please do me a favor.

INCORRECT: Are they doing progress on the new road?

CORRECT: Are they making progress on the new road?

INCORRECT: Have you done any interesting discoveries while you were doing your research?

CORRECT: Have you made any interesting discoveries while you were doing your research?

EXERCISES

Part A: Choose the correct answer.

The president usually _____ unless his press secretary approves it.

    (A) doesn't do a statement

    (B) doesn't make a statement

    (C) doesn't statement

    (D) no statement

Part B: Choose the incorrect word or phrase and correct it.

A one hundred-horsepower tractor can make the work of
          (A)   (B) (C)

a large number of horses.
    (D)

19   Prepositional Idioms

Prefer these idioms	Avoid these errors
accede to	accede on, by
according to	according
approve of	approve for
ashamed of	ashamed with
bored with	bored of
capable of	capable to
compete with	compete together
composed of	composed from
concerned with	concerned of
conscious of	conscious for
depend on	depend in, to
effects on	effects in
equal to	equal as
except for	excepting for
from now on	after now on
from time to time	for, when time to time
frown on	frown to
glance at, through	glance
incapable of	incapable to
in conflict	on conflict
inferior to	inferior with
in the habit of	in the habit to
in the near future	at the near future
knowledge of	knowledge on
near; next to	near to
of the opinion	in opinion
on top of	on top
opposite	opposite over
prior to	prior
regard to	regard of
related to	related with
respect for	respect of
responsible for	responsible
similar to	similar as
since	ever since

until	~~up until~~
with regard to	~~with regard of~~

EXAMPLES

INCORRECT: Excepting for the Gulf Coast region, most of the nation will have very pleasant weather tonight and tomorrow.

CORRECT: Except for the Gulf Coast region, most of the nation will have very pleasant weather tonight and tomorrow.

INCORRECT: In recent years, educators have become more concerned of bilingualism.

CORRECT: In recent years, educators have become more concerned with bilingualism.

INCORRECT: He always does what he pleases, without regard of the rules and regulations.

CORRECT: He always does what he pleases, without regard to the rules and regulations.

INCORRECT: The bank opposite over the university isn't open on Saturdays.

CORRECT: The bank opposite the university isn't open on Saturdays.

INCORRECT: The customs of other countries are not inferior with those of our own country.

CORRECT: The customs of other countries are not inferior to those of our own country.

EXERCISES

Part A: Choose the correct answer.

_____ discovery of insulin, it was not possible to treat diabetes.
- (A) Prior to the
- (B) Prior
- (C) The prior
- (D) To prior

Part B: Choose the incorrect word or phrase and correct it.

The price of gold depends in several factors, including supply
   (A)   (B)   (C)

and demand in relation to the value of the dollar.
            (D)

20 Parts of Speech

Although it is usually very easy to identify the parts of speech, word families can be confusing. Word families are groups of words with similar meanings and spellings. Each word in the family is a different part of speech. For example, *agreement* is a noun; *agreeable* is an adjective; to *agree* is a verb.

The endings of words can help you identify the part of speech.

Nouns Derived from Verbs

Verb	Ending	Noun
store	-age	storage
accept	-ance	acceptance
insist	-ence	insistence
agree	-ment	agreement
authorize	-sion/-tion	authorization

Nouns Derived from Adjectives

Adjective	Ending	Noun
convenient	-ce	convenience
redundant	-cy	redundancy
opposite	-tion	opposition
soft	-ness	softness
durable	-ty	durability

Adjectives Derived from Nouns

Noun	Ending	Adjective
possibility	-able/-ible	possible
intention	-al	intentional
distance	-ant	distant
frequency	-ent	frequent
juice	-y	juicy

Adverbs Derived from Adjectives

Adjective	Ending	Adverb
efficient	-ly	efficiently

EXAMPLES

INCORRECT: The agreeing is not legal unless everyone signs his name.

CORRECT: The agreement is not legal unless everyone signs his name.

INCORRECT: Even young children begin to show able in mathematics.

CORRECT: Even young children begin to show ability in mathematics.

INCORRECT: Arranging have been made for the funeral.
CORRECT: Arrangements have been made for the funeral.

INCORRECT: A free educating is guaranteed to every citizen.
CORRECT: A free education is guaranteed to every citizen.

INCORRECT: The develop of hybrids has increased yields.
CORRECT: The development of hybrids has increased yields.

EXERCISES

Part A: Choose the correct answer.

Unless protected areas are established, the Bengal tiger, the blue whale, and the California condor face_____ of extinction.

(A) possible
(B) the possibility
(C) to be possible
(D) possibly

Part B: Choose the incorrect word or phrase and correct it.

<u>Because</u> blood from different individuals may <u>different</u> in the
  (A)   (B)

type of antigen on the surface of the red cells and the type of

antibody in the plasma, a dangerous reaction <u>can occur</u> between
                                               (C)

the donor <u>and</u> recipient in a blood transfusion.
        (D)

TYPES OF QUESTIONS

Multiple Choice Questions

All of the questions on both the Paper and Pencil TOEFL and the Computer-Based TOEFL are multiple choice. There are no computer-assisted questions with special directions.

Although the structure questions in this book are numbered, and the answer choices are lettered A, B, C, and D, the same questions on the CD-ROM that supplements the larger version of this book, *Barron's How to Prepare for the TOEFL,* are not numbered and lettered. You need the numbers and letters in the book to refer to the Answer Key, the Explanatory Answers, and the Transcript for the

Listening Section. On the CD-ROM, you can refer to other chapters by clicking on the screen. The questions on the CD-ROM are like those on the Computer-Based TOEFL.

Paper and Pencil TOEFL

1. If water is heated to 121 degrees F, _____ as steam.
   (A) it will boil and escape
   (B) it is boiling and escaping
   (C) it boil and escape
   (D) it would boil and escape

2. If water freezes, it has become a solid.
   $\quad$ (A) $\qquad$ (B) $\quad$ (C) $\quad$ (D)

Answer Sheet

1. ● Ⓑ Ⓒ Ⓓ
2. Ⓐ Ⓑ ● Ⓓ

Computer-Based TOEFL

If water is heated to 121 degrees F,
_____ as steam.
   ● it will boil and escape
   ○ it is boiling and escaping
   ○ it boil and escape
   ○ it would boil and escape

If water freezes, it has become

a solid.

Computer Tutorial for the Structure Section

In order to succeed on the Computer-Based TOEFL, you must understand the computer vocabulary used for the test, and you must be familiar with the icons on the computer screens that you will see on the test. First, review the vocabulary that you learned in the Tutorial for Section 1 on page 66. The same vocabulary is used for Section 2. Then study the computer screens in this Tutorial.

Testing Tools: Review of Vocabulary, Icons, and Keys

The following words are from the list of general vocabulary for the Computer-Based TOEFL introduced in the previous chapter. Using the word list, fill in the blanks in the ten sentences.

Arrow	Mouse
Click	Mouse Pad
Confirm Answer	Next
Dismiss Directions	Oval
Help (Question mark)	Time (Clock)
Icon	

1. A _____ is a small control with a button on it.

2. A _____ is a rectangular pad where you move the mouse.

3. An _____ is a marker on the screen that shows you where you are moving on the computer.

4. To _____ is to depress the button on the mouse. You _____ the mouse to make changes on the screen.

5. An _____ is a small picture or word or phrase in a box. Move the arrow to the _____ to tell the computer what to do.

6. Click on _____ to remove the directions from the screen.

7. Click on an _____ to choose an answer to one of the multiple choice questions.

8. Click on _____ , then click on _____ to see the next question.

9. Click on _____ to see a list of the icons and directions.

10. Click on _____ to hide or show the time you have left to finish the section of the test you are working on.

Computer Screens for Section 2

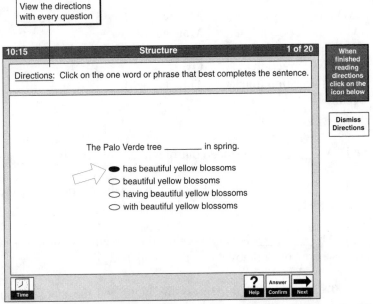

View the directions with every question

| 10:15 | Structure | 1 of 20 |

When finished reading directions click on the icon below

Directions: Click on the one word or phrase that best completes the sentence.

Dismiss Directions

The Palo Verde tree _____ in spring.

- ● has beautiful yellow blossoms
- ○ beautiful yellow blossoms
- ○ having beautiful yellow blossoms
- ○ with beautiful yellow blossoms

Time

? Help   Answer Confirm   Next

TIP: There are only two types of questions in Section 2. After you have read and understood the directions for both types of questions in this Tutorial, you will not need to read the top part of the screen every time.

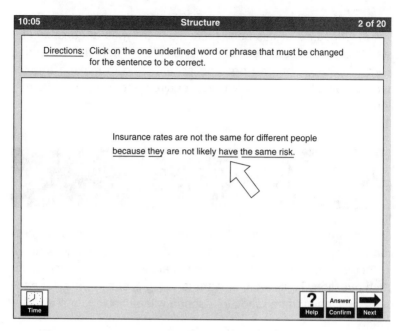

TIP: Be sure to click on **Next** before you click on **Answer Confirm**. If you do not click on these two icons in the correct order, the next question will not appear.

Simulations for Section 2

In order to prepare for the experience that you will have on the Computer-Based TOEFL, you can use the CD-ROM that supplements the larger version of this book, *Barron's How to Prepare for the TOEFL*. Locate the Structure Section on Model Tests 5–8. The computer will simulate the Structure Section on the Computer-Based TOEFL. These Model Tests are computer-assisted.

As part of your study plan, be sure to review all of the questions in all of the Model Tests. Use the Explanatory Answers on pages 385–432. Refer to the Review of Structure on pages 75–202 of this book. Finally, if you have the CD-ROM, take the Cumulative Model Test. This test is computer-adaptive, which means that the computer will select questions for you at your level of language proficiency.

If you choose not to purchase the larger version of this book, or you do not have a computer, you can still simulate some of the features of the Computer-Based TOEFL. Section 2 in Model Tests 3–4 in Chapter 7 of this book presents both types of questions for the Structure Section randomly. This is different from the Paper and Pencil TOEFL. You can become accustomed to making a quick decision about the kind of answer required—completion or correction.

Advice for the Structure Section: Computer-Based TOEFL

Become familiar with the directions. The two types of questions will appear at random. If you forget how to answer, look at the top of the screen. Directions will appear at the top of every screen for each question. To save time, learn to recognize the format for each question type, and be ready to respond without looking at the directions.

Move efficiently through the questions. In order to go to the next question, you must click on **Next** and then **Confirm Answer**. If you only click on **Next**, you will not be able to move to the next question. A screen will remind you to return to the previous question. You must enter an answer before you go to the next question. Click on **Return to Question** to move back to the question that you did not answer.

Change your answer before you confirm it. After you click on your answer and see the dark oval or dark box, you can still change your answer. Just click on a different choice. But remember that you cannot change your answer after you click on **Confirm Answer**. This means that you cannot go back to previous questions and change the answers. You must choose your answer, click on your choice, click on **Next**, click on **Confirm Answer**, and move to the next question.

Do your best. The computer will select the questions on this section of the test based on your responses. You will begin with questions that are considered of average difficulty. You will receive easier questions if you are not able to answer the average questions. You will receive more difficult questions if you are able to answer the average questions. You receive more points for the more difficult questions. Just do your best, and you will receive the most points for your level of structure ability.

Understand the **Help** *screen.* The **Help** screen has a question mark on it. It is mostly designed to repeat directions. Be careful. You can waste a lot of time on this screen. If you click on **Help** and you want to go back to the question you were answering, look at the box in the bottom right corner. Click on **Return to Where I Was.**

Get help from the test administrator. If you think that your computer is not performing correctly, notify one of the test administrators immediately. There should be several in the room. They cannot help you with the answers on the TOEFL, but they can help you use the computer. That is why they are there. Tell the administrator, "Excuse me. My computer won't _____ ." Show the administrator the problem on the computer.

Stay focused. There is only one test question on the screen at any time. Focus on it. If you need to rest your eyes or your neck muscles, don't look around at other people. Look down at your lap with your eyes closed. Then look up at the ceiling with your eyes closed. Then return to the question. Remember that you cannot return to previous questions, so give each question your full attention while it is on the screen. Then, get ready to focus on the next question.

REVIEW OF SECTION 3: READING

Overview of the Reading Section

QUICK COMPARISON
PAPER AND PENCIL TOEFL AND COMPUTER-BASED TOEFL
SECTION 3

Paper and Pencil TOEFL Reading Comprehension	*Computer-Based TOEFL Reading*
There are five reading passages with an average of ten questions after each passage.	There are three to six reading passages with an average of six to ten questions after each passage.
There are fifty questions.	There are fewer questions.
Everyone taking the TOEFL answers the same questions.	The computer does not select questions at your level of language proficiency. You will have the same questions as others who take the same form of the test.
There are no pictures or visual cues.	There may be pictures in the questions that refer to the content of the reading passage.
All of the questions are multiple choice.	Most of the questions are multiple choice, but some of the questions have special directions.
Every question has only one answer.	Some of the questions have two answers.

You answer on a paper answer sheet, filling in ovals marked (A), (B), (C), and (D).

You click on the screen in the oval that corresponds to the answer you have chosen, or you follow the directions on the screen.

You have fifty-five minutes to complete the section.

You have seventy to ninety minutes to complete the section.

You can return to previous passages and questions, erase, and change answers on your answer sheet.

You can return to previous passages and questions, change answers, and answer questions you have left blank.

You may not take notes.

You may not take notes.

Review of Problems and Questions for the Reading Section

This Review can be used to prepare for both the Paper and Pencil TOEFL and the Computer-Based TOEFL. For the most part, the same types of problems are tested on both the Paper and Pencil TOEFL and the Computer-Based TOEFL. Most of the questions on both the Paper and Pencil TOEFL and the Computer-Based TOEFL are multiple choice.

Some of the questions on the Computer-Based TOEFL are computer-assisted. Although the computer-assisted questions in this book are numbered, and the answer choices are lettered A, B, C, and D, the same questions on the CD-ROM that supplements the larger version of this book, *Barron's How to Prepare for the TOEFL*, are not numbered and lettered. You need the numbers and letters in the book to refer to the Answer Key, the Explanatory Answers, and the Transcript for the Listening Section. On the CD-ROM, you can refer to other chapters by clicking on the screen. The CD-ROM and the following examples are like those on the Computer-Based TOEFL. The computer-assisted questions have special directions on the screen.

Previewing

Research shows that it is easier to understand what you are reading if you begin with a general idea of what the passage is about. Previewing helps you form a general idea of the topic in your mind.

To preview, read the first sentence of each paragraph and the last sentence of the passage. You should do this as quickly as possible. Remember, you are not reading for specific information, but for an impression of the *topic*.

EXERCISE

DIRECTIONS: Preview the following passage. Focus on the first sentence in each paragraph and the last sentence of the passage. Can you identify the topic? Check your answer using the key on page 371.

A black hole is a region of space created by the total gravitational collapse of matter. It is so intense that nothing, not even light or radiation, can escape. In other words, it is a one-way surface through which matter can fall inward but cannot emerge.

Some astronomers believe that a black hole may be formed when a large star collapses inward from its own weight. So long as they are emitting heat and light into space, stars support themselves against their own gravitational pull with the outward thermal pressure generated by heat from nuclear reactions deep in their interiors. But if a star eventually exhausts its nuclear fuel, then its unbalanced gravitational attraction could cause it to contract and collapse. Furthermore, it could begin to pull in surrounding matter, including nearby comets and planets, creating a black hole.

Reading for Main Ideas

By previewing, you can form a general idea of what a reading passage is about; that is, you identify the *topic.* By reading for main ideas, you identify the point of view of the author—that is, what the writer's *thesis* is. Specifically, what does the author propose to write about the topic? If you could reduce the reading to one sentence, what would it be?

Questions about the main idea can be worded in many ways. For example, the following questions are all asking for the same information: (1) What is the main idea? (2) What is the subject? (3) What is the topic? (4) What would be a good title?

EXERCISE

DIRECTIONS: The main idea usually occurs at the beginning of a reading passage. Look at the first two sentences in the following passage. Can you identify the main idea? What would be a good title for this passage? Check your answers using the key on page 372.

> For more than a century, despite attacks by a few opposing scientists, Charles Darwin's theory of evolution by natural selection has stood firm. Now, however, some respected biologists are beginning to question whether the theory accounts for major developments such as the shift from water to land habitation. Clearly, evolution has not proceeded steadily but has progressed by radical advances. Recent research in molecular biology, particularly in the study of DNA, provides us with a new possibility. Not only environmental change but also genetic codes in the underlying structure of DNA could govern evolution.

3   Using Contexts for Vocabulary

Before you can use a context, you must understand what a context is. In English, a context is the combination of vocabulary and grammar that surrounds a word. Context can be a sentence or a paragraph or a passage. Context helps you make a general *prediction* about meaning. If you know the general meaning of a sentence, you also know the general meaning of the words in the sentence.

Making predictions from contexts is very important when you are reading a foreign language. In this way, you can read and understand the meaning of a passage without stopping to look up every new word in a dictionary. On an examination like the TOEFL, dictionaries are not permitted in the room.

EXERCISE

<u>DIRECTIONS:</u> Read the following passage, paying close attention to the underlined words. Can you understand their meanings from the context without using a dictionary? Check your answers using the key on page 372.

At the age of sixty-six, Harland Sanders had to <u>auction</u> off everything he owned in order to pay his debts. Once the successful <u>proprietor</u> of a large restaurant, Sanders saw his business suffer from the construction of a new freeway that bypassed his establishment and rerouted the traffic that had <u>formerly</u> passed.

With an income of only $105 a month in Social Security, he packed his car with a pressure cooker, some chickens, and sixty pounds of the seasoning that he had developed for frying chicken. He stopped at restaurants, where he cooked chicken for owners to <u>sample</u>. If they liked it, he offered to show them how to cook it. Then he sold them the seasoning and collected a <u>royalty</u> of four cents on each chicken they cooked. The rest is history. Eight years later, there were 638 Kentucky Fried Chicken franchises, and Colonel Sanders had sold his business again—this time for over two million dollars.

4 Scanning for Details

After reading a passage on the TOEFL, you will be expected to answer six to ten questions. Most of them are multiple choice. First, read a question and find the important content words. Content words are usually nouns, verbs, or adjectives. They are called content words because they contain the content or meaning of a sentence.

Next, let your eyes travel quickly over the passage for the same content words or synonyms of the words. This is called *scanning*. By scanning, you can find a place in the reading passage where the answer to a question is found. Finally, read those specific sentences carefully and choose the answer that corresponds to the meaning of the sentences you have read.

EXERCISE

DIRECTIONS: First, read the following passage. Then, read the questions after the reading passage, and look for the content words. Finally, scan the passage for the same words or synonyms. Can you answer the questions? Check your answers using the key on pages 372–373.

To prepare for a career in engineering, a student must begin planning in high school. Mathematics and science should form the core curriculum. For example, in a school where sixteen credit hours are required for high school graduation, four should be in mathematics, one each in chemistry, biology, and physics. The remaining credits should include four in English and at least three in the humanities and social sciences. The average entering freshman in engineering should have achieved at least a 2.5 grade point average on a 4.0 scale in his or her high school. Although deficiencies can be corrected during the first year, the student who needs additional work should expect to spend five instead of four years to complete a degree.

1. What is the average grade point for an entering freshman in engineering?

2. When should a student begin planning for a career in engineering?

3. How can a student correct deficiencies in preparation?

4. How many credits should a student have in English?

5. How many credits are required for a high school diploma?

5 Making Inferences

Sometimes, in a reading passage, you will find a direct statement of fact. That is called evidence. But other times, you will not find a direct statement. Then you will need to use the evidence you have to make an inference. An *inference* is a logical conclusion based on evidence. It can be about the passage itself or about the author's viewpoint.

EXERCISE

DIRECTIONS: First, read the following passage. Then, read the questions after the passage, and make inferences. Can you find the evidence for your inference in the reading passage? Check your answers using the key on pages 373–374.

When an acid is dissolved in water, the acid molecule divides into two parts, a hydrogen ion and another ion. An ion is an atom or a group of atoms that has an electrical charge. The charge can be either positive or negative. If hydrochloric acid is mixed with water, for example, it divides into hydrogen ions and chlorine ions.

A strong acid ionizes to a great extent, but a weak acid does not ionize so much. The strength of an acid, therefore, depends on how much it ionizes, not on how many hydrogen ions are produced. It is interesting that nitric acid and sulfuric acid become greatly ionized whereas boric acid and carbonic acid do not.

1. What kind of acid is sulfuric acid?

2. What kind of acid is boric acid?

6   Identifying Exceptions

After reading a passage on the TOEFL, you will be asked to select from four possible answers the one that is NOT mentioned in the reading.

Use your scanning skills to locate related words and phrases in the passage and the answer choices.

EXERCISE

DIRECTIONS: First, read the following passage. Then, read the question after the reading passage. Last, scan the passage again for related words and phrases. Try to eliminate three of the choices. Check your answer using the key on page 374.

All music consists of two elements—expression and design. Expression is inexact and subjective, and may be enjoyed in a personal or instinctive way. Design, on the other hand is exact and must be analyzed objectively in order to be understood and appreciated. The folk song, for example, has a definite musical design which relies on simple repetition with a definite beginning and ending. A folk song generally consists of one stanza of music repeated for each stanza of verse.

Because of their communal, and usually uncertain origin, folk songs are often popular verse set to music. They are not always recorded, and tend to be passed on in a kind of musical version of oral history. Each singer revises and perfects the song. In part as a consequence of this continuous revision process, most folk songs are almost perfect in their construction and design. A particular singer's interpretation of the folk song may provide an interesting expression, but the simple design that underlies the song itself is stable and enduring.

1. All of the following are true of a folk song EXCEPT
   (A) there is a clear start and finish
   (B) the origin is often not known
   (C) the design may change in the interpretation
   (D) simple repetition is characteristic of its design

7 Locating References

After reading a passage on the TOEFL, you will be asked to find the antecedent of a pronoun. An antecedent is a word or phrase to which a pronoun refers. Usually, you will be given a pronoun such as "it," "its," "them," or "their," and you will be asked to locate the reference word or phrase in the passage.

First, find the pronoun in the passage. Then read the sentence using the four answer choices in place of the pronoun. The meaning of the sentence in the context of the passage will not change when you substitute the correct antecedent.

EXERCISE

DIRECTIONS: First find the pronoun in the following passage. Next, start reading several sentences before the sentence in which the pronoun is found, and continue reading several sentences after it. Then, substitute the words or phrases in the answer choices. Which one does not change the meaning of the sentence? Check your answer using the key on page 375.

The National Road, also known as the Cumberland Road, was constructed in the early 1800s to provide transportation between the established commercial areas of the East and Northwest Territory. By 1818, the road had reached Wheeling, West Virginia, 130 miles from its point of origin in Cumberland, Maryland. The cost was a monumental thirteen thousand dollars per mile.

Upon reaching the Ohio River, the National Road became one of the major trade routes to the western states and territories, providing Baltimore with a trade advantage over neighboring cities. In order to compete, New York state authorized the construction of the Erie Canal, and Philadelphia initiated a transportation plan to link it with Pittsburgh. Towns along the rivers, canals, and the new National Road became important trade centers.

1. The word its refers to
   (A) the Northwest Territory
   (B) 1818
   (C) the road
   (D) Wheeling, West Virginia

Referring to the Passage

After reading the passage on the TOEFL, you will be asked to find certain information in the passage, and identify it by line number.

First, read the question. Then refer to the line numbers in the answer choices to scan for the information in the question.

EXERCISE

DIRECTIONS: First, read the following passage. Then, refer back to the passage. Can you find the correct reference? Check your answer using the key on pages 375–376.

In September of 1929, traders experienced a lack of confidence in the stock market's ability to continue its phenomenal rise. Prices fell. For many inexperienced inves-

Line tors, the drop produced a panic. They had all their money
(5) tied up in the market, and they were pressed to sell before the prices fell even lower. Sell orders were coming in so fast that the ticker tape at the New York Stock Exchange could not accommodate all the transactions.

To try to reestablish confidence in the market, a power-
(10) ful group of New York bankers agreed to pool their funds and purchase stock above current market values. Although the buy orders were minimal, they were counting on their reputations to restore confidence on the part of the smaller investors, thereby affecting the number of sell orders. On
(15) Thursday, October 24, Richard Whitney, the Vice President of the New York Stock Exchange and a broker for the J.P. Morgan Company, made the effort on their behalf. Initially, it appeared to have been successful, then, on the following Tuesday, the crash began again and accelerated.
(20) By 1932, stocks were worth only twenty percent of their value at the 1929 high. The results of the crash had

extended into every aspect of the economy, causing a long and painful depression, referred to in American history as the Great Depression.

1. Where in the passage does the author refer to the reason for the stock market crash?

2. Where in the passage does the author suggest that there was a temporary recovery in the stock market?

CUMULATIVE REVIEW EXERCISE FOR READING COMPREHENSION

Read the following passage, using the skills you have learned. Preview, read for main ideas, and use contexts for vocabulary. To read faster, read phrases instead of words. Then, answer the questions that follow the passage. Scan for details and evidence. Make inferences.

The computer-based version of this reading passage is best viewed on the CD-ROM that supplements the larger version of this book, *Barron's How to Prepare for the TOEFL.* Scroll through the passage, using the skills that you have learned. Check your answers on the screen. If you choose not to purchase the larger version or if you do not have a computer, then use the print version shown with the following computer-assisted questions.

Although each baby has an individual schedule of development, general patterns of growth have been observed. Three periods of development have been identified, including early
Line infancy, which extends from the first to the sixth month; mid-
(5) dle infancy, from the sixth to the ninth month; and late infancy, from the ninth to the fifteenth month. Whereas the newborn is concerned with his or her inner world and responds primarily to hunger and pain, in early infancy the baby is already aware of the surrounding world. During the second
(10) month, many infants are awake more and can raise their heads to look at things. They also begin to smile at people. By four months, the baby is searching for things but not yet grasping them with its hands. It is also beginning to be wary of

strangers and may scream when a visiting relative tries to pick
(15) it up. By five months, the baby is grabbing objects and putting
them into its mouth. Some babies are trying to feed themselves with their hands.

In middle infancy, the baby concentrates on practicing a
great many speech sounds. It loves to imitate actions and
(20) examine interesting objects. At about seven months, it begins
to crawl, a skill that it masters at the end of middle infancy.

In late infancy, the baby takes an interest in games, songs,
and even books. Progress toward walking moves through
standing, balancing, bouncing in place, and walking with oth-
(25) ers. As soon as the baby walks well alone, it has passed from
infancy into the active toddler stage.

TYPES OF QUESTIONS

Multiple Choice Questions

Paper and Pencil TOEFL

1. What does this passage mainly discuss?
   (A) Growth in early infancy
   (B) The active toddler stage
   (C) How a baby learns to walk
   (D) The developmental stages of infancy

2. The word "primarily" in line 8 could best be replaced by
   (A) often
   (B) naturally
   (C) for the most part
   (D) in a loud way

3. According to this reading passage, what would a six-month-old baby like to do?

    (A) Smile at people

    (B) Crawl on the floor

    (C) Imitate actions

    (D) Play simple games

4. A baby in late infancy would be able to do all of the following EXCEPT

    (A) make many speech sounds

    (B) walk well alone

    (C) show interest in games

    (D) imitate actions

Answer Sheet

1. Ⓐ Ⓑ Ⓒ ●
2. Ⓐ Ⓑ ● Ⓓ
3. Ⓐ Ⓑ ● Ⓓ
4. Ⓐ ● Ⓒ Ⓓ

Computer-Based TOEFL

What does the passage mainly discuss?

    ○ Growth in early infancy

    ○ The active toddler stage

    ○ How a baby learns to walk

    ● The developmental stages of infancy

The word primarily could best be replaced by

    ○ often

    ○ naturally

    ● for the most part

    ○ in a loud way

According to this reading passage, what would a six-month-old baby like to do?

- ○ Smile at people
- ○ Crawl on the floor
- ● Imitate actions
- ○ Play simple games

A baby in late infancy would be able to do all of the following EXCEPT

- ○ make many speech sounds
- ● walk well alone
- ○ show interest in games
- ○ imitate actions

Computer-Assisted Questions

Location Questions

On some of the computer-assisted questions, you will be asked to locate information in the passage. These questions are like the multiple-choice questions on the Paper and Pencil TOEFL where you must locate information by identifying the line numbers in the passage. On the computer-assisted questions, you must click on the sentence or paragraph in the passage.

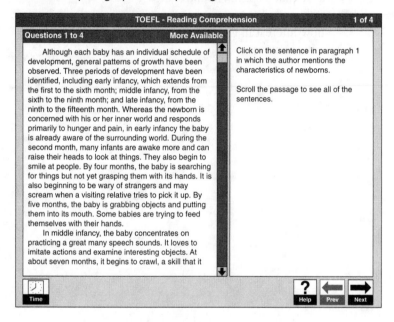

Synonyms

On some of the computer-assisted questions, you will be asked to locate synonyms in the reading passage. You must click on the word or phrase in the passage.

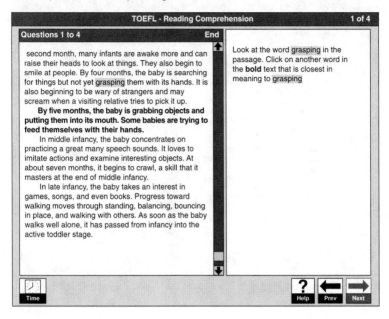

TOEFL - Reading Comprehension   1 of 4

Questions 1 to 4   End

second month, many infants are awake more and can raise their heads to look at things. They also begin to smile at people. By four months, the baby is searching for things but not yet grasping them with its hands. It is also beginning to be wary of strangers and may scream when a visiting relative tries to pick it up.

By five months, the baby is grabbing objects and putting them into its mouth. Some babies are trying to feed themselves with their hands.

In middle infancy, the baby concentrates on practicing a great many speech sounds. It loves to imitate actions and examine interesting objects. At about seven months, it begins to crawl, a skill that it masters at the end of middle infancy.

In late infancy, the baby takes an interest in games, songs, and even books. Progress toward walking moves through standing, balancing, bouncing in place, and walking with others. As soon as the baby walks well alone, it has passed from infancy into the active toddler stage.

Look at the word grasping in the passage. Click on another word in the **bold** text that is closest in meaning to grasping

Time   Help   Prev   Next

Paraphrased Sentences

On some of the computer-assisted questions, you will be asked to identify paraphrases of sentences in the passage.

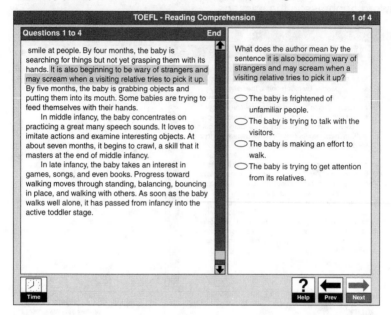

TOEFL - Reading Comprehension · 1 of 4

Questions 1 to 4 · End

smile at people. By four months, the baby is searching for things but not yet grasping them with its hands. It is also beginning to be wary of strangers and may scream when a visiting relative tries to pick it up. By five months, the baby is grabbing objects and putting them into its mouth. Some babies are trying to feed themselves with their hands.

In middle infancy, the baby concentrates on practicing a great many speech sounds. It loves to imitate actions and examine interesting objects. At about seven months, it begins to crawl, a skill that it masters at the end of middle infancy.

In late infancy, the baby takes an interest in games, songs, and even books. Progress toward walking moves through standing, balancing, bouncing in place, and walking with others. As soon as the baby walks well alone, it has passed from infancy into the active toddler stage.

What does the author mean by the sentence it is also becoming wary of strangers and may scream when a visiting relative tries to pick it up?

⃝ The baby is frightened of unfamiliar people.
⃝ The baby is trying to talk with the visitors.
⃝ The baby is making an effort to walk.
⃝ The baby is trying to get attention from its relatives.

Time · Help · Prev · Next

Reference Questions

On some of the computer-assisted questions, you will be asked to locate the nouns to which pronouns refer. These questions are like the multiple-choice questions on the Paper and Pencil TOEFL where you must choose the noun from four answer choices. On the computer-assisted questions, you must find the noun and click on it in the passage.

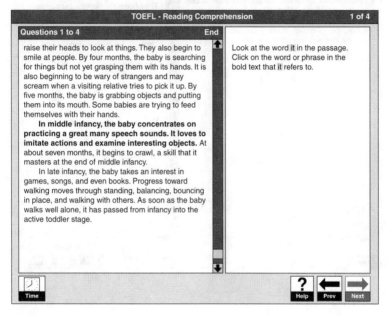

Sentence Insertion Questions

On some of the computer-assisted questions, you will be asked to locate the most logical place in the passage where a sentence could be inserted. You will have several options marked with a square (■) in the passage.

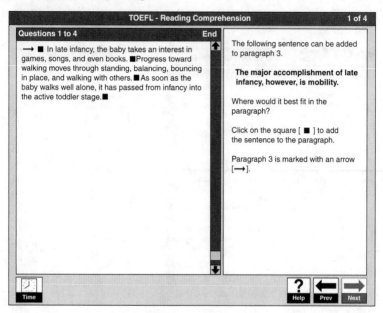

Questions 1 to 4 — End

→ ■ In late infancy, the baby takes an interest in games, songs, and even books. ■Progress toward walking moves through standing, balancing, bouncing in place, and walking with others. ■ As soon as the baby walks well alone, it has passed from infancy into the active toddler stage.■

The following sentence can be added to paragraph 3.

The major accomplishment of late infancy, however, is mobility.

Where would it best fit in the paragraph?

Click on the square [■] to add the sentence to the paragraph.

Paragraph 3 is marked with an arrow [→].

Time

? Help ← Prev → Next

Computer Tutorial for the Reading Section

Testing Tools: Vocabulary, Icons, and Keys

Specific Vocabulary for Section 3

Scroll   To move through reading passages on a screen. If the reading passage is long, new sentences will appear at the top and sentences that you have already read will disappear at the bottom.

Specific Icons for Section 3

Scroll Bar   An *icon* used to move the reading passages on the screen so that you can see a long passage. First move the *arrow* to the top of the **scroll bar**; then hold the *mouse button* down to move the **scroll bar** from the beginning of the reading passage to the end. Remember, you can see the words *beginning*, *more available*, and *end* at the top of the **scroll bar**. These words show you the place in the passage that is displayed on the screen.

Proceed   An *icon* at the bottom of the screen with the reading passage. *Click* on **Proceed** after you have read the passage in order to see the first question. Remember, you cannot use **Proceed** until you have scrolled down to the end of the passage.

Previous   An *icon* at the bottom of the screen with the questions. *Click* on **Previous** to see the previous question.

Computer Screens for Section 3

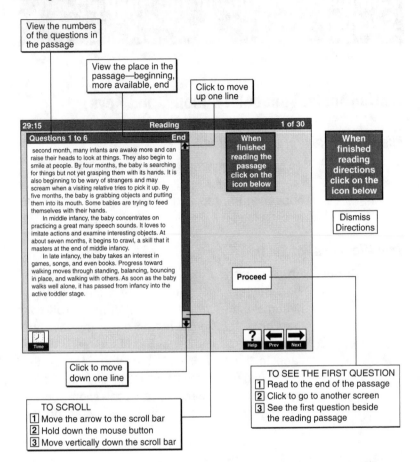

View the numbers of the questions in the passage

View the place in the passage—beginning, more available, end

Click to move up one line

29:15   Reading   1 of 30

Questions 1 to 6   End

second month, many infants are awake more and can raise their heads to look at things. They also begin to smile at people. By four months, the baby is searching for things but not yet grasping them with its hands. It is also beginning to be wary of strangers and may scream when a visiting relative tries to pick it up. By five months, the baby is grabbing objects and putting them into its mouth. Some babies are trying to feed themselves with their hands.

In middle infancy, the baby concentrates on practicing a great many speech sounds. It loves to imitate actions and examine interesting objects. At about seven months, it begins to crawl, a skill that it masters at the end of middle infancy.

In late infancy, the baby takes an interest in games, songs, and even books. Progress toward walking moves through standing, balancing, bouncing in place, and walking with others. As soon as the baby walks well alone, it has passed from infancy into the active toddler stage.

When finished reading the passage click on the icon below

When finished reading directions click on the icon below

Dismiss Directions

Proceed

Time

? Help   ← Prev   → Next

Click to move down one line

TO SCROLL
1. Move the arrow to the scroll bar
2. Hold down the mouse button
3. Move vertically down the scroll bar

TO SEE THE FIRST QUESTION
1. Read to the end of the passage
2. Click to go to another screen
3. See the first question beside the reading passage

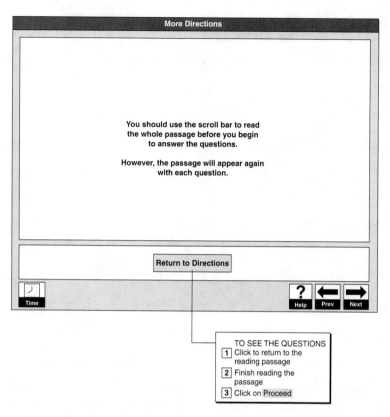

TIP: When you do not scroll to the end of the reading passage the first time you see it, this screen appears. You can spend a lot of time returning to the passage. Until you scroll to the bottom of the passage, you cannot see the questions.

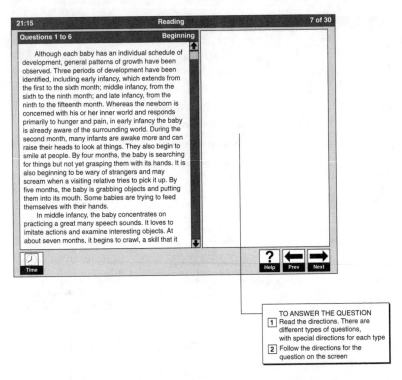

| 21:15 | Reading | 7 of 30 |

Questions 1 to 6   **Beginning**

Although each baby has an individual schedule of development, general patterns of growth have been observed. Three periods of development have been identified, including early infancy, which extends from the first to the sixth month; middle infancy, from the sixth to the ninth month; and late infancy, from the ninth to the fifteenth month. Whereas the newborn is concerned with his or her inner world and responds primarily to hunger and pain, in early infancy the baby is already aware of the surrounding world. During the second month, many infants are awake more and can raise their heads to look at things. They also begin to smile at people. By four months, the baby is searching for things but not yet grasping them with its hands. It is also beginning to be wary of strangers and may scream when a visiting relative tries to pick it up. By five months, the baby is grabbing objects and putting them into its mouth. Some babies are trying to feed themselves with their hands.

In middle infancy, the baby concentrates on practicing a great many speech sounds. It loves to imitate actions and examine interesting objects. At about seven months, it begins to crawl, a skill that it

Time

? Help **← Prev** **→ Next**

TO ANSWER THE QUESTION
1 Read the directions. There are different types of questions, with special directions for each type
2 Follow the directions for the question on the screen

TIP: The answer to the question on the right side of the screen is always found in the part of the passage visible on the left side of the screen. You do not have to scroll through the passage to find the answer.

Simulations for Section 3

In order to prepare for the experience that you will have on the Computer-Based TOEFL, you can use the CD-ROM that supplements the larger version of this book, *Barron's How to Prepare for the TOEFL*. Locate the Reading Section on Model Tests 5–8. The computer will simulate the Reading Section on the Computer-Based TOEFL. These model tests are computer-assisted. The Reading Section of the Computer-Based TOEFL is not computer-adaptive.

As part of your study plan, be sure to review all of the questions in all of the Model Tests. Use the Explanatory Answers on the CD-ROM or on pages 385–432.

If you choose not to purchase the larger version of this book, or if you do not have a computer, you can still simulate some of the features of the Computer-Based TOEFL. Section 3 of Model Tests 3–4 in Chapter 7 of this book is printed in two columns to give you the same kind of visual impression that you will have when you read from a computer screen. The on-screen directions for computer-assisted questions are also printed in the book.

Advice for the Reading Section: Computer-Based TOEFL

Practice reading on a computer screen. Reading on a computer screen is different from reading on a page. First, there is generally less text visible; second, you must scroll instead of turning pages; and finally, there may be quite a few icons or other distracting visuals surrounding the passage.

To become comfortable with reading on a computer screen, you should take advantage of every opportunity you have to practice. If you have a computer, spend time reading on the screen. Everything you read will help you improve this new skill.

Practice reading the kinds of topics you will find on the Reading Section. An inexpensive encyclopedia on CD-ROM would be a good investment. The kinds of passages found on the Computer-Based TOEFL are very similar to those found in a basic English encyclopedia.

If you do not have a computer, you may be able to locate software for an English encyclopedia at a local library where a computer is available for public use.

Become familiar with the directions for each of the question types. The different types of questions will appear at random. Directions will appear with each question, but if you already recognize the type of question presented, and you are familiar with the directions, you will save time. The less time you have to spend reading directions, the more time you will have to read the passages.

REVIEW OF
WRITING ESSAYS

Overview of the Writing Section

QUICK COMPARISON
PAPER AND PENCIL TOEFL AND COMPUTER-BASED TOEFL
ESSAY

Paper and Pencil TOEFL Test of Written English	*Computer-Based TOEFL Writing*
The essay, also called the Test of Written English (TWE), is offered five times each year. You must select a TOEFL test date when the TWE is scheduled if you need an essay score.	The essay is required as part of every TOEFL. You must write the essay as the last part of your TOEFL examination.
When you register for the TOEFL on one of the dates when the TWE is offered, you do not have to register separately for the TWE. It is offered at no additional cost.	When you register for the TOEFL, you are automatically registered for the Writing Section. It is offered at no additional cost.
There is only one topic for each essay.	There is only one topic for each essay.
Everyone taking the TOEFL writes an essay on the same topic.	The computer selects a topic for you. It may not be the same topic that is selected for someone else taking the TOEFL that day.

You do not know any of the topics for the essay.	All of the topics for the essay are published in the TOEFL *Information Bulletin* for Computer-Based Testing free of charge from ETS. They are also listed on the ETS web site at www.toefl.org.
Most of the topics ask you to agree or disagree with a statement or to express an opinion.	Most of the topics ask you to agree or disagree with a statement or to express an opinion.
There are three types of topics commonly used on the TWE: 1. *Argument.* Argue both sides of an issue, and take a position. 2. *Persuasion.* Agree or disagree with a statement, and support your opinion. 3. *Extension.* Based on several examples that support an argument, choose another example, and give reasons for the choice.	There are three types of topics commonly used on the Writing Section: 1. *Argument.* Argue both sides of an issue, and take a position. 2. *Persuasion.* Agree or disagree with a statement, and support your opinion. 3. *Extension.* Based on several examples that support an argument, choose another example, and give reasons for the choice.
The topics are very general and do not require any specialized knowledge of the subject to answer them.	The topics are very general and do not require any specialized knowledge of the subject to answer them.
You have thirty minutes to complete the essay.	You have thirty minutes to complete the essay.
You handwrite your essay on paper provided in the test materials.	You can choose to handwrite your essay on paper or type it on the computer.

You have one page to organize your essay. This page is not graded. You may organize in any way that is helpful to you—notes, a list, an outline, or a drawing. You may use your first language on this page.

Your essay will not be scored for neatness, but the readers must be able to understand what you have written.

You should write about 300 words, or three to five short paragraphs.

A scale from 1 to 6 is used to grade the essay.

The scale is printed on page 242.

Your essay will be scored by two professional teachers, reading independently. When the two scores differ by more than one point, a third teacher will read and score your essay.

The score is reported separately from the TOEFL score. It will not be included in the computation of the total TOEFL score and will not affect your score on the multiple choice TOEFL.

You have one page to organize your essay. This page is not graded. You may organize in any way that is helpful to you—notes, a list, an outline, or a drawing. You may use your first language on this page.

Your essay will not be scored for neatness, but the readers must be able to understand what you have written.

You should write about 300 words, or three to five short paragraphs.

A scale from 1 to 6 is used to grade the essay.

The scale is printed on page 242.

Your essay will be scored by two professional teachers, reading independently. When the two scores differ by more than one point, a third teacher will read and score your essay.

The score is combined with the score on the Structure Section. It will be factored in the section score at 50 percent.

Review of Strategies and Topics for the Writing Section

This Review can be used to prepare for both the Paper and Pencil TOEFL and the Computer-Based TOEFL. For the most part, the same types of topics are tested on both the Paper and Pencil TOEFL and the Computer-Based TOEFL. The essays on both the Paper and Pencil TOEFL and the Computer-Based TOEFL are scored using the same scale.

Three Steps for Writing Short Essays

There are three steps that most good writers follow in organizing their writing. You should use these steps when you write a short essay. First, tell your reader what you are going to write. Second, write it. Third, tell your reader what you wrote.

To look at these steps another way, your essay should have three parts:

1. A good beginning
2. Several good comments
3. A good ending

In this review of writing, we will discuss and give examples of the three parts of a short essay, using the types of topics that you will find on the TOEFL.

A Good Beginning

This is where you tell the reader what you are going to write. A good beginning has certain requirements.

A good beginning is short. Two or three sentences is enough to tell your reader how you plan to approach the topic.

A good beginning is direct. In the case of a comparison, state both sides of the argument in your first sentence. In a short composition, you don't have enough time for indirect approaches.

A good beginning is an outline. The second sentence usually outlines the organization. It gives the reader a general idea of your plan.

Good Comments

This is where you write.

Good comments include several points. A short essay may have between two and five points. Usually, the writer selects three. In the case of a comparison, three reasons is a standard argument.

Good comments are all related. All of the comments should relate to the general statement in the first sentence.

Good comments are logical. The points should be based on evidence. In the case of a comparison, the evidence should come from sources that can be cited, such as a television program that you have seen, an article that you have read in a magazine, a book that you have read, or a lecture that you have heard.

Good comments are not judgments. Opinions should be identified by phrases such as, "in my view," "in my opinion," or "it seems to me that." Furthermore, opinions should be based on evidence. Opinions that are not based on evidence are judgments. Judgments usually use words like "good" or "bad," "right" or "wrong." Judgments are not good comments.

A Good Ending

This is where you tell the reader what you wrote.

A good ending is a summary. The last sentence is similar to the first sentence. In a short essay, a good ending does not add new information. It does not introduce a new idea.

A good ending is not an apology. A good ending does not apologize for not having said enough, for not having had enough time, or for not using good English.

Scoring Scale for the Essay

The essay is scored on a scale of 1 to 6. A score between two points on the scale—5.5, 4.5, 3.5, 2.5, 1.5—can also be reported. The following guidelines are used by evaluators:

6 shows consistent proficiency	• Is well organized • Addresses the topic • Includes examples and details • Has few errors in grammar and vocabulary
5 shows inconsistent proficiency	• Is well organized • Addresses the topic • Includes fewer examples and details • Has more errors in grammar and vocabulary
4 shows minimal proficiency	• Is adequately organized • Addresses most of the topic • Includes some examples and details • Has errors in grammar and vocabulary that occasionally confuse meaning
3 shows developing proficiency	• Is inadequately organized • Addresses part of the topic • Includes few examples and details • Has many errors in grammar and vocabulary that confuse meaning
2 shows little proficiency	• Is disorganized • Does not address the topic • Does not include examples and details • Has many errors in grammar and vocabulary that consistently confuse meaning
1 shows no proficiency	• Is disorganized • Does not address the topic • Does not include examples and details • Has so many errors in grammar and vocabulary that meaning is not communicated

Example Essay

The following example essay would receive a score of 6. It is well organized, it addresses the topic, it includes examples and details, and it has some but not many errors in grammar and vocabulary.

Read and study this example essay before you complete the Model Tests.

Some students in the United States work while they are earning their degrees in college; others receive support from their families. How should a student's education be supported? Argue both sides of the issue and defend your position.

Notes

Some students in the United States work while they are earning their degrees; others receive support from their families. Both approaches
Line have advantages and disadvantages. In this
(5) essay, I will name some of the advantages of each approach, and I will argue in favor family support.

In a society where independence and individual accomplishment are value, a
(10) student who earned his degree by working would be greatly admired. Friends would praise him for his initiative and perseverence. Future employers might be impressed by his work record. He might derive greater
(15) satisfaction from his personal investment in it.

Line
(20)

On the other hand, in a society where cooperation and family dependence are value, a student who received support would be better understood. Friends would praise him for his efforts on behalf of his family. Future employers would not expect a work record from a student. He might feel greater

(25)

responsibility toward others in his family because the accomplishment was shared! Thus, not one but every family member would assured some opportunity or benefit.

(30)

For my part, I must argue in favor of family support. While I study at an American University, my older brother will send me money every month. When I finish my degree and find a good

(35)

job, I will send my younger sister to a school or university. It may not be a better way, but it is the way that my society rewards.

Evaluator's Comments

This writing sample is well organized with a good topic sentence and good support statements. It addresses the question, and does not digress from the topic. There is a logical progression of ideas and excellent language proficiency, as evidenced by a variety of grammatical structures and appropriate vocabulary. There are only a few grammatical errors that have been corrected below:

Line 7	in favor of
Line 9	are valued
Lines 18–19	are valued
Line 28	would be assured

Score: 6

Computer Tutorial for the Writing Section

Testing Tools: Vocabulary, Icons, and Keys

Specific Vocabulary for the Essay

Text All printed material on the screen. **Text** can refer to a word, a sentence, a paragraph, several paragraphs, or an essay.

Cursor The line that shows you where you can begin typing. When you move the *mouse,* the **cursor** appears. You can move the **cursor** on your essay by moving the *mouse* on your *mouse pad.*

Blinking Flashing on and off. The *cursor* is usually **blinking** to help you see it.

Highlight To select *text* in your essay that you want to edit. To **highlight**, move the *cursor* to the beginning of the place in your essay that you want to change. Hold down the mouse button and move to the end of the place in your essay that you want to change. Release the mouse button. The **highlighted** *text* should be shaded.

Keys The individual buttons on the keyboard used for typing and editing your essay.

Keys for the Essay

Arrow Keys Keys that let you move around in your essay. There is an **up arrow, down arrow, left arrow, and right arrow**. They are found between the letters and the numbers on the keyboard. Use the **arrow keys** to move up, down, left, or right.

Page Up,   Keys that let you see your essay if it is longer than
Page Down the screen. The **Page Up** and **Page Down** keys
               are above the *arrow keys* on the keyboard. Use
               Page Up to scroll to the beginning of your essay.
               Use **Page Down** to scroll to the end of your essay.

Backspace A key that moves you back one space at a time.
               Use the **Backspace** key to erase *text* from right to
               left.

Space Bar The long key at the bottom of the keyboard. Use
               the **Space Bar** two or three times to indent a para-
               graph. Remember, the *Tab* key does not function
               on your keyboard.

Icons for the Essay

Cut   An example of an *icon*. After you *highlight* the text
               you want to delete or move, click on **Cut**. The text
               will disappear. Use the **Cut** icon to delete text or
               as the first step in moving text.

Paste   An example of an *icon*. After you *cut* text, you can
               move the *cursor* to the place in the essay where
               you want to insert the text, and click on **Paste**. The
               text you *highlighted* will appear. Use the **Paste**
               icon as the second step in moving text.

Undo   An example of an *icon*. It lets you change your
               mind. For example, if you move a sentence, and
               then you want to move it back to the original place
               in your essay, click on **Undo**. **Undo** will return
               whatever you did last back to the way it looked
               before you made the change. Remember, **Undo**
               will only return your last change, not several
               changes.

Keyboard for the Essay

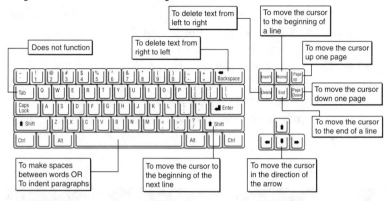

TIP: If you click the mouse, you can delete text. You may even delete your essay! If this happens, click on **Undo** immediately.

Computer Screen for the Essay

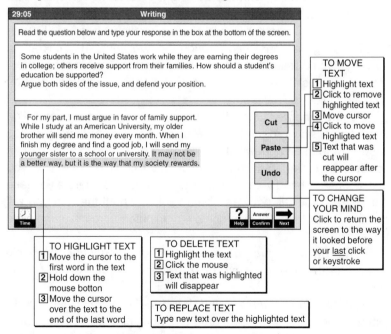

TIP: Be sure that you have completed the essay to your satisfaction before you click on **Answer Confirm.** After you click on **Answer Confirm**, you cannot continue writing or editing your essay.

Simulations for the Essay

In order to simulate the experience that you will have on the Computer-Based TOEFL, type the Model Test essays using the word processing program on the CD-ROM that supplements the larger version of this book, *Barron's How to Prepare for the TOEFL.* If you do not have a computer, handwrite the Model Test essays on paper. Be sure to complete your essay in thirty minutes.

As part of your study plan, it is a good idea to have an English teacher score your essays using the guidelines on page 242 of this book.

Advice for the Writing Section: Computer-Based TOEFL

Become familiar with the writing topics. All of the topics from the official TOEFL writing section are listed in the *TOEFL Information Bulletin* for Computer-Based Testing, available free from Educational Testing Service. Read through the questions and think about how you would respond to each of the topics. Since most of them require you to state an opinion, it is helpful to form a general opinion on each topic.

Decide whether you will handwrite or type your essay. The word processing program for the computer is very simple. If you know how to use Windows, it should be easy for you to adjust. But if you feel uncomfortable using the computer to write the essay, you may choose to handwrite it. By making your decision before you take the TOEFL, you will not waste time thinking about the way you will complete your test. You can use every minute to organize and write the essay.

Write on the topic you are assigned. If you write on a topic other than the one you have been assigned, your test will not be scored.

Get help from the test administrator. If you are having a problem with the word processing program, notify one of the test administrators immediately. There should be several in the room. They cannot help you with the answers on the TOEFL, but they can help you use the computer. That is why they are there. Tell the administrator, "Excuse me. I am trying to _____. What should I do?"

TOEFL
MODEL TESTS

There are three types of Model Tests to help you prepare for the TOEFL. They are the Paper and Pencil Model Test, the Computer-Assisted Model Test, and the Computer-Adaptive Model Test. The Paper and Pencil Model Test has questions like those that frequently appear on the Paper and Pencil TOEFL. Model Tests 1 and 2 in this book are Paper and Pencil Model Tests. The Computer-Assisted Model Test has questions like those that frequently appear on the Computer-Based TOEFL. Model Tests 3 and 4 in this book are Computer-Assisted Model Tests. They are designed to allow you to answer computer questions in the book. The Computer-Adaptive Model Test has questions like those that frequently appear on the Computer-Based TOEFL also, but in addition, the computer selects questions for you at your level of language proficiency. There is no Computer-Adaptive Model Test in *Pass Key to the TOEFL.*

The CD-ROM that supplements the larger version of this book, *Barron's How to Prepare for the TOEFL,* has four Paper and Pencil Model Tests, four Computer-Assisted Model Tests, and one Computer-Adaptive Model Test. The Computer-Assisted Model Tests are designed to allow you to answer either in the book or on the computer screen. The Computer-Adaptive Model Test is designed to allow you to repeat it until you are answering at a high level of proficiency.

After you complete the Model Tests in this book, you may wish to use *Barron's How to Prepare for the TOEFL,* and the CD-ROM that supplements it, to continue your preparation, and to practice answering questions on the computer.

MODEL TEST 1—ANSWER SHEET

Section 1

1 2 3 4 5 6 7 8 9 10 11 12 13 14 15 16 17 18 19 20 21 22 23 24 25 26 27

(A) (B) (C) (D) — repeated for each item

28 29 30 31 32 33 34 35 36 37 38 39 40 41 42 43 44 45 46 47 48 49 50

(A) (B) (C) (D) — repeated for each item

Section 2

1 2 3 4 5 6 7 8 9 10 11 12 13 14 15 16 17 18 19 20 21 22 23 24 25 26 27

(A) (B) (C) (D) — repeated for each item

28 29 30 31 32 33 34 35 36 37 38 39 40

(A) (B) (C) (D) — repeated for each item

Section 3

1 2 3 4 5 6 7 8 9 10 11 12 13 14 15 16 17 18 19 20 21 22 23 24 25 26 27

(A) (B) (C) (D) — repeated for each item

28 29 30 31 32 33 34 35 36 37 38 39 40 41 42 43 44 45 46 47 48 49 50

(A) (B) (C) (D) — repeated for each item

Cut here to remove answer sheet.

MODEL TEST 2—ANSWER SHEET

Section 1

1.	Ⓐ	Ⓑ	Ⓒ	Ⓓ
2.	Ⓐ	Ⓑ	Ⓒ	Ⓓ
3.	Ⓐ	Ⓑ	Ⓒ	Ⓓ
4.	Ⓐ	Ⓑ	Ⓒ	Ⓓ
5.	Ⓐ	Ⓑ	Ⓒ	Ⓓ
6.	Ⓐ	Ⓑ	Ⓒ	Ⓓ
7.	Ⓐ	Ⓑ	Ⓒ	Ⓓ
8.	Ⓐ	Ⓑ	Ⓒ	Ⓓ
9.	Ⓐ	Ⓑ	Ⓒ	Ⓓ
10.	Ⓐ	Ⓑ	Ⓒ	Ⓓ
11.	Ⓐ	Ⓑ	Ⓒ	Ⓓ
12.	Ⓐ	Ⓑ	Ⓒ	Ⓓ
13.	Ⓐ	Ⓑ	Ⓒ	Ⓓ
14.	Ⓐ	Ⓑ	Ⓒ	Ⓓ
15.	Ⓐ	Ⓑ	Ⓒ	Ⓓ
16.	Ⓐ	Ⓑ	Ⓒ	Ⓓ
17.	Ⓐ	Ⓑ	Ⓒ	Ⓓ
18.	Ⓐ	Ⓑ	Ⓒ	Ⓓ
19.	Ⓐ	Ⓑ	Ⓒ	Ⓓ
20.	Ⓐ	Ⓑ	Ⓒ	Ⓓ
21.	Ⓐ	Ⓑ	Ⓒ	Ⓓ
22.	Ⓐ	Ⓑ	Ⓒ	Ⓓ
23.	Ⓐ	Ⓑ	Ⓒ	Ⓓ
24.	Ⓐ	Ⓑ	Ⓒ	Ⓓ
25.	Ⓐ	Ⓑ	Ⓒ	Ⓓ
26.	Ⓐ	Ⓑ	Ⓒ	Ⓓ
27.	Ⓐ	Ⓑ	Ⓒ	Ⓓ
28.	Ⓐ	Ⓑ	Ⓒ	Ⓓ
29.	Ⓐ	Ⓑ	Ⓒ	Ⓓ
30.	Ⓐ	Ⓑ	Ⓒ	Ⓓ
31.	Ⓐ	Ⓑ	Ⓒ	Ⓓ
32.	Ⓐ	Ⓑ	Ⓒ	Ⓓ
33.	Ⓐ	Ⓑ	Ⓒ	Ⓓ
34.	Ⓐ	Ⓑ	Ⓒ	Ⓓ
35.	Ⓐ	Ⓑ	Ⓒ	Ⓓ
36.	Ⓐ	Ⓑ	Ⓒ	Ⓓ
37.	Ⓐ	Ⓑ	Ⓒ	Ⓓ
38.	Ⓐ	Ⓑ	Ⓒ	Ⓓ
39.	Ⓐ	Ⓑ	Ⓒ	Ⓓ
40.	Ⓐ	Ⓑ	Ⓒ	Ⓓ
41.	Ⓐ	Ⓑ	Ⓒ	Ⓓ
42.	Ⓐ	Ⓑ	Ⓒ	Ⓓ
43.	Ⓐ	Ⓑ	Ⓒ	Ⓓ
44.	Ⓐ	Ⓑ	Ⓒ	Ⓓ
45.	Ⓐ	Ⓑ	Ⓒ	Ⓓ
46.	Ⓐ	Ⓑ	Ⓒ	Ⓓ
47.	Ⓐ	Ⓑ	Ⓒ	Ⓓ
48.	Ⓐ	Ⓑ	Ⓒ	Ⓓ
49.	Ⓐ	Ⓑ	Ⓒ	Ⓓ
50.	Ⓐ	Ⓑ	Ⓒ	Ⓓ

Section 2

1.	Ⓐ	Ⓑ	Ⓒ	Ⓓ
2.	Ⓐ	Ⓑ	Ⓒ	Ⓓ
3.	Ⓐ	Ⓑ	Ⓒ	Ⓓ
4.	Ⓐ	Ⓑ	Ⓒ	Ⓓ
5.	Ⓐ	Ⓑ	Ⓒ	Ⓓ
6.	Ⓐ	Ⓑ	Ⓒ	Ⓓ
7.	Ⓐ	Ⓑ	Ⓒ	Ⓓ
8.	Ⓐ	Ⓑ	Ⓒ	Ⓓ
9.	Ⓐ	Ⓑ	Ⓒ	Ⓓ
10.	Ⓐ	Ⓑ	Ⓒ	Ⓓ
11.	Ⓐ	Ⓑ	Ⓒ	Ⓓ
12.	Ⓐ	Ⓑ	Ⓒ	Ⓓ
13.	Ⓐ	Ⓑ	Ⓒ	Ⓓ
14.	Ⓐ	Ⓑ	Ⓒ	Ⓓ
15.	Ⓐ	Ⓑ	Ⓒ	Ⓓ
16.	Ⓐ	Ⓑ	Ⓒ	Ⓓ
17.	Ⓐ	Ⓑ	Ⓒ	Ⓓ
18.	Ⓐ	Ⓑ	Ⓒ	Ⓓ
19.	Ⓐ	Ⓑ	Ⓒ	Ⓓ
20.	Ⓐ	Ⓑ	Ⓒ	Ⓓ
21.	Ⓐ	Ⓑ	Ⓒ	Ⓓ
22.	Ⓐ	Ⓑ	Ⓒ	Ⓓ
23.	Ⓐ	Ⓑ	Ⓒ	Ⓓ
24.	Ⓐ	Ⓑ	Ⓒ	Ⓓ
25.	Ⓐ	Ⓑ	Ⓒ	Ⓓ
26.	Ⓐ	Ⓑ	Ⓒ	Ⓓ
27.	Ⓐ	Ⓑ	Ⓒ	Ⓓ
28.	Ⓐ	Ⓑ	Ⓒ	Ⓓ
29.	Ⓐ	Ⓑ	Ⓒ	Ⓓ
30.	Ⓐ	Ⓑ	Ⓒ	Ⓓ
31.	Ⓐ	Ⓑ	Ⓒ	Ⓓ
32.	Ⓐ	Ⓑ	Ⓒ	Ⓓ
33.	Ⓐ	Ⓑ	Ⓒ	Ⓓ
34.	Ⓐ	Ⓑ	Ⓒ	Ⓓ
35.	Ⓐ	Ⓑ	Ⓒ	Ⓓ
36.	Ⓐ	Ⓑ	Ⓒ	Ⓓ
37.	Ⓐ	Ⓑ	Ⓒ	Ⓓ
38.	Ⓐ	Ⓑ	Ⓒ	Ⓓ
39.	Ⓐ	Ⓑ	Ⓒ	Ⓓ
40.	Ⓐ	Ⓑ	Ⓒ	Ⓓ

Section 3

1.	Ⓐ	Ⓑ	Ⓒ	Ⓓ
2.	Ⓐ	Ⓑ	Ⓒ	Ⓓ
3.	Ⓐ	Ⓑ	Ⓒ	Ⓓ
4.	Ⓐ	Ⓑ	Ⓒ	Ⓓ
5.	Ⓐ	Ⓑ	Ⓒ	Ⓓ
6.	Ⓐ	Ⓑ	Ⓒ	Ⓓ
7.	Ⓐ	Ⓑ	Ⓒ	Ⓓ
8.	Ⓐ	Ⓑ	Ⓒ	Ⓓ
9.	Ⓐ	Ⓑ	Ⓒ	Ⓓ
10.	Ⓐ	Ⓑ	Ⓒ	Ⓓ
11.	Ⓐ	Ⓑ	Ⓒ	Ⓓ
12.	Ⓐ	Ⓑ	Ⓒ	Ⓓ
13.	Ⓐ	Ⓑ	Ⓒ	Ⓓ
14.	Ⓐ	Ⓑ	Ⓒ	Ⓓ
15.	Ⓐ	Ⓑ	Ⓒ	Ⓓ
16.	Ⓐ	Ⓑ	Ⓒ	Ⓓ
17.	Ⓐ	Ⓑ	Ⓒ	Ⓓ
18.	Ⓐ	Ⓑ	Ⓒ	Ⓓ
19.	Ⓐ	Ⓑ	Ⓒ	Ⓓ
20.	Ⓐ	Ⓑ	Ⓒ	Ⓓ
21.	Ⓐ	Ⓑ	Ⓒ	Ⓓ
22.	Ⓐ	Ⓑ	Ⓒ	Ⓓ
23.	Ⓐ	Ⓑ	Ⓒ	Ⓓ
24.	Ⓐ	Ⓑ	Ⓒ	Ⓓ
25.	Ⓐ	Ⓑ	Ⓒ	Ⓓ
26.	Ⓐ	Ⓑ	Ⓒ	Ⓓ
27.	Ⓐ	Ⓑ	Ⓒ	Ⓓ
28.	Ⓐ	Ⓑ	Ⓒ	Ⓓ
29.	Ⓐ	Ⓑ	Ⓒ	Ⓓ
30.	Ⓐ	Ⓑ	Ⓒ	Ⓓ
31.	Ⓐ	Ⓑ	Ⓒ	Ⓓ
32.	Ⓐ	Ⓑ	Ⓒ	Ⓓ
33.	Ⓐ	Ⓑ	Ⓒ	Ⓓ
34.	Ⓐ	Ⓑ	Ⓒ	Ⓓ
35.	Ⓐ	Ⓑ	Ⓒ	Ⓓ
36.	Ⓐ	Ⓑ	Ⓒ	Ⓓ
37.	Ⓐ	Ⓑ	Ⓒ	Ⓓ
38.	Ⓐ	Ⓑ	Ⓒ	Ⓓ
39.	Ⓐ	Ⓑ	Ⓒ	Ⓓ
40.	Ⓐ	Ⓑ	Ⓒ	Ⓓ
41.	Ⓐ	Ⓑ	Ⓒ	Ⓓ
42.	Ⓐ	Ⓑ	Ⓒ	Ⓓ
43.	Ⓐ	Ⓑ	Ⓒ	Ⓓ
44.	Ⓐ	Ⓑ	Ⓒ	Ⓓ
45.	Ⓐ	Ⓑ	Ⓒ	Ⓓ
46.	Ⓐ	Ⓑ	Ⓒ	Ⓓ
47.	Ⓐ	Ⓑ	Ⓒ	Ⓓ
48.	Ⓐ	Ⓑ	Ⓒ	Ⓓ
49.	Ⓐ	Ⓑ	Ⓒ	Ⓓ
50.	Ⓐ	Ⓑ	Ⓒ	Ⓓ

1 1 1 1 1 1 1 1 1 1 1

Model Test 1
Paper and Pencil TOEFL

Section 1:
Listening Comprehension

50 QUESTIONS 40 MINUTES

In this section of the test, you will have an opportunity to demonstrate your ability to understand conversations and talks in English. There are three parts to this section with special directions for each part. Answer all the questions on the basis of what is stated or implied by the speakers in this test. When you take the actual TOEFL test, you will not be allowed to take notes or write in your test book. Try to work on this Model Test in the same way.

Part A

Directions: In Part A, you will hear short conversations between two people. After each conversation, you will hear a question about the conversation. The conversations and questions will not be repeated. After you hear a question, read the four possible answers in your book and choose the best answer. Then, on your answer sheet, find the number of the question and fill in the space that corresponds to the letter of the answer you have chosen.

1. (A) She will not go home for spring vacation.
   (B) She has not taken a vacation for a long time.
   (C) She does not plan to graduate.
   (D) She does not want to go home after graduation in May.

2. (A) At a butcher shop.
   (B) At a restaurant.
   (C) At a bookstore.
   (D) At a grocery store.

3. (A) The class.
   (B) The weekend.
   (C) Homework.
   (D) Books.

4. (A) That the man will not be able to sleep.
   (B) That someone will enter the back door while the man is sleeping.
   (C) That the lock on the door will break.
   (D) That the man will not be able to come back.

5. (A) She forgot her brother's birthday.
   (B) She does not have very much money.
   (C) She needs a gift for her brother.
   (D) Her brother did not like the present.

1 1 1 1 1 1 1 1 1 1 1 **1**

6. (A) He should have prepared more.
   (B) He is very worried.
   (C) He has been studying a lot.
   (D) He needs a few more days.

7. (A) She works at Sun Valley.
   (B) She does not like Mr. Miller.
   (C) Her husband is not well today.
   (D) She is Mrs. Adams.

8. (A) He believes that Jack will not be able to sell his house.
   (B) He believes that Jack was joking.
   (C) He agrees with the woman.
   (D) He believes that Jack will quit his job.

9. (A) Buy a textbook.
   (B) Come back later.
   (C) Go to the bookstore.
   (D) Drop his English class.

10. (A) She likes the weather.
    (B) She needs a new dress.
    (C) She wants to please the man.
    (D) She will wear the more comfortable dress.

11. (A) She does not like the class.
    (B) Her classmates are really great.
    (C) The professor is not very nice.
    (D) The class is interesting.

12. (A) She went to Atlanta.
    (B) She went to a convention.
    (C) She went to a hospital.
    (D) She stayed home.

13. (A) Make an appointment with a dentist.
    (B) Cancel her appointment with the dentist.
    (C) Postpone her appointment with the dentist.
    (D) See the dentist more often.

14. (A) He would rather have American food.
    (B) He has always liked American food.
    (C) He is accustomed to eating American food.
    (D) He ate American food more in the past.

15. (A) He should go to bed.
    (B) He did not know the time.
    (C) He is trying to bring his work up to date.
    (D) He is not sleepy yet.

16. (A) He intends to invite the woman to their home.
    (B) He does not want to see the woman.
    (C) He is not very polite to the woman.
    (D) He prefers seeing Connie.

17. (A) Spend some time with the man.
    (B) Make a list of the names.
    (C) Pass out the names.
    (D) Let someone else call the names.

18. (A) The woman has missed the deadline.
    (B) He will investigate the situation.
    (C) The deadline has been canceled.
    (D) An exception might be possible.

1 1 1 1 1 1 1 1 1 1 1

19. (A) The tickets are lost.
    (B) Judy was responsible for getting the tickets.
    (C) There were no tickets available.
    (D) He does not have his tickets yet.

20. (A) He is often wrong.
    (B) He usually recommends the freeway.
    (C) He is not a local radio personality.
    (D) He is a popular announcer.

21. (A) The book is confusing.
    (B) He is doing well in the class.
    (C) The teacher is not very clear.
    (D) The lectures are from the book.

22. (A) Randy is a confident person.
    (B) Randy is very fortunate.
    (C) She does not know Randy.
    (D) She is not sure whether she knows Randy.

23. (A) She wants to submit her paper early.
    (B) The answers on the paper are all correct.
    (C) The deadline has passed for the paper.
    (D) The paper is not quite finished.

24. (A) She prefers singing a solo.
    (B) She does not want to help the men.
    (C) She is not a good singer.
    (D) She does not like music.

25. (A) She does not like the class.
    (B) It is not a required class.
    (C) She has already taken the class.
    (D) The man will have to take the class.

26. (A) Get his car repaired.
    (B) Buy a different car.
    (C) Borrow a car.
    (D) Bring the car in.

27. (A) Study together.
    (B) Prepare for an oral final.
    (C) Review the quizzes.
    (D) Take the professor's advice.

28. (A) Make an appointment.
    (B) Give the man a pen.
    (C) Sign the form for the man.
    (D) Wait for the man.

29. (A) Revise her work.
    (B) Close the window.
    (C) Copy from the man.
    (D) Hand in the work.

30. (A) The computer made an error.
    (B) The payment is due on the fifth of every month.
    (C) The loan must be paid by the first of the month.
    (D) The loan had already been paid in full.

1 1 1 1 1 1 1 1 1 1 1

Part B

Directions: In this part of the test, you will hear longer conversations. After each conversation, you will hear several questions. The conversations and questions will not be repeated.

After you hear a question, read the four possible answers in your book and choose the best answer. Then, on your answer sheet, find the number of the question and fill in the space that corresponds to the letter of the answer you have chosen.

Remember, you are **not** allowed to take notes or write on your test pages.

31. (A) She is waiting for the man.
    (B) She is waiting for her mother.
    (C) She is waiting for a bus.
    (D) She is waiting for it to stop raining.

32. (A) Cold.
    (B) Very hot.
    (C) Cooler than the weather on the day of this conversation.
    (D) Drier than the weather on the day of this conversation.

33. (A) Florida.
    (B) New York.
    (C) California.
    (D) Indiana.

34. (A) Every ten minutes.
    (B) At twenty to one.
    (C) Every half-hour.
    (D) Once a day.

35. (A) To enroll in a class.
    (B) To ask his opinion about a university.
    (C) To find out who is chair of the selection committee.
    (D) To get a letter for graduate school.

36. (A) She might need to take his seminar.
    (B) She should do well in graduate school.
    (C) She had better go to another university.
    (D) She needs to apply before the end of April.

37. (A) The chair of the selection committee.
    (B) The entire selection committee.
    (C) Professor Hayes.
    (D) Dr. Warren.

38. (A) On May 1.
    (B) In three days.
    (C) Before the April 30th deadline.
    (D) Today.

1 1 1 1 1 1 1 1 1 1 1

Part C

Directions: In this part of the test, you will hear several short talks. After each talk, you will hear some questions. The talks and questions will not be repeated.

After you hear a question, read the four possible answers in your book and choose the best answer. Then, on your answer sheet, find the number of the question and fill in the space that corresponds to the letter of the answer you have chosen.

39. (A) A professor of religion.
    (B) A professor of business.
    (C) A guest lecturer in a drama class.
    (D) A guest lecturer in a writing class.

40. (A) By threatening to go to war.
    (B) By competing with farmers.
    (C) By keeping manufacturing processes secret.
    (D) By stealing plans from the colonies.

41. (A) He kept designs for English machinery from being used in the colonies.
    (B) He prevented Moses Brown from opening a mill.
    (C) He committed designs for English machinery to memory.
    (D) He smuggled drawings for English machines into the United States.

42. (A) A change from agriculture to industry began to occur in the United States.
    (B) A rise in prices for English goods was evidenced.
    (C) Many small farmers began to send their products to England.
    (D) Americans had to keep their manufacturing processes secret.

43. (A) The term "essay."
    (B) Prose writing.
    (C) Personal viewpoint.
    (D) Brainstorming.

44. (A) The work of Alexander Pope.
    (B) The difference between prose and poetry.
    (C) The general characteristics of essays.
    (D) The reason that the phrase "personal essay" is redundant.

1 1 1 1 1 1 1 1 1 1 1

45. (A) It is usually short.
    (B) It can be either prose or poetry.
    (C) It expresses a personal point of view.
    (D) It discusses one topic.

46. (A) They will prepare for a quiz.
    (B) They will write their first essay.
    (C) They will read works by Pope.
    (D) They will review their notes.

47. (A) To provide an overview of U.S. history from 1743 to 1826.
    (B) To discuss Jefferson's contribution to the American Revolution.
    (C) To analyze Jefferson's presidency.
    (D) To summarize Jefferson's life.

48. (A) Monarchist.
    (B) Federalist.
    (C) Republican.
    (D) Democrat.

49. (A) He received the most votes.
    (B) Congress approved him.
    (C) Aaron Burr withdrew from the race.
    (D) As vice president, he automatically became president.

50. (A) An effective public speaker.
    (B) An architect.
    (C) A literary draftsman.
    (D) A diplomat.

THIS IS THE END OF THE LISTENING COMPREHENSION SECTION OF TOEFL MODEL TEST 1.

DO NOT READ OR WORK ON ANY OTHER SECTION OF THE TEST.

2 **2** 2 **2** 2 **2** 2 **2** 2 **2** 2

Section 2:
Structure and Written Expression

40 QUESTIONS 25 MINUTES

This section is designed to measure your ability to recognize language that is appropriate for standard written English. There are two types of questions in this section, with special directions for each type.

Structure

Directions: Questions 1–15 are incomplete sentences. Beneath each sentence you will see four words or phrases, marked (A), (B), (C), and (D). Choose the **one** word or phrase that best completes the sentence. Then, on your answer sheet, find the number of the question and fill in the space that corresponds to the letter of the answer you have chosen. Fill in the space so that the letter inside the oval cannot be seen.

1. In simple animals, --------- reflex movement or involuntary response to stimuli.

   (A) behavior mostly
   (B) most is behavior
   (C) most behavior is
   (D) the most behavior

2. Although the weather in Martha's Vineyard isn't ---------- to have a year-round tourist season, it has become a favorite summer resort.

   (A) goodly enough
   (B) good enough
   (C) good as enough
   (D) enough good

3. According to the wave theory, --------- population of the Americas may have been the result of a number of separate migrations.

   (A) the
   (B) their
   (C) that
   (D) whose

4. It is presumed that rules governing the sharing of food influenced ----------- that the earliest cultures evolved.

   (A) that the way
   (B) is the way
   (C) the way
   (D) which way

2 2 2 2 2 2 2 2 2 2 2

5. Calculus, ----------- elegant and economical symbolic system, can reduce complex problems to simple terms.

   (A) it is an
   (B) that an
   (C) an
   (D) is an

6. Canada does not require that U.S. citizens obtain passports to enter the country, and ----------- .

   (A) Mexico does neither
   (B) Mexico doesn't either
   (C) neither Mexico does
   (D) either does Mexico

7. The poet ----------- just beginning to be recognized as an important influence at the time of his death.

   (A) being Walt Whitman
   (B) who was Walt Whitman
   (C) Walt Whitman
   (D) Walt Whitman was

8. ----------- the formation of the sun, the planets, and other stars began with the condensation of an interstellar cloud.

   (A) It accepted that
   (B) Accepted that
   (C) It is accepted that
   (D) That is accepted

9. As a general rule, the standard of living ----------- by the average output of each person in society.

   (A) is fixed
   (B) fixed
   (C) has fixed
   (D) fixes

10. The *Consumer Price Index* lists ------- .

    (A) how much costs every car
    (B) how much does every car cost
    (C) how much every car costs
    (D) how much are every car cost

11. The Ford Theater where Lincoln was shot ----------- .

    (A) must restore
    (B) must be restoring
    (C) must have been restored
    (D) must restored

12. Fast-food restaurants have become popular because many working people want -------- .

    (A) to eat quickly and cheaply
    (B) eating quickly and cheaply
    (C) eat quickly and cheaply
    (D) the eat quickly and cheaply

13. After seeing the movie *Centennial,* ----------- .

    (A) the book was read by many people
    (B) the book made many people want to read it
    (C) many people wanted to read the book
    (D) the reading of the book interested many people

2 **2** **2** **2** **2** **2** **2** **2** **2** **2** **2**

14. -----------, Carl Sandburg is also well known for his multi-volume biography of Lincoln.

   (A) An eminent American poet
   (B) He is an eminent American poet
   (C) An eminent American poet who is
   (D) Despite an eminent American poet

15. The examiner made us ----------- our identification in order to be admitted to the test center.

   (A) showing
   (B) show
   (C) showed
   (D) to show

Written Expression

Directions: In questions 16–40, each sentence has four underlined words or phrases. The four underlined parts of the sentence are marked (A), (B), (C), and (D). Identify the **one** underlined word or phrase that must be changed in order for the sentence to be correct. Then, on your answer sheet, find the number of the question and fill in the space that corresponds to the letter of the answer you have chosen.

16. A swarm of locusts is responsible the consumption of
                      (A)
   enough plant material to feed a million and a half people.
          (B)   (C)   (D)

17. Oyster farming has been practice in most parts of the world for many
             (A)   (B)   (C)   (D)
   years.

18. Those of us who smoke should have their lungs X-rayed regularly.
         (A)   (B)   (C)   (D)

19. After the team of geologists had drawn diagrams in their notebooks and
                                                        (A)
   wrote explanations of the formations which they had observed, they
    (B)   (C)
   returned to their campsite to compare notes.
                              (D)

2 **2** **2** **2** **2** **2** **2** **2** **2** **2** **2**

20. If Robert Kennedy <u>would have lived</u> a little longer, he <u>probably</u> would
                              (A)   (C)
    have <u>won</u> the election.
         (D)

21. <u>It</u> was Shirley Temple Black <u>which</u> <u>represented</u> her country in the United
    (A)   (B)   (C)
    Nations and <u>later</u> became an ambassador.
                 (D)

22. The prices <u>at</u> chain stores <u>are</u> as reasonable, <u>if not more</u> reasonable, <u>as</u>
                  (A)   (B)   (C)   (D)
    those at discount stores.

23. It is <u>extremely</u> important <u>for</u> an engineer <u>to know</u> to use a computer.
    (A)   (B)   (C)   (D)

24. <u>Historically</u> there <u>has been</u> <u>only</u> two major factions in the Republican
          (A)   (B)   (C)   (D)
    Party—the liberals and the conservatives.

25. Whitman wrote *Leaves of Grass* as a tribute to the Civil War soldiers who

    <u>had laid</u> on the battlefields and <u>whom</u> he <u>had seen</u> <u>while serving</u> as an
      (A)   (B)   (C)   (D)
    army nurse.

26. One of the first and <u>ultimately</u> the most important <u>purposeful</u> of a
                          (A)   (B)
    reservoir was <u>to control</u> <u>flooding</u>.
                    (C)   (D)

27. <u>The Chinese</u> were the first and <u>large</u> ethnic group <u>to work</u> on the
      (A)   (B)   (C)
    construction <u>of</u> the transcontinental railroad system.
                 (D)

28. The range of plant life on a mountainside <u>is</u> a <u>results</u> of <u>differences</u> in
                                              (A)   (B)   (C)
    temperature and precipitation at <u>varying</u> altitudes.
                                      (D)

2 2 2 2 2 2 2 2 2 2 2

29. Even a professional psychologist may have difficulty talking calm and
      (A)   (B)

    logically about his own problems.
            (C)   (D)

30. The more the relative humidity reading rises, the worst the heat affects us.
                                           (A)   (B)   (C) (D)

31. Because correlations are not causes, statistical data which are
                                    (A)   (B)

    extremely easy to misuse.
      (C)   (D)

32. Lectures for the week of March 22–26 will include the following: The
          (A)   (B)   (C)

    Causes of the Civil War, The Economy of the South, Battle Strategies,

    and The Assassinate Lincoln.
           (D)

33. Despite of many attempts to introduce a universal language, notably
      (A)   (B)   (C)

    Esperanto and Idiom Neutral, the effort has met with very little success.
                                                           (D)

34. As every other nation, the United States used to define its unit of
    (A)   (B)   (C)   (D)

    currency, the dollar, in terms of the gold standard.

35. It is necessary that one met with a judge before signing
                       (A)   (B)

    the final papers for a divorce.
       (C)   (D)

36. Until recently, women were forbidden by law from owning property.
       (A)   (B)   (C)   (D)

37. According to the graduate catalog, student housing is more cheaper than
      (A)   (B)   (C)   (D)

    housing off campus.

2 2 2 2 2 2 2 2 2 2 2

38. John Dewey thought that children <u>will learn</u> <u>better</u> through participating
                                    (A)   (B)
in experiences <u>rather than</u> through <u>listening to</u> lectures.
               (C)   (D)

39. <u>In England</u> <u>as early as</u> the <u>twelfth century</u>, young boys enjoyed <u>to play</u>
       (A)   (B)   (C)   (D)
football.

40. <u>Some</u> methods <u>to prevent</u> soil erosion <u>are</u> plowing parallel with the
       (A)   (B)   (C)
slopes of hills, <u>to plant</u> trees on unproductive land, and rotating crops.
                  (D)

THIS IS THE END OF THE STRUCTURE AND WRITTEN EXPRESSION SECTION OF TOEFL MODEL TEST 1.

IF YOU FINISH BEFORE 25 MINUTES HAS ENDED, CHECK YOUR WORK ON SECTION 2 ONLY.

DO NOT READ OR WORK ON ANY OTHER SECTION OF THE TEST.

STOP   STOP   STOP   **STOP**   STOP   STOP   STOP

3 3 3 3 3 3 3 3 3 3 3

Section 3:
Reading Comprehension

50 QUESTIONS 55 MINUTES

Directions: In this section you will read several passages. Each one is followed by a number of questions about it. For questions 1–50, you are to choose the **one** best answer, (A), (B), (C), or (D), to each question. Then, on your answer sheet, find the number of the question and fill in the space that corresponds to the letter of the answer you have chosen.

Answer all questions about the information in a passage on the basis of what is **stated** or **implied** in that passage.

Questions 1–10

Few men have influenced the development of American English to the extent that Noah Webster did. Born in West Hartford, Connecticut, in 1758, his name has become synonymous with
Line American dictionaries. Graduated from Yale in 1778, he was
(5) admitted to the bar in 1781 and thereafter began to practice law in Hartford. Later, when he turned to teaching, he discovered how inadequate the available schoolbooks were for the children of a new and independent nation.

In response to the need for truly American textbooks, Webster
(10) published *A Grammatical Institute of the English Language*, a three-volume work that consisted of a speller, a grammar, and a reader. The first volume, which was generally known as *The American Spelling Book*, was so popular that eventually it sold more than 80 million copies and provided him with a considerable income for
(15) the rest of his life. While teaching, Webster began work on the *Compendious Dictionary of the English Language*, which was published in 1806.

In 1807 Noah Webster began his greatest work, *An American Dictionary of the English Language*. In preparing the manuscript,
(20) he devoted ten years to the study of English and its relationship to other languages, and seven more years to the writing itself. Published in two volumes in 1828, *An American Dictionary of the English Language* has become the recognized authority for usage in the United States. Webster's purpose in writing it was to demonstrate
(25) that the American language was developing distinct meanings, pronunciations, and spellings from those of British English. He is responsible for advancing simplified spelling forms: *develop*

3 3 3 3 3 3 3 3 3 3 3

instead of the British form *develope*; *theater* and *center* instead of *theatre* and *centre*; *color* and *honor* instead of *colour* and *honour*.

(30)   In 1840 Webster brought out a second edition of his dictionary, which included 70,000 entries instead of the original 38,000. This edition has served as the basis for the many revisions that have been produced under the Webster name.

1. Which of the following would be the best title for the passage?

    (A) Webster's Work
    (B) Webster's Dictionaries
    (C) Webster's School
    (D) Webster's Life

2. The word "inadequate" in line 7 could best be replaced by

    (A) unavailable
    (B) expensive
    (C) difficult
    (D) unsatisfactory

3. Why did Webster write *A Grammatical Institute of the English Language*?

    (A) He wanted to supplement his income.
    (B) There were no books available after the Revolutionary War.
    (C) He felt that British books were not appropriate for American children.
    (D) The children did not know how to spell.

4. From which publication did Webster earn a lifetime income?

    (A) *Compendious Dictionary of the English Language*
    (B) *An American Dictionary of the English Language*
    (C) *An American Dictionary of the English Language: Second Edition*
    (D) *The American Spelling Book*

5. In how many volumes was *An American Dictionary of the English Language* published?

    (A) One volume
    (B) Two volumes
    (C) Three volumes
    (D) Four volumes

6. When was *An American Dictionary of the English Language* published?

    (A) 1817
    (B) 1807
    (C) 1828
    (D) 1824

3 3 3 3 3 3 3 3 3 3 3

7. According to the author, what was Webster's purpose in writing *An American Dictionary of the English Language*?

   (A) To respond to the need for new schoolbooks
   (B) To demonstrate the distinct development of the English language in America
   (C) To promote spelling forms based upon British models
   (D) To influence the pronunciation of the English language

8. The word "it" in line 24 refers to

   (A) language
   (B) usage
   (C) authority
   (D) dictionary

9. The word "distinct" in line 25 is closest in meaning to

   (A) new
   (B) simple
   (C) different
   (D) exact

10. According to this passage, which one of the following spellings would Webster have approved in his dictionaries?

    (A) *Develope*
    (B) *Theatre*
    (C) *Color*
    (D) *Honour*

Questions 11–20

     The San Andreas Fault is a fracture at the congruence of two major plates of the earth's crust, one of which supports most of the North American continent, and the other of which underlies the
Line coast of California and the ocean floor of the Pacific. The fault orig-
(5) inates about six hundred miles from the Gulf of California and runs north in an irregular line along the west coast to San Francisco, where it continues north for about two hundred more miles before angling into the ocean. In places, the trace of the fault is marked by a trench, or, in geological terms, a rift, and small ponds called sag
(10) ponds that dot the landscape. Its western side always moves north in relation to its eastern side. The total net slip along the San Andreas Fault and the length of time it has been active are matters of conjecture, but it has been estimated that, during the past fifteen million years, coastal California along the San Andreas Fault has moved
(15) about 190 miles in a northwesterly direction with respect to North America. Although the movement along the fault averages only a few inches a year, it is intermittent and variable. Some segments of the fault do not move at all for long periods of time, building up tremendous pressure that must be released. For this reason, tremors

3 3 3 3 3 3 3 3 3 3 **3**

(20) are not unusual along the San Andreas Fault, and some of them are classified as major earthquakes.

It is worth noting that the San Andreas Fault passes uncomfortably close to several major metropolitan areas, including Los Angeles and San Francisco. In addition, the San Andreas Fault has creat-
(25) ed smaller fault systems, many of which underlie the smaller towns and cities along the California Coast. For this reason, Californians have long anticipated the recurrence of what they refer to as the "Big One," a destructive earthquake that would measure near 8 on the Richter scale, similar in intensity to those that occurred in 1857
(30) and 1906. The effects of such a quake would wreak devastating effects on the life and property in the region. Unfortunately, as pressure continues to build along the fault, the likelihood of such an earthquake increases substantially.

11. What is the author's main purpose in the passage?

    (A) To describe the San Andreas Fault
    (B) To give a definition of a fault
    (C) To explain the reason for tremors and earthquakes
    (D) To classify different kinds of faults

12. The word "originates" in lines 4–5 could best be replaced by

    (A) gets wider
    (B) changes direction
    (C) begins
    (D) disappears

13. Where does the fault lie?

    (A) East of the Gulf of California
    (B) West of the Gulf of California
    (C) North of the Gulf of California
    (D) South of the Gulf of California

14. Which of the following words best describes the San Andreas Fault?

    (A) Straight
    (B) Deep
    (C) Wide
    (D) Rough

15. In which direction does the western side of the fault move?

    (A) West
    (B) East
    (C) North
    (D) South

16. The word "it" in line 7 refers to

    (A) San Francisco
    (B) ocean
    (C) coast
    (D) fault

3 3 3 3 3 3 3 3 3 3 3

17. The word "intermittent" in line 17 could best be replaced by which of the following?

    (A) dangerous
    (B) predictable
    (C) uncommon
    (D) occasional

18. The phrase "the Big One" refers to which of the following?

    (A) A serious earthquake
    (B) The San Andreas Fault
    (C) The Richter Scale
    (D) California

19. Along the San Andreas Fault, tremors are

    (A) small and insignificant
    (B) rare, but disastrous
    (C) frequent events
    (D) very unpredictable

20. How does the author define the San Andreas Fault?

    (A) A plate that underlies the North American continent
    (B) A crack in the earth's crust between two plates
    (C) Occasional tremors and earthquakes
    (D) Intense pressure that builds up

Questions 21–30

The body of an adult insect is subdivided into a head, a thorax of three segments, and a segmented abdomen. Ordinarily, the thorax bears three pairs of legs. One or two pairs of wings may be
Line attached to the thorax. Most adult insects have two large compound
(5) eyes, and two or three small simple eyes.

Features of the mouth parts are very helpful in classifying the many kinds of insects. A majority of insects have biting mouth parts or mandibles as in grasshoppers and beetles. Behind the mandibles are the maxillae, which serve to direct food into the
(10) mouth between the jaws. A labrum above and a labium below are similar to an upper and lower lip. In insects with sucking mouth parts, the mandibles, maxillae, labrum, and labium are modified to provide a tube through which liquid can be drawn. In a butterfly or moth, the coiled drinking tube is called the proboscis. Composed
(15) chiefly of modified maxillae fitted together, the proboscis can be extended to reach nectar deep in a flower. In a mosquito or an aphid, mandibles and maxillae are modified to sharp stylets with which the insect can drill through surfaces to reach juice. In a housefly, the expanding labium forms a spongelike mouth pad that
(20) it can use to stamp over the surface of food.

3 3 3 3 3 3 3 3 3 3 | **3**

21. What is the best title for this passage?

   (A) An Insect's Environment
   (B) The Structure of an Insect
   (C) Grasshoppers and Beetles
   (D) The Stages of Life of an Insect

22. What is the purpose of this passage?

   (A) To complain
   (B) To persuade
   (C) To entertain
   (D) To inform

23. How are insects classified?

   (A) By the environment in which they live
   (B) By the food they eat
   (C) By the structure of the mouth
   (D) By the number and type of wings

24. The word "majority" in line 7 is closest in meaning to

   (A) more than half
   (B) more than twelve
   (C) more than three
   (D) more than one

25. What is the purpose of the maxillae?

   (A) To bite or sting
   (B) To drill through surfaces to find nourishment
   (C) To put food between the jaws
   (D) To soak up nourishment like a sponge

26. The author compares labrum and labium to

   (A) an upper and lower lip
   (B) mandibles
   (C) maxillae
   (D) jaws

27. What is the proboscis?

   (A) Nectar
   (B) A tube constructed of modified maxillae
   (C) A kind of butterfly
   (D) A kind of flower

28. Which of the following have mandibles and maxillae that have been modified to sharp stylets?

   (A) Grasshoppers
   (B) Butterflies
   (C) Mosquitoes
   (D) Houseflies

29. The phrase "drill through" in line 18 could best be replaced by

   (A) penetrate
   (B) saturate
   (C) explore
   (D) distinguish

30. The word "it" in line 20 refers to

   (A) pad
   (B) food
   (C) housefly
   (D) mouth

3 3 3 3 3 3 3 3 3 3 | 3

Questions 31–40

Interest is the sum charged for borrowing money for a fixed period of time. Principal is the term used for the money that is borrowed, and the rate of interest is the percent per year of the principal charged for its use. Most of the profits for a bank are derived
Line
(5) from the interest that they charge for the use of their own or their depositors' money.

All problems in interest may be solved by using one general equation that may be stated as follows:

$$\text{Interest} = \text{Principal} \times \text{Rate} \times \text{Time}$$

(10)   Any one of the four quantities—that is, interest, principal, rate, or time—may be found when the other three are known. The time is expressed in years. The rate is expressed as a decimal fraction. Thus, 6 percent interest means six cents charged for the use of $1 of principal borrowed for one year. Although the time may be less
(15) than, equal to, or greater than one year, most applications for loans are for periods of less than one year. For purposes of computing interest for short periods, the commercial year or 360 days is commonly used, but when large sums of money are involved, exact interest is computed on the basis of 365 days.

31. With what topic is this passage primarily concerned?

(A) Profits
(B) Rate
(C) Interest
(D) Principal

32. The word "sum" in line 1 could best be replaced by

(A) amount
(B) institution
(C) customer
(D) formula

33. The word "fixed" in line 1 is closest in meaning to

(A) definite
(B) short
(C) repeated
(D) trial

34. The word "its" in line 4 refers to

(A) principal
(B) percent
(C) rate
(D) interest

35. At 4 percent interest for the use of $1 principal, how much would one pay?

(A) Six cents per year
(B) Twenty-five cents per year
(C) Four cents per year
(D) One cent per year

3 3 3 3 3 3 3 3 3 3 3

36. Which of the following would be a correct expression of an interest rate as stated in the equation for computing interest?

   (A) Four
   (B) .04
   (C) 4
   (D) 4/100

37. Most applications for loans are for

   (A) one year
   (B) less than one year
   (C) more than one year
   (D) 360 days

38. The word "periods" in line 16 refers to

   (A) time
   (B) loans
   (C) applications
   (D) interest

39. A commercial year is used to compute

   (A) exact interest
   (B) interest on large sums of money
   (C) interest on a large principal
   (D) interest for short periods of time

40. Which of the following is the best definition of interest?

   (A) Money borrowed
   (B) Rate × Time
   (C) A fee paid for the use of money
   (D) The number of years a bank allows a borrower in order to repay a loan

Questions 41–50

The protozoans, minute aquatic creatures, each of which consists of a single cell of protoplasm, constitute a classification of the most primitive forms of animal life. They are fantastically diverse,
Line but three major groups may be identified on the basis of their motil-
(5) ity. The Mastigophora have one or more long tails, which they use to project themselves forward. The Ciliata, which use the same basic means for locomotion as the Mastigophora, have a larger number of short tails. The Sarcodina, which include amoebae, float or row themselves about on their crusted bodies.
(10) In addition to their form of movement, several other features discriminate among the three groups of protozoans. For example, at least two nuclei per cell have been identified in the Ciliata, usually a large nucleus that regulates growth but decomposes during reproduction, and a smaller one that contains the genetic code necessary
(15) to generate the large nucleus.

3 3 3 3 3 3 3 3 3 3 3

Protozoans are considered animals because, unlike pigmented plants to which some protozoans are otherwise almost identical, they do not live on simple organic compounds. Their cell demonstrates all of the major characteristics of the cells of higher ani-

(20)   mals.

Many species of protozoans collect into colonies, physically connected to each other and responding uniformly to outside stimulae. Current research into this phenomenon along with investigations carried out with advanced microscopes may necessitate a redef-

(25)   inition of what constitutes protozoans, even calling into question the basic premise that they have only one cell. Nevertheless, with the current data available, almost 40,000 species of protozoans have been identified. No doubt, as the technology improves our methods of observation, better models of classification will be proposed.

41. With what topic is the passage primarily concerned?

(A) Colonies of protozoans
(B) Mastigophora
(C) Motility in protozoans
(D) Characteristics of protozoans

42. The word "minute" in line 1 could best be replaced by

(A) very common
(B) very fast
(C) very old
(D) very small

43. Where do protozoans probably live?

(A) Water
(B) Sand
(C) Grass
(D) Wood

44. What is protoplasm?

(A) A class of protozoan
(B) The substance that forms the cell of a protozoan
(C) A primitive animal similar to a protozoan
(D) An animal that developed from a protozoan

45. To which class of protozoans do the amoebae belong?

(A) Mastigophora
(B) Ciliata
(C) Sarcodina
(D) Motility

46. What is the purpose of the large nucleus in the Ciliata?

(A) It generates the other nucleus.
(B) It contains the genetic code for the small nucleus.
(C) It regulates growth.
(D) It reproduces itself.

3 3 3 3 3 3 3 3 3 3 3

47. Why are protozoans classified as animals?

 (A) They do not live on simple organic compounds.
 (B) They collect in colonies.
 (C) They respond uniformly to outside stimulae.
 (D) They may have more than one cell.

48. The word "uniformly" in line 22 is closest in meaning to

 (A) in the same way
 (B) once in a while
 (C) all of a sudden
 (D) in the long run

49. The word "they" in line 18 refers to

 (A) protozoans
 (B) microscopes
 (C) investigations
 (D) colonies

50. Which of the following statements is NOT true of protozoans?

 (A) There are approximately 40,000 species.
 (B) They are the most primitive forms of animal life.
 (C) They have a large cell and a smaller cell.
 (D) They are difficult to observe.

THIS IS THE END OF THE READING COMPREHENSION SECTION OF TOEFL MODEL TEST 1.

IF YOU FINISH BEFORE 55 MINUTES HAS ENDED, CHECK YOUR WORK ON SECTION 3 ONLY.

DO NOT READ OR WORK ON ANY OTHER SECTION OF THE TEST.

END OF TOEFL MODEL TEST 1.

To check your answers for Model Test 1, refer to the Answer Key on page 377. For an explanation of the answers, refer to the Explanatory Answers for Model Test 1 on pages 385–397.

THE TEST OF WRITTEN ENGLISH (TWE) FOLLOWS.

Test of Written English (TWE) Model Test 1

When you take a Model Test, you should use one sheet of paper, both sides. Time each Model Test carefully. After you have read the topic, you should spend 30 minutes writing. For results that would be closest to the actual testing situation, it is recommended that an English teacher score your test, using the guidelines on page 242 of this book.

Many people have learned a foreign language in their own country; others have learned a foreign language in the country in which it is spoken. Give the advantages of each and support your viewpoint.

Notes

1 1 1 1 1 1 1 1 1 1 1

Model Test 2
Paper and Pencil TOEFL

Section 1:
Listening Comprehension

50 QUESTIONS 40 MINUTES

In this section of the test, you will have an opportunity to demonstrate your ability to understand conversations and talks in English. There are three parts to this section with special directions for each part. Answer all the questions on the basis of what is stated or implied by the speakers in this test. When you take the actual TOEFL test, you will not be allowed to take notes or write in your test book. Try to work on this Model Test in the same way.

Part A

Directions: In Part A you will hear short conversations between two people. After each conversation, you will hear a question about the conversation. The conversations and questions will not be repeated. After you hear a question, read the four possible answers in your book and choose the best answer. Then, on your answer sheet, find the number of the question and fill in the space that corresponds to the letter of the answer you have chosen.

1. (A) Car repairs should be done at a garage.
   (B) The price was not too high.
   (C) The garage took advantage of the woman.
   (D) The car had serious problems.

2. (A) Have a party.
   (B) Attend the International Students' Association.
   (C) Go to work.
   (D) Get some rest.

3. (A) Leave immediately.
   (B) Watch the game on TV.
   (C) Start to play.
   (D) Eat a sandwich.

4. (A) He went to see the foreign student advisor.
   (B) He went to Washington.
   (C) He wrote to the Passport Office.
   (D) He reported it to the Passport Office.

5. (A) It is the policy of the bank.
   (B) The man was not helpful at all.
   (C) Her account at the bank is in order.
   (D) The check should be cashed.

1 1 1 1 1 1 1 1 1 1 1

6. (A) Ask Dr. Tyler to clarify the assignment.
   (B) Show a preliminary version to Dr. Tyler.
   (C) Let her see the first draft before Dr. Tyler sees it.
   (D) Talk to some of the other students in Dr. Tyler's class.

7. (A) Dr. Clark is a good teacher.
   (B) Statistics is a boring class.
   (C) Two semesters of statistics are required.
   (D) The students do not like Dr. Clark.

8. (A) He cannot do them.
   (B) They are finished.
   (C) It will be a difficult job.
   (D) They will be ready Saturday afternoon.

9. (A) A concert.
   (B) An art museum.
   (C) A flower shop.
   (D) A restaurant.

10. (A) He is at lunch.
    (B) He is at the office.
    (C) He is in class.
    (D) He is at home.

11. (A) Take the ten o'clock bus.
    (B) Come back in five minutes.
    (C) Go to New York another day.
    (D) Call the airport.

12. (A) A teacher.
    (B) A textbook.
    (C) An assignment.
    (D) A movie.

13. (A) Make corrections on the original.
    (B) Make copies.
    (C) Deliver the copies to Mr. Brown.
    (D) Find the original.

14. (A) She was Sally Harrison's cousin.
    (B) She was Sally Harrison's sister.
    (C) She was Sally Harrison's friend.
    (D) She was Sally Harrison.

15. (A) The desk drawer won't open.
    (B) The pen is out of ink.
    (C) She cannot find her pen.
    (D) She is angry with the man.

16. (A) John is usually late.
    (B) John will be there at eight-thirty.
    (C) John will not show up.
    (D) John is usually on time.

17. (A) She does not agree with the man.
    (B) She needs a larger home.
    (C) She regrets the cost of their vacation.
    (D) She thinks that houses are very expensive.

18. (A) He did not make a presentation.
    (B) He got confused during the presentation.
    (C) He should have spoken more loudly.
    (D) He did a very complete job.

1 1 1 1 1 1 1 1 1 1 1

19. (A) He has decided not to mail the invitations.
    (B) He wants to get Janet's opinion.
    (C) He is waiting for Janet to answer the phone.
    (D) He does not want to invite Janet.

20. (A) The baby is asleep.
    (B) The baby is very active.
    (C) The baby is not staying with the woman.
    (D) The baby is just about to start walking.

21. (A) The results of the tests are not available.
    (B) The experiment had unexpected results.
    (C) He has not completed the experiment yet.
    (D) It is taking a lot of time to do the experiment.

22. (A) She does not put much effort in her studies.
    (B) She is very likable.
    (C) She prefers talking to the woman.
    (D) She has a telephone.

23. (A) See the doctor.
    (B) Get another job.
    (C) Go to the counter.
    (D) Buy some medicine.

24. (A) She will try her best.
    (B) She has to save her money.
    (C) She is still undecided.
    (D) She needs an application.

25. (A) She is glad to meet Robert.
    (B) She is surprised to hear from Robert.
    (C) She does not enjoy talking with Robert.
    (D) She was ready to call Robert.

26. (A) The man must stop working.
    (B) There is a little more time.
    (C) The test is important.
    (D) It is time for the test.

27. (A) The woman's roommate took a different class.
    (B) The book is very expensive.
    (C) The textbook may have been changed.
    (D) The course is not offered this semester.

28. (A) Sally may get a bike for Christmas.
    (B) Sally already has a bike like that one.
    (C) Sally likes riding a bike.
    (D) Sally may prefer a different gift.

29. (A) He does not want to give Carol a ride.
    (B) He does not have a car.
    (C) He cannot hear well.
    (D) He does not know Carol.

30. (A) Take a break.
    (B) Go to work.
    (C) Do the other problems.
    (D) Keep trying.

1 1 1 1 1 1 1 1 1 1 1

Part B

Directions: In this part of the test, you will hear longer conversations. After each conversation, you will hear several questions. The conversations and questions will not be repeated.

After you hear a question, read the four possible answers in your book and choose the best answer. Then, on your answer sheet, find the number of the question and fill in the space that corresponds to the letter of the answer you have chosen.

Remember, you are **not** allowed to take notes or write on your test pages.

31. (A) Whether to introduce the metric system in the United States.
    (B) How the metric system should be introduced in the United States.
    (C) Which system is better— the English system or the metric system.
    (D) How to convert measurements from the English system to the metric system.

32. (A) Now the weather on radio and TV is reported exclusively in metrics.
    (B) Road signs have miles marked on them, but not kilometers.
    (C) Both the English system and the metric system are being used on signs, packages, and in weather reports.
    (D) Grocery stores use only metrics for their packaging.

33. (A) He thought that a gradual adoption would be better for everyone.
    (B) He thought that only metrics should be used.
    (C) He thought that only the English system should be used.
    (D) He thought that adults should use both systems, but that children should be taught only the metric system.

34. (A) Unfriendly.
    (B) Patronizing.
    (C) Uninterested.
    (D) Cooperative.

35. (A) To change his travel plans.
    (B) To arrange a time to pick up his tickets.
    (C) To reserve a hotel room.
    (D) To make a plane reservation.

1 1 1 1 1 1 1 1 1 1 1

36. (A) The man can save money by staying an extra night.
    (B) The man should have called earlier.
    (C) She needs the man to come into the office.
    (D) She will mail the tickets to the man.

37. (A) Travel on May 19 as planned.
    (B) Wait for a cheaper fare.
    (C) Stay an extra day in Atlanta.
    (D) Return on Sunday.

38. (A) Go back to his hotel.
    (B) Pack his suitcase.
    (C) Call a different travel agent.
    (D) Go to the travel agent's office in the afternoon.

Part C

Directions: In this part of the test, you will hear several short talks. After each talk, you will hear some questions. The talks and questions will not be repeated.

After you hear a question, read the four possible answers in your book and choose the best answer. Then, on your answer sheet, find the number of the question and fill in the space that corresponds to the letter of the answer you have chosen.

39. (A) Private industry.
    (B) Advances in medicine.
    (C) Space missions.
    (D) Technological developments.

40. (A) Contact lenses.
    (B) Cordless tools.
    (C) Food packaging.
    (D) Ultrasound.

41. (A) To monitor the condition of astronauts in spacecraft.
    (B) To evaluate candidates who wanted to join the space program.
    (C) To check the health of astronauts when they returned from space.
    (D) To test spacecraft and equipment for imperfections.

1 1 1 1 1 1 1 1 1 1 1

42. (A) Archaeologists and astro-
       nauts were compared.
    (B) Astronauts made pho-
        tographs of the earth later
        used by archaeologists.
    (C) Archaeologists have used
        advances in medical tech-
        nology developed for
        astronauts.
    (D) Space missions and under-
        water missions are very
        similar.

43. (A) Transportation on the
       Pacific Coast.
    (B) History of California.
    (C) Orientation to San Francisco.
    (D) Specifications of the Gol-
        den Gate Bridge.

44. (A) Golden Gate.
    (B) San Francisco de Asis Mis-
        sion.
    (C) Military Post Seventy-six.
    (D) Yerba Buena.

45. (A) Gold was discovered.
    (B) The Transcontinental Rail-
        road was completed.
    (C) The Golden Gate Bridge was
        constructed.
    (D) Telegraph communications
        were established with the
        East.

46. (A) Eighteen miles.
    (B) 938 feet.
    (C) One mile.
    (D) Between five and six miles.

47. (A) Transcendentalism.
    (B) Puritanism.
    (C) Ralph Waldo Emerson.
    (D) Nature.

48. (A) Seventeenth century.
    (B) Eighteenth century.
    (C) Nineteenth century.
    (D) Twentieth century.

49. (A) They stressed the impor-
       tance of the individual.
    (B) They supported the ideals
        of the Transcendental
        Club.
    (C) They believed that society
        was more important than
        the individual.
    (D) They established a com-
        mune at Brook Farm.

50. (A) A book by Emerson.
    (B) A history of Puritanism.
    (C) A novel by Nathaniel
        Hawthorne.
    (D) A book by Thoreau.

**THIS IS THE END OF THE LISTENING COMPREHENSION
SECTION OF TOEFL MODEL TEST 2.**

**DO NOT READ OR WORK ON ANY OTHER SECTION OF
THE TEST.**

2 2 2 2 2 2 2 2 2 2 2

Section 2:
Structure and Written Expression

40 Questions 25 Minutes

This section is designed to measure your ability to recognize language that is appropriate for standard written English. There are two types of questions in this section, with special directions for each type.

Structure

Directions: Questions 1–15 are incomplete sentences. Beneath each sentence you will see four words or phrases, marked (A), (B), (C), and (D). Choose the **one** word or phrase that best completes the sentence. Then, on your answer sheet, find the number of the question and fill in the space that corresponds to the letter of the answer you have chosen. Fill in the space so that the letter inside the oval cannot be seen.

1. Based on the premise that light was composed of color, the Impressionists came to the conclusion ---------- not really black.

   (A) which was that shadows
   (B) was shadows which
   (C) were shadows
   (D) that shadows were

2. ---------- a parliamentary system, the prime minister must be appointed on the basis of the distribution of power in the parliament.

   (A) The considered
   (B) To be considered
   (C) Considering
   (D) Considers

3. ---------- of the play *Mourning Becomes Electra* introduces the cast of characters and hints at the plot.

   (A) The act first
   (B) Act one
   (C) Act first
   (D) First act

4. As soon as -------- with an acid, salt, and sometimes water, is formed.

   (A) a base will react
   (B) a base reacts
   (C) a base is reacting
   (D) the reaction of a base

2 **2** **2** **2** **2** **2** **2** **2** **2** **2** **2**

5. The Internal Revenue Service ------- their tax forms by April 15 every year.

   (A) makes all Americans file
   (B) makes all Americans to file
   (C) makes the filing of all Americans
   (D) makes all Americans filing

6. Although one of his ships succeeded in sailing all the way back to Spain past the Cape of Good Hope, Magellan never completed the first circumnavigation of the world, and -------- .

   (A) most of his crew didn't too
   (B) neither most of his crew did
   (C) neither did most of his crew
   (D) most of his crew didn't also

7. To answer accurately is more important than ---------- .

   (A) a quick finish
   (B) to finish quickly
   (C) finishing quickly
   (D) you finish quickly

8. Weathering ---------- the action whereby surface rock is disintegrated or decomposed.

   (A) it is
   (B) is that
   (C) is
   (D) being

9. A telephone recording tells callers ---------.

   (A) what time the movie starts
   (B) what time starts the movie
   (C) what time does the movie start
   (D) the movie starts what time

10. The people of Western Canada have been considering ---------- themselves from the rest of the provinces.

    (A) to separate
    (B) separated
    (C) separate
    (D) separating

11. It costs about sixty dollars to have a tooth ---------- .

    (A) filling
    (B) to fill
    (C) filled
    (D) fill

12. Not until a student has mastered algebra ---------- the principles of geometry, trigonometry, and physics.

    (A) he can begin to understand
    (B) can he begin to understand
    (C) he begins to understand
    (D) begins to understand

13. Although Margaret Mead had several assistants during her long investigations of Samoa, the bulk of the research was done by ---------- alone.

    (A) herself
    (B) she
    (C) her
    (D) hers

2 2 2 2 2 2 2 2 2 2 2

14. ---------- war correspondent, Hemingway used his experiences for some of his most powerful novels.

   (A) But a
   (B) It is a
   (C) While
   (D) A

15. Thirty-eight national sites are known as parks, another eighty-two as monuments, and --------- .

   (A) the another one hundred seventy-eight as historical sites
   (B) the other one hundred seventy-eight as historical sites
   (C) seventy-eight plus one hundred more as historical sites
   (D) as historical sites one hundred seventy-eight

Written Expression

Directions: In questions 16–40, each sentence has four underlined words or phrases. The four underlined parts of the sentence are marked (A), (B), (C), and (D). Identify the **one** underlined word or phrase that must be changed in order for the sentence to be correct. Then, on your answer sheet, find the number of the question and fill in the space that corresponds to the letter of the answer you have chosen.

16. Interest in automatic data processing has grown rapid since the first large
        (A)   (B) (C) (D)
    calculators were introduced in 1950.

17. Vaslav Nijinsky achieved world recognition as both a dancer as well as
                (A)   (B)   (C)   (D)
    a choreographer.

18. Airports must be located near to major population centers for the
                 (A)   (B)
    advantage of air transportation to be retained.
                (C)   (D)

19. It is said that Einstein felt very badly about the application of his theories
     (A)   (B) (C)
    to the creation of weapons of war.
    (D)

2 2 2 2 2 2 2 2 2 2 2

20. The plants that <u>they belong to</u> the family of ferns are quite varied in <u>their</u>
          <u>(A)</u>   <u>(B)</u>   (C)   (D)
    size and structure.

21. <u>Despite of</u> the increase in air fares, most people <u>still</u> <u>prefer</u> <u>to travel</u> by
   <u>(A)</u>   (B) (C)   (D)
    plane.

22. All of <u>we</u> students must <u>have</u> an identification card in order to check
       <u>(A)</u>   <u>(B)</u>
    books <u>out of</u> the library.
     <u>(C)(D)</u>

23. Columbus Day <u>is celebrated</u> <u>on</u> the <u>twelve</u> of October <u>because</u> on that day
           <u>(A)</u>   <u>(B)</u>   <u>(C)</u>   <u>(D)</u>
    in 1492, Christopher Columbus first landed in the Americas.

24. One of <u>the most influence</u> newspapers in the U.S. is *The New York Times,*
       <u>(A)</u>   <u>(B)</u>   <u>(C)</u>
    which is <u>widely distributed</u> throughout the world.
           <u>(D)</u>

25. An unexpected <u>raise</u> in the cost of living <u>as well as</u> a decline in
            <u>(A)</u>   <u>(B)</u>
    employment opportunities has <u>resulted in</u> the <u>rapid</u> creation by Congress
                        <u>(C)</u>   <u>(D)</u>
    of new government programs for the unemployed.

26. It <u>is</u> imperative that a graduate student <u>maintains</u> a grade point average
  <u>(A)</u>   <u>(B)</u>
    <u>of</u> "B" in <u>his</u> major field.
 <u>(C)</u>   <u>(D)</u>

27. Coastal and inland waters <u>are inhabited</u> <u>not only</u> by fish but also by <u>such</u>
                   <u>(A)</u>   <u>(B)</u>   <u>(C)</u>
    <u>sea creature</u> as shrimps and clams.
   <u>(D)</u>

2 2 2 2 2 2 2 2 2 2 2

28. Economists have tried to discourage the use of the phrase
                     (A)   (B)
    "underdeveloped nation" and encouraging the more accurate phrase
                                 (C)   (D)
    "developing nation" in order to suggest an ongoing process.

29. A gas like propane will combination with water molecules in a saline
          (A)   (B)
    solution to form a solid called a hydrate.
             (C)   (D)

30. Although it cannot be proven, presumable the expansion of the universe
                      (A)   (B)   (C)
    will slow down as it approaches a critical radius.
                         (D)

31. Regardless of your teaching method, the objective of any conversation
    (A)
    class should be for the students to practice speaking words.
          (B)   (C)   (D)

32. A City University professor reported that he discovers a vaccine that has
                                                (A)   (B)
    been 80 percent effective in reducing the instances of tooth decay among
                                (C)   (D)
    small children.

33. American baseball teams, once the only contenders for the world
                             (A)
    championship, are now being challenged by either Japanese teams and
                             (B)   (C) (D)
    Venezuelan teams.

34. When they have been frightened, as, for example, by an electrical storm,
                   (A)   (B)   (C)
    dairy cows may refuse giving milk.
                          (D)

2 2 2 2 2 2 2 2 2 2 2

35. Miami, Florida is among the few cities in the United States that
                     (A)   (B)
    has been awarded official status as bilingual municipalities.
           (C)   (D)

36. No other quality is more important for a scientist to acquire as to observe
         (A)   (B)   (C)
    carefully.
      (D)

37. After the police had tried unsuccessfully to determine to who the car
             (A)   (B)   (C)
    belonged, they towed it into the station.
                        (D)

38. Fertilizers are used primarily to enrich soil and increasing yield.
                   (A)   (B)   (C)   (D)

39. If the ozone gases of the atmosphere did not filter out the ultraviolet rays
                                            (A)
    of the sun, life as we know it would not have evolved on earth.
                (B)   (C)   (D)

40. The regulation requires that everyone who holds a nonimmigrant visa
                                          (A) (B)
    reports an address to the federal government in January of each year.
     (C) (D)

THIS IS THE END OF THE STRUCTURE AND WRITTEN EXPRESSION SECTION OF TOEFL MODEL TEST 2.

IF YOU FINISH BEFORE 25 MINUTES HAS ENDED, CHECK YOUR WORK ON SECTION 2 ONLY.

DO NOT READ OR WORK ON ANY OTHER SECTION OF THE TEST.

STOP   STOP   STOP   **STOP**   STOP   STOP   STOP

3 3 3 3 3 3 3 3 3 3 3

Section 3:
Reading Comprehension

50 QUESTIONS 55 MINUTES

Directions: In this section you will read several passages. Each one is followed by a number of questions about it. For questions 1–50, you are to choose the **one** best answer, (A), (B), (C), or (D), to each question. Then, on your answer sheet, find the number of the question and fill in the space that corresponds to the letter of the answer you have chosen.

Answer all questions about the information in a passage on the basis of what is **stated** or **implied** in that passage.

Questions 1–10

Precipitation, commonly referred to as rainfall, is a measure of the quantity of water in the form of either rain, hail, or snow which reaches the ground. The average annual precipitation over the
Line whole of the United States is thirty-six inches. It should be under-
(5) stood however, that a foot of snow is not equal to a foot of precipitation. A general formula for computing the precipitation of snowfall is that ten inches of snow is equal to one inch of precipitation. In New York State, for example, twenty inches of snow in one year would be recorded as only two inches of precipitation. Forty inches
(10) of rain would be recorded as forty inches of precipitation. The total annual precipitation would be recorded as forty-two inches.
The amount of precipitation is a combined result of several factors, including location, altitude, proximity to the sea, and the direction of prevailing winds. Most of the precipitation in the United
(15) States is brought originally by prevailing winds from the Pacific Ocean, the Gulf of Mexico, the Atlantic Ocean, and the Great Lakes. Because these prevailing winds generally come from the West, the Pacific Coast receives more annual precipitation than the Atlantic Coast. Along the Pacific Coast itself, however, altitude
(20) causes some diversity in rainfall. The mountain ranges of the United States, especially the Rocky Mountain Range and the Appalachian Mountain Range, influence the amount of precipitation in their areas. East of the Rocky Mountains, the annual precipitation decreases substantially from that west of the Rocky Mountains. The
(25) precipitation north of the Appalachian Mountains is about 40 percent less than that south of the Appalachian Mountains.

3 3 3 3 3 3 3 3 3 3 3

1. What does this passage mainly discuss?

   (A) Precipitation
   (B) Snowfall
   (C) New York State
   (D) A general formula

2. Which of the following is another word that is often used in place of precipitation?

   (A) Humidity
   (B) Wetness
   (C) Rainfall
   (D) Rain-snow

3. The term *precipitation* includes

   (A) only rainfall
   (B) rain, hail, and snow
   (C) rain, snow, and humidity
   (D) rain, hail, and humidity

4. What is the average annual rainfall in inches in the United States?

   (A) Thirty-six inches
   (B) Thirty-eight inches
   (C) Forty inches
   (D) Forty-two inches

5. If a state has 40 inches of snow in a year, by how much does this increase the annual precipitation?

   (A) By two feet
   (B) By four inches
   (C) By four feet
   (D) By 40 inches

6. The phrase "proximity to" in line 13 is closest in meaning to

   (A) communication with
   (B) dependence on
   (C) nearness to
   (D) similarity to

7. Where is the annual precipitation highest?

   (A) The Atlantic Coast
   (B) The Great Lakes
   (C) The Gulf of Mexico
   (D) The Pacific Coast

8. Which of the following was NOT mentioned as a factor in determining the amount of precipitation that an area will receive?

   (A) Mountains
   (B) Latitude
   (C) The sea
   (D) Wind

9. The word "substantially" in line 24 could best be replaced by

   (A) fundamentally
   (B) slightly
   (C) completely
   (D) apparently

10. The word "that" in line 26 refers to

    (A) decreases
    (B) precipitation
    (C) areas
    (D) mountain ranges

3 3 3 3 3 3 3 3 3 3 3

Questions 11–20

> Course numbers are an indication of which courses are open to various categories of students at the University. Undergraduate courses with the numbers 100 or 200 are generally introductory
> *Line* courses appropriate for freshmen or sophomores, whereas courses
> *(5)* with the numbers 300 or 400 often have prerequisites and are open to juniors and seniors only. Courses with the numbers 800 or above are open only to graduate students. Certain graduate courses, generally those devoted to introductory material, are numbered 400 for undergraduate students who qualify to take them and 600 for grad-
> *(10)* uate students. Courses designed for students seeking a professional degree carry a 500 number for undergraduate students and a 700 number for graduate students. Courses numbered 99 or below are special interest courses that do not carry academic credit. If students elect to take a special interest course, it will not count toward
> *(15)* the number of hours needed to complete graduation requirements.
> A full-time undergraduate student is expected to take courses that total twelve to eighteen credit hours. A full-time graduate student is expected to take courses that total ten to sixteen credit hours. Students holding assistantships are expected to enroll for
> *(20)* proportionately fewer hours. A part-time graduate student may register for a minimum of three credit hours. An overload, that is, more than the maximum number of hours, may be taken with the approval of an academic advisor. To register for an overload, students must submit the appropriate approval form when registering.
> *(25)* Overloads above 24 hours will not be approved under any circumstances.

11. Where would this passage most likely be found?

    (A) In a syllabus
    (B) In a college catalog
    (C) In an undergraduate course
    (D) In a graduate course

12. What is the purpose of the passage?

    (A) To inform
    (B) To persuade
    (C) To criticize
    (D) To apologize

13. The word "prerequisites" in line 5 is closest in meaning to

    (A) courses required before enrolling
    (B) courses needed for graduation
    (C) courses that include additional charges
    (D) courses that do not carry academic credit

3 3 3 3 3 3 3 3 3 3 3

14. The word "those" in line 8 refers to

    (A) graduate students
    (B) graduate courses
    (C) introductory courses
    (D) course numbers

15. Which classification of students would be eligible to enroll in Mechanical Engineering 850?

    (A) A graduate student
    (B) A part-time student
    (C) A full-time student
    (D) An undergraduate student

16. If an undergraduate student uses the number 520 to register for an accounting course, what number would a graduate student probably use to register for the same course?

    (A) Accounting 520
    (B) Accounting 620
    (C) Accounting 720
    (D) Accounting 820

17. How is a student who registers for eight credit hours classified?

    (A) Full-time student
    (B) Graduate student
    (C) Part-time student
    (D) Non-degree student

18. Which of the following courses would not be included in the list of courses for graduation?

    (A) English 90
    (B) English 100
    (C) English 300
    (D) English 400

19. A graduate student may NOT

    (A) enroll in a course numbered 610
    (B) register for only one one-hour course
    (C) register for courses if he has an assistantship
    (D) enroll in an introductory course

20. The phrase "under any circumstances" in lines 25–26 is closest in meaning to

    (A) without cause
    (B) without permission
    (C) without exception
    (D) without a good reason

Questions 21–30

   During the nineteenth century, women in the United States organized and participated in a large number of reform movements, including movements to reorganize the prison system, improve
Line education, ban the sale of alcohol, and, most importantly, to free the
(5) slaves. Some women saw similarities in the social status of women and slaves. Women like Elizabeth Cady Stanton and Lucy Stone were feminists and abolitionists who supported the rights of both

3 3 3 3 3 3 3 3 3 3 **3**

women and blacks. A number of male abolitionists, including
William Lloyd Garrison and Wendell Philips, also supported the
(10) rights of women to speak and participate equally with men in anti-
slavery activities. Probably more than any other movement, aboli-
tionism offered women a previously denied entry into politics.
They became involved primarily in order to better their living conditions and the conditions of others.

(15)   When the Civil War ended in 1865, the Fourteenth and Fifteenth Amendments to the Constitution adopted in 1868 and 1870
granted citizenship and suffrage to blacks but not to women. Dis-
couraged but resolved, feminists influenced more and more women
to demand the right to vote. In 1869 the Wyoming Territory had
(20) yielded to demands by feminists, but eastern states resisted more
stubbornly than before. A women's suffrage bill had been presented to every Congress since 1878 but it continually failed to pass
until 1920, when the Nineteenth Amendment granted women the
right to vote.

21. With what topic is the passage
primarily concerned?

(A) The Wyoming Territory
(B) The Fourteenth and Fifteenth
     Amendments
(C) Abolitionists
(D) Women's suffrage

22. The word "ban" in line 4 most
nearly means to

(A) encourage
(B) publish
(C) prohibit
(D) limit

23. The word "supported" in line 7
could best be replaced by

(A) disregarded
(B) acknowledged
(C) contested
(D) promoted

24. According to the passage, why
did women become active in
politics?

(A) To improve the conditions
     of life that existed at the
     time
(B) To support Elizabeth Cady
     Stanton for president
(C) To be elected to public
     office
(D) To amend the Declaration of
     Independence

25. The word "primarily" in line 13
is closest in meaning to

(A) above all
(B) somewhat
(C) finally
(D) always

3 3 3 3 3 3 3 3 3 3 3

26. What had occurred shortly after the Civil War?

   (A) The Wyoming Territory was admitted to the Union.
   (B) A women's suffrage bill was introduced in Congress.
   (C) The eastern states resisted the end of the war.
   (D) Black people were granted the right to vote.

27. The word "suffrage" in line 17 could best be replaced by which of the following?

   (A) pain
   (B) citizenship
   (C) freedom from bondage
   (D) the right to vote

28. What does the Nineteenth Amendment guarantee?

   (A) Voting rights for blacks
   (B) Citizenship for blacks
   (C) Voting rights for women
   (D) Citizenship for women

29. The word "it" in line 22 refers to

   (A) bill
   (B) Congress
   (C) Nineteenth Amendment
   (D) vote

30. When were women allowed to vote throughout the United States?

   (A) After 1866
   (B) After 1870
   (C) After 1878
   (D) After 1920

Questions 31–40

    The *Acacia* is a genus of trees and shrubs of the Mimosa family. Although nearly five hundred species of *Acacia* have been identified, only about a dozen of the three hundred Australian varieties
Line grow well in the southern United States, and of these, only three are
(5) flowering. The *Bailey Acacia* has fernlike silver leaves and small, fragrant flowers arranged in rounded clusters. The *Silver Wattle*, although very similar to the *Bailey Acacia*, grows twice as high. The *Sydney Golden Wattle* is squat and bushy with broad, flat leaves and sharp spined twigs. Named for its bright, yellow flowers,
(10) the *Golden Wattle* is the most showy and fragrant of the Acacias. Another variety, the *Black Acacia* or *Blackwood*, has dark green leaves and unobtrusive blossoms. Besides being a popular tree for ornamental purposes, the *Black Acacia* is valuable for its dark wood, which is used in making cabinets and furniture, including
(15) highly prized pianos.

    The *Acacia's* unusual custom of blossoming in February has been commonly attributed to its Australian origins. In the Southern Hemisphere, of course, the seasons are reversed, and February,

3 3 3 3 3 3 3 3 3 3 3

which is wintertime in the United States, is summertime in Aus-
(20) tralia. Actually, however, the pale, yellow blossoms appear in
August in Australia. Whether growing in the Northern or Southern
Hemisphere, the *Acacia* will bloom in winter.

31. With which of the following topics is the passage primarily concerned?

(A) The *Black Acacia*
(B) Characteristics and varieties
of the *Acacia*
(C) Australian varieties of the
Acacia
(D) The use of *Acacia* wood in
ornamental furniture

32. How many species of *Acacia*
grow well in the southern United
States?

(A) Five hundred
(B) Three hundred
(C) Twelve
(D) Three

33. The word "these" in line 4 refers
to

(A) United States
(B) varieties
(C) species
(D) trees and shrubs

34. According to this passage, the
Silver Wattle

(A) is squat and bushy
(B) has unobtrusive blossoms
(C) is taller than the *Bailey
Acacia*
(D) is used for making furniture

35. In line 8, the word "flat" most
nearly means

(A) smooth
(B) pretty
(C) pointed
(D) short

36. The word "showy" in line 10
could best be replaced by

(A) strange
(B) elaborate
(C) huge
(D) fragile

37. Which of the following *Acacias*
has the least colorful blossoms?

(A) *Bailey Acacia*
(B) *Sydney Golden Wattle*
(C) *Silver Wattle*
(D) *Black Acacia*

38. Which of the following would
most probably be made from a
Black Acacia tree?

(A) A flower arrangement
(B) A table
(C) A pie
(D) Paper

39. The phrase "highly prized" in
line 15 is closest in meaning to

(A) valuable
(B) unique
(C) stylish
(D) attractive

3 3 3 3 3 3 3 3 3 3 | 3

40. When do *Acacia* trees bloom in Australia?

(A) February
(B) Summer
(C) August
(D) Spring

Questions 41–50

In 1626, Peter Minuit, governor of the Dutch settlements in North America known as New Amsterdam, negotiated with Canarsee Indian chiefs for the purchase of Manhattan Island for
Line merchandise valued at sixty guilders or about $24.12. He purchased
(5) the island for the Dutch West India Company.

The next year, Fort Amsterdam was built by the company at the extreme southern tip of the island. Because attempts to encourage Dutch immigration were not immediately successful, offers, generous by the standards of the era, were extended throughout Europe.
(10) Consequently, the settlement became the most heterogeneous of the North American colonies. By 1637, the fort had expanded into the village of New Amsterdam, and other small communities had grown up around it, including New Haarlem and Stuyvesant's Bouwery, and New Amsterdam began to prosper, developing char-
(15) acteristics of religious and linguistic tolerance unusual for the times. By 1643, it was reported that eighteen different languages were heard in New Amsterdam alone.

Among the multilingual settlers was a large group of English colonists from Connecticut and Massachusetts who supported the
(20) English King's claim to all of New Netherlands set out in a charter that gave the territory to his brother James, the Duke of York. In 1664, when the English sent a formidable fleet of warships into the New Amsterdam harbor, Dutch governor Peter Stuyvesant surrendered without resistance.

(25) When the English acquired the island, the village of New Amsterdam was renamed New York in honor of the Duke. By the onset of the Revolution, New York City was already a bustling commercial center. After the war, it was selected as the first capital of the United States. Although the government was eventually moved,
(30) first to Philadelphia and then to Washington, D.C., New York City has remained the unofficial commercial capital.

During the 1690s, New York became a haven for pirates who conspired with leading merchants to exchange supplies for their ships in return for a share in the plunder. As a colony, New York
(35) exchanged many agricultural products for English manufactured

3 3 3 3 3 3 3 3 3 3 3

goods. In addition, trade with the West Indies prospered. Three centuries after his initial trade with the Indians, Minuit's tiny investment was worth more than seven billion dollars.

41. Which of the following would be the best title for this passage?

(A) A History of New York City
(B) An Account of the Dutch Colonies
(C) A Biography of Peter Minuit
(D) The First Capital of the United States

42. What did the Indians receive in exchange for their island?

(A) Sixty Dutch guilders
(B) $24.12 U.S.
(C) Goods and supplies
(D) Land in New Amsterdam

43. Where was New Amsterdam located?

(A) In Holland
(B) In North America
(C) On the island of Manhattan
(D) In India

44. The word "heterogeneous" in line 10 could best be replaced by

(A) liberal
(B) renowned
(C) diverse
(D) prosperous

45. Why were so many languages spoken in New Amsterdam?

(A) The Dutch West India Company was owned by England.
(B) The Dutch West India Company allowed freedom of speech.
(C) The Dutch West India Company recruited settlers from many different countries in Europe.
(D) The Indians who lived there before the Dutch West India Company purchase spoke many languages.

46. The word "formidable" in line 22 is closest in meaning to

(A) powerful
(B) modern
(C) expensive
(D) unexpected

47. The name of New Amsterdam was changed

(A) to avoid a war with England
(B) to honor the Duke of York
(C) to attract more English colonists from Connecticut and Massachusetts
(D) to encourage trade during the 1690s

3 3 3 3 3 3 3 3 3 3 3

48. The word "it" in line 28 refers to
   - (A) Revolution
   - (B) New York City
   - (C) the island
   - (D) the first capital

49. Which city was the first capital of the new United States?

   - (A) New Amsterdam
   - (B) New York
   - (C) Philadelphia
   - (D) Washington

50. On what date was Manhattan valued at $7 billion?

   - (A) 1626
   - (B) 1726
   - (C) 1656
   - (D) 1926

THIS IS THE END OF THE READING COMPREHENSION SECTION OF TOEFL MODEL TEST 2.

IF YOU FINISH BEFORE 55 MINUTES HAS ENDED, CHECK YOUR WORK ON SECTION 3 ONLY.

DO NOT READ OR WORK ON ANY OTHER SECTION OF THE TEST.

STOP STOP STOP **STOP** STOP STOP STOP

END OF TOEFL MODEL TEST 2.

To check your answers for Model Test 2, refer to the Answer Key on page 378. For an explanation of the answers, refer to the Explanatory Answers for Model Test 2 on pages 397–409.

THE TEST OF WRITTEN ENGLISH (TWE) FOLLOWS.

Test of Written English (TWE) Model Test 2

When you take a Model Test, you should use one sheet of paper, both sides. Time each Model Test carefully. After you have read the topic, you should spend 30 minutes writing. For results that would be closest to the actual testing situation, it is recommended that an English teacher score your test, using the guidelines on page 242 of this book.

In your opinion, what is the best way to choose a marriage partner? Use specific reasons and examples why you think this approach is best.

Notes

How to Answer Questions for Model Tests 3–4

If you use the CD-ROM that supplements the larger version of this book, *Barron's How to Prepare for the TOEFL*, to take Model Tests 3 and 4, you will not need Answer Sheets. If you choose not to purchase the larger version or you do not have access to a computer, mark your responses to Model Tests 3 and 4 directly on the tests provided in the book.

For all multiple choice questions that require you to choose one answer, fill in the oval of the letter that corresponds to the answer you have chosen.

The Palo Verde tree _____ in spring.

Ⓐ has beautiful yellow
    blossoms
Ⓑ beautiful yellow blossoms
Ⓒ having beautiful yellow
    blossoms
Ⓓ with beautiful yellow
    blossoms

The Palo Verde tree _____ in spring.

● has beautiful yellow
    blossoms
Ⓑ beautiful yellow blossoms
Ⓒ having beautiful yellow
    blossoms
Ⓓ with beautiful yellow
    blossoms

For all questions that require you to choose two answers, mark an X in the squares that correspond to the answers you have chosen.

According to the professor what was the Hemingway style?

Click on two answers

[A] Powerful descriptions
[B] Imaginative details
[C] Short sentences
[D] Difficult symbolism

According to the professor what was the Hemingway style?

Click on two answers

[X] Powerful descriptions
[B] Imaginative details
[X] Short sentences
[D] Difficult symbolism

For questions that require you to click on sentences to move them into categories on charts, write letters on the charts that correspond to the sentences you have chosen.

How did Hemingway use his experience in different novels?

Click on the sentence.

Then click on the space where it belongs. Use each sentence only once.

A He was fishing in the of Gulf of Mexico.
B He was driving an ambulance in Italy.
C He was working as a newspaper reporter in Paris.

The Sun Also Rises	
A Farewell to Arms	
The Old Man and the Sea	

How did Hemingway use his experience in different novels?

Click on the sentence.

Then click on the space where it belongs. Use each sentence only once.

A He was fishing in the Gulf Mexico.
B He was driving an ambulance in Italy.
C He was working as a newspaper reporter in Paris.

The Sun Also Rises	C
A Farewell to Arms	B
The Old Man and the Sea	A

For all questions that require you to put events in order, write letters in the numbered boxes that correspond to the sequence you have chosen.

The professor briefly describes Hemingway's life as an author. Summarize the biographical data by putting the events in order.

Click on the sentence. Then click on the space where it belongs. Use each sentence only once.

- ⒜ Hemingway wrote about his experiences as an ambulance driver during the war
- ⒝ Hemingway received the Nobel prize for literature
- ⒞ Hemingway published *The Old Man and the Sea*
- ⒟ Hemingway was a newspaper reporter in Paris

1

2

3

4

The professor briefly describes Hemingway's life as an author. Summarize the biographical data by putting the events in order.

Click on the sentence. Then click on the space where it belongs. Use each sentence only once.

- ⒜ Hemingway wrote about his experiences as an ambulance driver during the war
- ⒝ Hemingway received the Nobel prize for literature
- ⒞ Hemingway published *The Old Man and the Sea*
- ⒟ Hemingway was a newspaper reporter in Paris

1 D

2 A

3 C

4 B

For all questions that require you to click on a word or phrase, circle the word or phrase in the passage.

Look at the word one in the passage. Click on the word or phrase in the bold text that one refers to.

Look at the word one in the passage. Click on the word or phrase in the bold text that one refers to.

Solar astronomers do know that the Sun is divided into five general layers or zones. Starting at the outside and going down into the sun, the zones are the corona, chromosphere, photosphere, convection zone, and finally the core. The first three zones are regarded as the Sun's atmosphere. But since the Sun has no solid surface, it is hard to tell where the atmosphere ends and the main body of the Sun begins.

The Sun's outermost layer begins about 10,000 miles above the visible surface and goes outward for millions of miles. This is the only part of the Sun that can be seen during an eclipse such as the one in February 1979. At any other time, the corona can be seen only when special instruments are used on cameras and telescopes to block the light from the photosphere.

The corona is a brilliant, pearly white, filmy light, about as bright as the full Moon. Its beautiful rays are a sensational sight during an eclipse. The corona's rays flash out in a brilliant fan that has wispy spikelike rays near the Sun's north and south poles. The corona is generally thickest at the Sun's equator.

The corona is made up of gases streaming

Solar astronomers do know that the Sun is divided into five general layers or zones. Starting at the outside and going down into the sun, the zones are the corona, chromosphere, photosphere, convection zone, and finally the core. The first three zones are regarded as the Sun's atmosphere. But since the Sun has no solid surface, it is hard to tell where the atmosphere ends and the main body of the Sun begins.

The Sun's outermost layer begins about 10,000 miles above the visible surface and goes outward for millions of miles. This is the only part of the Sun that can be seen during an eclipse **such as the one in February 1979.** At any other time, the corona can be seen only when special instruments are used on cameras and telescopes to block the light from the photosphere.

The corona is a brilliant, pearly white, filmy light, about as bright as the full Moon. Its beautiful rays are a sensational sight during an eclipse. The corona's rays flash out in a brilliant fan that has wispy spikelike rays near the Sun's north and south poles. The corona is generally thickest at the Sun's equator.

The corona is made up of gases streaming

For all questions that require you to click on a sentence, circle the sentence in the passage.

Click on the sentence in paragraph 4 or 5 in which the author compares the light of the Sun's outermost layer to that of another astronomical body.

Paragraphs 4 and 5 are marked with arrows [→]

Click on the sentence in paragraph 4 or 5 in which the author compares the light of the Sun's outermost layer to that of another astronomical body.

Paragraphs 4 and 5 are marked with arrows [→]

cameras and telescopes to block the light from the photosphere.

→ The corona is a brilliant, pearly white, filmy light, about as bright as the full Moon. Its beautiful rays are a sensational sight during an eclipse. The corona's rays flash out in a brilliant fan that has wispy spikelike rays near the Sun's north and south poles. The corona is generally thickest at the Sun's equator.

→ The corona is made up of gases streaming outward at tremendous speeds that reach a temperature of more than 2 million degrees Fahrenheit. The gas thins out as it reaches the space around the planets. By the time the gas of the corona reaches the Earth it has a relatively low density.

cameras and telescopes to block the light from the photosphere.

→ The corona is a brilliant, pearly white, filmy light, about as bright as the full Moon. Its beautiful rays are a sensational sight during an eclipse. The corona's rays flash out in a brilliant fan that has wispy spikelike rays near the Sun's north and south poles. The corona is generally thickest at the Sun's equator.

→ The corona is made up of gases streaming outward at tremendous speeds that reach a temperature of more than 2 million degrees Fahrenheit. The gas thins out as it reaches the space around the planets. By the time the gas of the corona reaches the Earth it has a relatively low density.

For all questions that require you to add a sentence, circle the square [■] where the sentence is to be inserted.

The following sentence can be added to paragraph 1.

At the center of the Earth's solar system lies the Sun.

Where would it best fit in paragraph 1? Click on the square [■] to add the sentence to the paragraph.

Paragraph 1 is marked with an arrow [→].

→ ■ The temperature of the Sun is over 10,000 degrees Fahrenheit at the surface, but it rises to perhaps more than 27,000,000° at the center. ■The Sun is so much hotter than the Earth that matter can exist only as a gas, except perhaps at the core. In the core of the Sun, the pressures are so great that, despite the high temperature, there may be a small solid core. ■However, no one really knows, since the center of the Sun can never be directly observed. ■

Solar astronomers do know that the Sun is divided into five general layers or zones. Starting at the outside and going down into the sun, the zones are the corona, chromosphere, photosphere, convection zone, and finally the core. The first three zones are regarded as the Sun's atmosphere. But since the Sun has no solid surface, it is hard to tell where the atmosphere ends and the main body of the Sun begins.

The Sun's outermost layer begins about 10,000 miles above the visible surface and goes outward for millions of miles. This is the only part of the Sun that can be seen during an eclipse such as the one in

The following sentence can be added to paragraph 1.

At the center of the Earth's solar system lies the Sun.

Where would it best fit in paragraph 1? Click on the square [■] to add the sentence to the paragraph.

Paragraph 1 is marked with an arrow [→].

→ (■)The temperature of the Sun is over 10,000 degrees Fahrenheit at the surface, but it rises to perhaps more than 27,000,000° at the center. ■The Sun is so much hotter than the Earth that matter can exist only as a gas, except perhaps at the core. In the core of the Sun, the pressures are so great that, despite the high temperature, there may be a small solid core. ■However, no one really knows, since the center of the Sun can never be directly observed. ■

Solar astronomers do know that the Sun is divided into five general layers or zones. Starting at the outside and going down into the sun, the zones are the corona, chromosphere, photosphere, convection zone, and finally the core. The first three zones are regarded as the Sun's atmosphere. But since the Sun has no solid surface, it is hard to tell where the atmosphere ends and the main body of the Sun begins.

The Sun's outermost layer begins about 10,000 miles above the visible surface and goes outward for millions of miles. This is the only part of the Sun that can be seen during an eclipse such as the one in

Model Test 3
Computer-Assisted TOEFL

Section 1:
Listening

The Listening section of the test measures the ability to understand conversations and talks in English. You will use headphones to listen to the conversations and talks. While you are listening, pictures of the speakers or other information will be presented on your computer screen. There are two parts to the Listening section, with special directions for each part.

On the day of the test, the amount of time you will have to answer all the questions will appear on the computer screen. The time you spend listening to the test material will not be counted. The listening material and questions about it will be presented only one time. You will not be allowed to take notes or have any paper at your computer. You will both see and hear the questions before the answer choices appear. You can take as much time as you need to select an answer; however, it will be to your advantage to answer the questions as quickly as possible. You may change your answer as many times as you want before you confirm it. After you have confirmed an answer, you will not be able to return to the question.

Before you begin working on the Listening section, you will have an opportunity to adjust the volume of the sound. You will not be able to change the volume after you have started the test.

QUESTION DIRECTIONS — Part A

In Part A of the Listening section, you will hear short conversations between two people. In some of the conversations, each person speaks only once. In other conversations, one or both of the people speak more than once. Each conversation is followed by one question about it.

Each question in this part has four answer choices. You should click on the best answer to each question. Answer the questions on the basis of what is stated or implied by the speakers.

1. What does the woman mean?

   Ⓐ She thinks the man is too tired to go to the movie.
   Ⓑ She really wants to go to the movie.
   Ⓒ She wants to go to class.
   Ⓓ She does not want to go to the movie.

2. What is the man going to do?

   Ⓐ He will borrow some typing paper from the woman.
   Ⓑ He will lend the woman some typing paper.
   Ⓒ He will type the woman's paper.
   Ⓓ He will buy some typing paper for the woman.

3. What can be inferred about the man?

   Ⓐ He is a student at the university.
   Ⓑ He is not driving a car.
   Ⓒ He knows the woman.
   Ⓓ He needs to go to the drug store.

4. What does the man imply?

   Ⓐ He could not stay with his parents.
   Ⓑ He did not want to change his plans.
   Ⓒ He will not go to summer school.
   Ⓓ He has completed all the courses.

5. What are the speakers discussing?

   Ⓐ The telephone
   Ⓑ An apartment
   Ⓒ Utilities
   Ⓓ Furniture

6. What does the woman imply?

   Ⓐ She likes Dr. Taylor's class.
   Ⓑ She is not sure how Dr. Taylor feels.
   Ⓒ She did not get an A on the paper.
   Ⓓ She is not doing very well in the class.

7. What does the man suggest that the woman do?

   Ⓐ Pay ten dollars an hour
   Ⓑ Be a subject in an experiment
   Ⓒ Ask Sandy to participate
   Ⓓ Go to a psychologist

8. What can be inferred about the study group meeting?

   Ⓐ The speakers did not go to the study group meeting.
   Ⓑ The woman went to the study group meeting, but the man did not.
   Ⓒ The man went to the study group meeting, but the woman did not.
   Ⓓ Both speakers went to the study group meeting.

9. What does the man mean?

   Ⓐ The woman can borrow his pen.
   Ⓑ A pen might be a good gift.
   Ⓒ Her advisor would probably like a card.
   Ⓓ A gift is not necessary.

10. What does the woman mean?

   Ⓐ She does not want to leave.
   Ⓑ She must stay.
   Ⓒ She did not like the dorm.
   Ⓓ She is undecided.

11. What does the woman imply?

    (A) She is not going home now.
    (B) She has already had some exercise.
    (C) She does not like to go to the gym.
    (D) She does not want to spend time with the man.

12. What does the woman imply?

    (A) The man may be taking on too much.
    (B) The job is more important than school.
    (C) The opportunity is very good.
    (D) The contract may not be valid.

13. What does the man suggest the woman do?

    (A) Call his family
    (B) Write a letter
    (C) Send postcards
    (D) Buy presents

14. What are the speakers discussing?

    (A) The length of time that it takes to get an answer from a university
    (B) Where the woman will go to school
    (C) States in the Midwest
    (D) The University of Minnesota

15. What will the woman probably do?

    (A) Buy a ticket
    (B) Go to room 27
    (C) Take a test in room 32
    (D) Show the man her ticket

16. What can be inferred about the woman?

    (A) She wasn't able to attend the reception.
    (B) She is an honors student.
    (C) She likes flowers very much.
    (D) She is a teacher.

17. What does the woman suggest that Terry do?

    (A) Try to be in class more often
    (B) Try to get the work done
    (C) Take the class twice
    (D) Take the class next term

18. What does the woman say about Margaret?

    (A) She is staying at a motel.
    (B) She is not working now.
    (C) She is saving her money for school.
    (D) She is studying very hard.

19. What does the man mean?

    (A) He does not like English.
    (B) Graduate school is easier than teaching.
    (C) It is not surprising that the woman is doing well.
    (D) The course is very interesting.

20. What problem do the students have?

    (A) They are going to make a group presentation.
    (B) They don't want to have Jane in their group.
    (C) Carl does not want to be in their group.
    (D) They are not good presenters.

QUESTION DIRECTIONS — Part B

In Part B of the Listening section, you will hear several longer conversations and talks. Each conversation or talk is followed by several questions. The conversations, talks, and questions will not be repeated.

The conversations and talks are about a variety of topics. You do not need special knowledge of the topics to answer the questions correctly. Rather, you should answer each question on the basis of what is stated or implied by the speakers in the conversations or talks.

For most of the questions, you will need to click on the best of four possible answers. Some questions will have special directions. The special directions will appear in a box on the computer screen.

21. What problem do the speakers have?

    Ⓐ They do not have a syllabus.
    Ⓑ They do not understand the requirement for the research paper.
    Ⓒ They do not have an appointment with the professor.
    Ⓓ They do not know the professor's office hours.

22. How much does the research paper count toward the grade for the course?

    Ⓐ It is not clear from the syllabus.
    Ⓑ It is valued at half of the total points for the course.
    Ⓒ It is worth ten points.
    Ⓓ It will count thirty points.

23. What did the professor say last week?

    Ⓐ She mentioned presentations.
    Ⓑ She discussed the syllabus.
    Ⓒ She answered questions.
    Ⓓ She made appointments.

24. What will the students probably do?

    Ⓐ Prepare a presentation of the research
    Ⓑ Make an appointment to see the professor
    Ⓒ Ask questions about the assignment in class
    Ⓓ Go to see the professor during office hours

25. What is the main purpose of this lecture?

    Ⓐ Captain Cook's life
    Ⓑ History of Hawaii
    Ⓒ Captain Cook's exploration of Hawaii
    Ⓓ Hawaiian culture

26. According to the lecturer, what were the two ships commanded by Captain Cook?

    Click on 2 answers.

    Ⓐ The Third Voyage
    Ⓑ The Resolution
    Ⓒ The Discovery
    Ⓓ The England

27. Why does the professor mention the name *Launo?*

   (A) It was the original name for the Hawaiian Islands before Cook's arrival.
   (B) It was the name of the king of Hawaii at the time of Cook's exploration.
   (C) It was the name of the god that the islanders believed Cook embodied.
   (D) It was the name of the welcome ceremony that the islanders gave Cook.

28. The professor briefly explains a sequence of events in the history of Hawaii.
   Summarize the sequence by putting the events in order.

   Click on a sentence. Then click on the space where it belongs.

   Use each sentence only once.

   A   Captain Cook and four of his crew were killed.
   B   The islanders and the crew began to fight.
   C   The king was to be taken hostage.
   D   A small boat was stolen from the crew.

   1 [   ]
   2 [   ]
   3 [   ]
   4 [   ]

29. What is an alloy?

   (A) Impure metals that occur accidentally
   (B) Metals melted into liquid form
   (C) A planned combination of metals for a specific purpose
   (D) Industrial metals that do not have to be very pure

30. What does the speaker say about the properties of alloys?

   Click on 2 answers.

   A   They are chosen for a particular purpose.
   B   They are combined in specific proportions.
   C   They are difficult to determine because there is more than one metal involved.
   D   They occur accidentally in nature.

31. Why does the speaker use the example of the aircraft industry?

   (A) To demonstrate how alloys can be used to solve industrial problems
   (B) To emphasize the importance of the aviation industry
   (C) To compare alloys and other mixtures
   (D) To illustrate how metals can be used without alloying them

32. What is the difference between combinations of metals in nature and alloys?

    Ⓐ Mixtures of metals in nature are very pure.
    Ⓑ Combinations of metals do not occur in nature.
    Ⓒ Metals combined in nature are mixed in random proportion.
    Ⓓ Alloys are mixtures, but metals that occur in nature are not.

33. What do the speakers mainly discuss?

    Ⓐ British English pronunciation
    Ⓑ Spelling patterns
    Ⓒ British and American English
    Ⓓ Movies

34. How are the words below referred to in the discussion?

    Click on a word. Then click on the empty box in the correct column. Use each word only once.

    Ⓐ color   Ⓑ theater
    Ⓒ centre   Ⓓ honour

American English spelling	
British English spelling	

35. What can be inferred about the word *flat* in British English?

    Ⓐ It has a different spelling from that of American English.
    Ⓑ It has a different meaning from that of American English.
    Ⓒ The pronunciation is so different that it cannot be understood by Americans.
    Ⓓ It is really about the same in American English.

36. On what did the class agree?

    Ⓐ British English and American English are the same.
    Ⓑ British English and American English are so different that Americans cannot understand Englishmen when they speak.
    Ⓒ British English and American English have different spelling and vocabulary but the same pronunciation.
    Ⓓ British English and American English have slightly different spelling, vocabulary, and pronunciation, but Americans and Englishmen still understand each other.

37. What is the presentation mainly about?

    Ⓐ The national department of education
    Ⓑ School boards
    Ⓒ Public schools in the United States
    Ⓓ Local control of schools

38. What surprised the presenter about her research?

    (A) Public schools are not the same throughout the United States.

    (B) The school board members are not professional educators.

    (C) The federal department is not the same as a department of education in many other countries.

    (D) The members of the school board serve without pay.

39. How does each of the persons identified below contribute to the operation of schools in the United States?

    Click on a word. Then click on the empty box in the correct row. Use each word only once.

    A   superintendent

    B   school board member

    C   resident of the district

governs the local school district	*B*
carries out the policies of the governing board	*A*
elects the members of the governing board	*C*

40. According to the speaker, what is the function of the department of education in the United States?

    Click on 2 answers.

    A   To support research projects

    B   To organize a national curriculum

    C   To monitor national legislation for schools

    D   To appoint local school boards

41. What kind of meal plan does the man decide to buy?

    Click on 2 answers.

    A   Breakfast

    B   Lunch

    C   Dinner

    D   Supper

42. How much does the plan cost?

    (A) Fourteen dollars a week

    (B) Thirty dollars a week

    (C) Thirty-six dollars a week

    (D) Forty-two dollars a week

43. Why do most residents order a pizza or go out to eat on Sundays?

    (A) Many of them live close enough to go home for the day.

    (B) They are tired of the food in the dormitory.

    (C) No meals are served on Sunday.

    (D) Some of them have dates on the weekend.

44. How will the man pay for the meals?

   Ⓐ He will pay the woman in cash for the first quarter.
   Ⓑ He will use his credit card to pay the woman.
   Ⓒ He will wait to receive a bill from the dormitory.
   Ⓓ He will write a check on a form provided by the woman.

45. What is hydroponics?

   Ⓐ Growing plants without soil
   Ⓑ Mixing nutrients in water
   Ⓒ Finding the chemical composition of soil
   Ⓓ Solving problems in the water system

46. According to the speaker, why are roots important to plants?

     Click on 2 answers.

   Ⓐ To absorb water and nutrients
   Ⓑ To take in oxygen
   Ⓒ To suspend the plants directly in the solution
   Ⓓ To filter out toxins

47. Why was the pump attached to the tank in this experiment?

   Ⓐ It was needed to mix the nutrients in the solution.
   Ⓑ It was used to pump out harmful chemicals.
   Ⓒ It was required to pump oxygen into the solution.
   Ⓓ It was necessary to anchor the plants.

48. What does the professor want the students to do with the specimen of the nutrient solution?

   Ⓐ Take a taste of it
   Ⓑ Make a drawing of it
   Ⓒ Observe it and draw conclusions
   Ⓓ Put it in the tank

49. Who was Harriet Tubman?

   Ⓐ She was one of the first freed slaves to work on the railroad.
   Ⓑ She was a slave who worked underground in the mines.
   Ⓒ She was a former slave who lived in Canada.
   Ⓓ She was a slave who escaped from her owners in Maryland during the Civil War.

50. What impressed the man about Harriet Tubman's story?

   Ⓐ She used the North Star to guide her to a free state.
   Ⓑ She returned to Maryland to help three hundred slaves escape.
   Ⓒ She founded the underground railroad.
   Ⓓ She was a slave for nineteen years.

Section 2: Structure

This section measures the ability to recognize language that is appropriate for standard written English. There are two types of questions in this section.

In the first type of question, there are incomplete sentences. Beneath each sentence, there are four words or phrases. You will choose the one word or phrase that best completes the sentence.

Clicking on a choice darkens the oval. After you click on **Next** and **Confirm Answer**, the next question will be presented.

The second type of question has four underlined words or phrases. You will choose the one underlined word or phrase that must be changed for the sentence to be correct.

Clicking on an underlined word or phrase will darken it. After you click on **Next** and **Confirm Answer**, the next question will be presented.

1. Gunpowder, in some ways
   ___(A)___
   the most effective of all the
   ___(B)___   ___(C)___
   explosive materials, were a
   ___(D)___
   mixture of potassium nitrate,

   charcoal, and sulfur.

2. As the demand increases,

   manufacturers who previously
   ___(A)___
   produced only a large, luxury

   car is compelled to make
   ___(B)___   ___(C)___
   a smaller model in order to
   ___(D)___
   compete in the market.

3. There are twenty species of wild
   ___(A)___
   roses in North America, all of

   which have prickly stems,
   ___(B)___
   pinnate leaves, and large

   flowers, which usually smell
   ___(C)___
   sweetly.
   ___(D)___

4. Professional people expect ------
   when it is necessary to cancel an
   appointment.

   (A) you to call them
   (B) that you would call them
   (C) your calling them
   (D) that you are calling them

5. In a new culture, many embarrassing situations occur ------- a misunderstanding.

   (A) for
   (B) of
   (C) because of
   (D) because

6. Factoring is the process of
   <u>A</u>
   <u>finding</u> two or more expressions
   <u>B</u>
   <u>whose</u> product is <u>equal as</u> the
   <u>C</u>   <u>D</u>
   given expression.

7. Schizophrenia, a behavioral

   disorder <u>typified by</u> a
   <u>A</u>
   <u>fundamental</u> break with reality,
   <u>B</u>
   may be <u>triggered</u> by genetic
   <u>C</u>
   predisposition, <u>stressful</u>, drugs,
   <u>D</u>
   or infections.

8. Sedimentary rocks are formed
   below the surface of the earth
   -------- very high temperatures
   and pressures.

   Ⓐ where there are
   Ⓑ there are
   Ⓒ where are there
   Ⓓ there are where

9. If Grandma Moses <u>having</u> been
   <u>A</u>
   able to continue <u>farming</u>, she
   <u>B</u>
   may never have <u>begun</u> to <u>paint</u>.
   <u>C</u>   <u>D</u>

10. A computer is usually chosen
    because of its simplicity of oper-
    ation and ease of maintenance
    ------ its capacity to store infor-
    mation.

    Ⓐ the same as
    Ⓑ the same
    Ⓒ as well as
    Ⓓ as well

11. Although the Red Cross <u>accepts</u>
    <u>A</u>
    blood from most donors, the

    nurses will not <u>leave</u> you <u>give</u>
    <u>B</u>   <u>C</u>
    blood if you have just <u>had</u> a
    <u>D</u>
    cold.

12. --------- that gold was discovered
    at Sutter's Mill and that the Cali-
    fornia Gold Rush began.

    Ⓐ Because in 1848
    Ⓑ That in 1848
    Ⓒ In 1848 that it was
    Ⓓ It was in 1848

13. Frost occurs in valleys and on
    low grounds --------- on adjacent
    hills.

    Ⓐ more frequently as
    Ⓑ as frequently than
    Ⓒ more frequently than
    Ⓓ frequently than

14. The native people of the

    Americas <u>are called</u> Indians
    <u>A</u>
    <u>because</u> when Columbus landed
    <u>B</u>
    in the Bahamas <u>in</u> 1492, he
    <u>C</u>
    thought that he <u>has reached</u> the
    <u>D</u>
    East Indies.

15. In the relatively short history of
          Ⓐ
    industrial developing
            Ⓑ
    in the United States, New York
        Ⓒ
    City has played a vital role.
         Ⓓ

16. When a body enters the earth's
    atmosphere, it travels ----------- .

    Ⓐ very rapidly
    Ⓑ in a rapid manner
    Ⓒ fastly
    Ⓓ with great speed

17. Employers often require that
    candidates have not only a
    degree ---------- .

    Ⓐ but two years experience
    Ⓑ also two years experience
    Ⓒ but also two years experi-
        ence
    Ⓓ but more two years experi-
        ence

18. The salary of a bus driver is
    much higher ----------- .

    Ⓐ in comparison with the
        salary of a teacher
    Ⓑ than a teacher
    Ⓒ than that of a teacher
    Ⓓ to compare as a teacher

19. Farmers look forward to
    ------------ every summer.

    Ⓐ participating in the county
        fairs
    Ⓑ participate in the county
        fairs
    Ⓒ be participating in the coun-
        ty fairs
    Ⓓ have participated in the
        county fairs

20. A turtle differs from all other
              Ⓐ   Ⓑ
    reptiles in that its body is encased

    in a protective shell of their own.
                     Ⓒ Ⓓ

Section 3: Reading

This section measures the ability to read and understand short passages similar in topic and style to those that students are likely to encounter in North American universities and colleges. This section contains reading passages and questions about the passages. There are several different types of questions in this section.

In the Reading section, you will first have the opportunity to read the passage.

You will use the scroll bar to view the rest of the passage.

When you have finished reading the passage, you will use the mouse to click on **Proceed**. Then the questions about the passage will be presented. You are to choose the one best answer to each question. Answer all questions about the information in a passage on the basis of what is stated or implied in that passage.

Most of the questions will be multiple choice questions. To answer these questions you will click on a choice below the question.

To answer some questions you will click on a word or phrase.

To answer some questions you will click on a sentence in the passage.

To answer some questions you will click on a square to add a sentence to the passage.

    The computer screens for selected questions in the Reading Section have been printed in this book to provide you with orientation to the format of the Computer-Based TOEFL. Use the screen to find the place in the original reading passage that corresponds to the question you are answering.

Perhaps it was his own lack of adequate schooling that inspired Horace Mann to work so hard for the important reforms in education that he accomplished. While he was still a boy, his father and older brother died, and he became responsible for supporting his family. Like most of the children in his town, he attended school only two or three months a year. Later, with the help of several teachers, he was able to study law and become a member of the Massachusetts bar, but he never forgot those early struggles.

While serving in the Massachusetts legislature, he signed a historic education bill that set up a state board of education. Without regret, he gave up his successful legal practice and political career to become the first secretary of the board. There he exercised an enormous influence during the critical period of reconstruction that brought into existence the American graded elementary school as a substitute for the older district school system. Under his leadership, the curriculum was restructured, the school year was increased to a minimum of six months, and mandatory schooling was extended to age sixteen. Other important reforms included the establishment of state normal schools for teacher training, institutes for inservice teacher education, and lyceums for adult education. He was also instrumental in improving salaries for teachers and creating school libraries.

Mann's ideas about school reform were developed and distributed in twelve annual reports to the state of Massachusetts that he wrote during his tenure as secretary of education. Considered quite radical at the time, the Massachusetts reforms later served as a model for the nation. Mann was recognized as the father of public education.

During his lifetime, Horace Mann worked tirelessly to extend educational opportunities to agrarian families and the children of poor laborers. In one of his last speeches he summed up his philosophy of education and life: "Be ashamed to die until you have won some victory for humanity." Surely, his own life was an example of that philosophy.

1. Which of the following titles would best express the main topic of the passage?

   (A) The Father of American Public Education
   (B) Philosophy of Education
   (C) The Massachusetts State Board of Education
   (D) Politics of Educational Institutions

2. Why does the author mention Horace Mann's early life?

   (A) As an example of the importance of an early education for success
   (B) To make the biography more complete
   (C) Because it served as the inspiration for his later work in education
   (D) In tribute to the teachers who helped him succeed

3. Look at the word **extended** in the passage. Click on another word or phrase in the **bold** text that is closest in meaning to extended.

   | More Available |

   While serving in the Massachusetts legislature, he signed a historic education bill that set up a state board of education. Without regret, he gave up his successful legal practice and political career to become the first secretary of the board. There he exercised an enormous influence during the critical period of reconstruction that brought into existence the American graded elementary school as a substitute for the older district school system. **Under his leadership, the curriculum was restructured, the school year was increased to a minimum of six months, and mandatory schooling was extended to age sixteen.** Other important reforms included the establishment of state normal schools for teacher training, institutes for inservice teacher education, and lyceums for adult education. He was also instrumental in improving salaries for teachers and creating school libraries.

   Mann's ideas about school reform were developed and distributed in twelve annual reports to the state of Massachusetts that he wrote during his tenure as secretary of education. Considered quite radical at the time, the Massachusetts reforms later served as a model for the nation. Mann was

4. With which of the following statements would the author most probably agree?

Ⓐ Horace Mann's influence on American education was very great.

Ⓑ A small but important influence on American education was exerted by Horace Mann.

Ⓒ Few educators fully understood Horace Mann's influence on American education.

Ⓓ The influence on American education by Horace Mann was not accepted or appreciated.

5. Horace Mann advocated all of the following EXCEPT

Ⓐ a state board of education
Ⓑ a district school system
Ⓒ classes for adults
Ⓓ graded elementary schools

6. The word struggles in paragraph 1 could best be replaced by

Ⓐ valuable experiences
Ⓑ happy situations
Ⓒ influential people
Ⓓ difficult times

> **Beginning**
>
> Perhaps it was his own lack of adequate schooling that inspired Horace Mann to work so hard for the important reforms in education that he accomplished. While he was still a boy, his father and older brother died, and he became responsible for supporting his family. Like most of the children in his town, he attended school only two or three months a year. Later, with the help of several teachers, he was able to study law and become a member of the Massachusetts bar, but he never forgot those early struggles.
>
> While serving in the Massachusetts legislature, he signed a historic education bill that set up a state board of education. Without regret, he gave up his successful legal practice and political career to become the first secretary of the board. There he exercised an enormous influence during the critical period of reconstruction that brought into existence the American graded elementary school as a substitute for the older district school system. Under his leadership, the curriculum was restructured, the school year was increased to a minimum of six months, and mandatory schooling was extended to age sixteen. Other important reforms included the

7. The word there refers to

Ⓐ the Massachusetts legislature
Ⓑ the state board of education
Ⓒ Mann's legal practice
Ⓓ his political career

> **More Available**
>
> able to study law and become a member of the Massachusetts bar, but he never forgot those early struggles.
>
> While serving in the Massachusetts legislature, he signed a historic education bill that set up a state board of education. Without regret, he gave up his successful legal practice and political career to become the first secretary of the board. There he exercised an enormous influence during the critical period of reconstruction that brought into existence the American graded elementary school as a substitute for the older district school system. Under his leadership, the curriculum was restructured, the school year was increased to a minimum of six months, and mandatory schooling was extended to age sixteen. Other important reforms included the establishment of state normal schools for teacher training, institutes for inservice teacher education, and lyceums for adult education. He was also instrumental in improving salaries for teachers and creating school libraries.
>
> Mann's ideas about school reform were developed and distributed in twelve annual reports to the state of Massachusetts that he wrote during his

8. The word mandatory in paragraph 2 is closest in meaning to

Ⓐ required
Ⓑ equal
Ⓒ excellent
Ⓓ basic

More Available

exercised an enormous influence during the critical
period of reconstruction that brought into existence the
American graded elementary school as a substitute
for the older district school system. Under his
leadership, the curriculum was restructured, the
school year was increased to a minimum of six
months, and mandatory schooling was extended to
age sixteen. Other important reforms included the
establishment of state normal schools for teacher
training, institutes for inservice teacher education, and
lyceums for adult education. He was also instrumental
in improving salaries for teachers and creating school
libraries.

Mann's ideas about school reform were
developed and distributed in twelve annual reports to
the state of Massachusetts that he wrote during his
tenure as secretary of education. Considered quite
radical at the time, the Massachusetts reforms later
served as a model for the nation. Mann was
recognized as the father of public education.

During his lifetime, Horace Mann worked tirelessly
to extend educational opportunities to agrarian
families and the children of poor laborers. In one of his
last speeches he summed up his philosophy of

---

9. The reforms that Horace Mann achieved

Ⓐ were not very radical for the time
Ⓑ were used only by the state of Massachusetts
Ⓒ were later adopted by the nation as a model
Ⓓ were enforced by the Massachusetts bar

10. Click on the paragraph that explains how the educational reforms were distributed.

Scroll the passage to see all of the paragraphs.

11. With which of the following statements would Horace Mann most probably agree?

Ⓐ Think in new ways.
Ⓑ Help others.
Ⓒ Study as much as possible.
Ⓓ Work hard.

Organic architecture—that is, natural architecture—may be varied in concept and form, but it is always faithful to natural principles. Organic architecture rejects rules imposed by individual preference or mere aesthetics in order to remain true to the nature of the site, the materials, the purpose of the structure, and the people who will ultimately use it. If these natural principles are upheld, then a bank cannot be built to look like a Greek temple. Form does not follow function; form is inseparable from function. In other words, a building should be inspired by nature's forms and constructed with materials that retain and respect the natural characteristics of the setting to create harmony with its natural environment. It should maximize people's contact with and utilization of the outdoors. Furthermore, the rule of functionalism is upheld; that is, the principle of excluding everything that serves no practical purpose.

Natural principles then, are principles of design, not style, expressed by construction that reflects unity, balance, proportion, rhythm, and scale. Like a sculptor, the organic architect views the site and materials as an innate form that develops organically from within. Truth in architecture results in a natural, spontaneous structure in total harmony with the setting. For the most part, these structures find their geometric shapes in the contours of the land and their colors in the surrounding palette of nature.

From the outside, an organic structure is so much a part of nature that it is often obscured by it. In other words, it may not be possible for the eye to easily separate the man-made structure from the natural terrain. Natural light, air, and view permeate the whole structure, providing a sense of communication with the outdoors. From the inside, living spaces open into each other. The number of walls for separate rooms is reduced to a minimum, allowing the functional spaces

> to flow together. Moreover, the interiors are sparse.
> Organic architecture incorporates built-in architectural
> features such as benches and storage areas to take
> the place of furniture.

12. According to the passage, what is another name for organic architecture?

   Ⓐ Natural architecture
   Ⓑ Aesthetic architecture
   Ⓒ Principle architecture
   Ⓓ Varied architecture

13. The word ultimately in paragraph 1 could best be replaced by

   Ⓐ fortunately
   Ⓑ eventually
   Ⓒ supposedly
   Ⓓ obviously

14. Look at the word it in the passage. Click on the word or phrase in the **bold** text that it refers to.

Beginning

Organic architecture—that is, natural architecture—may be varied in concept and form, but it is always faithful to natural principles. Organic architecture rejects rules imposed by individual preference or mere aesthetics in order to remain true to the nature of the site, the materials, the purpose of the structure, and the people who will ultimately use it. If these natural principles are upheld, then a bank cannot be built to look like a Greek temple. Form does not follow function; form is inseparable from function. In other words, a building should be inspired by nature's forms and constructed with materials that retain and respect the natural characteristics of the setting to create harmony with its natural environment. It should maximize people's contact with and utilization of the outdoors. Furthermore, the rule of functionalism is upheld; that is, the principle of excluding everything that serves no practical purpose.

Natural principles then, are principles of design, not style, expressed by construction that reflects unity, balance, proportion, rhythm, and scale. Like a sculptor, the organic architect views the site and materials as an innate form that develops organically

---

Beginning

Organic architecture—that is, natural architecture—may be varied in concept and form, but it is always faithful to natural principles. Organic architecture rejects rules imposed by individual preference or mere aesthetics in order to remain true to the nature of the site, the materials, the purpose of the structure, and the people who will ultimately use it. If these natural principles are upheld, then a bank cannot be built to look like a Greek temple. Form does not follow function; form is inseparable from function. In other words, a building should be inspired by nature's forms and constructed with materials that retain and respect the natural characteristics of the setting to create harmony with its natural environment. It should maximize people's contact with and utilization of the outdoors. Furthermore, the rule of functionalism is upheld; that is, the principle of excluding everything that serves no practical purpose.

Natural principles then, are principles of design, not style, expressed by construction that reflects unity, balance, proportion, rhythm, and scale. Like a sculptor, the organic architect views the site and materials as an innate form that develops organically from within. Truth in architecture results in a natural,

15. The word upheld in paragraph 1
is closest in meaning to

Ⓐ invalidated
Ⓑ disputed
Ⓒ promoted
Ⓓ perceived

Beginning

Organic architecture—that is, natural
architecture—may be varied in concept and form, but
it is always faithful to natural principles. Organic
architecture rejects rules imposed by individual
preference or mere aesthetics in order to remain true
to the nature of the site, the materials, the purpose of
the structure, and the people who will ultimately use it.
If these natural principles are upheld, then a bank
cannot be built to look like a Greek temple. Form does
not follow function; form is inseparable from function.
In other words, a building should be inspired by
nature's forms and constructed with materials that
retain and respect the natural characteristics of the
setting to create harmony with its natural environment.
It should maximize people's contact with and
utilization of the outdoors. Furthermore, the rule of
functionalism is upheld; that is, the principle of
excluding everything that serves no practical purpose.
    Natural principles then, are principles of design,
not style, expressed by construction that reflects unity,
balance, proportion, rhythm, and scale. Like a
sculptor, the organic architect views the site and
materials as an innate form that develops organically
from within. Truth in architecture results in a natural,

---

16. With which of the following
statements would the author
most probably agree?

Ⓐ Form follows function.
Ⓑ Function follows form.
Ⓒ Function is not important to
form.
Ⓓ Form and function are one.

17. The following examples are all
representative of natural architecture EXCEPT

Ⓐ a bank that is built to look
like a Greek temple
Ⓑ a bank built so that the
location is important to the
structure
Ⓒ a bank that is built to con-
form to the colors of the
natural surroundings
Ⓓ a bank that is built to be
functional rather than beautiful

18. Why does the author compare an
organic architect to a sculptor?

Ⓐ To emphasize aesthetics
Ⓑ To give an example of natural principles
Ⓒ To make a point about the
development of geometry
Ⓓ To demonstrate the importance of style

19. The word obscured in paragraph 3 is closest in meaning to

Ⓐ difficult to see
Ⓑ in high demand
Ⓒ not very attractive
Ⓓ mutually beneficial

End

from within. Truth in architecture results in a natural,
spontaneous structure in total harmony with the
setting. For the most part, these structures find their
geometric shapes in the contours of the land and their
colors in the surrounding palette of nature.
    From the outside, an organic structure is so much
a part of nature that it is often obscured by it. In other
words, it may not be possible for the eye to easily
separate the man-made structure from the natural
terrain. Natural light, air, and view permeate the whole
structure, providing a sense of communication with the
outdoors. From the inside, living spaces open into
each other. The number of walls for separate rooms is
reduced to a minimum, allowing the functional spaces
to flow together. Moreover, the interiors are sparse.
Organic architecture incorporates built-in architectural
features such as benches and storage areas to take
the place of furniture.

20. Look at the word contours in the passage. Click on another word or phrase in the **bold** text that is closest in meaning to contours .

End

from within. Truth in architecture results in a natural, spontaneous structure in total harmony with the setting. **For the most part, these structures find their geometric shapes in the contours of the land and their colors in the surrounding palette of nature.**

From the outside, an organic structure is so much a part of nature that it is often obscured by it. In other words, it may not be possible for the eye to easily separate the man-made structure from the natural terrain. Natural light, air, and view permeate the whole structure, providing a sense of communication with the outdoors. From the inside, living spaces open into each other. The number of walls for separate rooms is reduced to a minimum, allowing the functional spaces to flow together. Moreover, the interiors are sparse. Organic architecture incorporates built-in architectural features such as benches and storage areas to take the place of furniture.

---

21. Click on the sentence in paragraph 3 that describes the furnishings appropriate for natural architecture.

Paragraph 3 is marked with an arrow (→).

End

from within. Truth in architecture results in a natural, spontaneous structure in total harmony with the setting. For the most part, these structures find their geometric shapes in the contours of the land and their colors in the surrounding palette of nature.
→ From the outside, an organic structure is so much a part of nature that it is often obscured by it. In other words, it may not be possible for the eye to easily separate the man-made structure from the natural terrain. Natural light, air, and view permeate the whole structure, providing a sense of communication with the outdoors. From the inside, living spaces open into each other. The number of walls for separate rooms is reduced to a minimum, allowing the functional spaces to flow together. Moreover, the interiors are sparse. Organic architecture incorporates built-in architectural features such as benches and storage areas to take the place of furniture.

---

22. Which of the following statements best describes the architect's view of nature?

(A) Nature should be conquered.
(B) Nature should not be considered.
(C) Nature should be respected.
(D) Nature should be improved.

Although its purpose and techniques were often magical, alchemy was, in many ways, the predecessor of modern science, especially the science of chemistry. The fundamental premise of alchemy derived from the best philosophical dogma and scientific practice of the time, and the majority of educated persons in the period from 1400 to 1600 believed that alchemy had great merit.

The earliest authentic works on European alchemy are those of the English monk Roger Bacon and the German philosopher St. Albertus Magnus. In their treatises they maintained that gold was the perfect metal and that inferior metals such as lead and mercury were removed by various degrees of imperfection from gold. They further asserted that these base metals could be transmuted to gold by blending them with a substance even more perfect than gold. This elusive substance was referred to as the "philosopher's stone." The process was called transmutation.

Most of the early alchemists were artisans who were accustomed to keeping trade secrets and often resorted to cryptic terminology to record the progress of their work. The term *sun* was used for gold, *moon* for silver, and the five known planets for base metals. This convention of substituting symbolic language attracted a group of mystical philosophers who compared the search for the perfect metal with the struggle of mankind for the perfection of the soul. The philosophers began to use the artisan's terms in the mystical literature that they produced. Thus, by the fourteenth century, alchemy had developed two distinct groups of practitioners—the laboratory alchemist and the literary alchemist. Both groups of alchemists continued to work throughout the history of alchemy, but, of course, it was the literary alchemist who was most likely to produce a written record; therefore, much of what is known about the science of alchemy is derived from philosophers rather than from the alchemists who labored in laboratories.

Despite centuries of experimentation, laboratory alchemists failed to produce gold from other materials. However, they did gain wide knowledge of chemical substances, discovered chemical properties, and invented many of the tools and techniques that are still used by chemists today. Many of the laboratory alchemists earnestly devoted themselves to the scientific discovery of new compounds and reactions and, therefore, must be considered the legitimate forefathers of modern chemistry. They continued to call themselves alchemists, but they were becoming true chemists.

23. Which of the following is the main point of the passage?

(A) There were both laboratory and literary alchemists.
(B) Base metals can be transmuted to gold by blending them with a substance more perfect than gold.
(C) Roger Bacon and St. Albertus Magnus wrote about alchemy.
(D) Alchemy was the predecessor of modern chemistry.

24. The word authentic in paragraph 2 could best be replaced by

(A) valuable
(B) genuine
(C) complete
(D) comprehensible

Beginning

Although its purpose and techniques were often magical, alchemy was, in many ways, the predecessor of modern science, especially the science of chemistry. The fundamental premise of alchemy derived from the best philosophical dogma and scientific practice of the time, and the majority of educated persons in the period from 1400 to 1600 believed that alchemy had great merit.

The earliest authentic works on European alchemy are those of the English monk Roger Bacon and the German philosopher St. Albertus Magnus. In their treatises they maintained that gold was the perfect metal and that inferior metals such as lead and mercury were removed by various degrees of imperfection from gold. They further asserted that these base metals could be transmuted to gold by blending them with a substance even more perfect than gold. This elusive substance was referred to as the "philosopher's stone." The process was called transmutation.

Most of the early alchemists were artisans who were accustomed to keeping trade secrets and often resorted to cryptic terminology to record the progress of their work. The term sun was used for gold, moon

25. Look at the word those in the passage. Click on the word or phrase in the **bold** text that those refers to.

Although its purpose and techniques were often magical, alchemy was, in many ways, the predecessor of modern science, especially the science of chemistry. The fundamental premise of alchemy derived from the best philosophical dogma and scientific practice of the time, and the majority of educated persons in the period from 1400 to 1600 believed that alchemy had great merit.

The earliest authentic works on European alchemy are those of the English monk Roger Bacon and the German philosopher St. Albertus Magnus. In their treatises they maintained that gold was the perfect metal and that inferior metals such as lead and mercury were removed by various degrees of imperfection from gold. They further asserted that these base metals could be transmuted to gold by blending them with a substance even more perfect than gold. This elusive substance was referred to as the "philosopher's stone." The process was called transmutation.

Most of the early alchemists were artisans who were accustomed to keeping trade secrets and often resorted to cryptic terminology to record the progress of their work. The term sun was used for gold, moon

26. According to the alchemists, what is the difference between base metals and gold?

    Ⓐ Perfection
    Ⓑ Chemical content
    Ⓒ Temperature
    Ⓓ Weight

27. Look at the word asserted in the passage. Click on the word or phrase in the **bold** text that is closest in meaning to asserted.

Although its purpose and techniques were often magical, alchemy was, in many ways, the predecessor of modern science, especially the science of chemistry. The fundamental premise of alchemy derived from the best philosophical dogma and scientific practice of the time, and the majority of educated persons in the period from 1400 to 1600 believed that alchemy had great merit.

The earliest authentic works on European alchemy are those of the English monk Roger Bacon and the German philosopher St. Albertus Magnus. **In their treatises they maintained that gold was the perfect metal and that inferior metals such as lead and mercury were removed by various degrees of imperfection from gold. They further** asserted **that these base metals could be transmuted to gold by blending them with a substance even more perfect than gold.** This elusive substance was referred to as the "philosopher's stone." The process was called transmutation.

Most of the early alchemists were artisans who were accustomed to keeping trade secrets and often resorted to cryptic terminology to record the progress of their work. The term sun was used for gold, moon

28. According to the passage, what is the "philosopher's stone?"

    Ⓐ Lead that was mixed with gold
    Ⓑ An element that was never found
    Ⓒ Another name for alchemy
    Ⓓ A base metal

29. Why did the early alchemists use the terms *sun* and *moon*?

    Ⓐ To keep the work secret
    Ⓑ To make the work more literary
    Ⓒ To attract philosophers
    Ⓓ To produce a written record

30. Who were the first alchemists?

    Ⓐ Chemists
    Ⓑ Writers
    Ⓒ Artisans
    Ⓓ Linguists

31. The word cryptic in paragraph 3 could be replaced by which of the following?

    Ⓐ scholarly
    Ⓑ secret
    Ⓒ foreign
    Ⓓ precise

More Available

than gold. This elusive substance was referred to as the "philosopher's stone." The process was called transmutation.

Most of the early alchemists were artisans who were accustomed to keeping trade secrets and often resorted to cryptic terminology to record the progress of their work. The term sun was used for gold, moon for silver, and the five known planets for base metals. This convention of substituting symbolic language attracted a group of mystical philosophers who compared the search for the perfect metal with the struggle of mankind for the perfection of the soul. The philosophers began to use the artisan's terms in the mystical literature that they produced. Thus, by the fourteenth century, alchemy had developed two distinct groups of practitioners—the laboratory alchemist and the literary alchemist. Both groups of alchemists continued to work throughout the history of alchemy, but, of course, it was the literary alchemist who was most likely to produce a written record; therefore, much of what is known about the science of alchemy is derived from philosophers rather than from the alchemists who labored in laboratories.

Despite centuries of experimentation, laboratory

---

32. In paragraph 3, the author suggests that we know about the history of alchemy because

    Ⓐ the laboratory alchemists kept secret notes
    Ⓑ the literary alchemists recorded it in writing
    Ⓒ the mystical philosophers were not able to hide the secrets of alchemy
    Ⓓ the historians were able to interpret the secret writings of the alchemists

    Paragraph 3 is marked with an arrow (→).

More Available

than gold. This elusive substance was referred to as the "philosopher's stone." The process was called transmutation.

→ Most of the early alchemists were artisans who were accustomed to keeping trade secrets and often resorted to cryptic terminology to record the progress of their work. The term sun was used for gold, moon for silver, and the five known planets for base metals. This convention of substituting symbolic language attracted a group of mystical philosophers who compared the search for the perfect metal with the struggle of mankind for the perfection of the soul. The philosophers began to use the artisan's terms in the mystical literature that they produced. Thus, by the fourteenth century, alchemy had developed two distinct groups of practitioners—the laboratory alchemist and the literary alchemist. Both groups of alchemists continued to work throughout the history of alchemy, but, of course, it was the literary alchemist who was most likely to produce a written record; therefore, much of what is known about the science of alchemy is derived from philosophers rather than from the alchemists who labored in laboratories.

Despite centuries of experimentation, laboratory

---

33. With which of the following statements would the author most probably agree?

    Ⓐ Alchemy must be considered a complete failure.
    Ⓑ Some very important scientific discoveries were made by alchemists.
    Ⓒ Most educated people dismissed alchemy during the time that it was practiced.
    Ⓓ The literary alchemists were more important than the laboratory alchemists.

Human memory, formerly believed to be rather inefficient, is really much more sophisticated than that of a computer. Researchers approaching the problem from a variety of points of view have all concluded that there is a great deal more stored in our minds than has been generally supposed. Dr. Wilder Penfield, a Canadian neurosurgeon, proved that by stimulating their brains electrically, he could elicit the total recall of complex events in his subjects' lives. Even dreams and other minor events supposedly forgotten for many years suddenly emerged in detail.

The memory trace is the term for whatever is the internal representation of the specific information about the event stored in the memory. Assumed to have been made by structural changes in the brain, the memory trace is not subject to direct observation but is rather a theoretical construct that we use to speculate about how information presented at a particular time can cause performance at a later time. Most theories include the strength of the memory trace as a variable in the degree of learning, retention, and retrieval possible for a memory. One theory is that the fantastic capacity for storage in the brain is the result of an almost unlimited combination of interconnections between brain cells, stimulated by patterns of activity. Repeated references to the same information support recall. Or, to say that another way, improved performance is the result of strengthening the chemical bonds in the memory.

Psychologists generally divide memory into at least two types, short-term and long-term memory, which combine to form working memory. Short-term memory contains what we are actively focusing on at any particular time, but items are not retained longer than twenty or thirty seconds without verbal rehearsal. We use short-term memory when we look up a telephone number and repeat it to ourselves until we can place the call. On the other hand, long-term memory can store facts, concepts, and experiences after we stop thinking about them. All conscious processing of information, as for example, problem solving, involves both short-term and long-term memory. As we repeat, rehearse, and recycle information, the memory trace is strengthened, allowing that information to move from short-term memory to long-term memory.

34. Which of the following is the main topic of the passage?

   Ⓐ Wilder Penfield
   Ⓑ Neurosurgery
   Ⓒ Human memory
   Ⓓ Chemical reactions

35. The word formerly in paragraph 1 could best be replaced by

   Ⓐ in the past
   Ⓑ from time to time
   Ⓒ in general
   Ⓓ by chance

36. Compared with a computer, human memory is

   Ⓐ more complex
   Ⓑ more limited
   Ⓒ less dependable
   Ⓓ less durable

37. Look at the word that in the passage. Click on the word or phrase in the **bold** text that that refers to.

Beginning

Human memory, formerly believed to be rather inefficient, is really much more sophisticated than that of a computer. Researchers approaching the problem from a variety of points of view have all concluded that there is a great deal more stored in our minds than has been generally supposed. Dr. Wilder Penfield, a Canadian neurosurgeon, proved that by stimulating their brains electrically, he could elicit the total recall of complex events in his subjects' lives. Even dreams and other minor events supposedly forgotten for many years suddenly emerged in detail.

The memory trace is the term for whatever is the internal representation of the specific information about the event stored in the memory. Assumed to have been made by structural changes in the brain, the memory trace is not subject to direct observation but is rather a theoretical construct that we use to speculate about how information presented at a particular time can cause performance at a later time. Most theories include the strength of the memory trace as a variable in the degree of learning, retention, and retrieval possible for a memory. One theory is that the fantastic capacity for storage in the brain is the result of an almost unlimited combination of

---

Beginning

Human memory, formerly believed to be rather inefficient, is really much more sophisticated than that of a computer. Researchers approaching the problem from a variety of points of view have all concluded that there is a great deal more stored in our minds than has been generally supposed. Dr. Wilder Penfield, a Canadian neurosurgeon, proved that by stimulating their brains electrically, he could elicit the total recall of complex events in his subjects' lives. Even dreams and other minor events supposedly forgotten for many years suddenly emerged in detail.

The memory trace is the term for whatever is the internal representation of the specific information about the event stored in the memory. Assumed to have been made by structural changes in the brain, the memory trace is not subject to direct observation but is rather a theoretical construct that we use to speculate about how information presented at a particular time can cause performance at a later time. Most theories include the strength of the memory trace as a variable in the degree of learning, retention, and retrieval possible for a memory. One theory is that the fantastic capacity for storage in the brain is the result of an almost unlimited combination of

38. Look at the word sophisticated in the passage. Click on the word in the **bold** text that is closest in meaning to sophisticated.

> **Beginning**
>
> Human memory, formerly believed to be rather inefficient, is really much more sophisticated than that of a computer. **Researchers approaching the problem from a variety of points of view have all concluded that there is a great deal more stored in our minds than has been generally supposed. Dr. Wilder Penfield, a Canadian neurosurgeon, proved that by stimulating their brains electrically, he could elicit the total recall of complex events in his subjects' lives.** Even dreams and other minor events supposedly forgotten for many years suddenly emerged in detail.
>
> The memory trace is the term for whatever is the internal representation of the specific information about the event stored in the memory. Assumed to have been made by structural changes in the brain, the memory trace is not subject to direct observation but is rather a theoretical construct that we use to speculate about how information presented at a particular time can cause performance at a later time. Most theories include the strength of the memory trace as a variable in the degree of learning, retention, and retrieval possible for a memory. One theory is that the fantastic capacity for storage in the brain is the result of an almost unlimited combination of

39. With which of the following statements would the author most likely agree?

  (A) The mind has a much greater capacity for memory than was previously believed.
  (B) The physical basis for memory is clear.
  (C) Different points of view are valuable.
  (D) Human memory is inefficient.

40. How did Penfield stimulate dreams and other minor events from the past?

  (A) By surgery
  (B) By electrical stimulation
  (C) By repetition
  (D) By chemical stimulation

41. According to the passage, the capacity for storage in the brain

  (A) can be understood by examining the physiology of the brain
  (B) is stimulated by patterns of activity
  (C) has a limited combination of relationships
  (D) is not influenced by repetition

42. The word bonds in paragraph 2 means

  (A) promises
  (B) agreements
  (C) connections
  (D) responsibilities

> **More Available**
>
> Most theories include the strength of the memory trace as a variable in the degree of learning, retention, and retrieval possible for a memory. One theory is that the fantastic capacity for storage in the brain is the result of an almost unlimited combination of interconnections between brain cells, stimulated by patterns of activity. Repeated references to the same information support recall. Or, to say that another way, improved performance is the result of strengthening the chemical bonds in the memory.
>
> Psychologists generally divide memory into at least two types, short-term and long-term memory, which combine to form working memory. Short-term memory contains what we are actively focusing on at any particular time, but items are not retained longer than twenty or thirty seconds without verbal rehearsal. We use short-term memory when we look up a telephone number and repeat it to ourselves until we can place the call. On the other hand, long-term memory can store facts, concepts, and experiences after we stop thinking about them. All conscious processing of information, as for example, problem solving, involves both short-term and long-term memory. As we repeat, rehearse, and recycle

43. All of the following are true of a memory trace EXCEPT that

    (A) it is probably made by structural changes in the brain
    (B) it is able to be observed
    (C) it is a theoretical construct
    (D) it is related to the degree of recall

44. Why does the author mention looking up a telephone number?

    (A) It is an example of short-term memory.
    (B) It is an example of a weak memory trace.
    (C) It is an example of an experiment.
    (D) It is an example of how we move short-term memory to long-term memory.

45. Click on the sentence in paragraph 3 that defines working memory.

    Paragraph 3 is marked with an arrow (→).

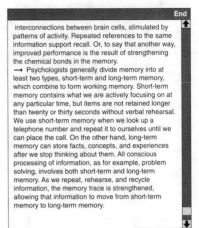

interconnections between brain cells, stimulated by patterns of activity. Repeated references to the same information support recall. Or, to say that another way, improved performance is the result of strengthening the chemical bonds in the memory.
→ Psychologists generally divide memory into at least two types, short-term and long-term memory, which combine to form working memory. Short-term memory contains what we are actively focusing on at any particular time, but items are not retained longer than twenty or thirty seconds without verbal rehearsal. We use short-term memory when we look up a telephone number and repeat it to ourselves until we can place the call. On the other hand, long-term memory can store facts, concepts, and experiences after we stop thinking about them. All conscious processing of information, as for example, problem solving, involves both short-term and long-term memory. As we repeat, rehearse, and recycle information, the memory trace is strengthened, allowing that information to move from short-term memory to long-term memory.

To check your answers for Model Test 3, refer to the Answer Key on page 379. For an explanation of the answers, refer to the Explanatory Answers for Model Test 3 on pages 410–421.

Writing Section Model Test 3

When you take a Model Test, you should use one sheet of paper, both sides. Time each Model Test carefully. After you have read the topic, you should spend 30 minutes writing. For results that would be closest to the actual testing situation, it is recommended that an English teacher score your test, using the guidelines on page 242 of this book.

Some people believe that it is very important to make large amounts of money, while others are satisfied to earn a comfortable living. Analyze each viewpoint and take a stand.

Notes

Model Test 4
Computer-Assisted TOEFL

Section 1:
Listening

The Listening section of the test measures the ability to understand conversations and talks in English. You will use headphones to listen to the conversations and talks. While you are listening, pictures of the speakers or other information will be presented on your computer screen. There are two parts to the Listening section, with special directions for each part.

On the day of the test, the amount of time you will have to answer all the questions will appear on the computer screen. The time you spend listening to the test material will not be counted. The listening material and questions about it will be presented only one time. You will not be allowed to take notes or have any paper at your computer. You will both see and hear the questions before the answer choices appear. You can take as much time as you need to select an answer; however, it will be to your advantage to answer the questions as quickly as possible. You may change your answer as many times as you want before you confirm it. After you have confirmed an answer, you will not be able to return to the question.

Before you begin working on the Listening section, you will have an opportunity to adjust the volume of the sound. You will not be able to change the volume after you have started the test.

QUESTION DIRECTIONS — Part A

In Part A of the Listening section, you will hear short conversations between two people. In some of the conversations, each person speaks only once. In other conversations, one or both of the people speak more than once. Each conversation is followed by one question about it.

Each question in this part has four answer choices. You should click on the best answer to each question. Answer the questions on the basis of what is stated or implied by the speakers.

1. What does the woman mean?

   (A) She does not know how to play tennis.
   (B) She has to study.
   (C) She does not like the man.
   (D) She does not qualify to play.

2. What does the woman mean?

   (A) She has no attendance policy.
   (B) The attendance policy is not the same for undergraduates and graduate students.
   (C) The grade will be affected by absences.
   (D) This class is not for graduate students.

3. What can be inferred about Bill?

   (A) He is a librarian.
   (B) He is a professor.
   (C) He is an accountant.
   (D) He is a reporter.

4. What does the woman say about Ali?

   (A) He is studying only at the American Language Institute.
   (B) He is taking three classes at the university.
   (C) He is a part-time student.
   (D) He is surprised.

5. What does the woman mean?

   (A) She will help the man.
   (B) She is not Miss Evans.
   (C) Dr. Warren has already gone.
   (D) The man should wait for Dr. Warren to answer the call.

6. What do we know from this conversation?

   (A) Mr. Adams is the new foreign student advisor.
   (B) The foreign student advisor is a man.
   (C) The foreign student advisor is married.
   (D) The foreign student advisor is not here.

7. What will the woman probably do?

   (A) Return home
   (B) Ask someone else about the shuttle
   (C) Make a telephone call
   (D) Board the bus

8. What does the woman mean?

   (A) She will go to the bookstore.
   (B) The books were too expensive.
   (C) There weren't any math and English books left.
   (D) She does not need any books.

9. What does the woman suggest the man do?

   (A) Take a different route
   (B) Leave earlier than planned
   (C) Wait until seven to leave
   (D) Stay at home

10. What does the woman mean?

    (A) The class with the graduate assistant is very enjoyable.
    (B) The students make a log of errors in the class.
    (C) The graduate assistant ridicules his students.
    (D) She is sorry that she took the class with the graduate assistant.

11. What does the man mean?

   Ⓐ He did not mean to insult the woman.
   Ⓑ What he said to Susan was true.
   Ⓒ The woman does not have an accent.
   Ⓓ Susan did not report the conversation accurately.

12. What does the woman agree to do for the man?

   Ⓐ Tell him the time
   Ⓑ Take care of his bag
   Ⓒ Help him find his books
   Ⓓ Go with him

13. What does the man mean?

   Ⓐ He has heard the woman talk about this often.
   Ⓑ He understands the woman's point of view.
   Ⓒ He is too tired to talk about it.
   Ⓓ He can hear the woman very well.

14. What does the woman imply?

   Ⓐ Mike does not have a car.
   Ⓑ Mike's brother is taking a break.
   Ⓒ Mike is in Florida.
   Ⓓ Mike is visiting his brother.

15. What does the woman advise the man to do?

   Ⓐ Get a job
   Ⓑ Finish the assignment
   Ⓒ Begin his project
   Ⓓ Pay his bills

16. What does the woman mean?

   Ⓐ She is not sure about going.
   Ⓑ She does not want to go to the show.
   Ⓒ She wants to know why the man asked her.
   Ⓓ She would like to go with the man.

17. What had the woman assumed about Bill and Carol?

   Ⓐ They would not get married.
   Ⓑ They were still away on their honeymoon.
   Ⓒ They didn't go on a honeymoon.
   Ⓓ They had not planned a large wedding.

18. What does the woman mean?

   Ⓐ She has already reviewed for the test.
   Ⓑ The test is important to her.
   Ⓒ The review session will not be helpful.
   Ⓓ The man does not understand her.

19. What will the man probably do?

   Ⓐ Telephone his sponsor
   Ⓑ Collect his check
   Ⓒ Help the woman look for his check
   Ⓓ Ask the woman to look again

20. What does the man mean?

   Ⓐ The university has been slow to respond.
   Ⓑ There are other universities.
   Ⓒ The situation is not that bad.
   Ⓓ The woman should keep trying.

QUESTION DIRECTIONS — Part B

In Part B of the Listening section, you will hear several longer conversations and talks. Each conversation or talk is followed by several questions. The conversations, talks, and questions will not be repeated.

The conversations and talks are about a variety of topics. You do not need special knowledge of the topics to answer the questions correctly. Rather, you should answer each question on the basis of what is stated or implied by the speakers in the conversations or talks.

For most of the questions, you will need to click on the best of four possible answers. Some questions will have special directions. The special directions will appear in a box on the computer screen.

21. What is Gary's problem?

    Ⓐ He is sick with the flu.
    Ⓑ He is in the hospital.
    Ⓒ He has missed some quizzes.
    Ⓓ He is behind in lab.

22. What does Gary want Margaret to do?

    Ⓐ Go to lab for him
    Ⓑ Let him copy her notes
    Ⓒ Help him study
    Ⓓ Be his lab partner

23. What does Margaret offer to do?

    Ⓐ Meet with him to clarify her notes
    Ⓑ Make a copy of the quizzes for him
    Ⓒ Read his notes before the next lab
    Ⓓ Show him how to do the lab experiments

24. What is Margaret's attitude in this conversation?

    Click on 2 answers.

    Ⓐ Helpful
    Ⓑ Worried
    Ⓒ Apologetic
    Ⓓ Friendly

25. What is the main topic of this lecture?

    Ⓐ Novelists of this century
    Ⓑ F. Scott Fitzgerald's work
    Ⓒ First novels by young authors
    Ⓓ Film versions of F. Scott Fitzgerald's novels

26. Why wasn't Fitzgerald more successful in his later life?

    Click on 2 answers.

    Ⓐ He had little natural talent.
    Ⓑ He was a compulsive drinker.
    Ⓒ The film versions of his books were not successful.
    Ⓓ He did not adjust to a changing world.

27. According to the lecturer, what do we know about the novels written by F. Scott Fitzgerald?

    Ⓐ They described the Jazz Age.
    Ⓑ They described the Deep South.
    Ⓒ They were based upon war experiences.
    Ⓓ They were written in stream-of-consciousness style.

28. What does the professor want the class to do after the lecture?

   Ⓐ Write a book report
   Ⓑ Read one of Fitzgerald's books
   Ⓒ Watch and discuss a video
   Ⓓ Research Fitzgerald's life

29. What is the main purpose of the talk?

   Ⓐ To explain chamber music
   Ⓑ To give examples of composers
   Ⓒ To congratulate the University Quartet
   Ⓓ To introduce madrigal singing

30. According to the speaker, which instruments are the most popular for chamber music?

   Click on 2 answers.

   Ⓐ Piano
   Ⓑ Brass
   Ⓒ Strings
   Ⓓ Percussion

31. Why does the speaker mention Johann Sebastian Bach?

   Ⓐ He was a famous composer.
   Ⓑ He composed the pieces that will be performed.
   Ⓒ He wrote vocal chamber music.
   Ⓓ He wrote trio sonatas.

32. What will the listeners hear next?

   Ⓐ A discussion of music from the eighteenth century
   Ⓑ A concert by the University Quartet
   Ⓒ An introduction to religious music
   Ⓓ A history of music from the Elizabethan Period

33. Why did the man go to the Chemical Engineering Department?

   Ⓐ To make an appointment
   Ⓑ To cancel his appointment
   Ⓒ To change his appointment time
   Ⓓ To rearrange his schedule so that he could keep his appointment

34. What does the woman say about Dr. Benjamin?

   Ⓐ He is busy on Wednesday.
   Ⓑ He will not be in on Wednesday.
   Ⓒ He does not schedule appointments on Wednesday.
   Ⓓ He will be moving his Wednesday appointment to Thursday this week.

35. What did the secretary offer to do?

    Ⓐ Give him an appointment at three o'clock on Wednesday
    Ⓑ Give him an appointment at either four-thirty on Wednesday or ten o'clock on Thursday
    Ⓒ Give him an appointment at lunch time
    Ⓓ Give him a new appointment earlier on the same day as his original appointment

36. What did the man decide to do?

    Ⓐ Make a new appointment later
    Ⓑ Cancel his regular appointment
    Ⓒ Rearrange his schedule to keep his original appointment
    Ⓓ Call back later when Dr. Benjamin is in

37. What is the main topic of this lecture?

    Ⓐ Health food
    Ⓑ The processing of bread
    Ⓒ Organic gardens
    Ⓓ Poisons

38. Which term is used to identify foods that have not been processed or canned?

    Ⓐ Refined foods
    Ⓑ Natural foods
    Ⓒ Organic foods
    Ⓓ Unprocessed foods

39. What happens to food when it is processed?

    Click on 2 answers.

    Ⓐ Some toxic chemicals may be added.
    Ⓑ The food is cooked.
    Ⓒ Vitamins are added to the food.
    Ⓓ The vitamin content is reduced.

40. Which word best describes the speaker's attitude toward health foods?

    Ⓐ Uninformed
    Ⓑ Convinced
    Ⓒ Uncertain
    Ⓓ Humorous

41. How did the professor define the Stone Age?

    Ⓐ The time when the first agricultural communities were established
    Ⓑ The time when the glaciers from the last Ice Age receded
    Ⓒ The time when prehistoric humans began to make tools
    Ⓓ The time when metals were introduced as material for tools and weapons

42. Identify the three time periods associated with the Stone Age.

Click on a phrase. Then click on the empty box in the correct row. Use each phrase only once.

A appearance of **Homo Sapiens**
B establishment of agricultural villages
C use of tools

Old Stone Age	
Middle Stone Age	
Late Stone Age	

43. Why did tools change during the Late Stone Age?

Ⓐ They began to be used for domestic purposes.
Ⓑ They were not strong enough for the cold weather.
Ⓒ They were adapted as farm tools.
Ⓓ They were more complex as humans became more creative.

44. What marked the end of the Stone Age?

Ⓐ The introduction of farming
Ⓑ The preference for metal tools
Ⓒ The decline of Neanderthals
Ⓓ The onset of the Ice Age

45. What is a trap?

Ⓐ A man-made storage area for oil
Ⓑ Gas and water that collect near oil deposits
Ⓒ An underground formation that stops the flow of oil
Ⓓ Cracks and holes that allow the oil to move

46. Select the diagram of the anticline trap that was described in the lecture.

Click on a diagram.

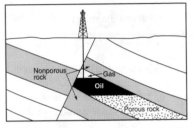

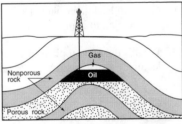

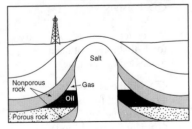

47. Identify the nonporous rock in the diagram.

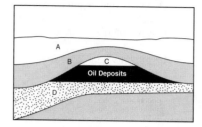

Click on the letter.

48. According to the speaker, how can geologists locate salt domes?

   Ⓐ They look for a bulge in an otherwise flat area.
   Ⓑ They look for an underground rock formation shaped like an arch.
   Ⓒ They look for salt on the surface of the area.
   Ⓓ They look for a large crack in the earth.

49. What is the woman's problem?

   Ⓐ She does not want to take the course.
   Ⓑ She does not know which professor to choose.
   Ⓒ She does not understand the course requirements.
   Ⓓ She does not want to take the man's advice.

50. Why did the woman decide to take the class with Dr. Robinson?

Click on 2 answers.

   A She has already taken classes with Dr. Robinson.
   B She prefers to take lecture classes.
   C She takes the class with the man.
   D She likes a more traditional approach to teaching.

Section 2: Structure

This section measures the ability to recognize language that is appropriate for standard written English. There are two types of questions in this section.

In the first type of question, there are incomplete sentences. Beneath each sentence, there are four words or phrases. You will choose the one word or phrase that best completes the sentence.

Clicking on a choice darkens the oval. After you click on **Next** and **Confirm Answer**, the next question will be presented.

The second type of question has four underlined words or phrases. You will choose the one underlined word or phrase that must be changed for the sentence to be correct.

Clicking on an underlined word or phrase will darken it. After you click on **Next** and **Confirm Answer**, the next question will be presented.

1. When friends insist on ------
   expensive gifts, it makes most
   Americans uncomfortable.

   Ⓐ them to accept
   Ⓑ their accepting
   Ⓒ they accepting
   Ⓓ they accept

2. Gilbert Stuart is considered by
   most art critics ------ greatest
   portrait painter in the North
   American colonies.

   Ⓐ that he was
   Ⓑ as he was
   Ⓒ who was the
   Ⓓ the

3. The extent to which an
            Ⓐ
   individual is a product of either

   heredity or environment

   cannot proved, but
       Ⓑ
   several theories have been
      Ⓒ   Ⓓ
   proposed.

4. A child in the first grade tends
   to be --------- all of the other
   children in the class.

   Ⓐ the same old to
   Ⓑ the same age than
   Ⓒ as old like
   Ⓓ the same age as

5. The bird's egg is such an efficient structure for protecting the
   embryo inside ------ difficult for
   the hatchling to break.

   Ⓐ that is
   Ⓑ that
   Ⓒ and is
   Ⓓ that it is

6. Jane Addams had already
                   Ⓐ
   established Hull House

   in Chicago and began her work
        Ⓑ   Ⓒ
   in the Women's Suffrage

   Movement when she was

   awarded the Nobel prize for
       Ⓓ
   peace.

7. The flag of the original first
                 Ⓐ
   colonies may or may not

   have been made by Betsy Ross
       Ⓑ   Ⓒ
   during the Revolution.
          Ⓓ

8. As a safety measure, the detona-
   tor for a nuclear device may be
   made of ------, each of which is
   controlled by a different
   employee.

   Ⓐ two equipments
   Ⓑ two pieces of equipments
   Ⓒ two pieces of equipment
   Ⓓ two equipment pieces

9. -------- that the English settled in
   Jamestown.

   Ⓐ In 1607 that it was
   Ⓑ That in 1607
   Ⓒ Because in 1607
   Ⓓ It was in 1607

10. The most common form of
    Ⓐ ─────────   Ⓑ
    treatment it is mass inoculation
                Ⓒ
    and chlorination of

    water sources.
    ─────────
       Ⓓ

11. An equilateral triangle is a trian-
    gle ------ and three angles of
    equal size.

    Ⓐ that have three sides of
       equal length
    Ⓑ it has three sides equally
       long
    Ⓒ that has three sides of equal
       length
    Ⓓ having three equal length
       sides in it

12. ------ are found on the surface of
    the moon.

    Ⓐ Craters and waterless seas
       that
    Ⓑ When craters and waterless
       seas
    Ⓒ Craters and waterless seas
    Ⓓ Since craters and waterless
       seas

13. Without alphabetical order,

    dictionaries would be
    ─────────   ────
       Ⓐ   Ⓑ
    impossibility to use.
    ─────────   ────
       Ⓒ   Ⓓ

14. ------ two waves pass a given
    point simultaneously, they will
    have no effect on each other's
    subsequent motion.

    Ⓐ So that
    Ⓑ They are
    Ⓒ That
    Ⓓ If

15. The Pickerel Frog, native to
    Ⓐ ───────
    Southern Canada and the

    Eastern United States,

    should be avoided because their
    ─────────────   ────
          Ⓑ   Ⓒ
    skin secretions are lethal to

    small animals and irritating to
                        ─────────
                            Ⓓ
    humans.

16. Staying in a hotel costs ------
    renting a room in a dormitory
    for a week.

    Ⓐ twice more than
    Ⓑ twice as much as
    Ⓒ as much twice as
    Ⓓ as much as twice

17. Unlike most Europeans, many
    Americans ------ a bowl of cereal
    for breakfast every day.

    Ⓐ used to eating
    Ⓑ are used to eat
    Ⓒ are used to eating
    Ⓓ use to eat

18. Scientists had previously
                 ─────────
                    Ⓐ
    estimated that the Grand Canyon

    in Arizona is ten million years
                 ──
                 Ⓑ
    old; but now, by using a more
                 ─────────
                    Ⓒ
    modern dating method, they

    agree that the age is closer to

    six million years.
    ─────────────
          Ⓓ

19. Although <u>jogging</u> is a good way
    (A)
    to lose weight and improve

    one's physical condition, <u>most</u>
    (B)
    doctors recommend that the

    potential jogger begin

    <u>in a correct manner</u> by <u>getting</u> a
    (C)   (D)
    complete checkup.

20. Some conifers, <u>that is,</u> <u>tree</u> that
    (A)   (B)   (C)
    have cones, <u>are</u> able to thrive on
              (D)
    poor, thin soil.

Section 3:
Reading

This section measures the ability to read and understand short passages similar in topic and style to those that students are likely to encounter in North American universities and colleges. This section contains reading passages and questions about the passages. There are several different types of questions in this section.

In the Reading section, you will first have the opportunity to read the passage.

You will use the scroll bar to view the rest of the passage.

When you have finished reading the passage, you will use the mouse to click on **Proceed**. Then the questions about the passage will be presented. You are to choose the one best answer to each question. Answer all questions about the information in a passage on the basis of what is stated or implied in that passage.

Most of the questions will be multiple choice questions. To answer these questions you will click on a choice below the question.

To answer some questions you will click on a word or phrase.

To answer some questions you will click on a sentence in the passage.

To answer some questions you will click on a square to add a sentence to the passage.

   The computer screens for selected questions in the Reading Section have been printed in this book to provide you with orientation to the format of the Computer-Based TOEFL. Use the screen to find the place in the original reading passage that corresponds to the question you are answering.

A geyser is the result of underground water under the combined conditions of high temperatures and increased pressure beneath the surface of the earth. Since temperature rises about 1°F for every sixty feet under the earth's surface, and pressure increases with depth, water that seeps down in cracks and fissures until it reaches very hot rocks in the earth's interior becomes heated to a temperature of approximately 290°F.

Water under pressure can remain liquid at temperatures above its normal boiling point, but in a geyser, the weight of the water nearer the surface exerts so much pressure on the deeper water that the water at the bottom of the geyser reaches much higher temperatures than does the water at the top of the geyser. As the deep water becomes hotter, and consequently, lighter, it suddenly rises to the surface and shoots out of the surface in the form of steam and hot water. In turn, the explosion agitates all the water in the geyser reservoir, creating further explosions. Immediately afterward, the water again flows into the underground reservoir, heating begins, and the process repeats itself.

In order to function, then, a geyser must have a source of heat, a reservoir where water can be stored until the temperature rises to an unstable point, an opening through which the hot water and steam can escape, and underground channels for resupplying water after an eruption.

Favorable conditions for geysers exist in regions of geologically recent volcanic activity, especially in areas of more than average precipitation. For the most part, geysers are located in three regions of the world: New Zealand, Iceland, and the Yellowstone National Park area of the United States. The most famous geyser in the world is Old Faithful in Yellowstone Park. Old Faithful erupts almost every hour, rising to a height of 125 to 170 feet and expelling more than ten thousand gallons during each eruption. Old Faithful earned its name because, unlike most geysers, it has never failed to erupt on schedule even once in eighty years of observation.

1. Which of the following is the main topic of the passage?

   (A) The Old Faithful geyser in Yellowstone National Park
   (B) The nature of geysers
   (C) The ratio of temperature to pressure in underground water
   (D) Regions of geologically recent volcanic activity

2. In order for a geyser to erupt

   (A) hot rocks must rise to the surface of the earth
   (B) water must flow underground
   (C) it must be a warm day
   (D) the earth must not be rugged or broken

3. Look at the word approximately in the passage. Click on another word or phrase in the **bold** text that is closest in meaning to approximately.

> Beginning
>
> A geyser is the result of underground water under the combined conditions of high temperatures and increased pressure beneath the surface of the earth. **Since temperature rises about 1°F for every sixty feet under the earth's surface, and pressure increases with depth, water that seeps down in cracks and fissures until it reaches very hot rocks in the earth's interior becomes heated to a temperature of approximately 290°F.**
>
> Water under pressure can remain liquid at temperatures above its normal boiling point, but in a geyser, the weight of the water nearer the surface exerts so much pressure on the deeper water that the water at the bottom of the geyser reaches much higher temperatures than does the water at the top of the geyser. As the deep water becomes hotter, and consequently, lighter, it suddenly rises to the surface and shoots out of the surface in the form of steam and hot water. In turn, the explosion agitates all the water in the geyser reservoir, creating further explosions. Immediately afterward, the water again flows into the underground reservoir, heating begins, and the process repeats itself.
>
> In order to function, then, a geyser must have a

4. As depth increases

   (A) pressure increases but temperature does not
   (B) temperature increases but pressure does not
   (C) both pressure and temperature increase
   (D) neither pressure nor temperature increases

5. The word it in paragraph 1 refers to

   Ⓐ water
   Ⓑ depth
   Ⓒ pressure
   Ⓓ surface

8. The word expelling in paragraph 4 is closest in meaning to

   Ⓐ heating
   Ⓑ discharging
   Ⓒ supplying
   Ⓓ wasting

Beginning

A geyser is the result of underground water under the combined conditions of high temperatures and increased pressure beneath the surface of the earth. **Since temperature rises about 1°F for every sixty feet under the earth's surface, and pressure increases with depth, water that seeps down in cracks and fissures until it reaches very hot rocks in the earth's interior becomes heated to a temperature of approximately 290°F.**

Water under pressure can remain liquid at temperatures above its normal boiling point, but in a geyser, the weight of the water nearer the surface exerts so much pressure on the deeper water that the water at the bottom of the geyser reaches much higher temperatures than does the water at the top of the geyser. As the deep water becomes hotter, and consequently, lighter, it suddenly rises to the surface and shoots out of the surface in the form of steam and hot water. In turn, the explosion agitates all the water in the geyser reservoir, creating further explosions. Immediately afterward, the water again flows into the underground reservoir, heating begins, and the process repeats itself.

In order to function, then, a geyser must have a

End

part, geysers are located in three regions of the world: New Zealand, Iceland, and the Yellowstone National Park area of the United States. The most famous geyser in the world is Old Faithful in Yellowstone Park. Old Faithful erupts almost every hour, rising to a height of 125 to 170 feet and expelling more than ten thousand gallons during each eruption. Old Faithful earned its name because, unlike most geysers, it has never failed to erupt on schedule even once in eighty years of observation.

6. Click on the paragraph that explains the role of water pressure in an active geyser.

   Scroll the passage to see all of the paragraphs.

7. How often does Old Faithful erupt?

   Ⓐ Every 10 minutes
   Ⓑ Every 60 minutes
   Ⓒ Every 125 minutes
   Ⓓ Every 170 minutes

9. According to the passage, what is required for a geyser to function?

   Ⓐ A source of heat, a place for water to collect, an opening, and underground channels
   Ⓑ An active volcano nearby and a water reservoir
   Ⓒ Channels in the earth and heavy rainfall
   Ⓓ Volcanic activity, underground channels, and steam

10. Why does the author mention New Zealand and Iceland in paragraph 4?

    (A) To compare areas of high volcanic activity
    (B) To describe the Yellowstone National Park
    (C) To provide examples of areas where geysers are located
    (D) To name the two regions where all geysers are found

    Paragraph 4 is marked with an arrow (→).

    End

    source of heat, a reservoir where water can be stored until the temperature rises to an unstable point, an opening through which the hot water and steam can escape, and underground channels for resupplying water after an eruption.
    → Favorable conditions for geysers exist in regions of geologically recent volcanic activity, especially in areas of more than average precipitation. For the most part, geysers are located in three regions of the world: New Zealand, Iceland, and the Yellowstone National Park area of the United States. The most famous geyser in the world is Old Faithful in Yellowstone Park. Old Faithful erupts almost every hour, rising to a height of 125 to 170 feet and expelling more than ten thousand gallons during each eruption. Old Faithful earned its name because, unlike most geysers, it has never failed to erupt on schedule even once in eighty years of observation.

11. What does the author mean by the statement Old Faithful earned its name because, unlike most geysers, it has never failed to erupt on schedule even once in eighty years of observation?

    (A) Old Faithful always erupts on schedule.
    (B) Old Faithful is usually predictable.
    (C) Old Faithful erupts predictably like other geysers.
    (D) Old Faithful received its name because it has been observed for many years.

The question has often been asked why the Wright brothers were able to succeed in an effort in which so many others had failed. Many explanations have been mentioned, but three reasons are most often cited. First, they were a team. Both men worked well together, read the same books, located and shared information, talked incessantly about the possibility of manned flight, and served as a consistent source of inspiration and encouragement to each other. Quite simply, two geniuses are better than one.

They were also both glider pilots. Unlike some other engineers who experimented with the theories of flight, Orville and Wilbur Wright experienced the practical side of their work by building and flying in kites and gliders. Each craft was slightly better than the last, incorporating in it the knowledge that they had gained from previous failures. They had realized from their experiments that the most serious problem in manned flight would be stabilizing and maneuvering the aircraft once it was airborne. While others concentrated their efforts on the problem of achieving lift for take-off, the Wright brothers focused on developing a three-axis control for guiding their aircraft. By the time that the brothers started to build an airplane, they were already among the best glider pilots in the world, and they knew the problems of flying first hand.

In addition, the Wright brothers had designed more effective wings for the airplane than had been previously engineered. Using a wind tunnel, they tested more than two hundred different wing designs, recording the effects of slight variations in shape on the pressure of air on the wings. The data from these experiments allowed the Wright brothers to construct a superior wing for their craft.

In spite of all these advantages, however, the Wright brothers might not have succeeded had they not been born at precisely the opportune moment in history. Attempts to achieve manned flight in the early nineteenth century were doomed because the steam engines that powered the aircrafts were too heavy in proportion to the power that they produced. But by the end of the nineteenth century, when the brothers were experimenting with engineering options, a relatively light internal combustion engine had already been invented, and they were able to bring the ratio of weight to power within acceptable limits for flight.

12. Which of the following is the main topic of the passage?

(A) The reasons why the Wright brothers succeeded in manned flight

(B) The advantage of the internal combustion engine in the Wright brothers' experiments

(C) The Wright brothers' experience as pilots

(D) The importance of gliders to the development of airplanes

13. The passage discusses all of the following reasons that the Wright brothers succeeded EXCEPT

(A) They worked very well together.

(B) They both had practical experience building other aircraft.

(C) They made extensive tests before they completed the design.

(D) They were well funded.

14. The word cited in paragraph 1 is closest in meaning to which of the following?

(A) disregarded

(B) mentioned

(C) considered

(D) proven

Beginning

The question has often been asked why the Wright brothers were able to succeed in an effort in which so many others had failed. Many explanations have been mentioned, but three reasons are most often cited. First, they were a team. Both men worked well together, read the same books, located and shared information, talked incessantly about the possibility of manned flight, and served as a consistent source of inspiration and encouragement to each other. Quite simply, two geniuses are better than one.

They were also both glider pilots. Unlike some other engineers who experimented with the theories of flight, Orville and Wilbur Wright experienced the practical side of their work by building and flying in kites and gliders. Each craft was slightly better than the last, incorporating in it the knowledge that they had gained from previous failures. They had realized from their experiments that the most serious problem in manned flight would be stabilizing and maneuvering the aircraft once it was airborne. While others concentrated their efforts on the problem of achieving lift for take-off, the Wright brothers focused on developing a three-axis control for guiding their

15. The word **incessantly** in paragraph 1 could best be replaced by which of the following?

    Ⓐ confidently
    Ⓑ intelligently
    Ⓒ constantly
    Ⓓ optimistically

Beginning

    The question has often been asked why the Wright brothers were able to succeed in an effort in which so many others had failed. Many explanations have been mentioned, but three reasons are most often cited. First, they were a team. Both men worked well together, read the same books, located and shared information, talked incessantly about the possibility of manned flight, and served as a consistent source of inspiration and encouragement to each other. Quite simply, two geniuses are better than one.

    They were also both glider pilots. Unlike some other engineers who experimented with the theories of flight, Orville and Wilbur Wright experienced the practical side of their work by building and flying in kites and gliders. Each craft was slightly better than the last, incorporating in it the knowledge that they had gained from their experiments that the most serious problem in manned flight would be stabilizing and maneuvering the aircraft once it was airborne. While others concentrated their efforts on the problem of achieving lift for take-off, the Wright brothers focused on developing a three-axis control for guiding their

---

16. What kind of experience did the Wright brothers have that distinguished them from their competitors?

    Ⓐ They were geniuses.
    Ⓑ They were glider pilots.
    Ⓒ They were engineers.
    Ⓓ They were inventors.

17. Click on the sentence in paragraph 2 that explains the most serious problem that the Wright brothers anticipated in constructing a manned aircraft.

Paragraph 2 is marked with an arrow (→).

More Available

consistent source of inspiration and encouragement to each other. Quite simply, two geniuses are better than one.
    → They were also both glider pilots. Unlike some other engineers who experimented with the theories of flight, Orville and Wilbur Wright experienced the practical side of their work by building and flying in kites and gliders. Each craft was slightly better than the last, incorporating in it the knowledge that they had gained from previous failures. They had realized from their experiments that the most serious problem in manned flight would be stabilizing and maneuvering the aircraft once it was airborne. While others concentrated their efforts on the problem of achieving lift for take-off, the Wright brothers focused on developing a three-axis control for guiding their aircraft. By the time that the brothers started to build an airplane, they were already among the best glider pilots in the world, and they knew the problems of flying first hand.
    In addition, the Wright brothers had designed more effective wings for the airplane than had been previously engineered. Using a wind tunnel, they tested more than two hundred different wing designs,

---

18. Look at the word **maneuvering** in the passage. Click on the word or phrase in the **bold** text that is closest in meaning to **maneuvering**.

More Available

practical side of their work by building and flying in kites and gliders. Each craft was slightly better than the last, incorporating in it the knowledge that they had gained from previous failures. **They had realized from their experiments that the most serious problem in manned flight would be stabilizing and maneuvering the aircraft once it was airborne. While others concentrated their efforts on the problem of achieving lift for take-off, the Wright brothers focused on developing a three-axis control for guiding their aircraft.** By the time that the brothers started to build an airplane, they were already among the best glider pilots in the world, and they knew the problems of flying first hand.
    In addition, the Wright brothers had designed more effective wings for the airplane than had been previously engineered. Using a wind tunnel, they tested more than two hundred different wing designs, recording the effects of slight variations in shape on the pressure of air on the wings. The data from these experiments allowed the Wright brothers to construct a superior wing for their craft.
    In spite of all these advantages, however, the Wright brothers might not have succeeded had they

19. Why does the author suggest that the experiments with the wind tunnel were important?

   Ⓐ Because they allowed the Wright brothers to decrease the weight of their airplane to acceptable limits

   Ⓑ Because they resulted in a three-axis control for their airplane

   Ⓒ Because they were important in the refinement of the wings for their airplane

   Ⓓ Because they used the data to improve the engine for their airplane

20. The word **they** in paragraph 3 refers to

   Ⓐ the Wright brothers

   Ⓑ aircraft

   Ⓒ engines

   Ⓓ attempts

21. The word **doomed** in paragraph 4 is closest in meaning to

   Ⓐ destined to fail

   Ⓑ difficult to achieve

   Ⓒ taking a risk

   Ⓓ not well planned

End

the pressure of air on the wings. The data from these experiments allowed the Wright brothers to construct a superior wing for their craft.

In spite of all these advantages, however, the Wright brothers might not have succeeded had they not been born at precisely the opportune moment in history. Attempts to achieve manned flight in the early nineteenth century were **doomed** because the steam engines that powered the aircrafts were too heavy in proportion to the power that they produced. But by the end of the nineteenth century, when the brothers were experimenting with engineering options, a relatively light internal combustion engine had already been invented, and they were able to bring the ratio of weight to power within acceptable limits for flight.

End

an airplane, they were already among the best glider pilots in the world, and they knew the problems of flying first hand.

In addition, the Wright brothers had designed more effective wings for the airplane than had been previously engineered. Using a wind tunnel, **they** tested more than two hundred different wing designs, recording the effects of slight variations in shape on the pressure of air on the wings. The data from these experiments allowed the Wright brothers to construct a superior wing for their craft.

In spite of all these advantages, however, the Wright brothers might not have succeeded had they not been born at precisely the opportune moment in history. Attempts to achieve manned flight in the early nineteenth century were doomed because the steam engines that powered the aircrafts were too heavy in proportion to the power that they produced. But by the end of the nineteenth century, when the brothers were experimenting with engineering options, a relatively light internal combustion engine had already been invented, and they were able to bring the ratio of weight to power within acceptable limits for flight.

22. In paragraph 4, the author suggests that the steam engines used in earlier aircraft had failed because

(A) They were too small to power a large plane.
(B) They were too light to generate enough power.
(C) They did not have internal combustion power.
(D) They did not have enough power to lift their own weight.

Paragraph 4 is marked with an arrow (→).

End

experiments allowed the Wright brothers to construct a superior wing for their craft.

→ In spite of all these advantages, however, the Wright brothers might not have succeeded had they not been born at precisely the opportune moment in history. Attempts to achieve manned flight in the early nineteenth century were doomed because the steam engines that powered the aircrafts were too heavy in proportion to the power that they produced. But by the end of the nineteenth century, when the brothers were experimenting with engineering options, a relatively light internal combustion engine had already been invented, and they were able to bring the ratio of weight to power within acceptable limits for flight.

The influenza virus is a single molecule composed of millions of individual atoms. Although bacteria can be considered a type of plant, secreting poisonous substances into the body of the organism they attack, viruses, like the influenza virus, are living organisms themselves. We may consider them regular chemical molecules since they have strictly defined atomic structure; but on the other hand, we must also consider them as being alive since they are able to multiply in unlimited quantities.

An attack brought on by the presence of the influenza virus in the body produces a temporary immunity, but, unfortunately, the protection is against only the type of virus that caused the influenza. Because the disease can be produced by any one of three types, referred to as A, B, or C, and many varieties within each type, immunity to one virus will not prevent infection by other types or strains. Protection from the influenza virus is also complicated by the fact that immunity to a specific virus persists for less than a year. Finally, because a virus may periodically change characteristics, the problem of mutation makes it difficult to carry out a successful immunization program. Vaccines are often ineffective against newly evolving strains.

Approximately every ten years, worldwide epidemics of influenza called pandemics occur. Thought to be caused by new strains of type-A virus, these pandemic viruses have spread rapidly, infecting millions of people.

Vaccines have been developed that have been found to be 70 to 90 percent effective for at least six months against either A or B types of the influenza virus, and a genetically engineered live-virus vaccine is under development. Currently, the United States Public Health Service recommends annual vaccination only for those at greatest risk of complications from influenza, including pregnant women and the elderly.

Nevertheless, many other members of the general population request and receive flu shots every year, and even more are immunized during epidemic or pandemic cycles.

23. Which of the following is the main topic of the passage?

Ⓐ The influenza virus
Ⓑ Immunity to disease
Ⓒ Bacteria
Ⓓ Chemical molecules

24. According to this passage, bacteria are

Ⓐ poisons
Ⓑ very small
Ⓒ larger than viruses
Ⓓ plants

25. Look at the word **themselves** in the passage. Click on the word or phrase in the **bold** text that **themselves** refers to.

> **Beginning**
>
> The influenza virus is a single molecule composed of millions of individual atoms. **Although bacteria can be considered a type of plant, secreting poisonous substances into the body of the organism they attack, viruses, like the influenza virus, are living organisms themselves. We may consider them regular chemical molecules since they have strictly defined atomic structure;** but on the other hand, we must also consider them as being alive since they are able to multiply in unlimited quantities.
>
> An attack brought on by the presence of the influenza virus in the body produces a temporary immunity, but, unfortunately, the protection is against only the type of virus that caused the influenza. Because the disease can be produced by any one of three types, referred to as A, B, or C, and many varieties within each type, immunity to one virus will not prevent infection by other types or strains. Protection from the influenza virus is also complicated by the fact that immunity to a specific virus persists for less than a year. Finally, because a virus may periodically change characteristics, the problem of mutation makes it difficult to carry out a successful immunization program. Vaccines are often ineffective

26. The word strictly in paragraph 1 could best be replaced by

Ⓐ unusually
Ⓑ completely
Ⓒ broadly
Ⓓ exactly

> **Beginning**
>
> The influenza virus is a single molecule composed of millions of individual atoms. Although bacteria can be considered a type of plant, secreting poisonous substances into the body of the organism they attack, viruses, like the influenza virus, are living organisms themselves. We may consider them regular chemical molecules since they have strictly defined atomic structure; but on the other hand, we must also consider them as being alive since they are able to multiply in unlimited quantities.
>
> An attack brought on by the presence of the influenza virus in the body produces a temporary immunity, but, unfortunately, the protection is against only the type of virus that caused the influenza. Because the disease can be produced by any one of three types, referred to as A, B, or C, and many varieties within each type, immunity to one virus will not prevent infection by other types or strains. Protection from the influenza virus is also complicated by the fact that immunity to a specific virus persists for less than a year. Finally, because a virus may periodically change characteristics, the problem of mutation makes it difficult to carry out a successful immunization program. Vaccines are often ineffective

27. Why does the author say that viruses are alive?

Ⓐ They have a complex atomic structure.
Ⓑ They move.
Ⓒ They multiply.
Ⓓ They need warmth and light.

28. The atomic structure of viruses

Ⓐ is variable
Ⓑ is strictly defined
Ⓒ cannot be analyzed chemically
Ⓓ is more complex than that of bacteria

29. The word unlimited in paragraph 1 could best be replaced by which of the following?

    Ⓐ very small
    Ⓑ very large
    Ⓒ very similar
    Ⓓ very different

More Available

poisonous substances into the body of the organism they attack, viruses, like the influenza virus, are living organisms themselves. We may consider them regular chemical molecules since they have strictly defined atomic structure; but on the other hand, we must also consider them as being alive since they are able to multiply in unlimited quantities.

An attack brought on by the presence of the influenza virus in the body produces a temporary immunity, but, unfortunately, the protection is against only the type of virus that caused the influenza. Because the disease can be produced by any one of three types, referred to as A, B, or C, and many varieties within each type, immunity to one virus will not prevent infection by other types or strains. Protection from the influenza virus is also complicated by the fact that immunity to a specific virus persists for less than a year. Finally, because a virus may periodically change characteristics, the problem of mutation makes it difficult to carry out a successful immunization program. Vaccines are often ineffective against newly evolving strains.

Approximately every ten years, worldwide epidemics of influenza called pandemics occur.

---

30. According to the passage, how does the body react to the influenza virus?

    Ⓐ It prevents further infection to other types and strains of the virus.
    Ⓑ It produces immunity to the type and strain of virus that invaded it.
    Ⓒ It becomes immune to types A, B, and C viruses, but not to various strains within the types.
    Ⓓ After a temporary immunity, it becomes even more susceptible to the type and strain that caused the influenza.

31. Look at the word strains in the passage. Click on another word or phrase in the **bold** text that is closest in meaning to strains .

More Available

only the type of virus that caused the influenza. Because the disease can be produced by any one of three types, referred to as A, B, or C, and many varieties within each type, **immunity to one virus will not prevent infection by other types or strains. Protection from the influenza virus is also complicated by the fact that immunity to a specific virus persists for less than a year. Finally, because a virus may periodically change characteristics, the problem of mutation makes it difficult to carry out a successful immunization program.** Vaccines are often ineffective against newly evolving strains.

Approximately every ten years, worldwide epidemics of influenza called pandemics occur. Thought to be caused by new strains of type-A virus, these pandemic viruses have spread rapidly, infecting millions of people.

Vaccines have been developed that have been found to be 70 to 90 percent effective for at least six months against either A or B types of the influenza virus, and a genetically engineered live-virus vaccine is under development. Currently, the United States Public Health Service recommends annual vaccination only for those at greatest risk of complications from

---

32. The passage discusses all of the following as characteristics of pandemics EXCEPT

    Ⓐ they spread very quickly
    Ⓑ they are caused by type-A virus
    Ⓒ they are regional outbreaks
    Ⓓ they occur once every ten years

33. The following sentence can be added to the passage.

> **Epidemics or regional outbreaks have appeared on the average every two or three years for type-A virus, and every four or five years for type-B virus.**

Where would it best fit into the passage?

Click on the square (■) to add the sentence to the passage.

Scroll the passage to see all of the choices.

End

mutation makes it difficult to carry out a successful immunization program. Vaccines are often ineffective against newly evolving strains.
 ■ Approximately every ten years, worldwide epidemics of influenza called pandemics occur. Thought to be caused by new strains of type-A virus, these pandemic viruses have spread rapidly, infecting millions of people.

Vaccines have been developed that have been found to be 70 to 90 percent effective for at least six months against either A or B types of the influenza virus, and a genetically engineered live-virus vaccine is under development. ■Currently, the United States Public Health Service recommends annual vaccination only for those at greatest risk of complications from influenza, including pregnant women and the elderly. ■ Nevertheless, many other members of the general population request and receive flu shots every year, and even more are immunized during epidemic or pandemic cycles.■

The Federal Reserve System is an independent agency of the United States government that helps oversee the national banking system. Since 1913 the Federal Reserve System, commonly called the Fed, has served as the central bank for the United States. It consists of twelve District Reserve Banks and their branch offices, along with several committees and councils. All national commercial banks are required by law to be members of the Fed, and all deposit-taking institutions are subject to regulation by the Fed regarding the amount of deposits that must be held in reserve and that, therefore, are not available for loans. The most powerful body is the seven-member Board of Governors in Washington, appointed by the President and confirmed by the Senate.

The System's primary function is to control monetary policy by influencing the cost and availability of money and credit through the purchase and sale of government securities. If the Federal Reserve provides too little money, interest rates tend to be high, borrowing is expensive, business activity slows down, unemployment goes up, and there is a danger of recession. If there is too much money, interest rates decline, and borrowing can lead to excess demand, pushing up prices and fueling inflation.

The Fed has several responsibilities in addition to controlling the money supply. In collaboration with the US Department of the Treasury, the Fed puts new coins and paper currency into circulation by issuing them to banks. It also supervises the activities of member banks abroad, and regulates certain aspects of international finance.

It has been said that the Federal Reserve is actually an informal fourth branch of the United States government because it is composed of national policy makers. However, in practice, the Federal Reserve does not stray far from the financial policies established by the executive branch of the government. Although it is true that the Fed does not depend on Congress for budget allocations, and therefore is free from the partisan politics that influences other governmental bodies, it is still responsible for frequent reports to the Congress on the conduct of monetary policies.

34. Which of the following is the most appropriate title for the passage?

(A) Banking
(B) The Federal Reserve System
(C) The Board of Governors
(D) Monetary Policies

35. The word oversee in paragraph 1 is closest in meaning to

(A) supervise
(B) maintain
(C) finance
(D) stimulate

Beginning

The Federal Reserve System is an independent agency of the United States government that helps oversee the national banking system. Since 1913 the Federal Reserve System, commonly called the Fed, has served as the central bank for the United States. It consists of twelve District Reserve Banks and their branch offices, along with several committees and councils. All national commercial banks are required by law to be members of the Fed, and all deposit-taking institutions are subject to regulation by the Fed regarding the amount of deposits that must be held in reserve and that, therefore, are not available for loans. The most powerful body is the seven-member Board of Governors in Washington, appointed by the President and confirmed by the Senate.

The System's primary function is to control monetary policy by influencing the cost and availability of money and credit through the purchase and sale of government securities. If the Federal Reserve provides too little money, interest rates tend to be high, borrowing is expensive, business activity slows down, unemployment goes up, and there is a danger of recession. If there is too much money, interest rates decline, and borrowing can lead to excess demand,

36. The word confirmed in paragraph 1 could best be replaced by

(A) modified
(B) considered
(C) examined
(D) approved

More Available

regarding the amount of deposits that must be held in reserve and that, therefore, are not available for loans. The most powerful body is the seven-member Board of Governors in Washington, appointed by the President and confirmed by the Senate.

The System's primary function is to control monetary policy by influencing the cost and availability of money and credit through the purchase and sale of government securities. If the Federal Reserve provides too little money, interest rates tend to be high, borrowing is expensive, business activity slows down, unemployment goes up, and there is a danger of recession. If there is too much money, interest rates decline, and borrowing can lead to excess demand, pushing up prices and fueling inflation.

The Fed has several responsibilities in addition to controlling the money supply. In collaboration with the US Department of the Treasury, the Fed puts new coins and paper currency into circulation by issuing them to banks. It also supervises the activities of member banks abroad, and regulates certain aspects of international finance.

It has been said that the Federal Reserve is actually an informal fourth branch of the United States

37. According to the passage, the principal responsibility of the Federal Reserve System is

(A) to borrow money
(B) to regulate monetary policies
(C) to print government securities
(D) to appoint the Board of Governors

38. The word securities in paragraph 2 is intended to mean

   (A) debts
   (B) bonds
   (C) protection
   (D) confidence

More Available

The most powerful body is the seven-member Board of Governors in Washington, appointed by the President and confirmed by the Senate.

The System's primary function is to control monetary policy by influencing the cost and availability of money and credit through the purchase and sale of government securities. If the Federal Reserve provides too little money, interest rates tend to be high, borrowing is expensive, business activity slows down, unemployment goes up, and there is a danger of recession. If there is too much money, interest rates decline, and borrowing can lead to excess demand, pushing up prices and fueling inflation.

The Fed has several responsibilities in addition to controlling the money supply. In collaboration with the US Department of the Treasury, the Fed puts new coins and paper currency into circulation by issuing them to banks. It also supervises the activities of member banks abroad, and regulates certain aspects of international finance.

It has been said that the Federal Reserve is actually an informal fourth branch of the United States government because it is composed of national policy makers. However, in practice, the Federal Reserve

---

39. What happens when the Federal Reserve provides too little money?

   (A) Demand for loans increases.
   (B) Unemployment slows down.
   (C) Interest rates go up.
   (D) Businesses expand.

40. In paragraph 2, the author suggests that inflation is caused by

   (A) high unemployment rates
   (B) too much money in the economy
   (C) very high fuel prices
   (D) a limited supply of goods

Paragraph 2 is marked with an arrow (→).

More Available

of Governors in Washington, appointed by the President and confirmed by the Senate.

→ The System's primary function is to control monetary policy by influencing the cost and availability of money and credit through the purchase and sale of government securities. If the Federal Reserve provides too little money, interest rates tend to be high, borrowing is expensive, business activity slows down, unemployment goes up, and there is a danger of recession. If there is too much money, interest rates decline, and borrowing can lead to excess demand, pushing up prices and fueling inflation.

The Fed has several responsibilities in addition to controlling the money supply. In collaboration with the US Department of the Treasury, the Fed puts new coins and paper currency into circulation by issuing them to banks. It also supervises the activities of member banks abroad, and regulates certain aspects of international finance.

It has been said that the Federal Reserve is actually an informal fourth branch of the United States government because it is composed of national policy makers. However, in practice, the Federal Reserve does not stray far from the financial policies

---

41. Look at the word them in the passage. Click on the word or phrase in the **bold** text that them refers to.

End

of recession. If there is too much money, interest rates decline, and borrowing can lead to excess demand, pushing up prices and fueling inflation.

The Fed has several responsibilities in addition to controlling the money supply. In collaboration with the US Department of the Treasury, the Fed puts new coins and paper currency into circulation by issuing them to banks. It also supervises the activities of member banks abroad, and regulates certain aspects of international finance.

It has been said that the Federal Reserve is actually an informal fourth branch of the United States government because it is composed of national policy makers. However, in practice, the Federal Reserve does not stray far from the financial policies established by the executive branch of the government. Although it is true that the Fed does not depend on Congress for budget allocations, and therefore is free from the partisan politics that influences other governmental bodies, it is still responsible for frequent reports to the Congress on the conduct of monetary policies.

42. Click on the paragraph that outlines the responsibilities of the Fed to banks overseas.

    Scroll the passage to see all of the paragraphs.

43. What does the author mean by the statement

    However, in practice, the Federal Reserve does not stray far from the financial policies established by the executive branch of the government?

    Ⓐ The Fed is more powerful than the executive branch of the government.
    Ⓑ The policies of the Fed and those of the executive branch of the government are not the same.
    Ⓒ The Fed tends to follow the policies of the executive branch of the government.
    Ⓓ The Fed reports to the executive branch of the government.

44. All of the following statements could be included in a summary of the passage EXCEPT:

    Ⓐ The Federal Reserve is an independent agency of the United States government.
    Ⓑ The Federal Reserve controls the flow of money and credit by buying and selling government securities.
    Ⓒ The Federal Reserve issues new coins and currency to banks.
    Ⓓ The Federal Reserve receives its yearly budget from Congress.

45. The following sentence can be added to the passage.

> **In fact, the Fed is not confined by the usual checks and balances that apply to the three official branches of government—the executive, the legislative, and the judicial.**

Where would it best fit in the passage?

Click on the square (■) to add the sentence to the passage.

Scroll the passage to see all of the choices.

them to banks. It also supervises the activities of member banks abroad, and regulates certain aspects of international finance.

■ It has been said that the Federal Reserve is actually an informal fourth branch of the United States government because it is composed of national policy makers. ■ However, in practice, the Federal Reserve does not stray far from the financial policies established by the executive branch of the government. ■ Although it is true that the Fed does not depend on Congress for budget allocations, and therefore is free from the partisan politics that influences other governmental bodies, it is still responsible for frequent reports to the Congress on the conduct of monetary policies. ■

To check your answers for Model Test 4, refer to the Answer Key on pages 380–381. For an explanation of the answers, refer to the Explanatory Answers for Model Test 4 on pages 421–432.

Writing Section Model Test 4

When you take a Model Test, you should use one sheet of paper, both sides. Time each Model Test carefully. After you have read the topic, you should spend 30 minutes writing. For results that would be closest to the actual testing situation, it is recommended that an English teacher score your test, using the guidelines on page 242 of this book.

Advances in transportation and communication like the airplane and the telephone have changed the way that nations interact with each other in a global society. Choose another technological innovation that you think is important. Give specific reasons for your choice.

Notes

ANSWER KEYS FOR THE TOEFL REVIEW EXERCISES AND MODEL TESTS

Answer Key—Exercises for Structure

Patterns

Problem		Part A	Part B
Problem	1	**(A)**	**(A)** have
Problem	2	**(C)**	**(A)** to evolve
Problem	3	**(D)**	**(B)** smoking
Problem	4	**(D)**	**(B)** permitting
Problem	5	**(C)**	**(A)** saw
Problem	6	**(A)**	**(B)** turns *or* will turn
Problem	7	**(A)**	**(C)** will have to pay *or* may have to pay
Problem	8	**(A)**	**(C)** unless they complete
Problem	9	**(D)**	**(B)** be used
Problem	10	**(B)**	**(A)** be
Problem	11	**(B)**	**(B)** for making *or* to make
Problem	12	**(C)**	**(C)** measured
Problem	13	**(A)**	**(A)** It is believed
Problem	14	**(D)**	**(C)** will have succeeded
Problem	15	**(B)**	**(B)** is losing
Problem	16	**(B)**	**(D)** should be discontinued
Problem	17	**(A)**	**(D)** for them
Problem	18	**(A)**	**(A)** which
Problem	19	**(C)**	**(C)** eight or ten computers
Problem	20	**(C)**	**(A)** Religion
Problem	21	**(B)**	**(A)** Space
Problem	22	**(C)**	**(A)** Progress
Problem	23	**(B)**	**(C)** pieces of equipment
Problem	24	**(C)**	**(A)** Spelling *or* To spell
Problem	25	**(B)**	**(A)** ~~it is~~
Problem	26	**(A)**	**(A)** The philosophy
Problem	27	**(D)**	**(B)** no
Problem	28	**(C)**	**(A)** Most of *or* Almost all of
Problem	29	**(C)**	**(A)** Sex education
Problem	30	**(A)**	**(B)** four-stage
Problem	31	**(A)**	**(B)** so expensive

Problem		*Part A*	*Part B*
Problem	32	**(B)**	**(B)** the same
Problem	33	**(C)**	**(D)** like
Problem	34	**(A)**	**(B)** differ from *or* are different from
Problem	35	**(C)**	**(A)** as much as
Problem	36	**(A)**	**(A)** more than
Problem	37	**(C)**	**(C)** as many as
Problem	38	**(C)**	**(B)** most
Problem	39	**(C)**	**(B)** worse
Problem	40	**(C)**	**(A)** the more intense
Problem	41	**(A)**	**(B)** like that of England
Problem	42	**(B)**	**(B)** besides
Problem	43	**(C)**	**(C)** because
Problem	44	**(D)**	**(D)** also easy to install
Problem	45	**(B)**	**(D)** complete
Problem	46	**(D)**	**(C)** the plane is
Problem	47	**(B)**	**(B)** does the same major league baseball team win
Problem	48	**(C)**	**(A)** since 1930
Problem	49	**(C)**	**(B)** as a whole
Problem	50	**(B)**	**(B)** that

Style

Problem		*Part A*	*Part B*
Problem	1	**(C)**	**(C)** were
Problem	2	**(C)**	**(B)** gave
Problem	3	**(B)**	**(B)** enables
Problem	4	**(C)**	**(A)** is
Problem	5	**(B)**	**(A)** There are
Problem	6	**(D)**	**(D)** its
Problem	7	**(B)**	**(C)** their
Problem	8	**(B)**	**(A)** Having designed
Problem	9	**(D)**	**(C)** find
Problem	10	**(C)**	**(B)** to develop
Problem	11	**(B)**	**(D)** to use as currency
Problem	12	**(B)**	**(B)** rapidly

Problem		Part A	Part B
Problem	13	**(B)**	**(A)** an old one *or* an ancient one
Problem	14	**(C)**	**(A)** ~~is~~
Problem	15	**(B)**	**(A)** raised
Problem	16	**(C)**	**(A)** lies
Problem	17	**(B)**	**(B)** sits
Problem	18	**(B)**	**(C)** do
Problem	19	**(A)**	**(B)** depends on
Problem	20	**(B)**	**(B)** differ

Answer Key—Exercises for Reading

Problem 1. Previewing

A black hole is a region of space created by the total gravitational collapse of matter. It is so intense that nothing, not even light or radiation, can escape. In other words, it is a one-way surface through which matter can fall inward but cannot emerge.

Some astronomers believe that a black hole may be formed when a large star collapses inward from its own weight. So long as they are emitting heat and light into space, stars support themselves against their own gravitational pull with the outward thermal pressure generated by heat from nuclear reactions deep in their interiors. But if a star eventually exhausts its nuclear fuel, then its unbalanced gravitational attraction could cause it to contract and collapse. Furthermore, it could begin to pull in surrounding matter, including nearby comets and planets, creating a black hole.

The topic is black holes.

Problem 2. Reading for Main Ideas

For more than a century, despite attacks by a few opposing scientists, Charles Darwin's theory of evolution by natural selection has stood firm. Now, however, some respected biologists are beginning to question whether the theory accounts for major developments such as the shift from water to land habitation. Clearly, evolution has not proceeded steadily but has progressed by radical advances. Recent research in molecular biology, particularly in the study of DNA, provides us with a new possibility. Not only environmental changes but also genetic codes in the underlying structure of DNA could govern evolution.

The main idea is that biologists are beginning to question Darwin's theory. A good title would be "Questions about Darwin's Theory."

Problem 3. Using Contexts for Vocabulary

1. *To auction* means to sell.

2. *Proprietor* means an owner.

3. *Formerly* means in the past.

4. *To sample* means to try or to taste.

5. *Royalty* means payment.

Problem 4. Scanning for Details

To prepare for a career in engineering, a student must begin planning in high school. Mathematics and science should form the core curriculum. For example, in a school where sixteen credit hours are required for high school graduation, four should be in mathematics, one each in chemistry, biology, and physics. The remaining credits should include four in English and at least three in the humanities and social sciences. The average entering freshman in engineering should have achieved at least a 2.5 grade point average on a 4.0 scale in his or her high school. Although deficiencies can be corrected during the first year, the student who needs additional work should expect to spend five instead of four years to complete a degree.

1. What is the average grade point for an entering freshman in engineering?

   2.5

2. When should a student begin planning for a career in engineering?

   in high school

3. How can a student correct deficiencies in preparation?

   by spending five years

4. How many credits should a student have in English?

   four

5. How many credits are required for a high school diploma?

   sixteen

Problem 5. Making Inferences

When an acid is dissolved in water, the acid molecule divides into two parts, a hydrogen ion and another ion. An ion is an atom or a group of atoms which has an electrical charge. The charge can be either positive or negative. If hydrochloric acid is mixed with water, for example, it divides into hydrogen ions and chlorine ions. A strong acid ionizes to a great extent, but a weak acid does not ionize so much. The strength of an acid, therefore, depends on how much it ionizes, not on how many hydrogen ions are produced. It is interesting that nitric acid and sulfuric acid become greatly ionized whereas boric acid and carbonic acid do not.

1. What kind of acid is sulfuric acid?

A strong acid ionizes to a great extent, and sulfuric acid becomes greatly ionized. Conclusion: Sulfuric acid is a strong acid!

2. What kind of acid is boric acid?

A weak acid does not ionize so much and boric acid does not ionize greatly. Conclusion: Boric acid is a weak acid.

Problem 6. Identifying Exceptions

All music consists of two elements—expression and design. Expression is inexact and subjective, and may be enjoyed in a personal or instinctive way. Design, on the other hand is exact and must be analyzed objectively in order to be understood and appreciated. The folk song, for example, has a definite musical <u>design</u> <u>which relies on simple repetition</u> with a <u>definite beginning and ending</u>. A folk song generally consists of one stanza of music repeated for each stanza of verse.

Because of their communal, and usually <u>uncertain origin</u>, folk songs are often popular verse set to music. They are not always recorded, and tend to be passed on in a kind of musical version of oral history. Each singer revises and perfects the song. In part as a consequence of this continuous revision process, most folk songs are almost perfect in their construction and design. A particular singer's interpretation of the folk song may provide an interesting expression, but the simple design that underlies the song itself is stable and enduring.

1. All of the following are true of a folk song EXCEPT

✓ There is a clear start and finish.
✓ The origin is often not known.
   The design may change in the interpretation.
✓ Simple repetition is characteristic of its design.

Problem 7. Locating References

The National Road, also known as the Cumberland Road, was constructed in the early 1800s to provide transportation between the established commercial areas of the
Line East and Northwest Territory. By 1818, the road had
(5) reached Wheeling, West Virginia, 130 miles from its point of origin in Cumberland, Maryland. The cost was a monumental thirteen thousand dollars per mile.

Upon reaching the Ohio River, the National Road became one of the major trade routes to the western states
(10) and territories, providing Baltimore with a trade advantage over neighboring cities. In order to compete, New York state authorized the construction of the Erie Canal, and Philadelphia initiated a transportation plan to link it with Pittsburgh. Towns along the rivers, canals, and the
(15) new National Road became important trade centers.

1. The word "its" in line 5 refers to *the road.*

2. The word "it" in line 13 refers to *the canal.*

Problem 8. Referring to the Passage

In September of 1929, traders experienced a lack of confidence in the stock market's ability to continue its phenomenal rise. Prices fell. For many inexperienced
Line investors, the drop produced a panic. They had all their
(5) money tied up in the market, and they were pressed to sell before the prices fell even lower. Sell orders were coming in so fast that the ticker tape at the New York Stock Exchange could not accommodate all the transactions.

To try to reestablish confidence in the market, a pow-
(10) erful group of New York bankers agreed to pool their funds and purchase stock above current market values. Although the buy orders were minimal, they were counting on their reputations to restore confidence on the part

of the smaller investors, thereby affecting the number of
(15) sell orders. On Thursday, October 24, Richard Whitney,
the Vice President of the New York Stock Exchange and a
broker for the J.P. Morgan Company, made the effort on
their behalf. Initially, it appeared to have been successful,
then, on the following Tuesday, the crash began again and
(20) accelerated. By 1932, stocks were worth only twenty percent of their value at the 1929 high. The results of the
crash had extended into every aspect of the economy,
causing a long and painful depression, referred to in
American history as the Great Depression.

1. Where in the passage does the author refer to the reason for
the stock market crash?   *Lines 1 - 4.*

2. Where in the passage does the author suggest that there was a
temporary recovery in the stock market?

Line 18.

Model Test 1—Paper and Pencil TOEFL

Section 1: Listening Comprehension

1. (A)	10. (D)	19. (B)	28. (C)	37. (B)	46. (B)
2. (B)	11. (A)	20. (A)	29. (A)	38. (C)	47. (D)
3. (C)	12. (D)	21. (A)	30. (B)	39. (B)	48. (C)
4. (B)	13. (A)	22. (B)	31. (C)	40. (C)	49. (B)
5. (C)	14. (C)	23. (A)	32. (C)	41. (C)	50. (A)
6. (C)	15. (C)	24. (C)	33. (A)	42. (A)	
7. (D)	16. (A)	25. (D)	34. (C)	43. (A)	
8. (D)	17. (D)	26. (B)	35. (D)	44. (C)	
9. (A)	18. (B)	27. (A)	36. (B)	45. (B)	

Section 2: Structure and Written Expression

1. (C)	8. (C)	15. (B)	22. (D)	29. (B)	36. (D)
2. (B)	9. (A)	16. (A)	23. (D)	30. (B)	37. (C)
3. (A)	10. (C)	17. (B)	24. (C)	31. (B)	38. (A)
4. (C)	11. (C)	18. (C)	25. (A)	32. (D)	39. (D)
5. (C)	12. (A)	19. (B)	26. (B)	33. (A)	40. (D)
6. (B)	13. (C)	20. (A)	27. (B)	34. (A)	
7. (D)	14. (A)	21. (B)	28. (B)	35. (A)	

Section 3: Reading Comprehension

1. (A)	10. (C)	19. (C)	28. (C)	37. (B)	46. (C)
2. (D)	11. (A)	20. (B)	29. (A)	38. (A)	47. (A)
3. (C)	12. (C)	21. (B)	30. (C)	39. (D)	48. (A)
4. (D)	13. (C)	22. (D)	31. (C)	40. (C)	49. (A)
5. (B)	14. (D)	23. (C)	32. (A)	41. (D)	50. (C)
6. (C)	15. (C)	24. (A)	33. (A)	42. (D)	
7. (B)	16. (D)	25. (C)	34. (A)	43. (A)	
8. (D)	17. (D)	26. (A)	35. (C)	44. (B)	
9. (C)	18. (A)	27. (B)	36. (B)	45. (C)	

Model Test 2—Paper and Pencil TOEFL

Section 1: Listening Comprehension

1. (B)	10. (C)	19. (B)	28. (D)	37. (A)	46. (C)
2. (C)	11. (A)	20. (B)	29. (A)	38. (D)	47. (A)
3. (A)	12. (C)	21. (B)	30. (A)	39. (D)	48. (C)
4. (A)	13. (A)	22. (A)	31. (B)	40. (A)	49. (C)
5. (B)	14. (B)	23. (D)	32. (C)	41. (D)	50. (D)
6. (B)	15. (C)	24. (A)	33. (D)	42. (B)	
7. (D)	16. (A)	25. (D)	34. (D)	43. (C)	
8. (D)	17. (C)	26. (A)	35. (D)	44. (D)	
9. (D)	18. (B)	27. (C)	36. (A)	45. (A)	

Section 2: Structure and Written Expression

1. (D)	8. (C)	15. (B)	22. (A)	29. (B)	36. (C)
2. (B)	9. (A)	16. (C)	23. (C)	30. (C)	37. (C)
3. (B)	10. (D)	17. (D)	24. (B)	31. (D)	38. (D)
4. (B)	11. (C)	18. (B)	25. (A)	32. (A)	39. (A)
5. (A)	12. (B)	19. (C)	26. (B)	33. (D)	40. (C)
6. (C)	13. (C)	20. (A)	27. (D)	34. (D)	
7. (B)	14. (D)	21. (A)	28. (C)	35. (C)	

Section 3: Reading Comprehension

1. (A)	10. (B)	19. (B)	28. (C)	37. (D)	46. (A)
2. (C)	11. (B)	20. (C)	29. (A)	38. (B)	47. (B)
3. (B)	12. (A)	21. (D)	30. (D)	39. (A)	48. (B)
4. (A)	13. (A)	22. (C)	31. (B)	40. (C)	49. (B)
5. (B)	14. (B)	23. (D)	32. (C)	41. (A)	50. (D)
6. (C)	15. (A)	24. (A)	33. (B)	42. (C)	
7. (D)	16. (C)	25. (A)	34. (C)	43. (B)	
8. (B)	17. (C)	26. (D)	35. (A)	44. (C)	
9. (A)	18. (A)	27. (D)	36. (B)	45. (C)	

Model Test 3—Computer-Assisted TOEFL

Section 1: Listening

1. **(D)**	14. **(B)**	27. **(C)**	40. **(A)(C)**
2. **(D)**	15. **(B)**	28. **(D)(C)(B)(A)**	41. **(B)(C)**
3. **(B)**	16. **(B)**	29. **(C)**	42. **(C)**
4. **(C)**	17. **(D)**	30. **(A)(B)**	43. **(C)**
5. **(B)**	18. **(C)**	31. **(A)**	44. **(C)**
6. **(B)**	19. **(C)**	32. **(C)**	45. **(A)**
7. **(C)**	20. **(A)**	33. **(C)**	46. **(A)(B)**
8. **(A)**	21. **(B)**	34. **(A)(B)(C)(D)**	47. **(C)**
9. **(B)**	22. **(D)**	35. **(B)**	48. **(C)**
10. **(D)**	23. **(A)**	36. **(D)**	49. **(D)**
11. **(B)**	24. **(C)**	37. **(D)**	50. **(B)**
12. **(A)**	25. **(C)**	38. **(A)**	
13. **(C)**	26. **(B)(C)**	39. **(B)(A)(C)**	

Section 2: Structure

1. **(D)**	5. **(C)**	9. **(A)**	13. **(C)**	17. **(C)**
2. **(B)**	6. **(D)**	10. **(C)**	14. **(D)**	18. **(C)**
3. **(D)**	7. **(D)**	11. **(B)**	15. **(B)**	19. **(A)**
4. **(A)**	8. **(A)**	12. **(D)**	16. **(A)**	20. **(C)**

Section 3: Reading

1. **(A)**	11. **(B)**	21. **sentence 7, paragraph 3**
2. **(C)**	12. **(A)**	22. **(C)**
3. **increased**	13. **(B)**	23. **(D)**
4. **(A)**	14. **(A)**	24. **(B)**
5. **(B)**	15. **(C)**	25. **(D)**
6. **(D)**	16. **(D)**	26. **(A)**
7. **(B)**	17. **(A)**	27. **maintained**
8. **(A)**	18. **(B)**	28. **(B)**
9. **(C)**	19. **(A)**	29. **(A)**
10. **sentence 1, paragraph 3**	20. **shapes**	30. **(C)**

31. **(B)**	37. **(D)**	43. **(B)**
32. **(B)**	38. **complex**	44. **(A)**
33. **(B)**	39. **(A)**	45. **sentence 1,**
34. **(C)**	40. **(B)**	**paragraph 3**
35. **(A)**	41. **(B)**	
36. **(A)**	42. **(C)**	

Model Test 4—Computer-Assisted TOEFL

Section 1: Listening

1. **(B)**	14. **(C)**	27. **(A)**	40. **(B)**
2. **(B)**	15. **(C)**	28. **(C)**	41. **(C)**
3. **(C)**	16. **(D)**	29. **(A)**	42. **(C)(A)(B)**
4. **(C)**	17. **(A)**	30. **(A)(C)**	43. **(C)**
5. **(C)**	18. **(C)**	31. **(B)**	44. **(B)**
6. **(C)**	19. **(A)**	32. **(B)**	45. **(C)**
7. **(C)**	20. **(D)**	33. **(C)**	46. **(B)**
8. **(C)**	21. **(D)**	34. **(A)**	47. **(B)**
9. **(B)**	22. **(B)**	35. **(B)**	48. **(A)**
10. **(C)**	23. **(A)**	36. **(C)**	49. **(B)**
11. **(A)**	24. **(A)(D)**	37. **(A)**	50. **(B)(D)**
12. **(B)**	25. **(B)**	38. **(B)**	
13. **(B)**	26. **(B)(D)**	39. **(A)(D)**	

Section 2: Structure

1. **(B)**	5. **(D)**	9. **(D)**	13. **(C)**	17. **(C)**
2. **(D)**	6. **(C)**	10. **(C)**	14. **(D)**	18. **(B)**
3. **(B)**	7. **(A)**	11. **(C)**	15. **(C)**	19. **(C)**
4. **(D)**	8. **(C)**	12. **(C)**	16. **(B)**	20. **(C)**

Section 3: Reading

1. **(B)**
2. **(B)**
3. **about**
4. **(C)**
5. **(A)**
6. **sentence 1, paragraph 2**
7. **(B)**
8. **(B)**
9. **(A)**
10. **(C)**
11. **(A)**
12. **(A)**
13. **(D)**
14. **(B)**
15. **(C)**
16. **(B)**
17. **sentence 4, paragraph 2**

18. **guiding**
19. **(C)**
20. **(C)**
21. **(A)**
22. **(D)**
23. **(A)**
24. **(D)**
25. **the viruses**
26. **(D)**
27. **(C)**
28. **(B)**
29. **(B)**
30. **(B)**
31. **types**
32. **(C)**
33. **"...for type-B virus. Approximately every..."**

34. **(B)**
35. **(A)**
36. **(D)**
37. **(B)**
38. **(B)**
39. **(C)**
40. **(B)**
41. **(C)**
42. **sentence 3, paragraph 3**
43. **(C)**
44. **(D)**
45. **"...policy makers. In fact, the Fed..."**

EXPLANATORY
ANSWERS FOR THE
TOEFL MODEL TESTS

Model Test 1—Paper and Pencil TOEFL

Section 1: Listening Comprehension

1. **(A)** Since the woman agrees with the man, it must be concluded that she will not go home for spring vacation. Choice (C) contradicts the fact that she will be graduating in May. Choices (B) and (D) are not mentioned and may not be concluded from information in the conversation.

2. **(B)** From the reference to serving *coffee* with *lunch*, it must be concluded that the conversation took place at a restaurant. Coffee may be bought at a grocery store, but it is not customary to serve lunch at any of the places referred to in Choices (A), (C), and (D).

3. **(C)** From the reference to *the assignment for Monday*, it must be concluded that the speakers are talking about homework. Choices (A), (B), and (D) are all mentioned in the conversation in reference to the assignment.

4. **(B)** Because of the woman's suggestion that the man lock the door at night and because the man assures her that no one will break in, it must be concluded that the woman thinks someone will enter. Choices (A), (C), and (D) are not mentioned and may not be concluded from information in the conversation.

5. **(C)** Since the man asks about her brother's birthday gift, and the woman has not purchased one yet, it must be concluded that she needs a gift for her brother. Choice (A) contradicts the fact that she has been thinking about what to get him for his birthday. Choice (D) contradicts the fact that her brother has not received the gift yet. Choice (B) is not mentioned and may not be concluded from information in the conversation.

6. **(C)** *Cramming* is an idiomatic expression that means studying a lot, especially just before a test. Choices (A), (B), and (D) contradict the fact that the man is confident about being ready for the test.

7. **(D)** Since the woman refers to Mr. Adams as her husband, it must be concluded that she is Mrs. Adams. Choice (A) refers to Mr. Miller, not to the woman. Choice (C) contradicts the fact that her husband is at work. Choice (B) is not mentioned and may not be concluded from information in the conversation.

8. **(D)** Because *don't be too sure* means that the speaker is skeptical, it must be concluded that the man doubts what the woman says. He believes that Jack will quit his job. Choices (B) and (C) refer to what the woman, not the man, believes. Jack is trying to sell his house, but Choice (A) is not mentioned and may not be concluded from information in the conversation.

9. **(A)** Since the man says that he needs a book for an English

course, it must be concluded that he will buy the textbook. Choice (C) contradicts the fact that he is already in the bookstore. Choice (D) contradicts the fact that he needs a book for the course. Choice (B) is not mentioned and may not be concluded from information in the conversation.

10. **(D)** Since the woman argues that the other dress is more comfortable, it must be concluded that she will wear the more comfortable one. Choice (B) contradicts the fact that she has a new dress. Choice (C) contradicts the fact that she prefers a dress that the man did not choose. Choice (A) is not mentioned and may not be concluded from information in the conversation.

11. **(A)** To *turn someone off* is an idiomatic expression that means the speaker does not like something or someone. Choice (D) contradicts the fact that the woman does not like the class. Choice (C) contradicts the fact that the woman thinks Professor Collins is a great person. Choice (B) is not mentioned and may not be concluded from information in the conversation.

12. **(D)** The woman said that she stayed home. Choices (A) and (B) refer to the place where the woman was planning to go, not to the place where she went. She had not been feeling well, but Choice (C) was not mentioned and may not be concluded from information in the conversation.

13. **(A)** To *not put off* is an idiomatic expression that means to stop postponing. Choices (B) and (C) contradict the fact that the

woman has not made an appointment yet. Choice (D) is not mentioned and may not be concluded from information in the conversation.

14. **(C)** To be *used to something* is an idiomatic expression that means to be accustomed to something. Choices (A), (B), and (D) are not paraphrases of the expression, and may not be concluded from information in the conversation.

15. **(C)** To *get caught up* is an idiomatic expression that means to bring work or assignments up to date. Choice (B) contradicts the fact that the man says he knows what time it is. Choices (A) and (D) are not mentioned and may not be concluded from information in the conversation.

16. **(A)** *Meaning to* is an idiomatic expression that means to intend. To "have someone over" means to invite them to one's home. Choice (B) contradicts the fact that he wants to invite her to his home. Choices (C) and (D) are not mentioned and may not be concluded from information in the conversation.

17. **(D)** To *pass* is an idiomatic expression that means to lose a turn. Choices (A), (B), and (C) are not paraphrases of the expression, and may not be concluded from information in the conversation.

18. **(B)** To *look into something* is an idiomatic expression that means to investigate. Choice (A) refers to the woman's conclusion, not to the man's intention. Choices (C) and (D) are not mentioned and may not be concluded from information in the conversation.

19. **(B)** To *take care of something* is an idiomatic expression that means to be responsible for it. Choices (A), (C), and (D) are not paraphrases of the expression, and may not be concluded from information in the conversation.

20. **(A)** Since the man says that they should take the opposite direction from the announcer's recommended route, he implies that the announcer is often wrong. Choices (B), (C), and (D) are not mentioned and may not be concluded from information in the conversation.

21. **(A)** To *get mixed up* is an idiomatic expression that means to become confused. Choice (C) contradicts the fact that the man understands the lectures. Choices (B) and (D) are not mentioned and may not be concluded from information in the conversation.

22. **(B)** To *have it made* is an idiomatic expression that means to be very fortunate. Choices (C) and (D) contradict the fact that when asked, the woman responds that she knows Randy. Choice (A) is not mentioned and may not be concluded from information in the conversation.

23. **(A)** To *turn in* is an idiomatic expression that means to submit. "Ahead of time" means early. Choice (C) contradicts the fact that she wants to turn in the paper before it is due. Choice (D) contradicts the fact that she is ready to turn the paper in. Choice (B) is not mentioned and may not be concluded from information in the conversation.

24. **(C)** Since the woman reminds the man that he has never heard her sing, she implies that she is not a good singer. Choice (A) refers to the man's suggestion, not to the woman's preference. Choices (B) and (D) are not mentioned and may not be concluded from information in the conversation.

25. **(D)** "You have to take it [the class] in order to graduate." Choice (A) refers to the man's attitude, not to the woman's opinion. Choice (B) contradicts the fact that the class is required for graduation. Choice (C) is not mentioned and may not be concluded from information in the conversation.

26. **(B)** "He'd better trade that car in [for a different car]." Choices (A), (C), and (D) are not mentioned and may not be concluded from information in the conversation.

27. **(A)** ". . . the T.A. said to get into a study group and quiz each other." Choice (B) refers to the type of exam that they will be given, not to the T.A.'s suggestion. Choice (C) refers to quizzes, but the T.A. suggests that they "quiz each other," which means to ask each other questions. Choice (D) contradicts the fact that the professor recommends studying alone, not in a group.

28. **(C)** Since the woman goes to get a pen, it must be concluded that she will sign the form. Choice (A) contradicts the fact that the woman says he doesn't need an appointment. Choice (B) refers to the pen that the woman, not the man, will use. Choice (D) contradicts the fact that the man is asked to wait for the woman.

29. **(A)** "I'd better make one more draft." A "draft" is a revision of written work. Choice (D) refers to the man's suggestion, not to what the woman is going to do. Choices (B) and (C) are not mentioned and may not be concluded from information in the conversation.

30. **(B)** "That's what I thought [that the computer. . . scheduled for the fifth]." Choice (C) refers to the woman's original statement, not to her final conclusion. Choice (D) contradicts the fact that payments are still due. Choice (A) refers to an error made by the woman, not the computer.

31. **(C)** "I'm waiting for the number seven [bus] myself." Choice (A) contradicts the fact that the woman and the man have never met before. Choice (D) contradicts the fact that she wishes it would rain and cool off. The woman moved to Florida with her mother, but Choice (B) is not mentioned and may not be concluded from information in the conversation.

32. **(C)** "I don't remember it ever being so hot and dry in March before." Choice (A) refers to the weather in Indiana, not in Florida. Choice (B) refers to the weather on the day of the conversation, which is noted as not being usual. Choice (D) contradicts the fact that the man cannot remember it ever being so hot and dry in March.

33. **(A)** "You're from Florida then." "I was born in New York, but I've lived here [in Florida] for ten years now." Choice (B) refers to the place where the man was born, not to where the conversation takes place. Choice (C) refers to the place where the woman would like to be, not to where she is now. Choice (D) refers to the place where the woman lived before she moved to Florida.

34. **(C)** "It never comes exactly on the half-hour as it should." The number in Choice (A) refers to the amount of time that the woman has been waiting, not to when the bus is scheduled to pass. Choice (B) refers to the time of the conversation. Choice (D) is not mentioned and may not be concluded from information in the conversation.

35. **(D)** ". . . I need three letters of recommendation. Would you be willing to write me one?" Choice (A) contradicts the fact that Betty is already in the professor's seminar class. Choice (C) refers to additional information that the professor gives to Betty, not to the purpose of her call. Choice (B) is not mentioned and may not be concluded from information in the conversation.

36. **(B)** "I think you are an excellent candidate for graduate school." Choice (A) contradicts the fact that Betty is already taking the seminar. Choice (D) contradicts the fact that the professor does not recall the deadline for applications. Choice (C) is not mentioned and may not be concluded from information in the conversation.

37. **(B)** "The committee meets on April 30." Choices (A) and (D) refer to the person who will

receive the letter, not to who will make the decision. Choice (C) refers to the person who will make a recommendation.

38. **(C)** "The committee meets on April 30, so all the materials must be submitted before then." Choice (A) contradicts the fact that the materials must be submitted before April 30. Choices (B) and (D) are not mentioned and may not be concluded from information in the conversation.

39. **(B)** Because the speaker talks about "trade," "manufacturing," and "competition," it must be concluded that he is a professor of business. It is not as probable that the professors and lecturers mentioned in Choices (A), (C), and (D) would discuss trade.

40. **(C)** "To maintain this favorable balance of trade, England went to fantastic lengths to keep secret the advanced manufacturing processes . . ." Choice (D) contradicts the fact that it was the colony (America), not England, that stole the plans. Choices (A) and (B) are not mentioned and may not be concluded from information in the talk.

41. **(C)** "Determined to take nothing in writing, Slater memorized the intricate designs for all the machines in an English textile mill. . . ." Choices (A) and (B) contradict the fact that Slater, in partnership with Brown, opened a mill in the United States in the state of Rhode Island. Choice (D) contradicts the fact that he took nothing in writing.

42. **(A)** ". . . in part as a result of Slater and Brown, America had

changed from a country of small farmers and craftsmen to an industrial nation . . . ." Choices (B), (C), and (D) are not mentioned and may not be concluded from information in the talk.

43. **(A)** "So many different kinds of writing have been called essays, it is difficult to define exactly what an essay is." Choices (B), (C), and (D) are secondary themes used to develop a definition of the essay.

44. **(C)** ". . . four characteristics that are true of most essays." Choices (A), (B), and (D) are secondary themes used to develop the main theme of the talk.

45. **(B)** ". . . an essay [is] a short, prose composition with a personal viewpoint that discusses one topic." Choice (B) contradicts the fact that an essay is written in prose, not poetry.

46. **(B)** ". . . let's brainstorm some topics for your first essay assignment." Choices (A), (C), and (D) are not mentioned and may not be concluded from information in the conversation.

47. **(D)** The main purpose of this talk is to summarize Jefferson's life. Choices (A), (B), and (C) are secondary themes in the life of Jefferson.

48. **(C)** "Although Jefferson was a Republican, he at first tried to cooperate with Alexander Hamilton, a Federalist. . . ." Choice (A) refers to Jefferson's opinion of Hamilton's political affiliation. Choice (B) refers to Hamilton, not Jefferson. Choice (D) is not mentioned and may not be concluded from information in the talk.

49. **(B)** "He [Jefferson] and Federalist Aaron Burr received an identical vote, but the Republican Congress elected to approve Jefferson as president." Choice (A) contradicts the fact that Jefferson and Burr received an identical vote. Choices (C) and (D) are not mentioned and may not be concluded from information in the conversation.

50. **(A)** "Thomas Jefferson was a statesman, a diplomat, an author, and an architect. . . . Not a gifted public speaker, he was most talented as a literary draftsman." Choices (B), (C), and (D) are all mentioned as attributes of Jefferson.

Section 2: Structure and Written Expression

1. **(C)** *Most* is used before a noncount noun to express a quantity that is larger than half the amount. A singular verb follows the noncount noun. Choice (A) does not have a verb. In Choice (B), the verb is before, not after the noun. In Choice (D), *the* is used before *most*.

2. **(B)** An adjective is used before *enough* to express sufficiency. In Choice (A), *goodly* is ungrammatical. The adverbial form of the adjective *good* is *well*. In Choice (C), *as* is unnecessary and incorrect. In Choice (D), the adjective is used after, not before *enough*.

3. **(A)** *The* can be used before a noncount noun that is followed by a qualifying phrase. *Population* should be *the population* before the qualifying phrase *of the Americas*.

4. **(C)** An adjective clause modifies a noun in the main clause. *That the earliest cultures evolved* modifies *the way*. Choice (A) is a clause marker *that* and a noun. Choice (B) is a verb and a noun. Choice (D) is a clause marker *which* and a noun.

5. **(C)** A sentence has a subject and a verb. Choice (A) is redundant because the subject pronoun *it* is used consecutively with the subject *calculus*. Choice (B) has the marker *that* to introduce a main clause. Choice (D) is redundant because it has a verb that replaces the main verb *can reduce*.

6. **(B)** Subject-verb order and a negative verb with *either* expresses negative agreement. Negative agreement with *neither* requires verb-subject order and an affirmative verb. In Choice (A), verb-subject order is reversed. In Choice (C), verb-subject order is reversed, and *neither* is used at the beginning, not at the end of the clause. In Choice (D) *either*, not *neither*, is used with verb-subject order and an affirmative verb. "Neither does Mexico" would also be correct.

7. **(D)** A sentence has a subject and a verb. Choice (A) does not have a verb. Choices (B) and (C) introduce a main clause subject and verb.

8. **(C)** The anticipatory clause *it is accepted that* introduces a subject and verb, *the formation . . . began.* Choices (A), (B), and (D)

are incomplete and ungrammatical.

9. **(A)** The word order for a passive sentence is a form of BE followed by a participle. Only Choice (A) has the correct word order. Choice (B) does not have a BE form. Choice (C) has a HAVE, not a BE form. Choice (D) is a present tense verb, not BE followed by a participle.

10. **(C)** Subject-verb order is used in the clause after a question word connector such as *how much*. In Choice (A), subject-verb order is reversed. In Choice (B), the auxiliary *does* is unnecessary and incorrect. In Choice (D), the verb *are* is repetitive. "The Consumer Price Index lists how much every car *is*" would also be correct.

11. **(C)** A logical conclusion about the past is expressed by *must have* and a participle. Choices (A), (B), and (D) are not logical because they imply that the theater will act to restore itself.

12. **(A)** The verb *to want* requires an infinitive complement. Choice (B) is an *-ing* form, not an infinitive. Choice (C) is a verb word. Choice (D) is ungrammatical.

13. **(C)** An introductory verbal phrase should immediately precede the noun that it modifies. Only Choice (C) provides a noun which could be logically modified by the introductory verbal phrase, *after seeing the movie*. Neither *the book* nor *the reading* could logically *see a movie* as would be implied by Choices (A), (B), and (D).

14. **(A)** An introductory phrase should immediately precede the subject noun that it modifies. It does not have a main verb. Choices (B) and (C) contain both subjects and verbs. Choice (D) does not modify the subject noun, *Carl Sandburg*.

15. **(B)** A form of *make* with someone such as *us* and a verb word expresses a causative. Choice (A) is an *-ing* form, not a verb word. Choice (C) is a past form. Choice (D) is an infinitive.

16. **(A)** *Responsible for* is a prepositional idiom. *Responsible the* should be *responsible for the*.

17. **(B)** A form of BE is used with the participle in passive sentences. *Practice* should be *practiced*.

18. **(C)** There must be agreement between pronoun and antecedent. *Their* should be *our* to agree with the second person antecedent *those of us*.

19. **(B)** *Wrote* should be *written* because the auxiliary *had* requires a participle. *Wrote* is a past form. *Written* is a participle.

20. **(A)** *Would have* and a participle in the result require *had* and a participle in the condition. Because *would have won* is used in the result, *would have* should be *had* in the condition.

21. **(B)** There must be agreement between pronoun and antecedent. *Which* should be *who* to refer to the antecedent *Shirley Temple Black*. *Which* refers to things. *Who* refers to persons.

22. **(D)** Comparative forms are usually followed by *than*. After the

comparative *more reasonable, as* should be *than.*

23. **(D)** *To know* should be *to know how* before the infinitive *to use. To know* is used before nouns and noun clauses. *To know how* is used before infinitives.

24. **(C)** *There* introduces inverted order, but there must still be agreement between subject and verb. *Has been* should be *have been* to agree with the plural subject *two major factions.*

25. **(A)** In order to refer to occupying a place on the battlefields, *lain* should be used. *To lay* means to put in a place, and the participle is *laid. To lie* means to occupy a place, and the participle is *lain.*

26. **(B)** *Purposeful* should be *purposes. Purposeful* is an adjective. *Purposes* is a noun.

27. **(B)** *Large* should be *largest.* Because there were more than two ethnic groups, a superlative form must be used.

28. **(B)** The determiner *a* is used before a singular count noun. *Results* should be *result.*

29. **(B)** Most adverbs of manner are formed by adding *-ly* to adjectives. *Calm* should be *calmly* to qualify the manner in which the talking should be done.

30. **(B)** When the degree of one quality, *the heat,* is dependent upon the degree of another quality, *the humidity,* two comparatives are used, each preceded by *the. The worst* should be *the worse* because it is a comparative.

31. **(B)** A dependent clause modifies an independent clause. *Which are* should be *are* to provide a verb for the subject *statistical data,* of the independent clause.

32. **(D)** Ideas in a series should be expressed by parallel structures. *The Assassinate* should be *The Assassination of* to provide for parallelism with the nouns *Causes, Economy,* and *Strategies.*

33. **(A)** *Despite of* is a combination of *despite* and *in spite of.* Either *despite* or *in spite of* should be used.

34. **(A)** Because it is a prepositional phrase, in a comparison *as every nation* should be *like every nation. As* functions as a conjunction. *Like* functions as a preposition.

35. **(A)** A verb word must be used in a clause after the phrase "It is necessary." *Met* should be *meet. Met* is a past form. *Meet* is a verb word.

36. **(D)** The verb *forbid* may be used with either an infinitive or an *-ing* complement. *From owning* should be *to own.* The *-ing* form *owning* would require the possessive pronoun modifier *their.*

37. **(C)** *More cheaper* should be *cheaper.* Because *cheap* is a one-syllable adjective, the comparative is formed by adding *-er. More* is used with two-syllable adjectives that do not end in *-y.*

38. **(A)** The verb *thought* establishes a point of view in the past. *Will* should be *would* in order to maintain the point of view.

39. **(D)** Because the verb *enjoy* requires an *-ing* form in the complement, *to play* should be *playing.*

40. **(D)** Ideas in a series should be expressed by parallel structures. *To plant* should be *planting* to provide for parallelism with the *-ing* forms *plowing* and *rotating*.

Section 3: Reading Comprehension

1. **(A)** "Webster's Work" is the best title because it states the main idea of the passage. Choice (B) is incorrect because Webster's dictionaries represent only part of the work referred to in the passage. Choices (C) and (D) are mentioned briefly in the discussion, but are not the most important topics.

2. **(D)** In the context of this passage, "inadequate" could best be replaced by "unsatisfactory." Choices (A), (B), and (C) are not accepted definitions of the word.

3. **(C)** ". . . he discovered how inadequate the available schoolbooks were for the children of a new and independent nation. . . . In response to the need for truly American textbooks, Webster published *A Grammatical Institute of the English Language*." Choice (A) is a result of having written *A Grammatical Institute*, not a reason for writing it. Choice (B) contradicts the fact that British books were available, but not appropriate. Choice (D) is not mentioned and may not be concluded from information in the passage.

4. **(D)** ". . . *The American Spelling Book* . . . provided him with a considerable income for the rest of his life." Choices (A), (B), and (C) are all publications by Webster, but the income afforded by each is not mentioned and may not be concluded from information in the passage.

5. **(B)** "Published in two volumes in 1828, *An American Dictionary of the English Language* . . . ." The numbers referred to in Choices (A), (C), and (D) are not mentioned and may not be concluded from information in the passage.

6. **(C)** "Published . . . in 1828, *An American Dictionary of the English Language* has become the recognized authority for usage . . . ." Choice (A) refers to the date that Webster finished his study of English and began writing the dictionary. Choice (B) refers to the date that Webster began work on the dictionary. Choice (D) refers to the date that Webster finished writing the dictionary, not to the date that it was published.

7. **(B)** "[His] purpose in writing [*An American Dictionary of the English Language*] was to demonstrate that the American language was developing distinct meanings, pronunciations, and spellings from those of British English." Choice (C) contradicts the fact that Webster promoted new spelling forms instead of the British forms that had been accepted by earlier authorities. Choice (D) occurred as a result of the publication, but it was not Webster's purpose in publishing *An American Dictionary of the English Language*. Choice (A) is not mentioned and may not be

concluded from information in the passage.

8. **(D)** "Webster's purpose in writing it [the dictionary] was to demonstrate that the American language was developing distinct meanings, pronunciations, and spellings from those of British English." Choices (A), (B), and (C) would change the meaning of the sentence.

9. **(C)** In the context of this passage, "distinct" is closest in meaning to "different." Choices (A), (B), and (D) are not accepted definitions.

10. **(C)** "He [Webster] is responsible for advancing the form . . . color . . . instead of colour." Choices (A), (B), and (D) are British English spellings.

11. **(A)** Choice (A) is the author's main purpose because the passage refers to the San Andreas Fault specifically. The general information referred to in Choices (B), (C), and (D) is not mentioned and may not be concluded from information in the passage.

12. **(C)** In the context of this passage, "originates" could best be replaced by "begins." Choices (A), (B), and (D) are not accepted definitions of the word.

13. **(C)** ". . . the San Andreas Fault . . . originates . . . six hundred miles from the Gulf of California and runs north. . . ." Choices (A), (B), and (D) contradict the fact that the fault runs north.

14. **(D)** ". . . the San Andreas Fault . . . runs north in an irregular line . . . ." The word *uneven* in Choice (D) means irregular. Choice (A) contradicts the fact that the line

is irregular. Choices (B) and (C) are not mentioned and may not be concluded from information in the passage.

15. **(C)** "Its western side always moves north in relation to its eastern side." Choices (A), (B), and (D) contradict the fact that the western side always moves north, not in any other direction.

16. **(D)** "Its western side always moves north in relation to its [the fault's] eastern side." Choices (A), (B), and (C) would change the meaning of the sentence.

17. **(D)** "Intermittent" means "occasional." Choices (A), (B), and (C) are not accepted definitions of the word.

18. **(A)** "Californians have long anticipated the recurrence of what they refer to as the 'Big One,' a destructive earthquake . . . ." Choices (B), (C), or (D) would change the meaning of the sentence.

19. **(C)** "Tremors are not unusual along the San Andreas Fault. . . ." Choice (B) contradicts the fact that tremors are not unusual. Choices (A) and (D) are not mentioned and may not be concluded from information in the passage.

20. **(B)** "The San Andreas Fault is a fracture at the congruence of two major plates of the earth's crust." Choice (A) refers to the plates, not to the fracture. Choices (C) and (D) refer to the results of the movement along the fracture, not to the fault.

21. **(B)** "The Structure of an Insect" is the best title because it states the main idea of the passage. Choice (C) is a secondary idea that is used to develop the main

idea. Choices (A) and (D) are not mentioned and may not be concluded from information in the passage.

22. **(D)** Because the passage is a statement of scientific facts written from an objective point of view, it must be concluded that the purpose is to inform. Choices (A) and (B) are improbable because the passage is not written from a subjective point of view. Choice (C) is improbable because of the scientific content.

23. **(C)** "Features of the mouth parts are very helpful in classifying the many kinds of insects." Choices (A), (B), and (D) are discussed, but not as a basis for classification.

24. **(A)** In the context of this passage, "majority" is closest in meaning to "more than half." Choices (B), (C), and (D) are not accepted definitions of the word.

25. **(C)** ". . . the maxillae which serve to direct food into the mouth between the jaws." Choice (A) refers to mandibles, not to maxillae. Choice (B) refers to sharp stylets. Choice (D) refers to the expanding labium.

26. **(A)** "A labrum above and a labium below are similar to an upper and lower lip." Choice (B) is compared to Choice (D). Choice (C) is discussed, but not compared to anything.

27. **(B)** ". . . the coiled drinking tube . . . called the proboscis . . . [is] composed . . . of modified maxillae." Choice (A) refers to food, not to the proboscis that is used in reaching it. Choices (C) and (D) are not mentioned and may

not be concluded from information in the passage.

28. **(C)** "In a mosquito or an aphid, mandibles and maxillae are modified to sharp stylets." The insect referred to in choice (A) has mandibles similar to jaws, not sharp stylets. The insect referred to in Choice (B) has a proboscis. The insect referred to in Choice (D) has a sponge-like mouth pad.

29. **(A)** In the context of this passage, "drill through" could best be replaced by "penetrate." Choices (B), (C), and (D) are not accepted definitions of the phrase.

30. **(C)** "In a housefly, the expanding labium forms a spongelike mouth pad that it [the housefly] can use to stamp over the surface of food." Choices (A), (B), and (D) would change the meaning of the sentence.

31. **(C)** The other choices are secondary ideas that are used to develop the primary topic, "interest." Choice (A) refers to the relationship of interest to banks. Choices (B) and (D) figure in the formula for computing interest.

32. **(A)** In the context of this passage, "sum" could best be replaced by "amount." Choices (B), (C), and (D) are not accepted definitions of the word.

33. **(A)** In the context of this passage, "fixed" is closest in meaning to "definite." Choices (B), (C), and (D) are not accepted definitions of the word.

34. **(A)** "Principal is the term used for the money that is borrowed, and the rate of interest is the percent per year of the principal charged for its [the principal's]

use." Choices (B), (C), and (D) would change the meaning of the sentence.

35. **(C)** "Interest = Principal × Rate × Time." One dollar at four percent for one year is $1 × .04 × 1, or $.04. Choices (A), (B), and (D) may not be computed on the basis of the formula in the passage.

36. **(B)** "The rate is expressed as a decimal fraction." Choices (A) and (C) are whole numbers, not decimal fractions. Choice (D) is a common, not a decimal, fraction.

37. **(B)** "Although the time may be less than, equal to, or greater than one year, most applications for loans are periods of less than one year." Choices (A) and (C) refer to other options, but not to the time for most applications. Choice (D) refers to the commercial year.

38. **(A)** In the context of this passage, "periods" refers to time. Choices (B), (C), and (D) are not accepted definitions of the word.

39. **(D)** "For purposes of computing interest for short periods, the commercial year or 360 days is commonly used. . ." Choices (A), (B), and (C) refer to situations that require the calendar year or 365 days, not the commercial year.

40. **(C)** "Interest is the sum charged for borrowing money." Choice (A) is a definition of principal, not interest. Choice (B) is a definition of the interest rate per time period. Choice (D) is not mentioned and may not be concluded from information in the passage.

41. **(D)** The primary topic is the characteristics of protozoans. Choices (A), (B), and (C) are important to the discussion and provide details that support the primary topic.

42. **(D)** In the context of this passage, "minute" could best be replaced by "very small." Choices (A), (B), and (C) are not accepted definitions of the word.

43. **(A)** "The protozoans, minute, aquatic creatures . . ." Choices (B), (C), and (D) contradict the fact that the protozoans are aquatic.

44. **(B)** "The protozoans . . . [consist] of a single cell of protoplasm. . . ." Choices (A), (C), and (D) contradict the fact that the cell of a protozoan is composed of protoplasm.

45. **(C)** "The Sarcodina, which include amoebae. . . ." Choices (A) and (B) refer to two other groups of protozoans that do not include amoebae. Choice (D) refers to the basis of classification for the three major groups of protozoans.

46. **(C)** ". . . a large nucleus that regulates growth but decomposes during reproduction. . ." Choice (A) refers to the small, not the large, nucleus. Choice (B) contradicts the fact that the small nucleus contains the genetic code for the large nucleus. Choice (D) contradicts the fact that the large nucleus decomposes during reproduction.

47. **(A)** "Protozoans are considered animals because. . .they do not live on simple organic compounds." Choices (B) and (C) refer to characteristics of some

protozoans, not to a reason why they are considered animals. Choice (D) contradicts the fact that they have only one cell, although current research is calling that into question.

48. **(A)** In the context of this passage, "uniformly" is closest in meaning to "in the same way." Choices (B), (C), and (D) are not accepted definitions of the word.

49. **(A)** "Current research into this phenomenon along with investigations carried out with advanced microscopes may neces- sitate a redefinition of what constitutes a protozoan, even calling into question the basic premise that they [protozoans] have only one cell." Choices (B), (C), and (D) would change the meaning of the sentence.

50. **(C)** Choice (A) is mentioned in lines 27–28. Choice (B) is mentioned in lines 2–3. Choice (D) is mentioned in lines 28–29. Protozoans consist of a single cell, although in the case of Ciliata, the cell may have a larger nucleus and a smaller nucleus.

Model Test 2—Paper and Pencil TOEFL

Section 1: Listening Comprehension

1. **(B)** *That's not too bad* is an idiomatic expression that means it is acceptable. Choice (C) contradicts the fact that the man feels the price was acceptable for the repairs. Choice (D) contradicts the fact that the car needed only a few minor repairs. Choice (A) is not mentioned and may not be concluded from information in the conversation.

2. **(C)** *I wish I could* is an idiomatic expression that means the speaker would like to but is not able to do something. Choice (A) refers to a party that the Association, not the woman, will have. Choice (B) refers to what the woman would like to do, not to what she will probably do. Choice (D) is not mentioned and may not be concluded from information in the conversation.

3. **(A)** Since they have just enough time to get there, it must be concluded that they will leave immediately. Choices (B), (C), and (D) are not mentioned and may not be concluded from information in the conversation.

4. **(A)** The man said that he went to see the foreign student advisor. Choice (D) refers to what the advisor did, not to what the man did himself. The Passport Office is in Washington, D.C., but Choices (B) and (C) are not mentioned and may not be concluded from information in the conversation.

5. **(B)** Since the woman thanks the man sarcastically, it must be concluded that the man was not helpful. Choice (A) refers to the man's comment, not to the woman's response. Choice (C) contradicts the fact that the woman does not have an account at the bank. Choice (D) refers to the woman's request, not to what she means by her response to the man.

6. **(B)** "I'd write a rough draft and ask Dr. Tyler to look at it." A "rough draft" is a preliminary version. Choice (C) contradicts the fact that the woman says to show the draft to Dr. Tyler, not to her. Choices (A) and (D) are not mentioned and may not be concluded from information in the conversation.

7. **(D)** To *put up with* is an idiomatic expression that means to tolerate. It must be concluded that the students do not like Dr. Clark. Choices (A), (B), and (C) are not paraphrases of the expression, and may not be concluded from information in the conversation.

8. **(D)** "Saturday afternoon would be the earliest that you could have them." Choice (A) contradicts the fact that the shirts will be ready on Saturday afternoon. Choice (B) contradicts the fact that the man cannot have the shirts on Friday morning. Choice (C) is not mentioned and may not be concluded from information in the conversation.

9. **(D)** From the references to *food* as well as to *music* and *flowers*, it must be concluded that the conversation took place at a restaurant. Music would be heard at a concert, and flowers would be found at a flower shop, but it is not customary to serve food at any of the places referred to in Choices (A), (B), and (C).

10. **(C)** According to Anne, Fred is in class. Choice (A) refers to the time when Fred will come home, not to where he is now. Choice (B) refers to where Larry is, not to where Fred is. Choice (D) refers to where Anne is.

11. **(A)** Since the man has asked for the next bus, and it leaves at ten o'clock, it must be concluded that he will take the ten o'clock bus. Choice (B) refers to his missing the first bus by five minutes, not to what he will do now. Choices (C) and (D) contradict the fact that the man asked for the next bus.

12. **(C)** The references to a *textbook* and a *movie* in Choices (B) and (D) relate to the assignment for the class. Choice (A) is not mentioned and may not be concluded from information in the conversation.

13. **(A)** "As soon as I make the final corrections on the original." Choice (B) refers to what the man asked the woman to do, not to what she will do. Choice (D) contradicts the fact that she was ready to make the corrections on the original. Choice (C) is not mentioned and may not be concluded from information in the conversation.

14. **(B)** Since the man asks whether the woman is Sally Harrison's sister, it must be concluded that he assumed the women were sisters. Choice (A) refers to who the

woman is, not to the man's assumption. Choices (C) and (D) contradict the fact that the woman is Sally Harrison's cousin.

15. **(C)** Since the woman says that she can't find her pen, it must be concluded that finding her pen is the problem. Choices (A), (B), and (D) are not mentioned and may not be concluded from information in the conversation.

16. **(A)** Because John agreed to arrive at eight-thirty but the man estimates that he won't arrive until nine o'clock, or one half-hour later, it must be concluded that John is usually late. Choice (B) refers to the time when John agreed to arrive, not to a conclusion that the man wants us to make. Choice (C) contradicts both the fact that John had agreed to come and the fact that the man estimates John's arrival at nine o'clock. Choice (D) contradicts the fact that the man estimates John's arrival one half-hour after he has agreed to arrive.

17. **(C)** "If only we hadn't spent so much money on our vacation [we would have money for the house]." Choice (B) may be true but it is not what the woman means by her comment. Choices (A) and (D) are not mentioned and may not be concluded from information in the conversation.

18. **(B)** To *not know up from down* is an idiomatic expression that means to get confused. Choice (A) contradicts the fact that the man and woman both saw the presentation. Choice (D) contradicts the fact that he was confused. Choice (C) is not men-

tioned and may not be concluded from information in the conversation.

19. **(B)** Since the man wants to talk to Janet, he implies that he wants to get her opinion. Choices (A), (C), and (D) are not mentioned and may not be concluded from information in the conversation.

20. **(B)** Since the woman can't keep up with the baby, it must be concluded that the baby is very active. Choice (D) contradicts the fact that the woman says the baby is walking. Choices (A) and (C) are not mentioned and may not be concluded from information in the conversation.

21. **(B)** ". . . it didn't turn out quite like I thought it would." Choice (A) contradicts the fact that the man knows how it turned out. Choice (C) contradicts the fact that the man says the experiment is finished. Choice (D) is not mentioned and may not be concluded from information in the conversation.

22. **(A)** Since the man expresses exasperation about the woman's attention to her classes, he implies that she does not put much effort in her studies. Choice (D) is true, but it is not what the man implies by his comment. Choices (B) and (C) are not mentioned and may not be concluded from information in the conversation.

23. **(D)** ". . . I'd try some over-the-counter medication. . ." Choice (A) refers to the woman's plan, not to the man's suggestion. Choice (B) refers to the idiom "do the job," which means to cure. Choice (C) refers to the

place to buy nonprescription medicine [over the counter], not to the man's suggestion.

24. **(A)** To *give it all you've got* is an idiomatic expression that means to try your best. Choices (B), (C), and (D) are not paraphrases of the expression, and may not be concluded from information in the conversation.

25. **(D)** *Just about to* is an idiomatic expression that means the person is ready. Choice (A) contradicts the fact that she greets Robert in a familiar way. Choices (B) and (C) are not mentioned and may not be concluded from information in the conversation.

26. **(A)** Since the woman denies the man's request for a few more minutes, it must be concluded that the man must stop working on the test. Choice (B) contradicts the fact that the man cannot have a few more minutes to finish. Choice (D) contradicts the fact that the test is in progress, not about to start. Choice (C) is not mentioned and may not be concluded from information in the conversation.

27. **(C)** Since the man thinks they are using a different book this semester, he implies that the textbook may have been changed. Choice (D) contradicts the fact that they are discussing plans for this semester. Choices (A) and (B) are not mentioned and may not be concluded from information in the conversation.

28. **(D)** Since the woman questions whether Sally would like a bike, she implies that Sally may prefer a different gift. Choice (A) refers to the man's idea, not to the woman's comment. Choices (B) and (C) are not mentioned and may not be concluded from information in the conversation.

29. **(A)** Since the man responds in dismay, it must be inferred that he does not want to give Carol a ride. Choice (B) contradicts the fact that the woman offered Carol a ride with the man. Choices (C) and (D) are not mentioned and may not be concluded from information in the conversation.

30. **(A)** ". . . get some rest and try it again later." Choices (B) and (D) contradict the fact that the woman recommends rest. Choice (C) is not mentioned and may not be concluded from information in the conversation.

31. **(B)** ". . .the question is not whether the metric system should be introduced in the United States, but rather, how it should be introduced." Choice (A) contradicts the fact that the question is not whether the metric system should be introduced. Choices (C) and (D) are not mentioned and may not be concluded from information in the discussion.

32. **(C)** "They [cans and packages] are marked in both ounces and grams. . . . And the weather reporters on radio and TV give the temperature readings in both degrees Fahrenheit and degrees Celsius now. . . . Some road signs have the distances marked in both miles and kilometers. . . ." Choice (A) contradicts the fact that the temperature readings are in both degrees Fahrenheit and degrees Celsius. Choice (B) contradicts the fact that the road signs have

distances marked in both miles and kilometers. Choice (D) contradicts the fact that cans and packages are marked in both ounces and grams.

33. **(D)** "I [Professor Baker] agree that a gradual adoption is better for those of us who have already been exposed to the English system of measurement. But I would favor teaching only metrics in the elementary schools." Choice (A) refers to the woman's suggestion, not to Professor Baker's opinion. The opinions expressed in Choices (B) and (C) are not mentioned and may not be concluded from information in the discussion.

34. **(D)** Because Professor Baker invites a free exchange of ideas, and does not criticize his students, it must be concluded that he is cooperative. The words in Choices (A), (B), and (C) do not describe Professor Baker's manner in the conversation.

35. **(D)** "I'm calling to make a reservation for a flight from Houston to Atlanta." Choices (A), (B), and (C) are all discussed, but they are not the main purpose of the conversation.

36. **(A)** ". . . if you stay over Saturday night and return on Sunday . . . the ticket will be even cheaper." Choice (B) contradicts the fact that the man is calling one month early. Choice (C) contradicts the fact that she offers to mail the tickets or save them for him in the office. Choice (D) refers to one or two alternatives, not to the woman's suggestion.

37. **(A)** "I'll just keep it [the reservation] for May 19th." Choices (B),

(C), and (D) refer to the alternatives, not to the decision that the man made.

38. **(D)** "I'll pick them up. . . . after two o'clock." Choices (A), (B), and (C) are not mentioned and may not be concluded from information in the conversation.

39. **(D)** ". . . an extensive research effort, which, in cooperation with private industry, has transferred technology to the international marketplace." Choices (A), (B), and (C) are secondary themes used to develop the main theme of the talk.

40. **(A)** "Hundreds of everyday products can be traced back to the space mission, including cordless electric tools, airtight food packaging. . . . ultrasound. . ." Choice (A) is not mentioned and may not be concluded from information in the talk.

41. **(D)** "First used to detect flaws in spacecraft, ultrasound is now standard equipment in almost every hospital. . ." Choice (A) refers to implants and pacemakers, not to ultrasound. Choices (B) and (C) are not mentioned and may not be concluded from information in the conversation.

42. **(B)** ". . . archaeologists have been able to explore the earth. . . cities. . . have been located . . . and the sea floor has been mapped using photographs from outer space." Choices (A), (C), and (D) are not mentioned and may not be concluded from information in the conversation.

43. **(C)** The tour guide discusses the history, economy, and landmarks of San Francisco. Choices (A), (B), and (D) are secondary

themes used to support the main purpose of the talk, an orientation to the City of San Francisco.

44. **(D)** ". . . the name was changed from Yerba Buena to San Francisco." Choice (A) refers to the name of the bridge, not a settlement. Choice (B) refers to a mission established before Yerba Buena was settled. Choice (C) refers to a military post established before the settlement of Yerba Buena.

45. **(A)** ". . . in 1848, with the discovery of gold, the population grew to ten thousand." Choice (B) refers to what happened in 1869, not 1848. Choice (C) refers to what happened in 1937. Choice (D) refers to what happened in 1862.

46. **(C)** "The bridge, which is more than one mile long, spans the harbor from San Francisco to Marin County. . . ." Choice (A) refers to the length of the Port of San Francisco, not to the length of the Golden Gate Bridge. Choice (B) refers to the altitude of the city. The number in Choice (D) refers to the number of tons of cargo handled at the Port of San Francisco every year.

47. **(A)** "Today we will discuss Transcendentalism. . . ." Choices (B), (C), and (D) are secondary themes that are used to develop the main theme of the lecture.

48. **(C)** "Today we will discuss Transcendentalism, which is a philosophical and literary movement that developed in New England in the early nineteenth century." Choices (A), (B), and (D) are not mentioned and may not be concluded from information in the talk.

49. **(C)** "This group [the Transcendental Club] was the advance guard of a reaction against the rigid Puritanism of the period, especially insofar as it emphasized society at the expense of the individual." Choices (A) and (D) refer to the Transcendental Club, not to the Puritans. Choice (B) contradicts the fact that the Transcendental Club reacted against the Puritans.

50. **(D)** "Thoreau built a small cabin along the shores of Walden Pond . . . he published an account of his experiences in *Walden*. . . ." Choices (A), (B), and (C) are not mentioned and may not be concluded from information in the talk.

Section 2: Structure and Written Expression

1. **(D)** A dependent clause modifies an independent clause. Choice (A) has two clause markers, *which* and *that*. Choice (B) is a verb followed by a noun and a clause marker. Choice (C) does not have a clause marker.

2. **(B)** A passive infinitive is used to express purpose. Choice (A) is a noun. Choice (C) is an *-ing* form. Choice (D) is a present verb.

3. **(B)** A cardinal number is used after a noun. *The* is used with an ordinal number before a noun. In Choices (A) and (C) an ordinal number is used after, not before a noun. Choice (D) is incomplete because it does not include *the* before the ordinal number.

4. **(B)** *As soon as* is an idiom that introduces a limit of time. The phrase *as soon as* is followed by a noun and a simple present verb. Choice (A) is a modal and a verb word, not a simple present verb. Choice (D) is a noun. Choice (C) uses a present but not a simple present form.

5. **(A)** A form of *make* with someone such as *all Americans* and a verb word expresses a causative. Choice (B) is an infinitive, not a verb word. Choice (D) is an *-ing* form. Choice (C) does not have a verb form.

6. **(C)** Negative agreement with *neither* requires verb-subject order and an affirmative verb. Affirmative agreement requires subject-verb order, an affirmative verb and *too* or *also*. Choices (A) and (D) have negative, not affirmative, verbs with *too* and *also*. Choice (B) reverses verb-subject order with *neither*.

7. **(B)** Ideas in a series should be expressed by parallel structures. Only *to finish* in Choice (B) provides for parallelism with the infinitive *to answer*. Choices (A), (C), and (D) are not parallel.

8. **(C)** *Weathering* is the subject of the verb *is*. Choices (A) and (B) are redundant and indirect. Choice (D) is an *-ing* form, not a verb.

9. **(A)** Subject-verb order is used in the clause after a question word connector such as *what time*. In Choice (B), subject-verb order is reversed. In Choice (C), the auxiliary *does* is unnecessary and incorrect. In Choice (D), the connector is after, not before the subject and verb.

10. **(D)** The verb *to consider* requires an *-ing* form in the complement. Choice (A) is an infinitive, not an *-ing* form. Choice (B) is a participle. Choice (C) is a verb word.

11. **(C)** A form of *have* with something such as a *tooth* and a participle expresses a causative. Choice (A) is an *-ing* form, not a participle. Choice (B) is an infinitive. Choice (D) is a verb word.

12. **(B)** A negative phrase introduces inverted order. *Not until* requires an auxiliary verb, subject, and main verb. In Choice (A), the subject precedes the auxiliary. In Choice (C), there is no auxiliary. In Choice (D), there is no auxiliary and no subject.

13. **(C)** Object pronouns are used after prepositions such as *by*. Choice (A) is a reflexive pronoun, not an object pronoun. Choices (B) and (D) are possessive pronouns. "The work was done *by herself*" without the repetitive word *alone* would also be correct.

14. **(D)** An appositive does not require connectors or an additional subject. Choices (A) and (C) include connecting conjunctions. Choice (B) is an anticipatory *it* clause, not an appositive.

15. **(B)** Consecutive order must be maintained, along with parallel structure.

16. **(C)** Most adverbs of manner are formed by adding *-ly* to adjectives. *Rapid* should be *rapidly* to qualify the manner in which

automatic data processing has grown.

17. **(D)** *As well as* should be *and*, which is used in correlation with *both*.

18. **(B)** *Near* does not require a preposition. *Near to* should be *near*. *Nearby* would also be correct.

19. **(C)** Because adjectives are used after verbs of the senses, *badly* should be *bad* after the verb *feel*. *Badly* functions as an adverb. *Bad* functions as an adjective.

20. **(A)** Repetition of the subject by a subject pronoun is redundant. *They* should be deleted.

21. **(A)** *Despite of* is a combination of *despite* and *in spite of*. *Despite of* should be either *despite* or *in spite of*.

22. **(A)** Object pronouns are used after prepositions. *We* should be *us* after the preposition *of*.

23. **(C)** Because dates require ordinal numbers, *twelve* should be *twelfth*.

24. **(B)** *Influence* should be *influential*. *Influence* is a noun. *Influential* is an adjective.

25. **(A)** In order to refer to an increase in the cost of living, *a rise* not *a raise* should be used. *A raise* is an increase in salary. *A rise* is an increase in price, worth, quantity, or degree.

26. **(B)** A verb word must be used in a clause after an impersonal expression. *Maintains* should be *maintain* after the impersonal expression *it is imperative*.

27. **(D)** *Such as* introduces the example *shrimps and clams*, which must refer to a plural antecedent. *Sea creature* should be *sea creatures*.

28. **(C)** Ideas in a series should be expressed by parallel structures. *Encouraging* should be *to encourage* to provide for parallelism with the infinitive *to discourage*.

29. **(B)** *Combination* should be *combine*. *Combination* is a noun. *Combine* is a verb.

30. **(C)** *Presumable* should be *presumably*. *Presumable* is an adjective. *Presumably* is an adverb.

31. **(D)** Using words with the same meaning consecutively is repetitive. *Words* should be deleted because *speaking* implies the use of *words*.

32. **(A)** The verb *reported* establishes a point of view in the past. *Discovers* should be *discovered* in order to maintain the point of view.

33. **(D)** *Either* should be *both*, which is used in correlation with the inclusive *and*.

34. **(D)** Because the verb *refuse* requires an infinitive in the complement, *giving* should be *to give*.

35. **(C)** There must be agreement between subject and verb. *Has* should be *have* to agree with the plural subject *the few cities*.

36. **(C)** Comparative forms are usually followed by *than*. After the comparative *more important*, *as* should be *than*.

37. **(C)** Object pronouns should be used after prepositions. *Who* should be *whom* after the preposition *to*.

38. **(D)** Ideas in a series should be expressed by parallel structures. *Increasing* should be *to increase* to provide for parallelism with the infinitive *to enrich*.

39. **(A)** *Would have* and a participle in the result requires *had* and a participle in the condition. Because *would not have evolved* is used in the result, *did not filter out* should be *had not filtered out* in the condition.

40. **(C)** A verb word must be used in a clause after the verb *to require*. *Reports* should be *report*. "Everyone who holds a nonimmigrant visa" is the subject of the clause.

Section 3: Reading Comprehension

1. **(A)** The other choices are secondary ideas that are used to develop the main idea, "precipitation." Choices (B), (C), and (D) provide details and examples.

2. **(C)** "Precipitation [is] commonly referred to as rainfall." Choices (A), (B), and (D) are not mentioned and may not be concluded from information in the passage.

3. **(B)** "Precipitation, commonly referred to as rainfall, is a measure of the quantity of water in the form of either rain, hail, or snow." Choice (A) is incomplete because it does not include hail and snow. Humidity referred to in Choices (C) and (D) is not mentioned and may not be concluded from information in the passage.

4. **(A)** "The average annual precipitation over the whole of the United States is thirty-six inches." Choice (B) refers to the formula for computing precipitation, not to the annual rainfall over the United States. Choice

(C) refers to the amount of rain recorded in New York State, not in the United States. Choice (D) refers to the total annual precipitation recorded in New York State.

5. **(B)** "A general formula for computing the precipitation of snowfall is that ten inches of snow is equal to one inch of precipitation." Forty inches of snow divided by 10 inches per one inch of precipitation is four inches, or one-third foot. Choices (A), (C), and (D) may not be computed on the basis of the formula in the passage.

6. **(C)** In the context of this passage, "proximity to" is closest in meaning to "nearness to." Choices (A), (B), and (D) are not accepted definitions of the phrase.

7. **(D)** ". . . the Pacific Coast receives more annual precipitation than the Atlantic Coast." Choices (A), (B), and (C) refer to the prevailing winds, not to the highest annual precipitation.

8. **(B)** Choice (A) is mentioned in lines 20–23. Choice (C) is mentioned in line 13. Choice (D) is mentioned in lines 13–14. Choice (B) is not mentioned and may not be concluded from information in the passage.

9. **(A)** In the context of this passage, "substantially" could best be replaced by "fundamentally." Choices (B), (C), and (D) are not accepted definitions of the word.

10. **(B)** "East of the Rocky Mountains, the annual precipitation decreases substantially from that [precipitation] west of the Rocky

Mountains." Choices (A), (C), and (D) would change the meaning of the sentence.

11. **(B)** Because the information relates to graduate courses, it is most probable that the passage would be found in a graduate catalog. Choice (A) contradicts the fact that the information is about graduate, not undergraduate, courses. It is less probable that this kind of information would be distributed in a class as in Choices (C) and (D).

12. **(A)** Because the style of the passage is objective, it must be concluded that the purpose of the passage is to inform. Choices (B), (C), and (D) would require a less objective style, with more subjective commentary.

13. **(A)** In the context of this passage, "prerequisites" is closest in meaning to "courses required before enrolling." Choices (B), (C), and (D) are not accepted definitions of the word.

14. **(B)** "Certain graduate courses, generally those [graduate courses] devoted to introductory material, are numbered 400 for undergraduate students who qualify to take them and 600 for graduate students." Choices (A), (C), and (D) would change the meaning of the sentence.

15. **(A)** "Courses with the numbers 800 or above are open only to graduate students." Choices (B) and (C) may refer to both graduate and undergraduate students. Part-time and full-time students are restricted on the basis of the number of hours that they may take, not on the basis of the courses that they may take.

Choice (D) contradicts the fact that courses numbered 800 or above are open to graduate, not undergraduate, students.

16. **(C)** "Courses designed for students seeking a professional degree carry a 500 number for undergraduate students and a 700 number for graduate students." The number in Choice (A) refers to an undergraduate, not to a graduate, registration. Choice (B) refers to an introductory course with an undergraduate equivalent of 420, not to a professional course with an undergraduate equivalent of 520. Choice (D) refers to a graduate course with no undergraduate equivalent.

17. **(C)** "A full-time graduate student is expected to take courses which total ten to sixteen credit hours . . . . A part-time graduate student must register for a minimum of five credit hours." The student referred to in Choice (A) would be required to register for a minimum of ten, not eight, credit hours. Choice (B) is ambiguous because it may refer to either a part-time or a full-time student. Choice (D) is not mentioned and may not be concluded from information in the passage.

18. **(A)** Choice (B) is mentioned in lines 3–4. Choice (C) is mentioned in lines 4–5. Choice (D) is mentioned in lines 4–5. Courses numbered 99 or below are special interest courses that do not carry academic credit and will not count toward the number of hours needed to complete graduation requirements.

19. **(B)** "A part-time graduate student must register for a minimum

of five credit hours." Choices (A) and (D) contradict the fact that introductory courses for graduate students are numbered 600. Choice (C) contradicts the fact that students holding assistantships are expected to enroll for fewer hours.

20. **(C)** In the context of this passage, "under any circumstances" is closest in meaning to "without exception." Choices (A), (B), and (D) are not accepted definitions of the phrase.

21. **(D)** Choices (A), (B), and (C) are important to the discussion, and provide details that support the main topic, "women's suffrage."

22. **(C)** In the context of this passage, "ban" most nearly means to "prohibit." Choices (A), (B), and (D) are not accepted definitions of the word.

23. **(D)** In the context of this passage, "supported" could best be replaced by "promoted." Choices (A), (B), and (C) are not accepted definitions of the word.

24. **(A)** "They [women] became involved primarily in order to better their living conditions and the conditions of others." Choices (B), (C), and (D) are not mentioned and may not be concluded from information in the passage.

25. **(A)** In the context of this passage, "primarily" is closest in meaning to "above all." Choices (B), (C), and (D) are not accepted definitions of the word.

26. **(D)** "When the Civil War ended . . .the Fifteenth Amendment . . . granted . . . suffrage to blacks. . ." *Suffrage* means the right to vote. Choice (B) contradicts the fact

that the bill was presented to Congress in 1878, not immediately after the Civil War. Choice (C) refers to the fact that the eastern states resisted the women's suffrage bill, not the end of the Civil War. Choice (A) is not mentioned and may not be concluded from information in the passage.

27. **(D)** *Suffrage* means the right to vote; the exercise of such a right. Choice (A) is a definition of the word *suffering*, not *suffrage*. Choices (B) and (C) are related to the word *suffrage*, but they are not accepted definitions of it.

28. **(C)** ". . . the Nineteenth Amendment granted women the right to vote." Choice (A) refers to the Fifteenth not the Nineteenth Amendment. Choice (B) refers to the Fourteenth Amendment. Choice (D) is not mentioned and may not be concluded from information in the passage.

29. **(A)** "A women's suffrage bill had been presented to every Congress since 1878 but it [the bill] continually failed to pass until 1920, when the Nineteenth Amendment granted women the right to vote." Choices (B), (C), and (D) would change the meaning of the sentence.

30. **(D)** ". . . 1920 when the Nineteenth Amendment granted women the right to vote." Choice (A) refers to the date when the Civil War ended. Choice (B) refers to the date when the Fifteenth Amendment was adopted granting blacks, not women, the right to vote. Choice (C) refers to the date when the bill to grant women the right to vote was

presented to Congress, not to the date that it was passed and became law.

31. **(B)** The other choices are secondary topics that are used to develop the primary topic, "characteristics and varieties of the *Acacia.*" Choices (A), (C), and (D) are important details and examples.

32. **(C)** "Only about a dozen of the three hundred Australian varieties grow well in the southern United States." Choice (A) refers to the number of species identified, not to the number that grow well in the United States. Choice (B) refers to the number of species that grow well in Australia, not in the southern United States. Choice (D) refers to the number of species that have flowers, not to the total number of species that grow well in the southern United States.

33. **(B)** "Although nearly five hundred species of *Acacia* have been identified, only about a dozen of the three hundred Australian varieties grow well in the southern United States, and of these [varieties], only three are flowering." Choices (A), (C), and (D) would change the meaning of the sentence.

34. **(C)** "The *Silver Wattle*, although very similar to the *Bailey Acacia*, grows twice as high." Choice (A) refers to the *Sydney Golden Wattle*, not to the *Silver Wattle*. Choices (B) and (D) refer to the *Black Acacia*.

35. **(A)** In the context of this passage, "flat" most nearly means "smooth." Choices (B), (C), and

(D) are not accepted definitions of the word.

36. **(B)** In the context of this passage, "showy" could best be replaced by "elaborate." Choices (A), (C), and (D) are not accepted definitions of the word.

37. **(D)** ". . . the *Black Acacia* or *Blackwood*, has dark green leaves and unobtrusive blossoms." The species referred to in Choices (A), (B), and (C) have fragrant clusters of yellow flowers.

38. **(B)** ". . .the *Black Acacia* is valuable for its dark wood, which is used in making cabinets and furniture." Choices (A), (C), and (D) are not mentioned and may not be concluded from information in the passage.

39. **(A)** In the context of this passage, "highly prized" is closest in meaning to "valuable." Choices (B), (C), and (D) are not accepted definitions of the phrase.

40. **(C)** ". . .the pale yellow blossoms appear in August in Australia." Choice (A) refers to the month that the *Acacia* blooms in the United States, not in Australia. Choices (B) and (D) refer to the reversal of seasons in the northern and southern hemispheres, but not to the blossoming of the *Acacia.*

41. **(A)** "A History of New York City" is the best title because it states the main idea of the passage. Choices (C) and (D) are details used to develop the main idea. Choice (B) is not specific enough.

42. **(C)** "Peter Minuit . . . negotiated with Indian chiefs for the purchase of Manhattan Island for

merchandise. . . ." Choices (A) and (B) refer to the value of the merchandise, not to what the Indians received. Choice (D) refers to where the Dutch settlements were located.

43. **(B)** ". . .Dutch settlements in North America known as New Amsterdam. . . ." Choice (C) refers to the location of the land that was purchased from the Indians. Choices (A) and (D) are not mentioned and may not be concluded from information in the passage.

44. **(C)** In the context of this passage, "heterogeneous" could best be replaced by "diverse." Choices (A), (B), and (D) are not accepted definitions of the word.

45. **(C)** ". . .offers, generous by the standards of the era, were extended throughout Europe. Consequently, the settlement became the most heterogeneous of the North American colonies." Choice (A) contradicts the fact that it was New Amsterdam, not the Dutch West India Company, that the English acquired. Choices (C) and (D) are not mentioned and may not be concluded from information in the passage.

46. **(A)** In the context of this passage, "formidable" is closest in mean-

ing to "powerful." Choices (B), (C), and (D) are not accepted definitions of the word.

47. **(B)** ". . . New Amsterdam was renamed New York in honor of the Duke." Choices (A), (C), and (D) are not mentioned and may not be concluded from information in the passage.

48. **(B)** "After the war, it [New York] was selected as the first capital of the United States." Choices (A), (C), and (D) would change the meaning of the sentence.

49. **(B)** "After the war, it [New York] was selected as the first capital of the United States." Choice (A) refers to the former name for New York, which had already been changed when it became the first capital. Choices (C) and (D) refer to cities that became the capital after New York.

50. **(D)** "Three centuries after his initial trade . . . Minuit's tiny investment was worth more than seven billion dollars." Choice (A) refers to the date that the Dutch purchased Manhattan Island from the Indians. Choice (B) refers to the date one century after the purchase. Choice (C) refers to the date three decades after the purchase.

Model Test 3—Computer-Assisted TOEFL

Section 1: Listening

1. **(D)** The woman offers to go to the movie in order to please the man, but she says that she is a little tired, indicating that she does not want to go out. Choice (A) is incorrect because it is the woman, not the man, who is tired. Choice (B) refers to what the man, not the woman, wants to do. Choice (C) is incorrect because the man suggests that they go out after dinner, not for dinner.

2. **(D)** The man offers to get some paper at the bookstore. Choice (A) is incorrect because it is the woman, not the man, who wants to borrow some typing paper. Choice (B) contradicts the fact that the man doesn't have any paper either. Choice (C) is not mentioned and may not be concluded from information in the conversation.

3. **(B)** ". . . walk three more blocks . . ." Since the woman gives directions for walking, it must be concluded that the man is not driving a car. Choice (C) contradicts the fact that the man calls the woman *Miss*. Choices (A) and (D) are not mentioned and may not be concluded from information in the conversation.

4. **(C)** To *fall through* is an idiomatic expression that means not to happen as planned. Choice (D) contradicts the fact that he

planned to go to summer school. Choices (A) and (B) are not mentioned and may not be concluded from information in the conversation.

5. **(B)** Choices (A), (C), and (D) are mentioned in reference to the main topic of discussion in the apartment.

6. **(B)** Since the woman mentions that Dr. Taylor does not interact with her in class despite her good grades, she implies that she is not sure how Dr. Taylor feels. Choices (C) and (D) contradict the fact that she was the only one who received an A on her paper. Choice (A) is not mentioned and may not be concluded from information in the conversation.

7. **(C)** Since the man inquires whether she has asked Sandy, he implies that she should ask her. Choice (A) refers to the payment for participation, not to the man's suggestion. Choice (B) refers to the woman's request, not to the man's suggestion. Choice (D) refers to the experiment in psychology, not to a person that the woman should see.

8. **(A)** Because *either* means that the speaker is including herself in her statement, it must be concluded that the woman did not go to the meeting. The man said that he did not go because of a headache. Choice (B) contradicts the use of the word *either* in the woman's question. Choice (C)

contradicts the man's negative response to the question of whether he went to the meeting. Choice (D) contradicts both the use of the word *either* and the man's negative response.

9. **(B)** "How about [buying] a nice pen?" Choice (C) refers to the card that the woman has already purchased, not to the man's idea. Choice (D) contradicts the fact that the man offers a suggestion for a gift. Choice (A) is not mentioned and may not be concluded from information in the conversation.

10. **(D)** To *not make up one's mind* is an idiomatic expression that means to be undecided. Choices (A) and (C) contradict the fact that she is still considering both alternatives. Choice (B) contradicts the fact that she has a choice.

11. **(B)** "I've probably had enough exercise for one day." Choice (A) contradicts the fact that they are on the way home. Choices (C) and (D) are not mentioned and may not be concluded from information in the conversation.

12. **(A)** Since the woman asks whether the man can work and go to school, she implies that he may be taking on too much. Choices (B), (C), and (D) are not mentioned and may not be concluded from information in the conversation.

13. **(C)** Since the man suggests that the woman buy postcards, it must be concluded that she should send postcards to her family. Choice (B) contradicts the fact that she does not have time to write a letter. Choice (A) refers

to the man's family, not to the woman's family. Choice (D) is not mentioned and may not be concluded from information in the conversation.

14. **(B)** Choices (A), (C), and (D) are all mentioned as they relate to the main topic of the conversation, "where the woman will go to school."

15. **(B)** Since the man says that ticket number 32 is in room 27, the woman will probably go to room 27. Choice (A) contradicts the fact that the woman already has a ticket. Choice (C) refers to the number of the ticket, not to the number of the room. Choice (D) contradicts the fact that the man has already seen her ticket.

16. **(B)** Since the teachers gave flowers to all of the honors students, and the woman has a flower, it must be concluded that she is an honors student. Choice (A) contradicts the fact that she has a flower that was presented at the reception. Choice (D) contradicts the fact that she received a flower for students. Choice (C) is not mentioned and may not be concluded from information in the conversation.

17. **(D)** ". . . Take it over next term." Choices (B) and (C) contradict the fact that the woman says to drop the class. Choice (A) is not mentioned and may not be concluded from information in the conversation.

18. **(C)** "To earn enough money for next year's tuition." Choice (A) refers to the place where Margaret works, not to where she stays. Choice (B) contradicts the fact that she is working at the

motel. Choice (D) is not mentioned and may not be concluded from information in the conversation.

19. **(C)** Since the woman used to teach English, the man is not surprised that she likes the course. *No wonder* is an idiomatic expression that means the information is logical. Choice (D) refers to the woman's interest, not to the course. Choices (A) and (B) are not mentioned and may not be concluded from information in the conversation.

20. **(A)** Since they are discussing potential group members and their value to a presentation, it must be concluded that they are planning to make a presentation. Choice (B) contradicts the fact that the second woman says they should ask Jane. Choices (C) and (D) are not mentioned and may not be concluded from information in the conversation.

21. **(B)** "I really don't know what Dr. Brown wants us to do. . . . The assignment was pretty vague." Choice (A) contradicts the fact that they looked in the syllabus. Choice (C) refers to the fact that the man was thinking of making an appointment with Dr. Brown to resolve the problem. Choice (D) contradicts the fact that the man was considering stopping by Dr. Brown's office during her office hours.

22. **(D)** ". . . it says under the course requirements . . . 'Research paper, thirty points.' " Choice (A) contradicts the fact that it says thirty points in the syllabus. Choice (B) contradicts the fact that thirty points is one-third, not

one-half of the total grade. Choice (C) contradicts the fact that it is thirty, not ten points.

23. **(A)** ". . . then she started talking about presentations." Choice (C) refers to the fact that the students are planning to ask questions in the next class, not to questions that were asked last week. Choices (B) and (D) are not mentioned and may not be concluded from information in the conversation.

24. **(C)** ". . . maybe we should ask about it in class tomorrow." Since the man agrees that she has a good idea, it must be concluded that they will ask questions about the assignment in class. Choices (B) and (D) were discussed earlier in the conversation before they decided to ask in class. Choice (A) contradicts the fact that they do not understand the assignment.

25. **(C)** "On his third exploratory voyage, as captain of two ships . . . Captain James Cook came upon . . . the Hawaiian Islands." Choices (A), (B), and (D) are secondary themes used to develop the main theme of the talk.

26. **(B)** **(C)** ". . . as captain in charge of two ships, the *Resolution* and the *Discovery*, he came upon a group of uncharted islands. . . ." Choice (A) refers to the fact that this was Cook's third voyage to explore the Pacific Ocean, not to the name of his ship. *England* in Choice (D) refers to the country that commissioned Cook, not to the name of his ship.

27. **(C)** "Some historians contend that the islanders welcomed Cook, believing that he was the god Launo, protector of peace

and agriculture." Choices (A), (B), and (D) are not mentioned and may not be concluded from information in the lecture.

28. **(D) (C) (B) (A)** ". . . Cook demanded that the king be taken as a hostage until the boat was returned. . . . In the fighting that followed, Cook and four other crewmen were killed."

29. **(C)** "Alloys are mixtures that have been deliberately combined in specific proportion for a definite purpose." Choice (A) refers to natural combinations of metals, not to alloys. Choice (B) is true, but incomplete because it does not mention the specific purposes. Choice (D) is not mentioned and may not be concluded from information in the conversation.

30. **(A) (B)** ". . . alloys are mixtures that have been deliberately combined in specific proportion for a definite purpose." Choice (D) refers to impure metals, not to alloys. Choice (C) is not mentioned and may not be concluded from information in the conversation.

31. **(A)** "In the aircraft industry, there is a need for metals that are both strong and light." Choice (D) contradicts the fact that the metals referred to are alloys. Choices (B) and (C) are not mentioned and may not be concluded from information in the conversation.

32. **(C)** "Both [alloys and combinations in nature] are mixtures, but alloys are mixtures that have been deliberately combined in specific proportion for a definite purpose." Choice (A) contradicts the fact that metals that occur accidentally in nature are impure. Choice (B) contradicts the fact that combinations of metals occur accidentally in nature. Choice (D) contradicts the fact that both alloys and combinations of metals that occur in nature are mixtures.

33. **(C)** "We all agree that British English and American English are different. Right? . . . But not so different that it prevents us from understanding each other." Choices (A), (B), and (D) are secondary points of discussion that are used to develop the main topic of the discussion.

34. **(A) (B) (C) (D)** "Words like *theater* and *center* end in *re* in England instead of *er* the way that we [Americans] spell them. . . . many words that end in *or* in American English are spelled *our* in British English, like *color* and *honor*."

35. **(B)** "I remember seeing an English movie where the actors kept calling their apartment a *flat*. Half of the movie was over before I realized what they were talking about." Choice (D) contradicts the fact that the man did not understand the word. Choices (A) and (C) are not mentioned and may not be concluded from information in the discussion.

36. **(D)** "We all agree that British English and American English are different. . . . But not so different that it prevents us from understanding each other." Choice (A) refers to the man's opinion at the beginning of the discussion, not to the opinion of the class at the conclusion of the

discussion. The opinions expressed in Choices (B) and (C) are not mentioned and may not be concluded from information in the discussion.

37. **(D)** "My report is on local control of schools." Choices (A), (B), and (C) are secondary themes used to develop the main theme of the report.

38. **(A)** ". . . I was surprised to learn that public schools in the United States are not the same in every state or even from community to community. . . ." Choices (B), (C), and (D) are all true, but they are not what surprised the presenter about her research.

39. **(B) (A) (C)** ". . . a governing board, called the school board, that makes the decisions . . . a superintendent . . . to carry out policies. . . . In most communities, the board is elected by the residents in their local school district."

40. **(A) (C)** "The function of the national department is . . . supporting research and projects, and supervising the compliance of schools with national legislation." Choice (B) contradicts the fact that the school board makes decisions about the curriculum in the local district. Choice (D) contradicts the fact that local school boards are elected by the people or appointed by the mayor.

41. **(B) (C)** "The two-meal plan includes lunch and dinner." Choice (A) contradicts the fact that there is no breakfast included. Choice (D) is not mentioned and may not be concluded from information in the conversation.

42. **(C)** "It's thirty-six dollars a week, which works out to about three dollars a meal." The number in Choice (A) refers to the number of meals that the man uses to calculate, not the cost. Choice (D) refers to the cost of two meals per day for seven days, not to the cost of a six-day plan. Choice (B) is not mentioned and may not be concluded from information in the conversation.

43. **(C)** ". . . we don't serve meals on Sunday." Choice (A) refers to the situation that some students have, but not to the reason that they eat out. Choices (B) and (D) are not mentioned and may not be concluded from information in the conversation.

44. **(C)** "Just fill out this form, and we'll bill you." Choice (B) refers to the man's question about credit cards, not to the way that he will pay. Choices (A) and (D) contradict the fact that the man will be billed.

45. **(A)** ". . . hydroponics is the science of growing plants without soil . . . ." Choice (B) refers to the nutrients that are used in the solution in order to grow the plants, not to a definition of hydroponics. Choices (C) and (D) are not mentioned and may not be concluded from information in the lecture.

46. **(A) (B)** ". . . for plants grown in soil, the roots not only absorb water and nutrients but also serve to anchor the plant . . . . oxygen is also taken in by the roots . . . ." Choice (C) contradicts the fact that hydroponic plants are not

placed directly in the water and nutrient solution. Choice (D) is not mentioned and may not be concluded from information in the lecture.

47. (**C**) "Because oxygen is also taken in by the roots, we had to attach an air pump to mix oxygen into the solution." Choice (D) contradicts the fact that the wood chips and wire mesh anchored the plants. Choices (A) and (B) are not mentioned and may not be concluded from information in the lecture.

48. (**C**) "I'd also like you to take a closer look at this specimen of nutrient solution. What conclusions can you draw?" Choice (B) confuses the word *draw* with the idiom *to draw conclusions.* Choices (A) and (D) are not mentioned and may not be concluded from information in the lecture.

49. (**D**) ". . . she escaped from her owners in Maryland . . . ." Tubman was a member of the underground railroad, but it was not mentioned whether she worked on the regular railroad or underground in a mine as in Choices (A) and (B). Choice (C) refers to the destination of many slaves who were helped by the underground railroad, not to Tubman's home.

50. (**B**) "What really impressed me though was the fact that after she escaped, she went back to Maryland nineteen times . . . [and] freed more than three hundred slaves." Choice (A) is true, but it is not what impressed the man. The number nineteen in Choice (D) refers to the number of times

that she returned to Maryland to help others, not to the number of years she spent in slavery. Choice (C) is not mentioned and may not be concluded from information in the conversation.

Section 2: Structure

1. (**D**) There must be agreement between subject and verb, not between the verb and words in the appositive after the subject. *Were* should be *was* to agree with the singular subject *gunpowder.*

2. (**B**) There must be agreement between subject and verb. *Is* should be *are* to agree with the plural subject *manufacturers.*

3. (**D**) Because adjectives are used after verbs of the senses, *sweetly* should be *sweet* after the verb *smell. Sweetly* is an adverb. *Sweet* is an adjective.

4. (**A**) The verb *to expect* requires an infinitive in the complement. Choices (B), (C), and (D) are not infinitives.

5. (**C**) *Because of* is used before nouns such as *a misunderstanding* to express cause. Choices (A) and (B) are not accepted for statements of cause. Choice (D) is used before a subject and verb, not a noun, to express cause.

6. (**D**) *Equal to* is a prepositional idiom. *As* should be *to.*

7. (**D**) Ideas in a series should be expressed by parallel structures. *Stressful* should be *stress* to provide for parallelism with the nouns *predisposition, drugs,* or *infection.*

8. (**A**) Subject-verb order is used in the clause after a question word

connector such as *where.* In Choice (B), there is no question word connector. In Choice (C), the subject-verb order is reversed. In Choice (D), the question word connector is used after, not before, the subject and verb.

9. (**A**) *May* and a verb word in the result require a past form in the condition. Because *may have* is used in the result, *having* should be *had* in the condition.

10. (**C**) *As well as* is used in correlation with the inclusive *and.* Choices (A) and (B) would be used in clauses of comparison, not correlation. Choice (D) is incomplete because it does not include the final word *as.*

11. (**B**) In order to refer to nurses not allowing you to give blood, *let* should be used. *To leave* means to go. *To let* means to allow.

12. (**D**) The anticipatory clause *it was in 1848 that* introduces a subject and verb, *gold was discovered.* Choice (A) may be used preceding a subject and verb without *that.* Choice (B) may be used as a subject clause preceding a main verb. Choice (C) is redundant and indirect. "Because in 1848 gold was discovered at Sutter's Mill, the California Gold Rush began," and "That in 1848 gold was discovered at Sutter's Mill was the cause of the California Gold Rush" would also be correct.

13. (**C**) Comparative forms for three-syllable adverbs are usually preceded by *more* and followed by *than.* Choice (A) is followed by *as.* Choice (B) is preceded by *as.*

Choice (D) is not preceded by *more.*

14. (**D**) The verb *thought* establishes a point of view in the past. *Has* should be *had* in order to maintain the point of view.

15. (**B**) *Developing* should be *development.* Although both are nouns derived from verbs, the *-ment* ending is preferred. *Developing* means progressing. *Development* means the act of developing or the result of developing.

16. (**A**) Most adverbs of manner are formed by adding *-ly* to adjectives. Choices (B) and (D) are redundant and indirect. Choice (C) is ungrammatical because the adverb *fast* does not have an *-ly* ending.

17. (**C**) *But also* is used in correlation with the inclusive *not only.* Choice (A) would be used in correlation with *not,* not in correlation with *not only.* Choices (B) and (D) are not used in correlation with another inclusive.

18. (**C**) Comparisons must be made with logically comparable nouns. Choices (A) and (D) are redundant and indirect. Choice (B) makes an illogical comparison of *a salary* with *a teacher.* Only Choice (C) compares two salaries.

19. (**A**) The verb phrase *to look forward to* requires an *-ing* form in the complement. Choices (B) and (D) are not *-ing* forms. Choice (C) is *be* and an *-ing* form.

20. (**C**) There must be agreement between pronoun and antecedent. *Their* should be *its* to agree with the singular antecedent *a turtle.*

Section 3: Reading

1. **(A)** "The Father of American Public Education" is the best title because it states the main idea of the passage. Choice (C) is a detail used to develop the main idea. Choices (B) and (D) are not specific enough.

2. **(C)** "Perhaps it was his own lack of adequate schooling that inspired Horace Mann to work so hard for the important reforms in education that he accomplished." Choice (A) contradicts the fact that Mann did not have benefit of an early education. Choice (B) contradicts the fact that the biography is limited to Horace Mann's work as an educator. Choice (D) contradicts the fact that the teachers are mentioned only briefly.

3. In the context of this passage, the word extended could best be replaced by increased. No other words or phrases in the **bold** text are close to the meaning of the word extended.

4. **(A)** "Mann was recognized as the father of public education." Choice (B) contradicts the fact that Horace Mann exercised an enormous influence. Choices (C) and (D) are unlikely since his influence resulted in a change in the school system.

5. **(B)** "There he exercised an enormous influence during the critical period of reconstruction that brought into existence the American graded elementary school as a substitute for the older district school system." Choice (A) refers to "the historic education bill that set up a state board of education" and to the fact that Mann served as first secretary of the board. Choice (C) refers to "the lyceums for adult education," which he founded. Choice (D) refers to the new system that was brought into existence under Mann's influence.

6. **(D)** In the context of this passage, struggles could best be replaced by difficult times. Choices (A), (C), and (B) are not accepted definitions of the word.

7. **(B)** ". . . to become first secretary of the board [of education]. There [at the board of education] he exercised an enormous influence . . . ." Choices (A), (C), and (D) would change the meaning of the sentence.

8. **(A)** In the context of this passage, mandatory is closest in meaning to required. Choices (B), (C), and (D) are not accepted definitions of the word.

9. **(C)** ". . . the Massachusetts reforms later served as a model for the nation." Choice (A) contradicts the fact that the reforms were considered quite radical at the time. Choice (B) contradicts the fact that they served as a model for the nation. Choice (D) is not mentioned and may not be concluded from information in the passage.

10. "Mann's ideas about school reform were developed and distributed in twelve annual reports to the state of Massachusetts . . . ." Quotation from sentence 1, paragraph 3.

11. **(B)** "Be ashamed to die until you have won some victory for humanity." Choices (A), (C), and

(D) are not mentioned specifically as part of Mann's philosophy.

12. (**A**) "Organic architecture, that is, natural architecture . . ." Choice (B) refers to the rule rejected by organic architecture, not to another name for it. Choices (C) and (D) refer to the fact that organic architecture may be varied but always remains true to natural principles. Neither principle architecture nor varied architecture was cited as another name for organic architecture, however.

13. (**B**) In the context of this passage, ultimately could best be replaced by eventually. Choices (A), (C), and (D) are not accepted definitions of the word.

14. (**A**) "Organic architecture—that is, natural architecture—may be varied in concept and form, but it [the architecture] is always faithful to natural principles." Other choices would change the meaning of the sentence.

15. (**C**) In the context of this passage, upheld is closest in meaning to promoted. Choices (A), (B), and (D) are not accepted definitions of the word.

16. (**D**) "Form does not follow function; form is inseparable from function." Choice (A) contradicts the fact that form does not follow function. Choices (B) and (C) contradict the fact that form is inseparable from function.

17. (**A**) "If these natural principles are upheld, then a bank cannot be built to look like a Greek temple." Choice (B) refers to the fact that natural principles require "total harmony with the setting." Choice (C) refers to the fact that

the colors are taken from "the surrounding palette of nature." Choice (D) refers to the fact that "the rule of functionalism is upheld."

18. (**B**) "Natural principles then, are principles of design, not style . . . . Like a sculptor, the organic architect views the site and materials as an innate form that develops organically from within." Choice (C) refers to the geometric themes mentioned later in the passage. Choice (D) contradicts the fact that the author emphasizes design, not style. Choice (A) is not mentioned and may not be concluded from information in the passage.

19. (**A**) In the context of this passage, obscured is closest in meaning to difficult to see. Choices (B), (C), and (D) are not accepted definitions of the word.

20. In the context of this passage, the word shapes is closest in meaning to contours. No other words or phrases in the **bold** text are close to the meaning of the word contours.

21. "Organic architecture incorporates built-in architectural features such as benches and storage areas to take the place of furniture." Quotation from sentence 7, paragraph 3.

22. (**C**) ". . . a building should . . . respect the natural characteristics of the setting to create harmony with its natural environment." Choices (A), (B), and (D) contradict the fact that nature should be respected.

23. (**D**) Choices (A), (B), and (C) are important to the discussion and provide details that support the

main point that alchemy was the predecessor of modern chemistry.

24. (**B**) In the context of the passage, authentic could best be replaced by genuine. Choices (A), (C), and (D) are not accepted definitions of the word.

25. (**D**) "The earliest authentic works on European alchemy are those [works] of the English monk Roger Bacon and the German philosopher St. Albertus Magnus." Other choices would change the meaning of the sentence.

26. (**A**) ". . . inferior metals such as lead and mercury were removed by various degrees of imperfection from gold." Choices (B), (C), and (D) are not mentioned and may not be concluded from information in the passage.

27. In the context of this passage, the word maintained is closest in meaning to asserted. No other words or phrases in the **bold** text are close to the meaning of the word asserted.

28. (**B**) ". . . base metals could be transmuted to gold by blending them with a substance even more perfect than gold. This elusive substance was referred to as the 'philosopher's stone.' " Choices (A) and (D) contradict the fact that the "philosopher's stone" was more perfect than gold. Choice (C) contradicts the fact that the "philosopher's stone" was an element that alchemists were searching for, not another name for their art.

29. (**A**) Because the early alchemists were "artisans who were accustomed to keeping trade secrets," it must be concluded that early

alchemists used cryptic terms like *sun* and *moon* to keep the work secret. Choices (B) and (C) refer to the fact that philosophers were attracted to alchemy and began to use the symbolic language in their literature, but they are not reasons why the alchemists used the terms. Choice (D) refers to the record of the progress of the work that was produced by alchemists, not to the reason for cryptic language.

30. (**C**) "Most of the early alchemists were artisans . . . ." Choice (B) refers to the second group, not the first group, of alchemists. Choices (A) and (D) are not mentioned and may not be concluded from information in the passage.

31. (**B**) In the context of this passage, cryptic could be replaced by secret. Choices (A), (C), and (D) are not accepted definitions of the word.

32. (**B**) ". . . it was the literary alchemist who was most likely to produce a written record; therefore, much of what is known about the science of alchemy is derived from philosophers rather than from the alchemists who labored in laboratories." Choice (A) is true, but it is not the reason that we know about the history of alchemy. Choices (C) and (D) are not mentioned and may not be concluded from information in the passage.

33. (**B**) ". . . they [laboratory alchemists] did gain a wide knowledge of chemical substances, discovered chemical properties, and invented many of the tools and techniques that are

still used by chemists today." Choice (A) contradicts the fact that the alchemists made scientific discoveries and were considered the legitimate forefathers of modern chemistry. Choice (C) contradicts the fact that the majority of educated persons in the period from 1400 to 1600 believed that alchemy had great merit. Although the author mentions the work of both laboratory and literary alchemists, Choice (D) is not mentioned and may not be concluded from information in the passage.

34. **(C)** The other choices are secondary ideas that are used to develop the main idea, "human memory." Choices (A), (B), and (D) are important to the discussion, but are not the main topic.

35. **(A)** In the context of this passage, formerly could best be replaced by in the past. Choices (B), (C), and (D) are not accepted definitions of the word.

36. **(A)** "Human memory . . . is really more sophisticated than that of a computer." Choice (B) contradicts the statement that human memory is more sophisticated. Choices (C) and (D) are not mentioned and may not be concluded from information in the passage.

37. **(D)** "Human memory, formerly believed to be rather inefficient, is really more sophisticated than that [the memory] of a computer." Other choices would change the meaning of the sentence.

38. In the context of this passage, the word complex is closest in meaning to sophisticated. No other words or phrases in the

bold text are close to the meaning of the word sophisticated.

39. **(A)** ". . . there is a great deal more stored in our minds than has been generally supposed." Choice (B) contradicts the statement that the physical basis for memory is not yet understood. Choice (C) refers to the fact that researchers have approached the problem from a variety of points of view, but it may not be concluded that different points of view are valuable. Choice (D) contradicts the statement that memory was formerly believed to be inefficient, but is really sophisticated.

40. **(B)** ". . . by stimulating their brains electrically, he could elicit the total recall of specific events." Choice (A) refers to the fact that Penfield was a neurosurgeon, but he did not rely on surgery to elicit dreams. Choice (C) refers to the procedure for supporting recall. Choice (D) refers to the way that performance is improved in memory, not to the procedure for eliciting dreams.

41. **(B)** ". . . the . . . capacity for storage in the brain is the result of an almost unlimited combination of interconnections . . . stimulated by patterns of activity." Choice (A) contradicts the fact that the physical basis for memory is not yet understood. Choice (C) contradicts the statement that storage in the brain is the result of an almost unlimited combination of interconnections. Choice (D) contradicts the fact that repeated references to the same information supports recall.

42. (**C**) Although Choices (A), (B), and (D) are definitions of the word bonds, the meaning in the context of the sentence is connections.

43. (**B**) "The memory trace is . . . made by structural changes in the brain . . . is not subject to direct observation . . . is rather a theoretical construct. . . . Repeated references to the same information supports recall." Choices (A), (C), and (D) are all mentioned in the passage. Choice (B) contradicts the fact that the memory trace is not subject to direct observation.

44. (**A**) "We use short-term memory when we look up a telephone number and repeat it to ourselves until we can place the call." Choices (B), (C), and (D) are not mentioned and may not be concluded from information in the passage.

45. "Psychologists generally divide memory into at least two types, short-term and long-term, which combine to form working memory." Quotation from sentence 1, paragraph 3.

Model Test 4—Computer-Assisted TOEFL

Section 1: Listening

1. (**B**) According to the woman, she has to study for her qualifying examinations. Choices (A) and (C) contradict the fact that the woman says she is tempted to go. Choice (D) is incorrect because the woman is taking a qualifying examination [for a degree]. She is not trying to qualify in order to play tennis.

2. (**B**) "I have an attendance requirement for undergraduates, but not for graduate students." Choice (A) contradicts the fact that she has a policy for undergraduates. Choice (C) contradicts the fact that the woman says "no" when she is asked whether attendance will count toward the grade. Choice (D) contradicts the fact that the woman has an attendance requirement for undergraduates, but not for this class, which implies that it is a graduate course.

3. (**C**) From the references to *financial reports, books,* and *accounts,* it must be concluded that the man is an accountant. It is not as probable that any of the persons referred to in Choices (A), (B), and (D) would be handling *accounts* and *financial reports.*

4. (**C**) The woman says that Ali is a part-time student this term. Choice (A) is incomplete because Ali is studying at the university and the American Language Institute. The number

in Choice (B) refers to the number of classes that Ali is taking at the Institute, not at the university. Choice (D) is incorrect because it is the man in the conversation, not Ali, who is surprised. The woman says that Ali's situation is not surprising.

5. (**C**) To *just miss* someone is an idiomatic expression that means that the person has already left. Choices (A), (B), and (D) are not paraphrases of the expression and may not be concluded from information in the conversation.

6. (**C**) Because the foreign student advisor is Mrs. Jones, not Miss Jones, we know that she is married. Choice (A) is incorrect because it is Mrs. Jones, not Mr. Adams, who is the new foreign student advisor. Choice (B) contradicts the fact that Mrs., not Mr., Jones is the foreign student advisor. In Choice (D), it is Mr. Adams, not the foreign student advisor, who is not here.

7. (**C**) Since the woman asks where she can find a telephone, she will probably make a phone call. Choice (D) contradicts the fact that the shuttle has already departed. Choices (A) and (B) are not mentioned and may not be concluded from information in the conversation.

8. (**C**) *Sold out* is an idiomatic expression that means there are none left. Choice (A) contradicts the fact that she has already tried to buy her books at the bookstore. Choice (D) contradicts the fact that she tried to buy the books. Choice (B) is not mentioned and may not be concluded

from information in the conversation.

9. (**B**) "You'd better leave a few minutes early." Choice (C) refers to the time the man has to be there, not to the time he should leave. Choices (A) and (D) are not mentioned and may not be concluded from information in the conversation.

10. (**C**) To *make fun of* is an idiomatic expression that means to ridicule. Choices (A), (B), and (D) are not paraphrases of the expression, and may not be concluded from information in the conversation.

11. (**A**) A *put down* is an idiomatic expression that means an insult. Choices (B), (C), and (D) are not paraphrases of the expression, and may not be concluded from information in the conversation.

12. (**B**) "Can you watch my book bag?" Choice (D) contradicts the fact that the man wants the woman to stay with his book bag. Choices (A) and (C) are not mentioned and may not be concluded from information in the conversation.

13. (**B**) *I hear you* is an idiomatic expression that means the speaker understands the other person's point of view. Choice (C) refers to the woman's feelings about the apartment, not to the man's feelings about the conversation. Choices (A) and (D) are not paraphrases of the expression, and may not be concluded from information in the conversation.

14. (**C**) Since Mike's brother is using the car while Mike is away, it must be concluded that Mike is in Florida as planned. Choice (A)

contradicts the fact that Mike's brother is using his car. Choice (B) refers to Mike, not to his brother. Choice (D) contradicts the fact that Mike's brother is here and Mike is in Florida.

15. (**C**) "You'd better start working on that project." Choice (B) contradicts the fact that the man has not started yet. Choices (A) and (D) are not mentioned and may not be concluded from information in the conversation.

16. (**D**) *Why not?* is an idiomatic expression that means the speaker agrees with the other person's plan. Choices (A), (B), and (C) are not paraphrases of the expression, and may not be concluded from information in the conversation.

17. (**A**) Since the woman registers surprise, it must be concluded that she thought the couple would not get married. Choices (B) and (C) contradict the fact that the woman made her comment about the wedding, not the honeymoon. The size of the wedding in Choice (D) is not mentioned and may not be concluded from information in the conversation.

18. (**C**) *What's the point?* is an idiomatic expression that means the speaker does not believe that the suggestion will be helpful. Choices (A), (B), and (D) are not paraphrases of the expression, and may not be concluded from information in the conversation.

19. (**A**) Since the woman says "I suggest that you call your sponsor," the man will probably do it. Choice (B) contradicts the fact

that the check isn't here. Choices (C) and (D) are not mentioned and may not be concluded from information in the conversation.

20. (**D**) *Don't give up* is an idiomatic expression that means keep trying. Choices (A), (B), and (C) are not paraphrases of the expression, and may not be concluded from information in the conversation.

21. (**D**) "I've been sick. . . . Now I'm worried about getting caught up." Choice (A) refers to the fact that the man has been sick, but he is not sick now. Choice (B) contradicts the fact that he stayed out of the hospital. Choice (C) contradicts the fact that he has not missed any quizzes.

22. (**B**) "I was hoping you'd let me make a copy of your notes." Choice (C) refers to the offer that she makes, not to what Gary asks Margaret to do. Choices (A) and (D) are not mentioned and may not be concluded from information in the conversation.

23. (**A**) ". . . why don't we get together . . . so that I can explain [my notes] to you." Choice (B) contradicts the fact that he hasn't missed any quizzes. Choices (C) and (D) are not mentioned and may not be concluded from information in the conversation.

24. (**A**) (**D**) Since Margaret agrees to let Gary borrow her notes, it must be concluded that she is helpful. Her attitude is positive and friendly. Choices (B) and (C) cannot be concluded from information in the conversation.

25. (**B**) The main topic of this talk is F. Scott Fitzgerald's work. The

other topics are secondary themes used to develop the main topic.

26. **(B) (D)** "Fitzgerald had a great natural talent, but he became a compulsive drinker. He never made the adjustments necessary to a maturing writer in a changing world." Choice (A) contradicts the fact that Fitzgerald had a great natural talent. Choice (C) contradicts the fact that his reputation is greater since the film version of his novel *The Great Gatsby* was released.

27. **(A)** "He wrote novels that describe the post-war American society . . . caught up in the rhythms of jazz." Choice (C) contradicts the fact that his novels describe post-war society, not war experiences. Choices (B) and (D) are not mentioned and may not be concluded from information in the talk.

28. **(C)** ". . . I am going to run the video version of *The Great Gatsby*, and then we'll divide up into groups to talk about it." Choices (A), (B), and (D) are not mentioned and may not be concluded from information in the talk.

29. **(A)** ". . . let me tell you a little bit about chamber music." Choice (B) is a detail used to develop the main purpose of the talk. Choices (C) and (D) are not mentioned and may not be concluded from information in the talk.

30. **(A) (C)** ". . . any combination of instruments can be used for chamber music. The most popular are the piano, strings, and woodwinds . . . ." Choices (B) and (D) are not mentioned and

may not be concluded from information in the talk.

31. **(B)** "This evening the University Quartet will perform two of the later pieces by Bach." Choices (A) and (D) are true, but they are not the reason that the speaker mentions Bach. Choice (C) contradicts the fact that Bach wrote music after vocal chamber music was popular.

32. **(B)** "Ladies and Gentlemen, the University Quartet." Choices (A), (C), and (D) are mentioned earlier in the talk.

33. **(C)** ". . . I was wondering whether he has an earlier appointment available on the same day [as my regular appointment]." Choice (A) contradicts the fact that he has an appointment at three o'clock on Wednesday. Choice (B) contradicts the fact that he asked for an early appointment. Choice (D) refers to what the man ultimately decided to do, not to the purpose of his call.

34. **(A)** ". . . Dr. Benjamin is tied up in a meeting until noon, and he has two appointments scheduled before yours. . . ." Choices (B), (C), and (D) contradict the fact that Dr. Benjamin has a meeting and appointments on Wednesday.

35. **(B)** "There is a later appointment time open . . . at four-thirty . . . or . . . Thursday morning at ten." Choice (A) refers to the man's regular appointment time, not to the new appointment that the secretary offered to make. Choice (D) refers to what the man wanted to do, not to what

the secretary offered to do. Choice (C) was not mentioned and may not be concluded from information in the conversation.

36. **(C)** "I think I'll just rearrange my own schedule so I can keep my regular appointment." Choices (A), (B), and (D) are not mentioned and may not be concluded from information in the conversation.

37. **(A)** "Health food is a general term applied to all kinds of foods that are considered more healthful than the types of food widely sold in supermarkets." Although Choices (B), (C), and (D) are all mentioned in the talk, they are secondary ideas used to develop the main idea.

38. **(B)** "A narrower classification of health food is natural food. This term [natural food] is used to distinguish between types of the same food. Fresh fruit is a natural food, but canned fruit, with sugars and other additives, is not." Choice (A) refers to foods like refined sugar, but is not mentioned as a term to distinguish between types of the same food. Choice (C) refers to food grown on a particular kind of farm. Choice (D) refers to organic foods that are not refined after harvest.

39. **(A) (D)** ". . . the allegations that processed foods contain chemicals, some of which are . . . toxic, and that vitamin content is greatly reduced in processed foods." Choice (C) contradicts the fact that vitamin content is reduced. Choice (B) is not mentioned and may not be concluded from information in the talk.

40. **(B)** "Eat health foods, preferably the organic variety." Choice (A) contradicts the fact that the speaker has provided detailed information in the talk. Choice (C) contradicts the fact that the speaker recommends eating health foods. Choice (D) may not be concluded from the manner in which the talk was delivered.

41. **(C)** ". . . the Stone Age is the time . . . when prehistoric people started to make tools and weapons." Choice (A) refers to an event in the Late Stone Age, not to a defining feature of the Stone Age. Choice (D) contradicts the fact that the introduction of metals marked the end of the Stone Age. Choice (B) is not mentioned and may not be concluded from information in the discussion.

42. **(C) (A) (B)** ". . . the use of flint for tools . . . was the beginning of the Old Stone Age . . . Homo Sapiens emerged . . . [which] marks . . . the beginning of the Middle Stone Age . . . it was during the . . . Late Stone Age [that agricultural] villages started to develop. . . ."

43. **(C)** "Some of the tools previously used for hunting were adapted for rudimentary farming. . . ." Choice (A) contradicts the fact that tools for domestic purposes were being used during the Old Stone Age. Choices (B) and (D) are not mentioned and may not be concluded from information in the discussion.

44. **(B)** ". . . the introduction of metals was usually considered the defining event that brought an end to the Stone Age." Choice

(A) refers to Chuck's idea, not to the event that marked the end of the Stone Age. Choices (C) and (D) occurred much earlier.

45. **(C)** ". . . oil moves up . . . until it reaches a nonporous rock deposit which will not allow it to continue moving. The oil becomes trapped under the nonporous rock deposit." Choice (A) contradicts the fact that traps are underground formations that occur in nature. Choice (B) is true, but it is not the definition of a trap. Choice (D) contradicts the fact that the trap stops the flow of oil through the cracks and holes.

46. **(B)** Choice (A) is a diagram of a fault trap, not an anticline trap. Choice (C) is a diagram of a salt dome trap.

47. **(B)** ". . . in all traps, the oil is collected in the porous rock and trapped underground by the nonporous rock." Choice (B) is the nonporous rock where the oil collects. Choice (A) is above ground. Choice (C) is a water and gas deposit. Choice (D) is porous rock.

48. **(A)** ". . . a bulge in a flat surface may signal the presence of a salt dome." Choice (B) refers to an anticline trap, not a salt dome. Choices (C) and (D) are not mentioned and may not be concluded from information in the lecture.

49. **(B)** ". . . I have a choice between Dr. Perkins and Dr. Robinson." Choice (D) contradicts the fact that she asks for the man's advice and tells him that it was helpful. Choices (A) and (C) are not mentioned and may not be concluded from information in the conversation.

50. **(B) (D)** "I'd call [Robinson] traditional. . . . If you like to listen to lectures and take notes . . . I'd say Robinson." Since the woman decides to take the class with Dr. Robinson, it must be concluded that she prefers lectures and a more traditional approach to teaching. Choice (A) contradicts the fact that she does not know about either of the professors. Choice (C) contradicts the fact that the man is recalling information about the professor, which implies that he has already taken the class that the woman is going to take.

Section 2: Structure

1. **(B)** The verb phrase *to insist on* requires an *-ing* form in the complement. *-Ing* forms are modified by possessive pronouns. Choice (A) is an infinitive modified by an object pronoun. Choice (C) is an *-ing* form, but it is modified by a subject, not a possessive pronoun. Choice (D) is a verb word.

2. **(D)** *The* must be used with a superlative. Choices (A), (B), and (C) are wordy and ungrammatical.

3. **(B)** A form of BE is used with the participle in passive sentences. *Cannot proved* should be *cannot be proved*.

4. **(D)** *The same* is used with a quality noun such as *age*, and *as* in comparisons. *As* is used with a quality adjective such as *old*, and *as*. Choice (A) is a quality

adjective, not a noun, with *to*. In Choice (B), *the same* is used with *than*, not *as*. "As old as" would also be correct.

5. (**D**) *Such* is used with a noun phrase to express cause before *that* and a subject and verb that expresses result. Choice (A) does not have a subject. Choice (B) does not have a subject or verb. Choice (C) is not a *that* clause.

6. (**C**) *Began* should be *begun* because the auxiliary *had* requires a participle. *Began* is a past form. *Begun* is a participle.

7. (**A**) Using words with the same meaning consecutively is repetitive. *First* should be deleted because *original* means *first*.

8. (**C**) Singular and plural expressions of noncount nouns such as *equipment* occur in idiomatic phrases, often *piece* or *pieces of*. Choices (A), (B), and (D) are not idiomatic.

9. (**D**) The anticipatory clause *it was in 1607 that* introduces a subject and verb, *the English settled*. Choice (A) is wordy and indirect. Choice (B) may be used as part of a subject clause preceding a main verb. Choice (C) may be used without *that* preceding a subject and verb. "That in 1607 the English settled in Jamestown *has changed* the history of the Americas," and "Because in 1607 the English settled in Jamestown, *the history* of the Americas *has changed*" would also be correct.

10. (**C**) Repetition of the subject by a subject pronoun is redundant. *It* should be deleted.

11. (**C**) There must be agreement between subject and verb. *Have* should be *has* to agree with the singular subject *triangle*.

12. (**C**) A sentence has a subject and a verb. Choice (A) is the subject, but there is no main clause verb. Choices (B) and (D) introduce a main clause subject and verb.

13. (**C**) *Impossibility* should be *impossible*. *Impossibility* is a noun. *Impossible* is an adjective.

14. (**D**) For scientific results, a present form in the condition requires a present or future form in the result. Only Choice (D) introduces a conditional.

15. (**C**) There must be agreement between pronoun and antecedent. *Their* should be *its* to refer to the singular antecedent *Pickerel Frog*.

16. (**B**) Multiple comparatives like *twice* are expressed by the multiple followed by the phrase *as much as*. Choice (A) is a multiple number followed by the phrase *more than*. Choices (C) and (D) reverse the order of the multiple number and the phrase.

17. (**C**) *Used to* requires a verb word. When preceded by a form of BE, *used to* requires an *-ing* form. In Choice (A), *used to* requires a verb word, not an *-ing* form. In Choice (B), *used to* preceded by a form of BE may be used with an *-ing* form, not an infinitive. Choice (D) uses the incorrect form, *use to*.

18. (**B**) The adverb *previously* establishes a point of view in the past. *Is* should be *was* in order to maintain the point of view.

19. (**C**) Redundant, indirect phrases should be avoided. *In a correct manner* is a redundant pattern.

The adverb *correctly* is simple and more direct.

20. (C) The noun in the appositive must agree with the antecedent. *Tree* should be *trees* to agree with the antecedent *conifers*.

Section 3: Reading

1. (B) The other choices are secondary ideas used to develop the main idea, "the nature of geysers." Choices (A), (C), and (D) are subtopics that provide details and examples.

2. (B) "A geyser is the result of underground water under the combined conditions of high temperatures and increased pressure beneath the surface of the earth." Choice (A) contradicts the fact that water, not hot rocks, rises to the surface. Choice (C) contradicts the fact that the hot rocks are in the earth's interior, not on the surface. Choice (D) contradicts the fact that the water seeps down in cracks and fissures in the earth.

3. In the context of this passage, approximately could best be replaced by about. No other words or phrases in the **bold** text are close to the meaning of the word approximately.

4. (C) "Since temperature rises . . . and pressure increases with depth . . ." Choices (A), (B), and (D) contradict the fact that both temperature and pressure increase with depth.

5. (A) "Since temperature rises about 1° F for every sixty feet under the earth's surface, and pressure increases with depth, water that seeps down in cracks

and fissures until it [water] reaches very hot rocks in the earth's interior becomes heated to a temperature of approximately 290° F." Choices (B), (C), and (D) would change the meaning of the sentence.

6. "Water under pressure . . ." Quotation from sentence 1, paragraph 2.

7. (B) "Old Faithful erupts almost every hour." The number in Choice (A) refers to the number of thousand gallons of water that is expelled during an eruption, not to the number of minutes between eruptions. The numbers in Choices (C) and (D) refer to the number of feet to which the geyser rises during an eruption.

8. (B) In the context of this passage, expelling is closest in meaning to discharging. Choices (A), (C), and (D) are not accepted definitions of the word.

9. (A) ". . . a geyser must have a source of heat, a reservoir where water can be stored . . . an opening through which the hot water and steam can escape, and underground channels. . . . Favorable conditions for geysers exist in regions of geologically recent volcanic activity . . . in areas of more than average precipitation." Choice (C) includes some of, but not all, the necessary conditions. Choices (B) and (D) contradict the fact that the volcanic activity should be recent, but not active.

10. (C) "For the most part, geysers are located in three regions of the world: New Zealand, Iceland, and the Yellowstone National

Park area of the United States."
Choice (A) contradicts the fact
that no comparisons are made
among the areas. Choice (B) contradicts the fact that Yellowstone
National Park is in the United
States, not in New Zealand or
Iceland. Choice (D) contradicts
the fact that geysers are also
found in a third region, the Yellowstone National Park area of
the United States.

11. (**A**) Choice (A) is a restatement
of the sentence referred to in the
passage. *Never failed* means
always. Choices (B), (C), and
(D) would change the meaning
of the original sentence.

12. (**A**) Choice (A) is the author's
main point because the reasons
for success are referred to
throughout the passage. Choices
(B), (C), and (D) are each specific reasons for success.

13. (**D**) Choice (A) refers to the fact
that the Wright brothers were "a
team." Choice (B) refers to the
fact that they were "among the
best glider pilots in the world."
Choice (C) refers to the "experiments [that] allowed the Wright
brothers to construct a superior
wing for their craft." Choice (D)
is not mentioned and may not be
concluded from information in
the passage.

14. (**B**) In the context of this passage,
cited is closest in meaning to
mentioned. Choices (A), (C),
and (D) are not accepted definitions of the word.

15. (**C**) Incessantly means constantly. Choices (A), (B), and
(D) are not accepted definitions
of the word.

16. (**B**) "They were also both glider
pilots. Unlike some other engineers who experimented with the
theories of flight, [they] experienced the practical side . . . ."
Choices (A), (C), and (D) were
all true of the Wright brothers,
but these experiences were not
different from those of their
competitors.

17. "They had realized from their
experiments that the most serious
problems in manned flight would
be stabilizing and maneuvering
the aircraft once it was airborne."
Quotation from sentence 4, paragraph 2.

18. In the context of this passage, the
word guiding is closest in meaning to maneuvering. No other
words or phrases in the **bold** text
are close to the meaning of the
word maneuvering.

19. (**C**) "The data from these experiments [using the wind tunnel]
allowed the Wright brothers to
construct a superior wing for
their craft." Choice (A) contradicts the fact that the light internal combustion engine had
already been invented by someone else. Choice (B) contradicts
the fact that they developed a
three-axis control while experimenting with gliders, not with
the wind tunnel. Choice (D) contradicts the fact that they used the
data to improve the wings, not
the engine for their airplane.

20. (**C**) "Attempts to achieve manned
flight in the early nineteenth century were doomed because the
steam engines that powered the
aircraft were too heavy in proportion to the power that they

[the engines] produced." Choices (A), (B), and (D) would change the meaning of the sentence.

21. (**A**) In the context of this passage, doomed is closest in meaning to destined to fail. Choices (B), (C), and (D) are not accepted definitions of the word.

22. (**D**) ". . . they were able to bring the ratio of weight to power within acceptable limits for ·flight." From the reference to the ratio of weight to power and *acceptable limits*, it must be concluded that previous engines did not have acceptable limits of weight to power and, thus, did not have enough power to lift their own weight. Choice (B) contradicts the fact that the engines were relatively heavy. Choice (C) contradicts the fact that they were experimenting with internal combustion engines. The size in Choice (A) is not mentioned and may not be concluded from information in the passage.

23. (**A**) The other choices are secondary ideas used to develop the main idea, "the influenza virus." Choices (B), (C), and (D) are subtopics that provide details and examples.

24. (**D**) ". . . bacteria can be considered a type of plant . . . ." Choice (A) refers to the secretions of bacteria, not to the bacteria themselves. Although it may be true that bacteria are very small, as in Choice (B), or larger than viruses, as in Choice (C), this information is not mentioned and may not be concluded from reading the passage.

25. ". . . viruses, like the influenza virus, are living organisms [the viruses] themselves." Other choices would change the meaning of the sentence.

26. (**D**) In the context of this passage, strictly could best be replaced by exactly. Choices (A), (B), and (C) are not accepted definitions of the word.

27. (**C**) ". . . we must also consider them [viruses] as being alive since they are able to multiply in unlimited quantities." Choice (A) is the reason that we must consider them as regular chemical molecules, not the reason that we must consider them as being alive. Choices (B) and (D) are not mentioned and may not be concluded from information in the passage.

28. (**B**) ". . . they [viruses] have strictly defined atomic structure . . . ." Choice (A) contradicts the fact that viruses have a strictly defined atomic structure. Choice (C) contradicts the fact that we may consider them as regular chemical molecules. Although Choice (D) is implied, it may not be concluded from information in the passage.

29. (**B**) Unlimited means without limits; very large. Choices (A), (C), and (D) are not accepted definitions of the word.

30. (**B**) ". . . the protection is against only the type of virus that caused the influenza." Choices (A) and (C) contradict the fact that the protection is against only the one type of virus. Choice (D) is not mentioned and may not be concluded from information in the passage.

31. In the context of this passage, the word types is closest in meaning to strains. No other words or phrases in the **bold** text are close to the meaning of the word strains.

32. (**C**) ". . . every ten years . . . pandemics occur. Thought to be caused by new strains of type-A virus, these pandemics spread rapidly." Choices (A), (B), and (D) are all mentioned in the passage. Choice (C) refers to epidemics, not to pandemics.

33. "Epidemics or regional outbreaks have appeared on the average' every two or three years for type-A virus, and every four or five years for type-B virus. Approximately every ten years, worldwide epidemics of influenza called pandemics also occur." The connection between the two sentences is the reference to "epidemics" and the transition word "also." The second sentence with the word "also" must be mentioned after the first sentence.

34. (**B**) The other choices are secondary ideas that are used to develop the main idea, "The Federal Reserve System." Choices (A), (C), and (D) are important to the discussion as they relate to the Federal Reserve System.

35. (**A**) In the context of this passage, oversee is closest in meaning to supervise. Choices (B), (C), and (D) are not accepted definitions of the word.

36. (**D**) In the context of this passage, confirmed could best be replaced by approved. Choices (A), (B), and (C) are not accepted definitions of the word.

37. (**B**) "The System's primary function is to control monetary policy by influencing the cost and availability of money and credit through the purchase and sale of government securities." Choice (A) refers to the effect of regulation on the public, not to the System's responsibility. Choice (D) contradicts the statement that the Board of Governors is appointed by the President. Choice (C) is not mentioned and may not be concluded from information in the passage.

38. (**B**) Although Choices (A), (C), and (D) are definitions of the word securities, the meaning in the context of the sentence is bonds.

39. (**C**) "If the Federal Reserve provides too little money, interest rates tend to be high, borrowing is expensive, business activity slows down, unemployment goes up . . . ." Choice (A) contradicts the fact that interest rates are high and borrowing is expensive. Choice (B) contradicts the fact that unemployment goes up. Choice (D) contradicts the fact that business activity slows down.

40. (**B**) "If there is too much money, interest rates decline, and borrowing can lead to excess demand, pushing up prices and fueling inflation." Choice (A) contradicts the statement that during times of too little money, unemployment goes up. Choice (C) misinterprets the word *fuel* to mean *oil*. Choice (D) is not mentioned and may not be concluded from information in the passage.

41. (**C**) "In collaboration with the US Department of the Treasury, the Fed puts new coins and paper currency into circulation by issuing them [coins and paper currency] to banks." Other choices would change the meaning of the sentence.

42. "It [the Fed] also supervises the activities of member banks abroad, and regulates certain aspects of international finance." Quotation from sentence 3, paragraph 3.

43. (**C**) Choice (C) is a restatement of the sentence referred to in the passage. *Not stray* means follow. Choices (A), (B), and (D) would change the meaning of the original sentence.

44. (**D**) Choice (A) refers to the fact that the "Federal Reserve System is an independent agency of the United States government that helps oversee the national banking system." Choice (B) refers to the fact that the Federal Reserve's ". . . primary function is to control monetary policy . . . through the purchase and sale of government securities." Choice (C) refers to the fact that "the Fed puts new coins and paper currency into circulation by issuing them to banks." Choice (D) contradicts the fact that "the Fed does not depend on Congress for budget allocations" although it does send "frequent reports to the Congress."

45. "It has been said that the Federal Reserve is actually an informal branch of the United States government because it is composed of national policy makers. In fact, the Fed is not confined by the usual checks and balances that apply to the three official branches of government—the executive, the legislative, and the judicial." The connection between the two sentences is the reference to an "informal branch" in the first sentence and a reference to "the three official branches of government" in the second sentence.

TRANSCRIPT FOR THE LISTENING SECTIONS OF THE TOEFL MODEL TESTS

The following is the transcript of the Listening Sections for all of the four TOEFL Model Tests in this book. Note that the Listening Sections always appear as Section 1 of the examinations.

When you take the Model Tests in this book as a preliminary step in your preparation for the actual examination, you may use either the compact disc that supplements this book or the cassette tapes that supplement the larger version of this book, *Barron's How to Prepare for the TOEFL.* The compact disc includes audio for Model Tests Three and Four. The cassette tapes include audio for Model Tests One, Two, Three, and Four, as well as four additional Model Tests printed in *Barron's How to Prepare for the TOEFL.*

If you have someone read the TOEFL transcript to you, be sure that he or she understands the timing sequences. The reader should work with a stopwatch or with a regular watch with a second hand in order to keep careful track of the timed pauses between questions. The total amount of time for each section is noted both on the transcript and on the Model Tests. In addition, the time for the pauses between questions is also given on the transcript. Be sure that the reader speaks clearly and at a moderately paced rate. For results that would be closest to the actual testing situation, it is recommended that three persons be asked to read, since some of the Listening Sections include dialogues.

Model Test 1
Paper and Pencil TOEFL

Section 1:
Listening Comprehension

50 QUESTIONS 40 MINUTES

In this section of the test, you will have an opportunity to demonstrate your ability to understand conversations and talks in English. There are three parts to this section with special directions for each part. Answer all the questions on the basis of what is stated or implied by the speakers in this test. When you take the actual TOEFL test, you will not be allowed to take notes or write in your test book. Try to work on this Model Test in the same way.

Part A

Directions: In Part A, you will hear short conversations between two people. After each conversation, you will hear a question about the conversation. The conversations and questions will not be repeated. After you hear a question, read the four possible answers in your book and choose the best answer. Then, on your answer sheet, find the number of the question and fill in the space that corresponds to the letter of the answer you have chosen.

1. Man: It doesn't make any sense for us to go home for spring vacation now.
   Woman: Especially since we'll be graduating in May.
   Narrator: What does the woman mean?

(Note: There should be a 12-second pause after each test question in this section.)

2. Woman: Shall I bring you your coffee now or would you rather have it with your lunch?
   Man: I'd like it now, please.
   Narrator: Where did this conversation most probably take place?

3. Man: Could you please explain the assignment for Monday, Miss Smith?
   Woman: Certainly. Read the next chapter in your textbook and come to class prepared to discuss what you've read.
   Narrator: What are the speakers talking about?

4. Woman: If I were you, I'd be more careful about locking the back door at night.
   Man: Don't worry. No one will break in.
   Narrator: What did the woman imply?

5. Man: Did you buy a birthday present for your brother?
   Woman: I've been thinking about getting him a CD. He likes classical music.
   Narrator: What is the woman's problem?

6. Woman: Are you ready for this?
   Man: I should be. I've been cramming for the past three days.
   Narrator: What does the man mean?

7. Man: Good morning. I'd like to speak to Mr. Adams, please. This is Edward Miller at the Sun Valley Health Center.
   Woman: Mr. Miller, my husband isn't at home. I can give you his business phone if you'd like to call him at work, though.
   Narrator: What can be inferred about the woman?

8. Woman: Jack must have been joking when he said that he was going to quit his job.
   Man: Don't be too sure. He told me that he was trying to sell his house.
   Narrator: What does the man mean?

9. Man: I need a book for English two-twenty-one.
    Woman: All of the textbooks are on the shelves in the back of the store.
    Narrator: What will the man probably do?

10. Man: I was hoping that you'd wear your new dress. It's much prettier.
    Woman: But this one is more comfortable for hot weather.
    Narrator: What can be inferred about the woman?

11. Man: What do you think of Professor Collins?
    Woman: I think he's a great person, but the class just turns me off.
    Narrator: What does the woman mean?

12. Man: I thought that you were going to the convention in Atlanta last Saturday.
    Woman: I was planning to, but I haven't been feeling well.
    Narrator: What can be inferred about the woman?

13. Man: Have you made an appointment with the dentist yet?
    Woman: No. And I really can't put it off anymore.
    Narrator: What will the woman probably do?

14. Woman: How do you like American food?
    Man: I'm used to it now.
    Narrator: What does the man mean?

15. Woman: Are you still studying? It's two o'clock in the morning.
    Man: I know. I just can't seem to get caught up.
    Narrator: What does the man mean?

16. Woman: Let's get together sometime soon.
    Man: Yes. Connie and I have been meaning to have you over.
    Narrator: What does the man mean?

17. Man: It's your turn to call the names on the list if you want to.
    Woman: I think I'll pass this time.
    Narrator: What is the woman going to do?

18. Woman: I'm pretty sure that the deadline for applications has passed.
    Man: Why don't you let me look into it for you?
    Narrator: What does the man mean?

19. Woman: Did you get your tickets?
    Man: I talked to Judy about it, and she took care of it for me.
    Narrator: What does the man mean?

20. Woman: Maybe we should take Front Street this morning. The radio announcer said that traffic was very heavy on the freeway.

    Man: Well, if he says to take Front Street, we should go the other way.

    Narrator: What does the man imply about the radio announcer?

21. Woman: What seems to be the problem?

    Man: Well I understand the lectures but I get mixed up when I try to read the book.

    Narrator: What does the man mean?

22. Man: Do you know Randy Johnson?

    Woman: Yes. He sure has it made, doesn't he?

    Narrator: What does the woman mean?

23. Man: This paper isn't due until next week.

    Woman: Yes, I know. But I wanted to turn it in ahead of time if that's all right.

    Narrator: What does the woman mean?

24. Man: Why don't you do the solo?

    Woman: You've never heard me sing, have you?

    Narrator: What does the woman imply?

25. Man: I can't stand this class!

    Woman: Well, you might as well get used to it. You have to take it in order to graduate.

    Narrator: What does the woman say about the class?

26. Man: That was Dale on the phone. His car broke down on the way here, so he won't be able to make it.

    Woman: He'd better trade that car in.

    Narrator: What does the woman suggest that Dale do?

27. Woman: How are you going to get ready for an oral final?

    Man: The professor said we should study alone, but the T.A. said to get into a study group and quiz each other.

    Narrator: What did the T.A. suggest the students do?

28. Man: I need an advisor's signature on my course request form. Could I make an appointment, please?

    Woman: Oh, well, you don't need to make an appointment. Just wait here. I'll get a pen.

    Narrator: What is the woman going to do?

29. Man: This copy looks good. Why don't you just hand it in?
    Woman: I'd better make one more draft.
    Narrator: What is the woman going to do?

30. Woman: Your loan payment is due on the first. Oh, sorry, the computer has you scheduled for the fifth.
    Man: That's good. That's what I thought.
    Narrator: What had the man assumed about the loan payment?

Part B

Directions: In this part of the test, you will hear longer conversations. After each conversation, you will hear several questions. The conversations and questions will not be repeated.

After you hear a question, read the four possible answers in your book and choose the best answer. Then, on your answer sheet, find the number of the question and fill in the space that corresponds to the letter of the answer you have chosen.

Remember, you are **not** allowed to take notes or write on your test pages.

Questions 31–34. Listen to a conversation between two strangers.

Man: Excuse me. Have you been waiting long?
Woman: About ten minutes.
Man: Did you notice whether the number seven bus has gone by?
Woman: Not while I've been standing here. I'm waiting for the number seven myself.
Man: Good. Hot today, isn't it?
Woman: Yes, it is. I wish that it would rain and cool off.
Man: Me too. This is unusual for March. I don't remember it ever being so hot and dry in March before.
Woman: You're from Florida then.
Man: Not really. I was born in New York, but I've lived here for ten years now.
Woman: My mother and I have just moved here from Indiana.
Man: Pretty cold in Indiana, isn't it?
Woman: Yes. That's why we moved. But we didn't know that it would be so hot here. We should have gone to California. Do you think that we've missed the bus?
Man: No. It's always a little late.
Woman: I have twenty to one, but my watch is a little fast.
Man: Don't worry. It never comes exactly on the half-hour like it should.

Narrator: 31. Why is the woman waiting?

(Note: There should be a 12-second pause after each test question in this section.)

32. According to the conversation, what kind of weather is usual for March?

33. Where does this conversation take place?

34. How often is the bus scheduled to pass their stop?

Questions 35–38. Listen to a telephone call to a professor.

Woman:	Hello, Professor Hayes. This is Betty Peterson. I'm in your senior seminar this semester.
Man:	Oh, yes, Betty. How are you?
Woman:	Just fine, thanks. I'm calling because I'm applying for graduate school, and I need three letters of recommendation. Would you be willing to write me one?
Man:	Why yes, Betty. I'd be happy to. I think you are an excellent candidate for graduate school. Are you applying here or to another university?
Woman:	Here. That's why I think your letter is so important. Everyone on the selection committee knows and respects you.
Man:	Let's see, Dr. Warren is the chair of that committee, isn't she?
Woman:	Yes. So, if you would just write the letter to her, that would be great.
Man:	Okay. And when do you need this? I don't recall the deadline for applications.
Woman:	The committee meets on April 30, so all the materials must be submitted before then.
Man:	All right. I'll send it directly to her office.
Woman:	Thank you. I really appreciate it.
Man:	You're welcome. Glad to do it.
Narrator:	35. Why did Betty call Professor Hayes?

36. What does Professor Hayes think about Betty?

37. Who will decide whether Betty is accepted to the program?

38. When does Betty need to submit all her materials?

Part C

Directions: In this part of the test, you will hear several short talks. After each talk, you will hear some questions. The talks and questions will not be repeated.

After you hear a question, read the four possible answers in your book and choose the best answer. Then, on your answer sheet, find the number of the question and fill in the space that corresponds to the letter of the answer you have chosen.

Questions 39–42. Listen to a lecture by a history professor.

I know that this is probably a digression from the topic of today's lecture, but it is worth noting that although England no longer ruled her former colonies after the eighteenth century, she controlled trade with them by selling products so cheaply that it was not possible for the new countries to manufacture and compete with English prices. To maintain this favorable balance of trade, England went to fantastic lengths to keep secret the advanced manufacturing processes upon which such a monopoly depended.

Enterprising Americans made all kinds of ingenious attempts to smuggle drawings for the most modern machines out of England, but it was an Englishman, Samuel Slater, who finally succeeded.

Although textile workers were forbidden to emigrate, Slater traveled to the United States in secret. Determined to take nothing in writing, he memorized the intricate designs for all the machines in an English textile mill, and in partnership with Moses Brown, a Quaker merchant, recreated the mill in Rhode Island.

Forty-five years later, in part as a result of the initial model by Slater and Brown, America had changed from a country of small farmers and craftsmen to an industrial nation in competition with England.

Narrator:　　39. Who is the speaker?

(Note: There should be a 12-second pause after each test question in this section.)

40. According to the speaker, how did England control trade in the eighteenth century?

41. What did Samuel Slater do?

42. What happened as a result of the Slater-Brown partnership?

<u>Questions 43–46</u>. Listen to a talk by a college instructor in an English class.

So many different kinds of writing have been called essays, it is difficult to define exactly what an essay is. Perhaps the best way is to point out four characteristics that are true of most essays. First, an essay is about one topic. It does not start with one subject and digress to another and another. Second, although a few essays are long enough to be considered a small book, most essays are short. Five hundred words is the most common length for an essay. Third, an essay is written in prose, not poetry. True, Alexander Pope did call two of his poems essays, but that word is part of a title, and after all, the "Essay on Man" and the "Essay on Criticism" really are not essays at all. They are long poems. Fourth, and probably most important, an essay is personal. It is the work of one person whose purpose is to share a thought, idea, or point of view. Let me also state here that since an essay is always personal, the term "personal essay" is redundant. Now, taking into consideration all of these characteristics, perhaps we can now define an essay as a short, prose composition with a personal viewpoint that discusses one topic. With that in mind, let's brainstorm some topics for your first essay assignment.

Narrator:	43. What is the instructor defining?
	44. What is the main point of the talk?
	45. According to the talk, which of the characteristics are NOT true of an essay?
	46. What will the students probably do as an assignment?

<u>Questions 47–50</u>. Listen to a talk by a tour guide for Jefferson's home.

Not a gifted public speaker, Thomas Jefferson was most talented as a literary draftsman. Sent to Congress by the Virginia Convention in 1775, he was elected to the committee to draft a declaration of independence from England. Although John Adams and Benjamin Franklin also served on the committee, the composition of the Declaration of Independence belongs indisputably to Jefferson. In 1779, Jefferson was elected governor of the state of Virginia, an office he held until Congress appointed him to succeed Franklin as US minister to France. Upon returning to Washington, he accepted the position of secretary of state.

Although Jefferson was a Republican, he at first tried to cooperate with Alexander Hamilton, a Federalist who was first among President Washington's advisors. When he concluded that Hamilton was really in favor of a monarchy, hostility between the two men sharpened.

Having served as vice-president in John Adams' administration, Jefferson ran for president in the election of 1800. He and Federalist Aaron Burr received an identical vote, but the Republican Congress elected to approve Jefferson as president. The most outstanding accomplishment of his administration was the purchase of the Louisiana Territory from France in 1803. He was easily re-elected in 1804. When he left office four years later, he returned here to Monticello, where he promoted the formation of a liberal university for Virginia.

Narrator: 47. What is the main purpose of this talk?

48. Jefferson was a member of which political group?

49. How did Jefferson become president?

50. According to the lecturer, what was it that Jefferson was NOT?

Model Test 2
Paper and Pencil TOEFL

Section 1:
Listening Comprehension

50 QUESTIONS 40 MINUTES

In this section of the test, you will have an opportunity to demonstrate your ability to understand conversations and talks in English. There are three parts to this section with special directions for each part. Answer all the questions on the basis of what is stated or implied by the speakers in this test. When you take the actual TOEFL test, you will not be allowed to take notes or write in your test book. Try to work on this Model Test in the same way.

Part A

Directions: In Part A, you will hear short conversations between two people. After each conversation, you will hear a question about the conversation. The conversations and questions will not be repeated. After you hear a question, read the four possible answers in your book and choose the best answer. Then, on your answer sheet, find the number of the question and fill in the space that corresponds to the letter of the answer you have chosen.

1. Woman: You'd better take the car to the garage from now on. They charged me seventy-five dollars for a few minor repairs.
   Man: That's not too bad.
   Narrator: What does the man mean?

(Note: There should be a 12-second pause after each test question in this section.)

2. Man: The International Students' Association is having a party Saturday night. Can you come or do you have to work at the hospital?
   Woman: I wish I could.
   Narrator: What will the woman probably do?

3. Woman: I think that the game starts at eight.
   Man: Good. We have just enough time to get there.
   Narrator: What will the speakers probably do?

4. Woman: What did you do after you lost your passport?
   Man: I went to see the foreign student advisor, and he reported it to the Passport Office in Washington.
   Narrator: What did the man do after he lost his passport?

5. Man: If you don't have an account here, I can't cash your check. I'm sorry, but that's the way it is.
   Woman: Well, thanks a lot! You're a big help!
   Narrator: What does the woman mean?

6. Man: I'm not sure what Dr. Tyler wants us to do.
   Woman: If I were you, I'd write a rough draft and ask Dr. Tyler to look at it.
   Narrator: What does the woman suggest the man do?

7. Man: Dr. Clark is the only one teaching statistics this term.
   Woman: You mean we have to put up with her for another semester?
   Narrator: What does the woman mean?

8. Man: Do you think that you can have these shirts finished by Friday morning?
   Woman: I'm sorry. I couldn't possibly get them done by then. Saturday afternoon would be the earliest that you could have them.
   Narrator: What does the woman say about the shirts?

9. Woman: The music and the flowers are lovely.
   Man: Yes. I hope that the food is good.
   Narrator: What kind of place are the speakers probably talking about?

10.	Man:	Hello, Anne. This is Larry at the office. Is Fred at home?
	Woman:	No, Larry. He's in class now. He'll be home for lunch though.
	Narrator:	What do we know about Fred?

11.	Man:	When does the next bus leave for New York?
	Woman:	Buses leave for New York every half-hour. You just missed the nine-thirty bus by five minutes.
	Narrator:	What will the man probably do?

12.	Woman:	Did we have an assignment for Monday? I don't have anything written down.
	Man:	Nothing to read in the textbook, but we have to see a movie and write a paragraph about it.
	Narrator:	What are the speakers discussing?

13.	Man:	Make thirty copies for me and twenty copies for Mr. Brown.
	Woman:	As soon as I make the final corrections on the original.
	Narrator:	What is the woman probably going to do?

14.	Man:	Excuse me. Are you Sally Harrison's sister?
	Woman:	No, I'm not. I'm her cousin.
	Narrator:	What had the man assumed about the woman?

15.	Woman:	I can't find my pen. It was right here on the desk yesterday and now it's gone. Have you seen it?
	Man:	Yes. I put it in the desk drawer.
	Narrator:	What is the woman's problem?

16.	Woman:	When is John coming?
	Man:	Well, he said he'd be here at eight-thirty, but if I know him, it will be at least nine o'clock.
	Narrator:	What does the man imply about John?

17.	Man:	I suppose we should look for a bigger house, but I don't see how we can afford one right now.
	Woman:	If only we hadn't spent so much money on our vacation this year.
	Narrator:	What does the woman mean?

18.	Man:	Did you see Jack's presentation?
	Woman:	Yes. What happened? He didn't seem to know up from down.
	Narrator:	What does the woman imply about Jack?

19. Woman: Shall I send out the invitations?
    Man: Let's hold off on that until I can talk to Janet.
    Narrator: What does the man mean?

20. Man: How's the baby? Is she walking yet?
    Woman: Oh, yes. I can't keep up with her!
    Narrator: What does the woman mean?

21. Woman: How is your experiment coming along?
    Man: It's finished, but it didn't turn out quite like I thought it would.
    Narrator: What does the man mean?

22. Woman: Barbara sure likes to talk on the phone.
    Man: If only she liked her classes as well!
    Narrator: What does the man imply about Barbara?

23. Woman: My allergies are really bothering me. I guess I'll have to go to the doctor.
    Man: If I were you, I'd try some over-the-counter medications first. They usually do the job.
    Narrator: What does the man suggest the woman do?

24. Man: What did you decide about the scholarship? Did you fill out the application?
    Woman: I'm going to give it all I've got.
    Narrator: What does the woman mean?

25. Man: Hello, Anne. This is Robert.
    Woman: Oh, hi, Robert. I was just about to call you.
    Narrator: What does the woman mean?

26. Man: Could I have a few more minutes to finish?
    Woman: I'm afraid not. It's a timed test.
    Narrator: What does the woman mean?

27. Woman: The best part is I can use my roommate's book.
    Man: I'm not so sure about that. I think they're using a different book this semester.
    Narrator: What does the man imply?

28. Man: I'm going to get Sally a bike for Christmas.
    Woman: Are you sure she'd like one?
    Narrator: What does the woman imply?

29. Woman: Carol needs a ride downtown, and I said you'd take her.
    Man: Oh no. Please say you didn't!
    Narrator: What can be inferred about the man?

30. Man: I just can't get the answer to this problem! I've been
                  working on it for three hours.
    Woman: Maybe you should get some rest and try it again later.
    Narrator: What does the woman suggest that the man do?

Part B

Directions: In this part of the test, you will hear longer conversations. After
each conversation, you will hear several questions. The conversations and
questions will not be repeated.

After you hear a question, read the four possible answers in your book and
choose the best answer. Then, on your answer sheet, find the number of the
question and fill in the space that corresponds to the letter of the answer you
have chosen.

Remember, you are **not** allowed to take notes or write on your test pages.

Questions 31–34. Listen to a class discussion.

Baker: It seems to me that the question is not whether the metric
            system should be introduced in the United States, but
            rather, how it should be introduced.
Woman: I think that it should be done gradually to give everyone
            enough time to adjust.
Man: Yes. Perhaps we could even have two systems for a while.
            I mean, we could keep the English system and use metrics
            as an optional system.
Woman: That's what they seem to be doing. When you go to the
            grocery store, look at the labels on the cans and packages.
            They are marked in both ounces and grams.
Man: Right. I've noticed that too. And the weather reporters on
            radio and TV give the temperature readings in both
            degrees Fahrenheit and degrees Celsius now.
Woman: Some road signs have the distances marked in both miles
            and kilometers, especially on the interstate highways.
            What do you think, Professor Baker?
Baker: Well, I agree that a gradual adoption is better for those of
            us who have already been exposed to the English system
            of measurement. But I would favor teaching only metrics
            in the elementary schools.
Man: I see your point. It might be confusing to introduce two
            systems at the same time.

Narrator: 31. What is the topic under discussion?

(Note: There should be a 12-second pause after each test question in this section.)

32. What changes in measurement in the United States have the students observed?

33. What was Professor Baker's opinion?

34. Which word best describes Professor Baker's attitude toward his students?

Questions 35–38. Listen to a telephone call to a travel agent.

Man:	Hi. This is Roger Jackson. I'm calling to make a reservation for a flight from Houston to Atlanta.
Woman:	Yes, Mr. Jackson. And what day would you like to travel?
Man:	Oh, not until next month. I want to leave on May 15th and return on May 19th. I thought maybe if I called in advance I could get a better fare.
Woman:	Yes, you can. But if you stay over Saturday night and return on Sunday, May 20th, the ticket will be even cheaper.
Man:	Really? How much cheaper?
Woman:	Almost fifty dollars.
Man:	Hmnn. But I would have an extra night in a hotel. No. That's okay. I'll just keep it for May 19th.
Woman:	All right. Do you have a seating preference?
Man:	I'd rather have a window seat.
Woman:	Good. There is one available. And do you want me to mail these tickets or will you pick them up?
Man:	I'll pick them up. When can I have them?
Woman:	Any time after two o'clock.
Man:	Great!
Narrator:	35. What is the main purpose of the telephone call?
	36. What does the woman suggest?
	37. What does the man decide to do?
	38. What will the man probably do?

Part C

Directions: In this part of the test, you will hear several short talks. After each talk, you will hear some questions. The talks and questions will not be repeated.

After you hear a question, read the four possible answers in your book and choose the best answer. Then, on your answer sheet, find the number of the question and fill in the space that corresponds to the letter of the answer you have chosen.

Questions 39–42. Listen to "Breakthroughs in Science," a weekly radio program.

Since the National Aeronautical and Space Administration was established in 1961, NASA has been engaged in an extensive research effort, which, in cooperation with private industry, has transferred technology to the international marketplace. Hundreds of everyday products can be traced back to the space mission, including cordless electrical tools, airtight food packaging, water purification systems, and even scratch coating for eye glasses.

In addition, many advances in medical technology can be traced back to NASA laboratories. First used to detect flaws in spacecraft, ultrasound is now standard equipment in almost every hospital for diagnosis and assessment of injuries and disease; equipment first used by NASA to transmit images from space to earth is used to assist in cardiac imaging, and lasers first used to test satellites are now used in surgical procedures. Under-the-skin implants for the continuous infusion of drugs, and small pacemakers to regulate the heart were originally designed to monitor the physical condition of astronauts in space.

Finally, with the help of images that were obtained during space missions, and NASA technology, archaeologists have been able to explore the earth. Cities lost under desert sands have been located and rediscovered, and the sea floor has been mapped using photographs from outer space.

Narrator: 39. What is the talk mainly about?

(Note: There should be a 12-second pause after each test question in this section.)

              40. Which of the products listed are NOT mentioned as part of the technology developed for space missions?

              41. According to the speaker, why did NASA develop medical equipment?

              42. Why does the speaker mention archaeology?

Questions 43–46. Listen to a talk by a tour guide on a bus.

The first permanent settlement was made at this site in 1776, when a Spanish military post was established on the end of that peninsula. During the same year, some Franciscan Fathers founded the Mission San Francisco de Asis on a hill above the post. A trail was cleared from the military post to the mission, and about halfway between the two, a station was established for travelers called *Yerba Buena*, which means "good herbs."

For thirteen years the village had fewer than one hundred inhabitants. But in 1848, with the discovery of gold, the population grew to ten thousand. That same year, the name was changed from Yerba Buena to San Francisco.

By 1862 telegraph communications linked San Francisco with eastern cities, and by 1869, the first transcontinental railroad connected the Pacific coast with the Atlantic seaboard. Today San Francisco has a population of almost three million. It is the financial center of the West, and serves as the terminus for trans-Pacific steamship lines and air traffic. The port of San Francisco, which is almost eighteen miles long, handles between five and six million tons of cargo annually.

And now, if you will look to your right, you should just be able to see the Golden Gate Bridge. The bridge, which is more than one mile long, spans the harbor from San Francisco to Marin County and the Redwood Highway. It was completed in 1937 at a cost of thirty-two million dollars and is still one of the largest suspension bridges in the world.

Narrator: 43. What is the main purpose of this talk?

44. According to the tour guide, what was the settlement called before it was renamed San Francisco?

45. According to the tour guide, what happened in 1848?

46. How long is the Golden Gate Bridge?

Questions 47–50. Listen to a talk by an English professor.

Transcendentalism began with the formation in 1836 of the Transcendental Club in Boston, Massachusetts, by a group of artists and writers. This group advanced a reaction against the rigid Puritanism of the period, especially insofar as it emphasized society at the expense of the individual.

One of the most distinguished members of the club was Ralph Waldo Emerson, who served as editor of the literary magazine *Dial*. His writing stressed the importance of the individual. In one of his best-known essays, "Self-Reliance," he appealed to intuition as a source of ethics, asserting that people should be the judge of their own actions, without the rigid restrictions of society.

From 1841 to 1843, Emerson entertained in his home the naturalist and author Henry David Thoreau who also became a member of the Transcendental Club. Probably more than any other member, he demonstrated by his life-style the ideas that the group advanced. He preferred to go to jail rather than to pay taxes to the federal government for a war of which he did not approve.

Upon leaving Emerson's home, Thoreau built a small cabin along the shores of Walden Pond near Concord, Massachusetts, where he lived alone for two years. Devoting himself to the study of nature and to writing, he published an account of his experiences in *Walden*, a book which is generally acknowledged as the most original and sincere contribution to literature by the Transcendentalists.

Narrator: 47. What does the lecturer mainly discuss?

48. During which century did the literary movement develop?

49. According to the lecturer, what did the Puritans do?

50. What is *Walden?*

Model Test 3
Computer-Assisted TOEFL

Section 1:
Listening

The Listening section of the test measures the ability to understand conversations and talks in English. On the actual TOEFL, you will use headphones to listen to the conversations and talks. While you are listening, pictures of the speakers or other information will be presented on your computer screen. There are two parts to the Listening section, with special directions for each part.

On the day of the test, the amount of time you will have to answer all the questions will appear on the computer screen. The time you spend listening to the test material will not be counted. The listening material and questions about it will be presented only one time. You will not be allowed to take notes or have any paper at your computer. You will both see and hear the questions before the answer choices appear. You can take as much time as you need to select an answer; however, it will be to your advantage to answer the questions as quickly as possible. You may change your answer as many times as you want before you confirm it. After you have confirmed an answer, you will not be able to return to the question.

Before you begin working on the Listening section, you will have an opportunity to adjust the volume of the sound. You will not be able to change the volume after you have started the test.

QUESTION DIRECTIONS—Part A

In Part A of the Listening section, you will hear short conversations between two people. In some of the conversations, each person speaks only once. In other conversations, one or both of the people speak more than once. Each conversation is followed by one question about it.

Each question in this part has four answer choices. You should click on the best answer to each question. Answer the questions on the basis of what is stated or implied by the speakers.

1.	Man:	Let's go to the movies after class.
	Woman:	Well, I'll go if you really want to, but I'm a little bit tired.
	Narrator:	What does the woman mean?
2.	Woman:	I'm out of typing paper. Will you lend me some?
	Man:	I don't have any either, but I'll be glad to get you some when I go to the bookstore.
	Narrator:	What is the man going to do?
3.	Man:	Excuse me, Miss. Could you please tell me how to get to the University City Bank?
	Woman:	Sure. Go straight for two blocks, then turn left and walk three more blocks until you get to the drugstore. It's right across the street.
	Narrator:	What can be inferred about the man?
4.	Woman:	Are you still going to summer school at the university near your parent's house?
	Man:	That plan kind of fell through because there weren't enough courses.
	Narrator:	What does the man imply?
5.	Man:	How much is the rent for the apartment?
	Woman:	It's six hundred and fifty dollars a month unfurnished or eight hundred dollars a month furnished. Utilities are seventy-five dollars extra, not including the telephone. It's

expensive, but it's worth it because it's within walking distance from the university.

Narrator: What are the speakers discussing?

6. Man: Dr. Taylor must have really liked your paper. You were about the only one who got an A.
Woman: But he never seems to call on me in class.
Narrator: What does the woman imply?

7. Woman: Do you know anyone who would like to participate in a psychology experiment? It pays ten dollars an hour.
Man: Have you asked Sandy?
Narrator: What does the man suggest that the woman do?

8. Woman: Didn't you go to the study group meeting last night either?
Man: No. I had a slight headache.
Narrator: What can be inferred about the study group meeting?

9. Woman: I have a card, but now I need a farewell gift for my advisor.
Man: How about a nice pen?
Narrator: What does the man mean?

10. Man: Are you going to move out of the dorm next semester?
Woman: I just can't seem to make up my mind.
Narrator: What does the woman mean?

11. Man: You and I should stop by the gym on the way home.
Woman: I don't think so. I've probably had enough exercise for one day.
Narrator: What does the woman imply?

12. Man: I signed the contract.
Woman: Do you really think you can work and go to school full time?
Narrator: What does the woman imply?

13. Woman: I owe everyone in my family a letter, but I really don't have time to sit down and write them and it's too expensive to call.
Man: Why don't you just buy some postcards?
Narrator: What does the man suggest the woman do?

14. Man: Have you heard from any schools yet?
Woman: Yes, I was accepted at Kansas State, the University of Oklahoma, and the University of Nebraska, but I'm going

to wait until I hear one way or another from the University of Minnesota.

	Narrator:	What are the speakers discussing?

15. Woman: I thought I was supposed to take the test in Room 32.
    Man: No. Ticket number 32 is in Room 27.
    Narrator: What will the woman probably do?

16. Man: Where did you get the flower?
    Woman: At the Honors Reception. The teachers gave them to all of the honors students.
    Narrator: What can be inferred about the woman?

17. Man: Terry is really having trouble in Dr. Wise's class. She's missed too much to catch up.
    Woman: If I were Terry, I'd drop the course, and take it over next semester.
    Narrator: What does the woman suggest that Terry do?

18. Man: Why does Margaret have to work so many hours at the motel?
    Woman: To earn enough money for next semester's tuition.
    Narrator: What does the woman say about Margaret?

19. Woman: I used to teach English before I came back to graduate school.
    Man: No wonder you like this course!
    Narrator: What does the man mean?

20. Man: We should ask Carl to be in our group.
    Woman: We probably ought to ask Jane, too. She's really good at making presentations.
    Narrator: What problem do the students have?

QUESTION DIRECTIONS—Part B

In Part B of the Listening section, you will hear several longer conversations and talks. Each conversation or talk is followed by several questions. The conversations, talks, and questions will not be repeated.

The conversations and talks are about a variety of topics. You do not need special knowledge of the topics to answer the questions correctly. Rather, you should answer each question on the basis of what is stated or implied by the speakers in the conversations or talks.

For most of the questions, you will need to click on the best of four possible answers. Some questions will have special directions. The special directions will appear in a box on the computer screen.

Narrator:	Listen to part of a conversation between two students on campus.
Man:	To tell the truth, I really don't know what Dr. Brown wants us to do. The assignment was pretty vague.
Woman:	I know. I've already looked in the syllabus, but all it says under the course requirements is "Research paper, thirty points."
Man:	Thirty points? I hadn't realized that it counted so much. That's almost one-third of the grade for the course.
Woman:	That's why I'm so worried about it. At first I thought she wanted us to do library research, and write it up; then she started talking about presentations. Last week she said there would be time during the next to the last class for us to present.
Man:	I was thinking about making an appointment to see her, or just stopping by during her office hours.
Woman:	You could do that. But since so many of us are confused, maybe we should ask about it in class tomorrow. I'll bet we won't be the only ones with questions either.
Man:	That's a good idea.
Narrator:	Now get ready to answer the questions.

21. What problem do the speakers have?

22. How much does the research paper count toward the grade for the course?

23. What did the professor say last week?

24. What will the students probably do?

Narrator:	Listen to part of a lecture in a world history class. Today the professor will talk about exploration and discovery. She will focus on the Hawaiian Islands.

On his third exploratory voyage, as captain of two ships, the *Resolution* and the *Discovery*, Captain James Cook came upon a group of uncharted islands that he named the Sandwich Islands as a tribute to his friend, the Earl of Sandwich. Today the islands are known as the Hawaiian Islands.

Some historians contend that the islanders welcomed Cook, believing that he was the god Launo, protector of peace and agriculture. I have that name written on the board for you. Of course, it didn't take long for them to realize that Launo had not returned.

These islanders were short, strong people, with a well-organized social system. The men fished and raised crops, including taro, coconuts, sweet potatoes, and sugarcane. The women cared for the children and made clothing—loin cloths for the men and short skirts for the women. The natives were eager to exchange food and supplies for iron nails and tools, and Cook was easily able to restock his ship.

Because of a severe storm in which the *Resolution* was damaged, it was necessary to return to Hawaii. Now sure that Cook and his crew were men and not gods, the natives welcomed them less hospitably. Besides, diseases brought by the English had reached epidemic proportions. When a small boat was stolen from the *Discovery*, Cook demanded that the king be taken as a hostage until the boat was returned. In the fighting that followed, Cook and four other crewmen were killed.

Narrator: Now get ready to answer the questions.

25. What is the main purpose of this lecture?

26. According to the lecturer, what were the two ships commanded by Captain Cook?

27. Why does the professor mention the name *Launo*?

28. The professor briefly explains a sequence of events in the history of Hawaii. Summarize the sequence by putting the events in order.

Narrator: Listen to part of a lecture in an engineering class. The professor will discuss alloys.

An alloy is a substance that is formed by combining a metal with other metals, or nonmetals. For example, brass is an alloy of the metals copper and zinc, and steel is an alloy of the metal iron with the nonmetal carbon.

The special characteristics of metals, such as hardness, strength, flexibility, and weight are called its properties. By the process of alloying, it is possible to create materials with the exact combination of properties for a particular use. In the aircraft industry, there is a need for metals that are both strong and light. Steel is strong but too heavy, whereas aluminum is light but not strong. By alloying aluminum with copper and other metals, a material that is strong enough to withstand the stresses of flight, but light enough to reduce the cost of fuel to lift the craft is created. By alloying steel with nickel and chromium, the steel alloy that results is not only lighter but also stronger than solid steel.

Of course, there is an important difference between the alloys we have used in our examples and the combination of metals that occur accidentally as impure metals. Both are mixtures, but alloys are mixtures that have been deliberately combined in specific proportion for a definite purpose.

Narrator:	Now get ready to answer the questions.
	29. What is an alloy?
	30. What does the speaker say about the properties of alloys?
	31. Why does the speaker use the example of the aircraft industry?
	32. What is the difference between combinations of metals in nature and alloys?
Narrator:	Listen to part of a discussion in an English class.
John:	British English and American English are really about the same, aren't they?
Mary:	I don't think so. It seems to me that some of the spellings are different.
Baker:	You're right, Mary. Words like *theater* and *center* end in *re* in England instead of in *er*, the way that we spell them. Let me write that on the board. Can you think of any more examples?
Mary:	The word *color*?
Baker:	Good. In fact, many words that end in *or* in American English are spelled *our* in British English, like *color* and *honor.*
John:	I'm still not convinced. I mean, if someone comes here from England, we can all understand what he's saying. The spelling doesn't really matter that much.
Baker:	Okay. Are we just talking about spelling? Or are there some differences in pronunciation and meaning too?
Mary:	Professor Baker?
Baker:	Yes?
Mary:	I remember seeing an English movie where the actors kept calling their apartment a *flat*. Half of the movie was over before I realized what they were talking about.
John:	So there are slight differences in spelling and some vocabulary.

Mary:	And pronunciation, too. You aren't going to tell me that you sound like Richard Burton.
John:	Richard Burton wasn't English. He was Welsh.
Mary:	Okay. Anyway, the pronunciation is different.
Baker:	I think that what we are really disagreeing about is the extent of the difference. We all agree that British English and American English are different. Right?
Mary:	Yes.
John:	Sure.
Baker:	But not so different that it prevents us from understanding each other.
John:	Well, that's what I mean.
Mary:	That's what I mean, too.

| Narrator: | Now get ready to answer the questions. |

33. What do the speakers mainly discuss?

34. How are the words below [see answer choices] referred to in the discussion?

35. What can be inferred about the word *flat* in British English?

36. On what did the class agree?

| Narrator: | Listen to part of a talk in an education class. A student is giving a presentation about local control of schools. |

My report is on local control of schools. First, I was surprised to learn that public schools in the United States are not the same in every state or even from community to community within the state. The reason for differences in organization, curriculum, and school policies is because each school district has a governing board, called the school board, that makes the decisions about the way the schools in their district will be run. Of course, a superintendent is selected by the board to carry out policies and the superintendent is usually a professional educator, but the board, often made up of community leaders who are not professional educators, must approve the recommendations of the superintendent.

There are two ways to organize a school board. In most communities, the board is elected by the residents in their local school district. And the members usually serve without pay for three to five years. But in some districts, the school board is appointed by the mayor.

Of course, the federal government has an interest in improving education on a national level, even though schools are controlled locally. But the function of the national department is very different from a department of education in many parts of the world. This national agency is primarily involved in collecting demographics, supporting research and projects, and supervising the compliance of schools with national legislation.

Narrator:	Now get ready to answer the questions.
	37. What is the presentation mainly about?
	38. What surprised the presenter about her research?
	39. How does each of the persons identified below [see answer choices] contribute to the operation of schools in the United States?
	40. According to the speaker, what is the function of the department of education in the United States?
Narrator:	Listen to part of a conversation between a student and a secretary in a college dormitory.
Man:	I want to buy a meal ticket.
Woman:	Okay. Which plan do you want?
Man:	You mean there is more than one?
Woman:	Sure. You can buy one meal a day, two meals a day, or three meals a day.
Man:	Oh. If I buy two meals a day, can I choose which meals?
Woman:	Not really. The two-meal plan includes lunch and dinner. No breakfast.
Man:	Great. That's what I would have wanted anyway. How much is that?
Woman:	It's thirty-six dollars a week, which works out to about three dollars a meal.
Man:	Wait a minute. Fourteen meals at three dollars would be forty-two dollars, wouldn't it?
Woman:	Yes, but we don't serve meals on Sunday.
Man:	Oh.
Woman:	Most residents order a pizza or go out to eat on Sundays. Of course, some students live close enough to go home for the day.
Man:	Okay. I'll take the two-meal plan. Do I pay by the quarter or by the week?
Woman:	By the quarter.

Man: Fine. Do you take credit cards?

Woman: Yes, but you don't have to pay now. Just fill out this form, and we'll bill you.

Narrator: Now get ready to answer the questions.

            41. What kind of meal plan does the man decide to buy?

            42. How much does the plan cost?

            43. Why do most residents order a pizza or go out to eat on Sundays?

            44. How will the man pay for the meals?

Narrator: Listen to part of a lecture in a botany class. The professor is talking about hydroponics.

As you will recall, hydroponics is the science of growing plants without soil, using a solution of nutrients in water. Of course, good soil has the nutrients necessary for plant growth, but when plants are grown without soil, all the nutrients must be provided in another way. This solution contains potassium nitrate, ammonium sulfate, magnesium sulfate, monocalcium phosphate, and calcium sulfate. Don't try to write down all of that now. You can refer to your lab workbook for the list of substances and the proportions needed for proper plant growth.

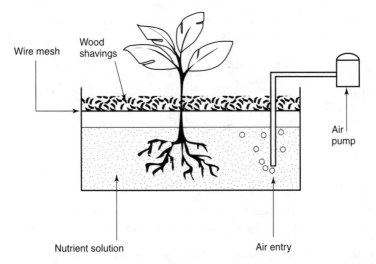

For now, let's look at the diagram that we worked on last time when we began our hydroponics experiment. Your drawing should look more or less like this one. As you know, for plants grown in soil, the roots not only absorb water and nutrients but also serve to anchor the plant. That is why the roots of our hydroponic plants are not placed directly in the water and nutrient solution. We used wood chips held in place by a wire mesh to anchor the plants and allow us to suspend the roots in the tank below that contains the water and nutrient solution. Because oxygen is also taken in by the roots, we had to attach an air pump to mix oxygen into the solution. And you can see the way that the pump was attached to the tank.

During our break this morning, I'd like you to come over to the hydroponics area and examine the experiment close up. I'd also like you to take a closer look at this specimen of nutrient solution. What do you notice about this? What conclusions can you draw?

Narrator:	Now get ready to answer the questions.

45. What is hydroponics?

46. According to the speaker, why are roots important to plants?

47. Why was the pump attached to the tank in this experiment?

48. What does the professor want the students to do with the specimen of the nutrient solution?

Narrator:	Listen to part of a conversation between two students on campus.
Man:	Did you watch "American Biography" last night?
Woman:	No, I had class. Did you?
Man:	Yes. Actually, it was an assignment for my history class, and it was excellent. It featured Harriet Tubman.
Woman:	Who is Harriet Tubman?
Man:	Don't feel bad. I didn't know either until I watched the show. She was a member of the underground railroad. You know, the organization that helped runaway slaves escape to free states or to Canada in the mid eighteen hundreds, just before and during the Civil War.
Woman:	Oh, I know who you mean. She had been a slave herself, hadn't she?
Man:	Right. According to the program, when she escaped from her owners in Maryland, she felt for moss on the north side of trees, and followed the North Star until she got to Philadelphia.

Woman:	No kidding.
Man:	What really impressed me though was the fact that after she escaped, she went back to Maryland nineteen times to lead others to freedom. I think they said she freed more than three hundred slaves.
Woman:	That sounds interesting. I'm sorry I missed it.
Man:	Sometimes they rerun the biographies.
Woman:	Well I'll watch for it then. Thanks for telling me about it.
Narrator:	Now get ready to answer the questions.

49. Who was Harriet Tubman?

50. What impressed the man about Harriet Tubman's story?

Model Test 4
Computer-Assisted TOEFL

Section 1:
Listening

The Listening section of the test measures the ability to understand conversations and talks in English. You will use headphones to listen to the conversations and talks. While you are listening, pictures of the speakers or other information will be presented on your computer screen. There are two parts to the Listening section, with special directions for each part.

On the day of the test, the amount of time you will have to answer all the questions will appear on the computer screen. The time you spend listening to the test material will not be counted. The listening material and questions about it will be presented only one time. You will not be allowed to take notes or have any paper at your computer. You will both see and hear the questions before the answer choices appear. You can take as much time as you need to select an answer; however, it will be to your advantage to answer the questions as quickly as possible. You may change your answer as many times as you want before you confirm it. After you have confirmed an answer, you will not be able to return to the question.

Before you begin working on the Listening section, you will have an opportunity to adjust the volume of the sound. You will not be able to change the volume after you have started the test.

QUESTION DIRECTIONS—Part A

In Part A of the Listening section, you will hear short conversations between two people. In some of the conversations, each person speaks only once. In other conversations, one or both of the people speak more than once. Each conversation is followed by one question about it.

Each question in this part has four answer choices. You should click on the best answer to each question. Answer the questions on the basis of what is stated or implied by the speakers.

1. Man: What are you going to do this weekend? Maybe we can play some tennis.
   Woman: Don't tempt me. I have to study for my qualifying examinations. I take them on Monday.
   Narrator: What does the woman mean?

2. Man: Does attendance count toward the grade in this class?
   Woman: No. I have an attendance requirement for undergraduates, but not for graduate students.
   Narrator: What does the woman mean?

3. Woman: How do you like your new job, Bill?
   Man: Fine. This week I have been reading the financial reports and studying the books. Next week I will probably start to handle some of the accounts.
   Narrator: What can be inferred about Bill?

4. Man: Have you talked to Ali lately? I thought that he was studying at the American Language Institute, but yesterday I saw him going into the chemistry lab in the engineering building.
   Woman: That is not surprising. Ali is a part-time student this term. He is taking three classes at the Institute and one class at the university.
   Narrator: What does the woman say about Ali?

5. Man: Hello, Miss Evans? This is Paul Thompson. I would like to talk with Dr. Warren, please.
   Woman: Oh, Paul. You just missed her.
   Narrator: What does the woman mean?

6. Man: I would like to see Mr. Adams, please.
   Woman: Mr. Adams is not here anymore. Mrs. Jones is the foreign student advisor now.
   Narrator: What do we know from this conversation?

7. Man: I am sorry. The last campus shuttle has already left.
    Woman: Oh. All right. Can you please tell me where I can find a
              telephone?
    Narrator: What will the woman probably do?

8. Man: Have you bought your books yet?
    Woman: I tried to, but the math and English books were sold out.
    Narrator: What does the woman mean?

9. Man: I don't have to be there until seven.
    Woman: The traffic is really bad though. You'd better leave a few
              minutes early.
    Narrator: What does the woman suggest the man do?

10. Man: You don't like the new graduate assistant, do you?
    Woman: No. He makes fun of his students' mistakes.
    Narrator: What does the woman mean?

11. Woman: Susan told me what you said about my accent.
    Man: I don't know what she told you, but I really didn't mean it
              as a put-down.
    Narrator: What does the man mean?

12. Man: I'll be right back. Can you watch my book bag for a
              minute?
    Woman: Sure. I'll be glad to.
    Narrator: What does the woman agree to do for the man?

13. Woman: I'm really tired of spending every weekend studying.
    Man: I hear you.
    Narrator: What does the man mean?

14. Man: Is that Mike's car? I thought you said that Mike was
              spending spring break in Florida.
    Woman: That's Mike's brother. He's using the car while Mike's
              away.
    Narrator: What does the woman imply?

15. Woman: You'd better start working on that project. It's due in a
              week.
    Man: I will. I'll get it done.
    Narrator: What does the woman advise the man to do?

16. Man: Do you want to go to the International Talent Show?
    Woman: Sure. Why not?
    Narrator: What does the woman mean?

17.	Man:	Did you know that Bill and Carol are back from their honeymoon?
	Woman:	So they *did* get married after all.
	Narrator:	What had the woman assumed about Bill and Carol?

18.	Man:	Are you going to the review session for the test?
	Woman:	What's the point?
	Narrator:	What does the woman mean?

19.	Woman:	Your check isn't here. I suggest that you call your sponsor.
	Man:	Okay. I'll be back.
	Narrator:	What will the man probably do?

20.	Woman:	I still haven't heard from Columbia University yet.
	Man:	I know it looks grim right now, but don't give up!
	Narrator:	What does the man mean?

QUESTION DIRECTIONS—Part B

In Part B of the Listening section, you will hear several longer conversations and talks. Each conversation or talk is followed by several questions. The conversations, talks, and questions will not be repeated.

The conversations and talks are about a variety of topics. You do not need special knowledge of the topics to answer the questions correctly. Rather, you should answer each question on the basis of what is stated or implied by the speakers in the conversations or talks.

For most of the questions, you will need to click on the best of four possible answers. Some questions will have special directions. The special directions will appear in a box on the computer screen.

| | Narrator: | Listen to part of a conversation between two students on campus. |

	Woman:	Where have you been? I've missed you in lab.
	Man:	I've been sick.
	Woman:	Nothing serious, I hope.
	Man:	Well, I stayed out of the hospital, but to tell the truth, I was in pretty bad shape. Some kind of flu.
	Woman:	That's too bad. Are you better now?
	Man:	Well enough to start thinking about school again. Now I'm worried about getting caught up.
	Woman:	Let's see, how many labs have you missed?
	Man:	Margaret, I got sick three weeks ago, so I am really behind.
	Woman:	Let me look at my notebook. I've got it right here.

Man:	Oh, great. I was hoping you'd let me make a copy of your notes.
Woman:	Sure. You can do that, Gary. And I have some good news for you. You haven't missed any quizzes. We haven't had any since you've been gone. Listen, after you have a chance to look at my notes, why don't we get together? If there's anything you don't understand, maybe I can explain it to you. It's hard trying to read someone else's notes.
Man:	That would be perfect. I hate to bother you though.
Woman:	No bother. I'm sure you'd do it for me.
Narrator:	Now get ready to answer the questions.

21. What is Gary's problem?

22. What does Gary want Margaret to do?

23. What does Margaret offer to do?

24. What is Margaret's attitude in this conversation?

Narrator:	Listen to part of a lecture in an American literature class. The professor is talking about American novelists in the twentieth century. He is focusing on F. Scott Fitzgerald.

There have been a number of important American novelists in this century, but I have chosen F. Scott Fitzgerald for our class because he is one of the more interesting ones. Born in 1896 and educated at Princeton, he wrote novels that describe the post-war American society, very much caught up in the rhythms of jazz.

In 1920, the same year that he published his first book, *This Side of Paradise*, he married Zelda Sayre, also a writer. His most famous book, *The Great Gatsby*, appeared in 1925.

Fitzgerald had a great natural talent, but unfortunately he became a compulsive drinker. A brilliant success in his youth, he never made the adjustments necessary to a maturing writer in a changing world. His later novels, *All the Sad Young Men*, *Tender Is the Night*, and *The Last Tycoon*, were less successful, so that when he died in 1940 his books were out of print and he had been almost forgotten. His reputation now is far greater than it was in his lifetime, especially since the film version of his novel *The Great Gatsby* was released.

Now, with that introduction, I am going to run the video version of *The Great Gatsby*, and then we'll divide up into groups to talk about it.

Narrator: Now get ready to answer the questions.

             25. What is the main topic of this lecture?

             26. Why wasn't Fitzgerald more successful in his later life?

             27. According to the lecturer, what do we know about the novels written by F. Scott Fitzgerald?

             28. What does the professor want the class to do after the lecture?

Narrator: The university quartet has been invited to play for a music appreciation class. Listen to a talk by the director of the quartet.

Before the concert begins, let me tell you a little bit about chamber music. From medieval times through the eighteenth century, musicians in Europe had two options for employment—the church or the nobility. So when they were not performing at religious functions, they were playing in the chambers of stately homes. And they came to be known as chamber players.

Chamber music is written to be performed by a small group, more than one, but fewer than a dozen musicians. Pieces for more than eight players are unusual though, and it is rare to see a conductor. It may surprise you to know that any combination of instruments can be used for chamber music. The most popular are the piano, strings, and woodwinds, but chamber music has been written for other instruments as well.

Early chamber music, let's say the sixteenth and seventeenth centuries, was often written for the recorder, harpsichord, and viola. During the Elizabethan Period, there were many talented composers of chamber music, including William Byrd and Orlando Gibbons. And at that time, vocal chamber music, called madrigal singing, was very popular. Later, both Johann Sebastian Bach and George Frederick Handel wrote trio sonatas for chamber groups. This evening the University Quartet will perform two of the later pieces by Bach.

Ladies and gentlemen, the University Quartet.

Narrator: Now get ready to answer the questions.

             29. What is the main purpose of the talk?

30. According to the speaker, which instruments are the most popular for chamber music?

31. Why does the speaker mention Johann Sebastian Bach?

32. What will the listeners hear next?

Narrator:	Listen to part of a conversation between a student and a secretary in the chemical engineering department.
Woman:	May I help you?
Man:	Yes. My name is Bob Stephens and I have an appointment with Dr. Benjamin at three o'clock on Wednesday.
Woman:	Three o'clock on Wednesday? Yes. I see it here on his calendar.
Man:	Well, I was wondering whether he has an earlier appointment available on the same day.
Woman:	I'm sorry, Mr. Stephens, but Dr. Benjamin is tied up in a meeting until noon, and he has two appointments scheduled before yours when he gets back from lunch.
Man:	Oh.
Woman:	There is a later appointment time open though, at four-thirty, if that would help you. Or you could see him Thursday morning at ten.
Man:	Hmmm. No thank you. I think I'll just rearrange my own schedule so I can keep my regular appointment.
Narrator:	Now get ready to answer the questions.

33. Why did the man go to the Chemical Engineering Department?

34. What does the woman say about Dr. Benjamin?

35. What did the secretary offer to do?

36. What did the man decide to do?

Narrator:	Listen to part of a lecture in a health class. The professor will be talking about nutrition. She will focus on health food.

Health food is a general term applied to all kinds of foods that are considered more healthful than the types of foods widely sold in supermarkets. For example, whole grains, dried beans, and corn oil are health foods. A narrower classification of health foods is natural food. This term is used to distinguish between types of the same food. Fresh fruit is a natural food, but canned fruit, with sugars and other additives, is not. The most precise term of all and the narrowest classification within health foods is organic food, used to describe food that has been grown on a particular kind of farm. Fruits and vegetables that are grown in gardens treated only with organic fertilizers, that are not sprayed with poisonous insecticides, and that are not refined after harvest, are organic foods.

In choosing the type of food you eat, then, you have basically two choices: inorganic, processed foods, or organic, unprocessed foods. A wise decision should include investigation of the allegations that processed foods contain chemicals, some of which are proven to be toxic, and that vitamin content is greatly reduced in processed foods.

Narrator:	Now get ready to answer the questions.
	37. What is the main topic of this lecture?
	38. Which term is used to identify foods that have not been processed or canned?
	39. What happens to food when it is processed?
	40. Which word best describes the speaker's attitude toward health foods?
Narrator:	Listen to part of a class discussion in an anthropology class. The professor is talking about the Stone Age.
Professor:	So, as you will recall, the Stone Age is the time, early in the development of human cultures, before the introduction of metals, when prehistoric people started to make stone tools and weapons. Can anyone remember the exact dates for the Stone Age? Chuck?
Chuck:	Well, you said that the exact dates would vary for different parts of the world.
Professor:	That's exactly right. I did. But in general, the use of flint for tools was widespread about two million years ago. That was the beginning of the Paleolithic Period, which is also referred to as the Old Stone Age. What can you tell me about the humanoid creatures that were alive during this period? Yes, Beverly?
Beverly:	They were Neanderthals, and they were nomads. And they survived by hunting and gathering.

Professor:	Very good. Beverly, can you tell us anything about the tools that they made?
Beverly:	Yes, they were primarily general purpose tools such as axes, knives, and arrowheads that they used for hunting.
Professor:	Correct. But we have also found some interesting tools for specific domestic purposes as well. Bone implements were being introduced in the Old Stone Age, and we have reason to believe that they were actually making sewing needles. Any ideas on why that might be so? Chuck?
Chuck:	The Ice Age. They must have been cold.
Professor:	That's true. The last Ice Age was about 13000 B.C. which is at the end of the Paleolithic Period. Do you remember anything else about that time that is of particular importance? Beverly?
Beverly:	Neanderthal man began to decline, and Homo Sapiens emerged.
Professor:	Right. This marks the end of the Old Stone Age and the beginning of the Middle Stone Age, or the Mesolithic Period. In fact, "Meso" means "middle." Now let's think about the changing climate and the emergence of Homo Sapiens. How would this influence the kind of tools that would be produced? Any ideas, Chuck?
Chuck:	Well, with the more moderate climate, Homo Sapiens didn't have to wander so far to hunt and gather. Wasn't it in the Middle Stone Age that agricultural villages started to develop?
Professor:	Actually, it was during the Neolithic Period or the Late Stone Age, about 8000 B.C. But you are on the right track. Some of the tools previously used for hunting were adapted for rudimentary farming even during the Middle Stone Age before farming communities started to develop.
Chuck:	So was it farming that marked the end of the Stone Age then?
Professor:	It was influential. But the introduction of metals was usually considered the defining event that brought an end to the Stone Age. As metals started to challenge stone as the material of choice for tools, mankind entered a new era.
Narrator:	Now get ready to answer the questions.
	41. How did the professor define the Stone Age?
	42. Name the three time periods associated with the Stone Age.

43. Why did tools change during the Late Stone Age?

44. What marked the end of the Stone Age?

Narrator: Listen to part of a lecture in a geology class. The professor is talking about oil deposits.

Most crude oil is found in underground formations called traps. In a trap, the oil collects in porous rocks, along with gas and water. Over time, the oil moves up toward the surface of the earth through cracks and holes in the porous rock until it reaches a nonporous rock deposit which will not allow it to continue moving. The oil becomes trapped under the nonporous rock deposit.

There are several different types of traps, but today we will talk about the three most common ones—the anticline trap, the salt dome trap, and the fault trap.

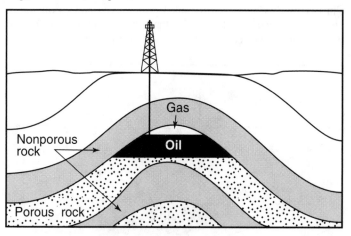

Look at this diagram. Here is an example of an anticline. As you can see, the oil is trapped under a formation of rock that resembles an arch. In this anticline, the petroleum is trapped under a formation of nonporous rock with a gas deposit directly over it. This is fairly typical of an anticline.

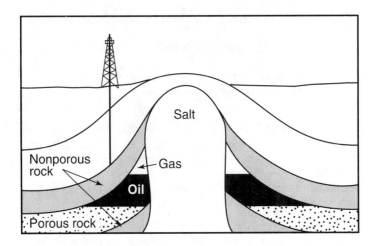

Now, let's look at a diagram of a salt dome. This salt dome shows how a cylinder-shaped salt deposit has pushed up through a layer of sedimentary rocks, causing them to arch and fracture. The oil deposits have collected along the sides of the salt dome.

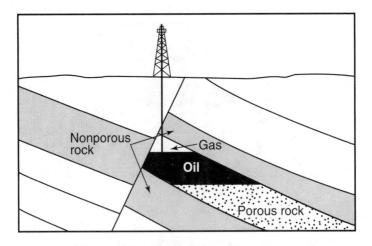

Finally, I want to show you a fault trap. This diagram represents a fracture in the earth that has shifted a nonporous rock formation on top of a porous formation. Remember, as in all traps, the oil is collected in the porous rock and trapped underground by the nonporous rock.

Geologists study the terrain for indications of possible oil traps. For example, a bulge in a flat surface may signal the presence of a salt dome.

Narrator:	Now get ready to answer the questions.

45. What is a trap?

46. Select the diagram of the anticline trap that was described in the lecture.

47. Identify the nonporous rock in the diagram.

48. According to the speaker, how can geologists locate salt domes?

Narrator:	Listen to part of a conversation between two students on campus.
Man:	Who is teaching the class?
Woman:	Actually, I have a choice between Dr. Perkins and Dr. Robinson. Do you know anything about them?
Man:	Sure. I've taken classes with both of them.
Woman:	So what do you think?
Man:	They are both good in their own way. But it depends on how you learn best, because they approach the class from two entirely different points of view.
Woman:	I've heard that Robinson is very strict.
Man:	You could say that. I'd call it traditional. He lectures every day, gives quizzes every week, leading up to a comprehensive final exam, multiple choice as I recall.
Woman:	How about Perkins?
Man:	More relaxed. Uses group discussion and projects instead of quizzes. And I'm pretty sure his final is short essay.
Woman:	Which one would you advise me to take?
Man:	I really can't say. If you like to listen to lectures and take notes, and if you do well on objective tests, I'd say Robinson. But if you enjoy working in groups, and you do better on essay exams, then I'd recommend Perkins.
Woman:	Thanks. This was helpful. I think I'll sign up for Robinson's class.
Narrator:	Now get ready to answer the questions.

49. What is the woman's problem?

50. Why did the woman decide to take the class with Dr. Robinson?

NOTES

NOTES

BARRON'S BOOKS AND CASSETTES TO HELP YOU SUCCEED IN ESL AND TOEFL EXAMS

Where the Action Is: An Easy ESL Approach to Pure Regular Verbs
• A clear, easy-to-follow guide complete with charts that instruct ESL students to use and understand pure regular verbs in speaking, reading and writing. Six practice test and answer keys are included. $7.95, Canada $10.50.

Barron's ESL Guide to American Business English
• Focused to fit the needs of ESL students. Paperback handbook describes a variety of business writings and sample correspondence. Review section covers the basics of English grammar. $13.95, Canada $17.95.

Write English Right
• A workbook with two cassettes presents exercises, assignment worksheets, and drills for TOEFL and ESL students. Accompanying cassettes feature oral exercises on English words that sound alike but have different meanings. $24.95, Canada $32.50. Book only $8.95, Canada $11.95.

American Accent Training
• Concentrates on spoken English, American style, with exercises in American speech rhythms and inflections. Exercises prompt ESL students to listen and imitate, in order to be better understood by Americans, while also increasing listening comprehension. Package consists of book and three 90-minute cassettes in a durable case. $39.95, Canada $49.95.

Writing a Research Paper American Style: An ESL/EFL Handbook
• Instructs advanced high school, college, and graduate students who have little experience in writing academic papers in English. Explains Modern Language Association and American Psychological Association rules, outlines documentation techniques, gives helpful grammar tips, and much more. $9.95, Canada $12.95.

Minimum Essentials of English, 2nd
• A concise 48-page summary of English grammar, rules, and language forms. An indispensable aid and style sheet to help with all written assignments. Pages are punched to fit a three-ring notebook binder. $6.95, Canada $9.50.

Please send me the following titles:

____ Where the Action Is,
(0-7641-0509-4), $7.95, Canada $10.50.

____ Barron's ESL Guide to American Business English,
(0-7641-0594-9), $13.95, Canada $17.95.

____ Write English Right 2-Cassette Package,
(0-8120-8018-1), $24.95, Canada $32.50.

____ Write English Right Book,
(0-8120-1462-6), $8.95, Canada $11.95.

____ American Accent Training,
(0-8120-7763-6), $39.95, Canada $49.95.

____ Writing a Research Paper American Style,
(0-8120-9637-1), $9.95, Canada $12.95.

____ Minimum Essentials of English, 2nd
(0-7641-0745-3), $6.95, Canada $9.50.

BARRON'S EDUCATIONAL SERIES, INC.
250 Wireless Blvd. • Hauppauge, NY 11788
In Canada: Georgetown Book Warehouse
34 Armstrong Ave. • Georgetown, Ontario
L7G 4R9

I am enclosing a check or money order for $_____ which includes an additional 15% for postage and shipping (minimum charge $4.95). New York State residents add sales tax to total.

Charge To My: ☐ Mastercard ☐ Visa ☐ American Express
☐ Carte Blanche ☐ Diners Club

Account # _____ Exp. Date _____

Signature_____

Name _____

Address _____

City _____State_____ Zip_____

If not satisfied, please return books within 15 days of the date of purchase for full refund. Prices are subject to change without notice. All books are paperback editions, and may be purchased at local bookstores or direct from Barron's.

Visit our website at: www.barronseduc.com

(#6a) R 2/99

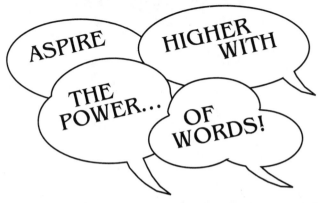

1-800-475-8295

A- little or some ex

3- some exp.

C- considerat ex

W- willing to

U- unwilling t

51, Lenox Pointe
Atlanta, Ga
30 324